TENTH EDITION

Financing Education in a Climate of Change

Vern Brimley, Jr.
Brigham Young University

Rulon R. Garfield
Brigham Young University

PEARSON

Boston ■ New York ■ San Francisco
Mexico City ■ Montreal ■ Toronto ■ London ■ Madrid ■ Munich ■ Paris
Hong Kong ■ Singapore ■ Tokyo ■ Cape Town ■ Sydney

Senior Editor: *Arnis E. Burvikovs*
Series Editorial Assistant: *Erin E. Reilly*
Marketing Manager: *Erica DeLuca*
Production Editor: *Annette Joseph*
Editorial Production Service: *Lynda Griffiths*
Composition Buyer: *Linda Cox*
Manufacturing Buyer: *Linda Morris*
Electronic Composition: *Omegatype Typography, Inc.*
Cover Administrator: *Linda Knowles*

For related titles and support materials, visit our online catalog at www.ablongman.com.

Between the time website information is gathered and then published, it is not unusual for some sites to have closed. Also, the transcription of URLs can result in typographical errors. The publisher would appreciate notification where these errors occur so that they may be corrected in subsequent editions.

ISBN-10: 0-205-51179-1
ISBN-13: 978-0-205-51179-2

Library of Congress Cataloging-in-Publication Data
Brimley, Vern.
    Financing education in a climate of change / Vern Brimley, Jr., Rulon R.
      Garfield.—10th ed.
      p.   cm.
    Includes bibliographical references and index.
    ISBN 0-205-51179-1
      1. Education—United States—Finance. I. Garfield, Rulon R. II. Title.
  LB2825.B86 2008
  379.1'0973—dc22

                                  2006053286

Printed in the United States of America

10 9 8 7 6 5   RRD-VA   11 10 09

To Dawn and Shirley

CONTENTS

PREFACE

The challenge in researching and updating *Financing Education in a Climate of Change* for the tenth edition has been exciting and stimulating. The opportunity to have reviewers make positive suggestions and to receive input from professors and comments from students who use the text is satisfying. Changes from those sources are included in this new edition. In the brief span since the last edition many events have transpired that influenced education and affected school finance policy. A continuing war, terrorist acts, escalating oil prices, and global economic factors have had an impact. Hurricanes Katrina and Rita in the southern states and natural disasters in other parts of the country have been devastating. Caused actions, including continued violence in the schools, are alarming. These and other factors have resulted in concerns for educators in attempting to meet the needs of our changing society.

The No Child Left Behind Act (NCLB) has had a marked effect on the education climate in the nation. A court case in Connecticut challenged the law on the basis of it being an "unfunded mandate," while other states have balked at meeting compliance standards. The act's effect on the structure of authority on the education scene has been dramatic. The relationship between the federal government and state governments has become strained. Mandates issued at the federal level requiring compliance at the state and local levels has challenged the concept of federalism. Hearings have been held with congressional leaders with input from many sources seeking to change the law. Some restrictions were modified by Congress in 2006, although the *authority* question has not been completely resolved. A review of the concept of federalism and the influence NCLB has on education finance are expanded in this tenth edition.

A new period in education finance has emerged with the courts and legislatures struggling to determine the *authority* issue. New York's highest court established a dollar figure for capital and operation projects in New York City schools to adequately provide revenue for a "sound basic education" for students. The legislature funded the capital amount, resulting in further judicial actions to require the funding of the maintenance and operations amount. In several other court cases state legislatures were left with the responsibility of not only funding schools *adequately* but also determining what definition of *adequate* would meet the requirements of their state constitutions. Education policy groups are attempting to identify the leadership role and responsibility they must assume in this power play. Both the courts and the legislatures have continued to have an influence on *choice* issues with establishing charter schools, vouchers, and some tax credits to businesses and individuals who make a contribution to private foundations.

Local control of schools is being challenged by outside agencies. Some states have passed legislation that requires that 65 percent of revenues be reflected in expenditures at the school level. State and federal requirements are usurping power from local boards and some states are taking over the jurisdiction of *failing* schools. Mayors in several large cities are attempting to have schools in their area function under a board over which they have control.

Many school districts in the country are unprepared to meet the requirements of Statements 45 through 47 from the Governmental Accounting Standards Board (GASB). The Statements require that districts must have revenues in reserve to cover costs of retirement and health plans for retirees rather than paying for such costs on a pay-as-you-go basis. Education budgets have been affected and retirement benefits scaled down or dropped from compensation packages. Rather than lose future benefits, many district personnel have retired, causing a much larger turnover of teachers, administrators, and auxiliary staff than in previous years. Also, added in this edition is an update of accounting and auditing practices with an examination of the Comprehensive Annual Financial Report (CAFR), which is now required in all school districts.

Previous editions of *Financing Education in a Climate of Change* have discussed the developmental stages of school finance theory and practice. This new edition adds a sixth stage that reflects the past two to three decades. It describes an *amalgam* of complexities that indicate the unique characteristics of the era.

As in previous editions, models and figures have been updated. New demographics and other information relevant to the study of school finance are included, showing interesting present and future projections that need to be studied and clarified for the student in relation to administrative decisions. The theme that still permeates this book is that education is an investment in human capital. This concept has more recently drawn the attention of economists who are taking a greater interest in education finance matters and studying it in relation to the benefit education provides to society and the impact it has on economic growth. The integrity of previous editions is maintained, with the goal of providing information for the student that is relevant, practicable, and applicable to the current education scene.

Education equity has not in any sense been totally achieved on a nationwide scale, but increasing clarification of the principle and the emphasis by court mandates and legislative actions have carried it to a new point of practice in a number of states. Democracy is best served by extending to all children an equal opportunity to attend schools adequate for the achievement of self-realization, economic sufficiency, civic responsibility, and effective human relationships. Some of the unsolved problems of financing public education include providing high-quality education that is equitable to all students, regardless of place of residence or degree of parental affluence, and furnishing adequate funds with maximum fairness to all taxpayers.

Financing Education in a Climate of Change is intended as a text for a basic course in school finance at the graduate level. It also has great value for undergraduate students in education, providing an overview of education finance principles. Practicing school administrators, teachers, school board members, legislators, and others interested in school finance issues will find information on how to finance education adequately and equitably. Since the chief school administrator is responsible for the overall school program and the financial reporting of the school district, some aspects of school business administration are included in the book.

Our aim as authors of the text is to make the study of education finance a worthwhile and enjoyable experience. There is a great deal of information that can be somewhat overwhelming to the student. For practicing administrators and instructors of the course, our goal is to make the information user-friendly and easily understood. The basic information in the book has been maintained and has been very useful for students and instructors. The historical coverage has been extremely beneficial to both students and researchers and remains intact. A Resource Study Guide, financial data for text simulations and questions, and an outline of important federal education programs for teachers and students are available online at **www.ablongman.com/edleadership**. In addition, an excellent **PowerPoint** package is available for the tenth edition that will be very beneficial for class presentations.

As in previous editions we have many to thank for the assistance they have given. Especially, we thank readers, instructors, and students who have made comments for the improvement of this edition, and those who have graciously allowed the use of some of their materials. This book is a cooperative effort among scholars, experienced editors and publishers, insightful reviewers, researchers, computer consultants, and designers. We thank all whose suggestions have improved this work, including Reed R. Garfield, Janet J. Tanner, Burt R. Garfield, Elyse Rasmussen, J. D. Willardson, Lynda Griffiths, and, at Allyn and Bacon, Arnis Burvikovs, Erin Reilly, and Annette Joseph. Special thanks to Richard Young and LeGrand Richards both of Brigham Young University. We also gratefully acknowledge the reviewers of this tenth edition: Marilyn Hirth, Purdue University; Lora Knutson, Governor's State University; and Joseph Herbert Torres, New Mexico State University. Continued gratitude to the late Percy Burrup, who made the foundation of this work possible. His influence still remains.

V. B.
R. R. G.

1 The Economics of Education

As a former educator and school board member, and as a parent, I am personally convinced that improving education is vital to the future of our economy and in the cultural, social, political, and personal aspects of our lives as well.

—Ben S. Bernanke, 2007

Education is an investment in human capital. Education occurs in various settings—in formal education, on-the-job training, professional seminars, and personally directed study. Through education we develop literacy, the ability to numerate, and the skills to solve problems. We achieve self-realization, economic sufficiency, civic responsibility, and satisfactory human relationships. As with all investments, it takes resources to create human capital and provide schooling for children, youths, and adults of the United States. There is an element of risk. Resources may be misallocated, investment decisions made incorrectly, and no one can be certain that recipients of the education product will achieve the maximum of their human potential. It is imperative that equitable and adequate finance be provided to education to achieve those goals, in spite of that risk.

The increase of human capital is largely responsible for the remarkable social and economic development of the United States over the two centuries of its existence. The costs that are required to create human capital through our education system are mostly worthwhile. The most important producer of human capital in the United States is the public education system. Public education is the conduit that transfers resources from the private sector to education consumers. The human capital generated in public schools and elsewhere is needed to ensure a dynamic economy, provide an adequate standard of living, reinforce domestic security, as well as sustain the United States prominence in the world.

Alan Greenspan, former Chairman of the Board of Governors, Federal Reserve System, said the nation must invest in human capital and that it is "critical that the quality of education in elementary and secondary schools be improved."[1] He declared:

> Even the most significant advances in information and technology will not produce additional economic value without human creativity and intellect. Certainly, if we are to remain preeminent in transforming knowledge into economic value, the U.S. system of education must remain the world's leader in generating scientific and technological breakthroughs

1

and in preparing workers to meet the need for skilled labor. . . . Education must realize the potential for bringing lasting benefits to the economy.[2]

Education as Human Capital

Economists now recognize the importance of investment in education for developing the nation's human capital. Early economists such as David Ricardo and Thomas Malthus emphasized the roles of land, labor, and capital in creating economic growth, and they gave only passing attention to the economic importance of education.

More recently, economists have emphasized the value of education as a factor in stimulating economic growth. Education is now popularly referred to as investment in human capital. Such leaders in the field as John Kenneth Galbraith, Harold Groves, Milton Friedman, Theodore Schultz, Gary Becker, George Psacharopoulos, and Charles Benson have documented the relationship between education and economic growth. They have deplored the waste of the labor force and human resources that automatically accompanies inadequate education, regardless of its causes. Schultz has given an excellent definition of human capital:

> Human capital has the fundamental attributes of the basic economic concept of capital; namely, it is a source of future satisfactions, or of future earnings, or both of them. What makes it human capital is the fact that it becomes an integral part of a person. But we were taught that land, capital, and labor are the basic factors of production. Thus we find it hard to think of the useful skills and knowledge that each of us has acquired as forms of capital.[3]

Since human capital has the fundamental characteristics of any form of economic capital and it is a part of the person possessing it, such capital deteriorates with inactivity. It does not disappear completely until the death or complete incapacity of the person possessing it. It often needs to be reactivated and updated to lessen its degree of obsoleteness or the extent of its inadequateness.

Creation of Wealth and Education

Human capital is essential to the creation of wealth. Economists use models to analyze growth that focus on increases in labor, physical capital, and technological progress. Technological progress explains nearly all economic growth and wealth creation, and it relies heavily on increases in human capital. Increasing human capital through quality education is therefore vitally important.

Increases in human capital mean there are more educated workers. Educated workers take more pride in their work, are faster and more creative, have more basic job skills, and acquire new skills more rapidly than less educated workers. Educated workers are more productive. They have less absenteeism, are less likely to shirk, and understand the goals of their employer.

Human capital begets more human and physical capital. People with more education are more likely to continue training, to have personally directed studies, and to participate in professional seminars. They are more likely to have children who consume high levels of education. Those who have a college education generally earn nearly twice as much as high school dropouts and consequently have more to invest in physical capital. Investment benefits society through the greater production of goods and services. Thus, education creates a virtuous circle—the condition in which a favorable circumstance or result gives rise to another that subsequently supports the first. The more education, the more wealth is developed, the more wealth, the more funds are available for investment, the more investment, the more wealth is available for investment in physical and human capital.

The wonders of modern technology have been made possible largely because of education. The position the United States holds in technical improvements is the result of an educational system and a society that encourages research, creativity, and practical application. Much of today's wealth is tied to technology, and technology is advanced through education.

Every area of resources—human, physical, and financial—has been improved and refined through education. Even the environment is better appreciated and preserved through education. Methods of mining, lumbering, and other forms of natural resource production and use have been improved through the development of skills and training, and more wealth is produced through better use of resources. Improvements in productivity mean that more wealth is created with a smaller impact on the natural world.

Human capital allows greater productivity in management. As managers and leaders learn about leadership skills, they are better able to make decisions leading to more production, less dissatisfaction among workers, and more efficient accomplishment of the organization's goals. Effective management of labor, capital, technology, and natural resources promotes wealth.

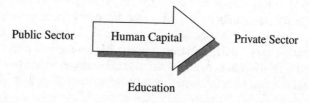

Education: An Important Industry

A common and certainly defensible description of education is that it is an industry in the sense that it utilizes money and other valuable resources to develop its product. Although it is this country's largest industry, education produces only intangibles in the form of nonmaterial services that are valuable but difficult to measure. It is an industry where extensive data are readily available to determine the inputs to education but where no research or empirical study has yet found a satisfactory way to measure, or even to approximate, its total output. In public education, there is no profit motive. Education is usually provided in government schools, which are dependent on the private economy for financial support. The United States is a world leader in education, with about 25 percent of its population involved in one way or another. "Citizens of the United States have the highest number of years in formal education of any wealthy country."[4] With regard to expenditures, statistics from the United States Department of Education show that 7.9 percent of the gross domestic product goes toward all educational institutions—an all-time high (see Table 1.1). The United States spends more per pupil on education than any other wealthy country; as a percentage of the gross domestic product (GDP), only Iceland spends more.[5]

Historically, education has been the largest public function—and the country's biggest business—when viewed in terms of the numbers of people and dollars of income involved in its operation. The expansion of educational services and the greatly increasing costs of education year after year have had an effect on the nation's economy. It is not likely that this condition will change.

Education requires resources in order to provide for the needs of students: teachers, administrators, facilities, equipment and supplies, and property. The resources to provide education depend on the private economy. The interconnection between education (providing the human capital to engender economic strength) and the economy (providing funds for education) is a reality. All over the world educational achievement and economic success are clearly linked. The struggle to raise a nation's living standard is fought first and foremost in the classroom. Certainly, no one needs to be convinced that education matters. The jobs in industry, in manufacturing, in services, and in providing homeland security for the nation require citizens who are well educated.

Interest in the economics of education is said to date back to the time of Plato; numerous economists and educators have given in-depth consideration to this relationship. They have established and documented the fact that increases in education bring increases in productivity and gains in social, political, and economic life. They support the idea that education costs are necessary and real investments in human capital.

Since educational institutions collectively are this country's biggest disbursers of public money, and since education is the greatest contributor to economic productivity, the positive relation of education to economic growth is real and obvious. Educators and economists have understood this close and interdependent relationship for some time.

One modern-day school finance writer who gives emphasis to the economics of education was Charles S. Benson. His book received popular acceptance and established a relation between education and economics that has been recognized by most school finance writers since that time. His point of view is summarized here:

TABLE 1.1 Total Expenditures of Educational Institutions Related to the Gross Domestic Product, by Level of Institution: Selected Years, 1929–30 to 2003–04

			Total Expenditures for Education in Current Dollars					
			All Educational Institutions		All Elementary and Secondary Schools		All Colleges and Universities	
Year	Gross Domestic Product (in Billions of Current Dollars)	School Year	Amount, in Millions	As a Percent of Gross Domestic Product	Amount, in Millions	As a Percent of Gross Domestic Product	Amount, in Millions	As a Percent of Gross Domestic Product
1	2	3	4	5	6	7	8	9
1929	$103.6	1929–30	—				$632	0.6
1939	92.2	1939–40	—				758	0.8
1949	267.3	1949–50	$8,911	3.3	$6,249	2.3	2,662	1.0
1959	506.6	1959–60	23,860	4.7	16,713	3.3	7,147	1.4
1969	984.6	1969–70	68,459	7.0	43,183	4.4	25,276	2.6
1970	1,038.5	1970–71	75,741	7.3	48,200	4.6	27,541	2.7
1975	1,638.3	1975–76	118,706	7.2	75,101	4.6	43,605	2.7
1980	2,789.5	1980–81	182,849	6.6	112,325	4.0	70,524	2.5
1985	4,220.3	1985–86	269,485	·6.4	161,800	3.8	107,685	2.6
1990	5,803.1	1990–91	412,652	7.1	248,930	4.3	163,722	2.8
1995	7,397.7	1995–96	529,596	7.2	318,246	4.3	211,350	2.9
1996	7,816.9	1996–97	560,571	7.2	339,151	4.3	221,420	2.8
1997	8,304.3	1997–98	594,715	7.2	361,415	4.4	233,300	2.8
1998	8,747.0	1998–99	633,038	7.2	384,038	4.4	249,000	2.8
1999	9,268.4	1999–00	680,038	7.3	411,538	4.4	268,500	2.9
2000	9,817.0	2000–01	734,311	7.5	442,011	4.5	292,300	3.0
2001	10,128.0	2001–02[1]	782,500	7.7	467,900	4.6	314,600[2]	3.1
2002	10,487.0	2002–03[1]	823,100	7.8	490,900	4.7	332,100[2]	3.2
2003	11,004.0	2003–04[2]	865,500	7.9	514,300	4.7	351,200[2]	3.2

—Not available.
[1]Preliminary data for public elementary and secondary schools and estimates for colleges and universities.
[2]Estimated.

Source: U.S. Department of Education, National Center for Education Statistics. (This table was prepared in April 2005.)

Throughout the world, both philosophers and men of affairs appear to have reached consensus on this point: education is a major force for human betterment. Quality of education is intimately related to its financing. How much resources are made available, and how effectively these resources are used stand as crucial questions in determining the degree to which education meets the aspirations that people hold for it.[6]

It is now a seldom-disputed fact that expending adequate funds for education will provide economic dividends to society. Quality education is expensive, but it brings commensurate benefits to individuals, families, business and professional people, and social agencies and institutions.

A cursory look at the political and economic philosophies in relation to education of Karl Marx, John Maynard Keynes, John Kenneth Galbraith, Milton Friedman and Adam Smith illustrates that they all saw the need for and the power of education even though their recommended role of government (and education) varies. Marx said that the central government should have absolute control. With the other four, perspectives differed from government assisting in cases of economic depression (Keynes), to more support of the public sector and more government resources being derived from the affluent private sector (Galbraith), to government intervention generally hampering progress (Friedman), to limiting government (Smith) (see Table 1.2).

Each of these philosophers felt that education was important; the differences involve the how and the what. According to Marx, education should be free to the student, state controlled, and financed by taxation and administered by the central government. It exists to train citizens in the value system of the government. Keynes believed the government had to provide an education, but he was famous for saying that education is the inculcation of the incomprehensible into the indifferent by the incompetent. Galbraith maintains that education is vital for technical and human advancement and must be supported to a more significant level by the resources that are abundant in the affluent private economy. Friedman saw education as excessively controlled by government; he believes the solution is the individual's freedom to choose what education is most suitable, using a voucher to shop for that education. Smith sees education as one of the essential services of government.

When seeking financial support for the schools, educators must understand the diverse philosophies and communicate across the political spectrum by using concepts that resonate within the particular politician's philosophy. More and more educational leaders understand that all major social forces must not only recognize each other's objectives and circumstances but also work cooperatively to solve one another's problems. Until recent years, educators, economists, and political leaders have been largely indifferent to each other's needs and problems.

A Public-Sector Responsibility

Education is produced in the private sector of the economy as well as in the public sector. Government, through taxation, produces most educational services consumed in the United States; however, private individuals, companies, and churches sponsor many schools. In certain other countries, education is largely a product of the private sector.

Schools in the private sector operate under a different set of theories and rules than those in the public sector. Educational organizations in the private sector are more responsive to consumer demand. Private educational organizations that fail to meet consumer demand see a reduction in pupils that leads to a reduction in resources available to hire staff, acquire buildings and property, and create endowments. The ability of private schools to meet consumer demand largely determines how much financial support is available for future operations. The desires, needs, and even whims of potential purchasers are soon met in the private sector, for to ignore such would mean a loss of revenue and profits. Inefficiency, incompetence, or other internal deficiencies are readily made known and usually lead to changes in schools in the competitive marketplace.

Government institutions, which include public schools, do not react as quickly or as obediently to consumer demand, external pressure, and public criticism as their counterparts in the competitive world. Local, state, and federal governments use tax funds to pay for their part of the education pattern. These tax funds are disbursed with little reliance on consumer demand to guide financial decisions. Also, the pluralism built into the U.S. constitutional order may make it more difficult to efficiently allocate resources to education. There is considerable variation from community to community in the quality of the schools, the needs of the students, and the availability of resources. For this reason, states should provide guidance and resources to help local districts and schools meet their goals.[7]

On September 11, 2001, terrorists struck the country with a devastating attack. That tragic event required an emphasis shift, and fighting terrorism became the major focus of the nation. In 2005, unprecedented destruction occurred when massive hurricanes ripped through several states, ending school operations and displacing students. To restart school programs and to care for and return students to their former educational venues $1.1 billion was appropriated. The Department of Education indicated that Louisiana, Mississippi, and Texas shared those funds. Reflecting 9/11, concern was raised about the country's ability to survive in the community of nations. It was postulated that Americans did not have the wherewithal to develop the skills necessary to protect the citizenry. Furthermore, the ability of the country to sufficiently solve ponderous weather and shifting student enrollment problems was questioned.

In this interacting, cooperating, and sometimes confusing education enterprise, some recipients may receive advantages over others; other recipients may suffer disadvantages. This is inevitable in a process where there are innate and fundamental differences in student ability, interest, and desire to learn—as well as differences in the many other factors that make up America's school milieu. In the country's federal system, public education is designed to produce equity (fairness) in the treatment of students. Although the terms are often used interchangeably, *equity* and *equality* are not synonyms. Although some degree of inequality will exist, it should be minimized.

Allocating economic resources to education is one of the primary responsibilities of local, state, and federal lawmaking bodies. Fortunately, the educational establishment now recognizes that decisions concerning resource allocation are made in the political arena.

TABLE 1.2   Political and Economic Continuum

	Marx	**Keynes**
Government or Economy	*Communist*	*Government Intervention*
Role of Government	Central government has total control; sets policy and goals in all aspects of society; strong bureaucracy.	Government will help the economy in depression or recession by public works projects, etc. Deficits accumulated thereby will be repaid during good economic times.
Educational Perspective	Free public education, controlled and financed by centralized government. Trains in value system of the government.	Education is the inculcation of the incomprehensible into the indifferent by the incompetent.
Taxes	Highly graduated progressive tax on income.	Progressive tax to redistribute wealth so the poor can spend more and the wealthy save less.
Property	Abolition of private ownership of property.	Private property essential; however, government is the most important element of the economy.
Vantage Point in History	Reaction to exploitation of workers in the Industrial Revolution. History is determined by economic conditions.	Predicted ruin of Europe's economy because of harsh economic conditions imposed on Germany by the Treaty of Versailles. Capitalism usually better than alternatives.

Galbraith	Friedman	Smith
Liberal	*Conservative*	*Capitalist*
Government is a dominant factor in society. Limit overproduction by private sector. Provide affluence for all citizens.	Government interventions have hampered programs. Should reduce bureaucracy because people who are free to choose without bureaucratic influence create a better quality of life.	The invisible hand of competition will run the economy in a natural way. Government should govern only—no government interference in business or trade, just preserve law and order, defend the nation, enforce justice. Least government is best.
Education is vital for technical advances and growth. Education must be encouraged for future research and development.	Government overgoverns education. Voucher system for education. Education is essential in maintaining free enterprise, political freedom, and open economy.	Education is one of the essential government services to make capitalism work; competition between schools. Local education control, compulsory education at elementary level.
Public economy is starved; private economy is bloated. Tax the affluent society (private sector) more to provide needed public services, education, etc.	Private economy is starved; public economy is bloated. Tax reform encourages investment in private sector.	Taxes should reflect ability to pay, not be arbitrary; should be convenient and efficient. Needed to provide for essential government services.
Private ownership has been oversold through advertising; the affluence of private sector has cheated public needs. Fiscal policy is essential.	People must be free to own and exchange goods. Monetary policy, not fiscal policy, is essential in shaping economic events.	Private property is essential to freedom; if state owns, freedom vanishes.
Conventional wisdom always in danger of becoming obsolete. Rejects orthodox views of economics. Quality of life, not gross national product, should be the measure of economic achievement.	Freedom is more important than prosperity. However, freedom is the best environment for economic prosperity; monetary policy leads to stability.	Wrote *The Wealth of Nations* in 1776, but its major impact came in early 1800s. Reaction to British mercantilism; tariffs and limited "free" trade.

Economics and Social Progress

Profits are earned when revenues, generated by sales, exceed costs. Profits are meaningful only in the private sector of the economy. When consumers and producers engage in market transactions, the resulting profits are signals private firms use to make investment, hiring, and strategic decisions. With the resources generated in the private sector, the public sector, including education, receives the financial resources it requires to operate. Therefore, a system of diverting funds from the private sector to the public sector must exist. The most common system to accomplish this, although far from perfect, is taxation.

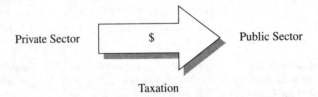

Private Sector $ Public Sector

Taxation

The reliance on taxation to provide funds for education requires a recognition and understanding of the relationship between public education and the field of economics. Educational leaders at all levels cannot continue to give mere fleeting glances and incidental references to fundamental economic theories and principles if they are to be effective in helping solve, or reduce, the complex and persistent problems involved in financing education adequately and equitably. Some knowledge of economics and its partnership role with education is therefore deemed to be important for school finance students as well as practitioners. For that reason, this book begins with a brief discussion of some of the fundamental principles and concepts of economics that have practical application to the broad field of school finance.

The effects of compulsory school attendance laws, taxation laws, changes in the economy, clamor for improvement in government-sponsored schools, and social pressures can be understood with a basic grasp of economic principles. Since education is vital to interests of the individual and broader society, the state has the right and the responsibility to provide education opportunities broadly and to ensure that those opportunities are accessed by every child. Parents and guardians have the responsibility to ensure that their children and wards take advantage of the schooling provided by the public.

There are diverse ways of measuring or rating the degree of advancement or upward progress of a society. One way is to apply the economic dimension that attempts to determine the degree or percentage of total human effort that is being diverted to production of the goods and services required for survival such as food, clothing, and shelter. This measure of human effort is then added to the effort devoted to producing goods and services that make life more comfortable but are not required for survival, such as entertainment, travel, and education. Societies at the low end of the social–progress continuum devote all or nearly all their efforts to producing essential goods and services. As societies develop economically, the percentage of human effort expended to produce goods and services not required for subsistence increases.

As societies reach the point where all the material requirements for survival are met, production and consumption decisions are devoted to satisfy other desires. Society has no ability to judge which desires should be met or how to allocate scarce resources. Through free exchange in the marketplace, individual consumers signal producers which goods and services they desire. Education is one of those desires that is highly sought after as societies advance above basic survival. In the economic history of more-developed countries, one finds the importance of education services and the strong consumer demand for increased educational services. Early education entrepreneurs provided schools, books, and other opportunities to meet the demand for education. In the 1800s and thereafter, governments began to recognize the value of providing basic education to more children. Countries around the world are at various points on the education–economic development continuum.

Thus, it appears that the greater the degree of advancement of a society, the greater its potential for producing additional goods and services, including education. Those countries that lack resources or people with technical ability must spend most of their time and effort in producing goods for subsistence and survival. In turn, they will have commensurately little time and ability to produce a good educational system. A report from the World Bank stated:

> Although exceptions are made, in general the emphasis in low-income countries is on the development of low-cost basic education to lay the requisite foundation of science, language, mathematics, and other cognitive skills. In middle-income countries, where first-level education is already widely available, educational quality is emphasized, and with it the expansion of facilities to meet the needs of an increasingly sophisticated economy. As the absorptive capacity of an economy grows, the priority tends to shift toward providing higher level technical skills, as well as developing skills in science, technology, information processing, and research.[8]

A country that strives to produce quality educational services is constantly improving the foundation on which advances in economic productivity and wealth are built. Countries that make only minimal effort in education usually produce only the goods and services necessary for a meager, subsistence existence. The educational system, then, is both a very important result and determinant of the social and economic progress of a nation.

As stated in *The Economist:* "In the advanced economies of America and Europe, today's chief economic worry is that jobs and industries will be lost to new competition from Asia, Latin America, and Eastern Europe. It is commonplace that, among these emerging economies, the most successful are the ones that have educated most of their workers up to, and in many cases well beyond, levels typically achieved in the West."[9]

Produces Nonfree Services

Any college student can attest to the fact that education is not a free commodity in the economic sense. When consideration is given to the indirect costs, what economists call *opportunity costs* (the income lost while attending school), as well as the direct costs (living expenses, fees, textbooks, computers, materials, and tuition), there is no need for an additional reminder that education is far from free.

As a purchaser of educational services, the student recognizes education as a consumer good, paying money for the avowed purpose of consuming as much education as possible for the money spent. On the other hand, because education creates human capital, education can be treated as a producer good. The increase in human capital generated by education allows for a greater production of goods and services, not the least of which is more education. Instructors must first be educated before they can teach.

As the college graduate receives an academic degree and moves into the world of work, no stock of accumulated physical capital is evident from educational experiences. The investment has been made in nontangible goods and services—human capital, that, it is hoped, will be used to provide consumers with valuable goods and services which follows from the necessary process of earning a living. The human capital is bundled with the goods and services provided in the market. A good such as a house, for example, has embedded in the rooms and conveniences the educational attainment of architects, mortgage lenders, carpenters, plumbers, electricians, and many others.

These educational services acquired in school may be used and reused almost without limit and are therefore described as multiple-use goods or services. In contrast with machines, equipment, and other physical goods that depreciate with use, the durability or utility of educational services normally appreciates with use.

Although much learning is sought and obtained for its intrinsic and cultural value, most education is sought to increase the ability of the student to engage in some useful occupation or profession and thus to produce goods and services for the marketplace. This process is an economic one, since it provides the means to satisfy wants as a consumer as well as to produce goods and services for other consumers. An education adds to the richness of life for its recipients, allows for more informed decision making, and changes the scope of consumption decisions to products that require more education to access such as books, magazines, works of art, and musical compositions. Thus, education is literally a consumer's good as well as a producer's good.

Stimulates Economic Growth

Education is important to increases in economic productivity. Wealth in the economy is created by increasing the amount of labor or capital available for production or by improving the productivity of their use. Labor increases are determined by demographics, capital increases are determined by savings and investment, and productivity increases are enhanced by increases in knowledge. The only durable way to increase wealth is by improving capital and labor productivity. One may think of education as a necessary condition for economic growth but it is not a sufficient condition.

In the quest for economic growth and higher productivity, it is important to recognize that other investment projects have legitimate claims to investment dollars. Legislative leaders find themselves under pressure from educational advocates as they attempt to make decisions to establish and support public educational institutions to divert resources from other worthy investments. These leaders understand only too well that education, as an industry, does not and cannot operate in a vacuum without reference to the broader economy. To become effective, educators must be cognizant of the philosophy of individual politicians, economic principles, political theories, and related disciplines. Educators must understand that politicians are their clients as much as students are. Whether it be a school board member making programmatic or salary decisions, a legislator determining the level of school support, a member of Congress, or the president of the United States, each is influential in determining fiscal matters that affect the educational program.

Although the United States has been blessed with a strong, vibrant economy and a well-educated citizenry, the demands that can be made on the private sector have limits. The spiraling costs of the services of government and its institutions have sharpened competition for the tax dollar more than ever before. As an important economic service with increasing responsibility to the people of the nation, education would seem to have established itself as a strong and deserving competitor for the economic resources responsible for its support.

The Scope of Educational Services

Economics has a concept called *consumer sovereignty.* In a competitive market, consumers will determine with their purchasing decisions what goods and services will be provided. If entrepreneurs desire to create new goods or services, they must ensure that there exists an adequate demand. Without consumer demand, entrepreneurs cannot repay their suppliers nor earn a profit and the enterprise fails. It is the willingness to pay for a good that creates the supply. Demand for education, however, is unlike the demands for most other goods and services. In education, the consumers of education, the students, generally do not pay for their education. Rather, funds for education are primarily provided through taxes collected by the government.

The quality and quantity of educational services are determined in large measure by the wishes of government officials, by the pleasant or unpleasant experiences voters have had with education in their own lives, by groups with interest in education such as parents, teachers, and administrators, and by taxpayers who seek to lower their share of the tax burden. The degree of satisfaction of students is often secondary to the concerns of taxpayers who determine the extent of such services available. Thus, educational expenditures are often determined in a right-to-left direction—in much the same way as a customer who is short of cash might approach the menu in a luxurious restaurant.

The individuals who determine the supply of education to be made available often have no children or other family who are students or have a direct relationship with any of the individuals of any education interest group. For that reason, school board members, other elected officials, and government administrators who are responsible for the supply of education may approach school finance with a neutral or even a negative attitude. Their decisions may be made in terms of a real or imagined financial tax burden to the exclusion of more relevant and necessary educational needs. This often results in exaggerated criticism of increases in educational expenditures, especially in areas where there is little objective evidence of commensurate results. Regular and substantial increases in financial inputs are necessary to keep pace with inflation and to increase and improve quality. Teacher and administrative salaries must keep pace with inflation. Increasing teacher quality also requires a financial commitment.

The Marginal Dollar Principle

How does a free society determine the amount of resources it will spend for such an important service of government as education? Theoretically, it could be done in the same way an individual decides how to allocate scarce resources among competing goods and services in a free market. The individual considers the marginal utility of prospective goods and services. The utility is the pleasure or satisfaction that the consumer achieves in consuming a good or service.

It is important to understand what economists call *diminishing marginal utility*. The utility of additional units of a particular good or service decreases as additional units are consumed. For example, an individual will have a smaller increase in utility with the purchase of a third car than with the purchase of a second one, and the second car adds much less additional utility than the first. Diminishing marginal utility explains the paradox that water, which is essential for life, is relatively cheap, whereas diamonds, which fulfill no basic human need, are very expensive. To a man suffering extreme thirst, a little water might command a very high price, but to the average water consumer, the last gallon has very little value.

Diminishing marginal utility is important in education. The public may place high value on the purchase of elementary education for all its children at public expense and give high priority to this undertaking, but may put less emphasis on education for four years of high school and still less emphasis on providing funds for higher education. The public may feel, too, that the expenditure of the first $10,000 per pupil per year is highly desirable, but an additional $1,000 might be less desirable, and that expending a further $1,000 might be undesirable or unwise—for it might require taking funds away from other, seemingly more important, goods or services.

The marginal dollar is the dollar that would be better spent for some other good or service. Thus, allocating funds for education becomes a problem of determining at what point an additional amount proposed as an expenditure for education would bring greater satisfaction or worth if it were spent for other goods or services.

Education has specific problems allocating resources while recognizing diminishing marginal utility. As McLure has noted:

> The theory of marginal utility cannot be applied as clearly in education as in some other operations. It is difficult, for example, to determine when the addition of one more staff member may or may not produce results which would be equal to or less than the value of the money paid the person. In industry, however, the addition of one worker would be at the margin if the increased income would be equal to the cost of the worker.[10]

Economists who are becoming more involved in studying this relationship in education are classifying the concept as "value added."

The Point of Diminishing Returns

Undoubtedly, there is a point of diminishing returns in the expenditure of funds for education—a point beyond which additional expenditures will yield very little or no additional educational returns. Where this point is—in terms of expenditures per pupil—has not yet been determined. The problem with education is that the information needed to determine educational returns is not available. One reason is that education is not bought and sold like other commodities.

Determining the relation of the per-pupil expenditures for education to the quality of the product has proved to be a popular, but elusive, research subject for many years. There is considerable disagreement among researchers on whether a direct relationship exists between dollars spent and student performance. Such divergence of opinion has caused some to believe that public education has already reached the marginal dollar limit and a point of diminishing returns. The lack of unanimity among scholars does not diminish that whatever improvements can be made to make education more effective, more extensive, and more applicable to the lives of U.S. citizens should be made.

To say that resource inputs can and do make a difference in students' educational outcomes is still a matter of interpretation. It is normal for people, especially overburdened taxpayers, to compare the costs and apparent productivity of various public institutions or industries—particularly those in direct competition with each other for scarce tax dollars. Such comparisons may reflect unfavorably on education for reasons not under the control of those involved.

The problem of producing spectacular improvements in education with the allocation of additional funds is another matter. Greatly increased expenditures for education have not, cannot, and will not produce such large or fantastic increases or improvements in its products. The nature of the learning process being what it is, increases in learning effectiveness can be anticipated only in small percentages, regardless of the magnitude of the financial increments applied to the improvement process. It is unlikely that the field of education, even with the application of almost limitless resources, will ever have available ways of multiplying the quantity or the quality of learning that human beings can achieve in a predetermined amount of time.

Economic Benefits of Education

Right or wrong, the main thrust of expenditures for public education is toward transmitting known information to individual consumers. Since the generally accepted philosophy of education requires that all citizens have a high-quality education through most of their preadult life, the costs of a formal education program must, of necessity, be proportionately higher for the United States than for countries that are disposed to release their youths at an earlier age. But what of the benefits of education to individuals under a system that requires participation for such an extended period?

Many studies have been conducted and estimates made to determine the economic benefits that accrue to the average person with varying amounts of formal education. Universally, these reports indicate the high pecuniary benefits of education (see Table 1.3).

The educated person enjoys a broader range of job opportunities than his or her less well-educated counterpart. Since unemployment is usually closely related to lack of education and adequate work skills, education provides some security against joblessness in periods of change or a slackening of business and industrial activity. However, no figures can be quoted to indicate the economic benefits of education to individuals in such matters as growth in vocational alternatives, growth in vocational and avocational interests, and greater appreciation for cultural and intellectual pursuits.

Many people view education strictly in terms of costs, legislative allocations, and percentage of taxes. If education is considered as an investment in human capital, the problem becomes one of extracting sufficient resources from the present economy to provide educational opportunities to the populace now that will be adequate to pay dividends to society in the future. If one considers only the taxes paid by individuals who make more money, the benefit to the state is significant. The Campaign for Educational Equity (CEE) maintains:

- Annual losses exceed $50 billion in federal and state income taxes for all 23,000,000 U.S. high school dropouts ages 18 to 67.
- America loses $192 billion—1.6 percent of GDP—in combined income and tax revenue losses with each cohort of 18-year-olds who never complete high school. Health-related losses for the estimated 600,000 high school dropouts in 2004 totaled at least $58 billion, or nearly $100,000 per student.
- High school dropouts have a life expectancy that is 9.2 years shorter than that of high school graduates.
- America could save between $7.9 billion and $10.8 billion annually by improving educational attainment among all recipients of Temporary Assistance for Needy Families (TANF), food stamps, and housing assistance.
- Increasing the high school completion rate by just 1 percent for all men ages 20 to 60 would save the United States up to $1.4 billion per year in reduced costs from crime.
- The economic benefits of participation in model preschool programs range as high as $7 for each dollar invested.
- College graduates are three times more likely to vote than Americans without a high school degree, while those who earn more are far more likely to be affiliated with a political organization.[11]

In addition to these benefits there is significant pecuniary advantage to the individual. Economic benefits, in terms of average earnings per person in the United States relative to education level achieved in 2006, were as follows:

- A male junior high school dropout earned $14,066 less per year than a high school graduate. In lifetime earnings, that amounts to $492,310 (see Table 1.3).
- A male high school dropout earned $9,446 less per year than a high school graduate. In lifetime earnings, that equates to $330,680.
- A male high school graduate earned $21,495 less annually than a college graduate did. In lifetime earnings, that equals $752,325.

TABLE 1.3 Median Annual Income of Year-round, Full-time Workers 25 Years Old and Over, by Highest Level of Educational Attainment and Sex: 1995 through 2004

		Elementary/Secondary			College			Bachelor's or Higher Degree			
Sex and Year	Total	Less than 9th Grade	Some High School, No Completion	High School Completion (includes equivalency)	Some College, No Degree	Associate's Degree	Total	Bachelor's Degree	Master's Degree	Professional Degree	Doctor's Degree
1	2	3	4	5	6	7	8	9	10	11	12
					Current Dollars						
Males											
1995	34,551	18,354	22,185	29,510	33,883	35,201	50,481	45,266	55,216	79,667	65,336
2000	41,059	20,789	25,095	34,303	40,337	41,952	61,868	56,334	68,322	99,411	80,250
2001	41,617	21,361	26,209	34,723	41,045	42,776	62,223	55,929	70,899	100,000	86,965
2002	41,152	20,919	25,903	33,206	40,851	42,856	61,700	56,077	67,281	100,000	83,305
2003	41,939	21,217	26,468	35,412	41,348	42,871	62,075	56,502	70,640	100,000	87,131
2004	42,085	21,659	26,277	35,725	41,895	44,404	62,797	57,220	71,530	100,000	82,401
Females											
1995	24,875	13,577	15,825	20,463	23,997	27,311	35,259	32,051	40,263	50,000	48,141
2000	30,327	15,798	17,919	24,970	28,697	31,071	42,706	40,415	50,139	58,957	57,081
2001	31,356	16,691	19,156	25,303	30,418	32,153	44,776	40,994	50,669	61,748	62,123
2002	31,010	16,510	19,307	25,182	29,400	31,625	43,245	40,853	48,890	57,018	65,715
2003	31,565	16,907	18,938	26,074	30,142	32,253	45,116	41,327	50,163	66,491	67,214
2004	31,990	17,023	19,162	26,029	30,816	33,481	45,911	41,681	51,316	75,036	68,875

Source: Prepared by the Bureau of Labor Statistics, U.S. Department of Labor. (Printed June 11, 2006.)

- Increasing education for males at the master's, doctorate, and professional levels showed similar gains (see Figure 1.1).
- A female junior high school dropout earned $9,006 less per year than a high school graduate. That amounts to $315,210 in lifetime earnings.
- A female high school dropout earned $6,867 less per year than a high school graduate. That equates to $240,345 in lifetime earnings.
- A female high school graduate earned $15,652 less annually than a college graduate did. That equals $547,820 in lifetime earnings.
- Increasing education for females at the master's, doctorate, and professional levels showed similar gains (see Figure 1.1).
- There were 55,469,000 male workers and 39,072,000 female workers with income.

Workers are limited because of lack of education—the more education they receive, the more money they make. The relationship of education and earnings is positive for males and females. However, males have a higher median annual income. Also, males at the professional level make more than those with a doctorate. Females usually follow this same pattern.

FIGURE 1.1   Mean Average Earnings per Person in the United States, Age 25 and Over, in Full-Time Employment, by Gender: 2004.

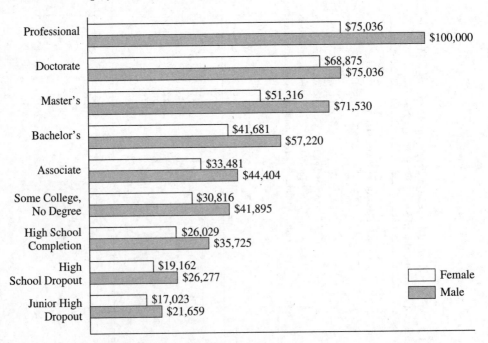

Source: U.S. Department of Commerce, Bureau of the Census, Current Population Reports, Series P-60, "Money Income of Households, Families, and Persons in the United States." (This figure was prepared in October 2005.) Retrieved May 17, 2006.

Increasing Expenditures and the Economy

It is well established that human capital is more important than natural resources in wealth creation. Fortunate indeed is a nation that has extensive natural resources; however, the nation with highly developed human resources is even more fortunate. A nation with high educational development will overcome to a great degree any lack of natural resources, but no nation having a poor educational system, even with tremendous stores of natural wealth, has been able to approach high individual economic productivity. Countries such as Japan, Taiwan, Singapore, and Finland are examples of high-income countries with a strong tradition of quality education and few or very limited natural resources. On the other extreme are countries such as Nigeria, Brazil, Saudi Arabia, and Indonesia with abundant natural resources but that fail to provide adequate education for their citizens. As a result, these countries with abundant natural resources are too slowly improving the incomes and well-being of their citizens.

Expenditures Benefit Individuals and Society

It is clear that the returns to education expenditures are shared by the individual student and society at large. The amount that society and the individual benefit from education varies with the amount of education. Early elementary education—basic reading, writing, and math skills—aids society enormously. Through elementary education, society acquires voters who are more easily informed, patients who are better able to take advantage of health services, and individuals who more readily communicate. With regard to students, they acquire very few skills that will differentiate them in the marketplace. Those marketable skills are acquired later in secondary and higher education. As such, the returns to education start out favoring social returns, but in college and graduate and professional schools, the individual benefits by acquiring marketable skills and captures the larger share of the returns to education.

It is true that many of the benefits of education cannot be measured with standard economic measures. An individual gains social mobility, a higher status, more appreciation for arts and culture, and the ability to participate more fully in the democratic process. In addition, benefits accrue to the individual's family, neighborhood, business, society, and culture that cannot be measured in dollars and cents. Children of college graduates are more likely to attend college and be successful in college, creating a family education cycle. The whole of society benefits from scientific inventions. Business organizations benefit from higher skilled and motivated workers.

Generally, the more education a person attains, the more income he or she will have. As income rises, so do income and property taxes and thus more resources are available for government-provided goods and services such as education. As income increases, more services can be provided even without increasing the tax burden on individuals.

Education expenditures, particularly those for teacher and administrative salaries (75 to 80 percent of the total education spending of current expenditures), quickly find their way back into the private economy through normal flow in the economic system. Thus, their withdrawal from the private sector in the form of taxes paid, their passage into and through the public sector via the payroll, and their return to the sector of their beginnings usually form a cycle that is operative in such a short period of time that the original withdrawal effect on the economy is minimal.

Noneconomic Benefits of Education

The positive economic effects of good education are extremely important. Much is said and written about education as an investment in people. Sometimes, however, in an effort to show its economic investment characteristics, people may inadvertently overlook the social benefits or the noneconomic benefits of education. A republic must stake its chances for a free democratic society on a viable education system. Uninformed and illiterate people are not able to govern themselves. Students must understand the philosophical foundation and the federalism nature of the United States Constitution, the framework of government, their role in continuing the nation's political system, and the dangers of anarchy. The foundation of representative government is a population of well-informed and responsible citizens with knowledge to cast a rational vote for candidates for public office. Those for whom they vote must make decisions about the education system, national defense, communication, and international affairs, which makes it clear that an educated citizenry is an essential national requirement.

Perpetuating our form of government is just one of the many noneconomic benefits of education. Another is that schools are a source of moral values. The principles of honesty, integrity, morality, compassion, and observing rules and laws are still taught, directly or indirectly, in the schools. Although religious instruction is for the churches, ethical values such as tolerance, rejecting prejudice, and equality are studied in school classrooms. Informed and perceptive minds are nurtured in the school setting.

Individuals also learn to appreciate and patronize the arts, benefiting all. Education preserves a nation's culture and a people's sense of identity. Only through education can the history and traditions of a people be preserved and the standard of living (as measured by quantity of money and quality of life) be enhanced.

Education Produces External Benefits

As previously stated, education produces benefits for society beyond the benefits obtained by its recipients. Therefore, it is said that education possesses externalities. Externalities may be positive or negative. A negative externality is something like pollution. Individuals value steel and therefore companies produce it for consumers; however, iron ore and coal must be mined, which scars landscapes and creates pollution, and steel is transported to consumers on trains or trucks that emit pollution. The consumer of steel does not pay for the pollution generated in the production of steel. It is society as a whole that pays the cost of this pollution. Education is a good example of a positive externality. The benefits that are produced are not all captured by the student.

A healthier society, a more informed electorate, and a more productive labor force are a few of the examples of benefits that the student shares with society.

This positive education externality is used to justify financing education through taxation rather than by fee collecting, rate bills, or tuition charges. Also, the purchaser of elementary education would not be the student but the student's parents or guardians. One cannot assume that parents and/or guardians always take into account the best interest of the student. The large societal benefit of elementary education is such that society does not permit individuals to refrain from purchasing it. Society, through government, sets a minimum level of education that every child should acquire. Some parents or guardians would purchase little or no education if allowed to exercise their individual options.

To ensure that an adequate amount of education is produced and consumed, education is supported financially by a form of tax. Income taxes are based on some measure of ability to pay. Property taxes are based on the value of real estate. Sales taxes depend on the level of consumption. These tax systems presume no direct relation between the amount of taxes paid and the amount of public goods or services that are received by the taxpayer. To a great degree, the systems deny the individual the right of choice of the type, amount, or method of educational services he or she is required to assume.

It is evident that individuals are not only concerned with the amount of education they consume but are also concerned with the extent of education others consume. Standards of living are raised and economic growth is enhanced by the externalities that are generated by the education of the members of a social group. Individuals will reap additional personal benefits when most citizens have an adequate education. If few in society obtain adequate education, many in a society will suffer lost income and well-being.

Exclusion or Free Rider Principle

Most goods and services produced by the private market cannot be consumed simultaneously by others. An apple bought at the grocery store can only be eaten once, a barber cannot cut the hair of two heads at once. The private sector is very adept at producing these types of goods. These goods and services provide benefits only to the consumer and cannot be enjoyed by others. Other types of goods, called *public goods* by economists, can be enjoyed by many simultaneously. The community police force provides benefits for every citizen in the community by reducing crime. The reduction in criminals benefits every citizen of the community. The ability of a consumer to enjoy exclusively a good or service is commonly referred to as the *exclusion principle*. Likewise, a consumer who enjoys a good or service that is provided to the community as a whole without paying for that service is known as a *free rider*. Examples of public goods are defense, police, vaccinations, and the courts.

Education allows for free riders. There is a large social benefit if the vast majority of individuals acquire adequate education. Individuals may garner many of these benefits without spending their income or foregoing income to continue schooling.

Everyone benefits from education when the results are lower social costs, increased wealth, greater income and sales tax revenue, and development of the five elements that expand the economy: resources, labor, capital, technology, and management. It is thereby impossible to assess costs in terms of potential benefits to purchasers and at the same time exclude nonpurchasers from similar benefits.

Externalities Justify the Ability Principle

The problem of financing education is different from that of marketing most other goods and services. The existence of externalities and free riders changed the method of financing education from the benefit principle to the ability principle. The lessons learned in the pre–public school era in this matter should not be forgotten. Unfortunately, some individuals in every society would not be partakers of education if it were purchasable only on a voluntary basis. They must be required by government to obtain it in some minimum quantity by compulsory school attendance laws. A second important factor is that not only does education benefit individuals in proportion to their purchase or consumption of it, but it pervades society and indirectly affects all citizens. These effects lead to higher standards of living and allow greater consumption of cultural goods and services.

It is impossible to measure the benefits that come to the person or to society from individual purchases of educational services. That being true, the most defensible approach is to assume that all individuals in society benefit to about the same degree or extent. On that basis, the costs of education should be paid by all members of society in terms of their ability to pay. Under this ability principle, the wealthy pay more for the services of government, but their comparative burden is no greater than that borne by the less affluent.

Taxation and Education

To tax individuals in direct relation to the benefits they receive from the service or commodity that is provided by that tax would seem to be defensible, provided that the benefit is observable and to a high degree measurable, and provided further that they alone benefit from the tax they pay. Proponents of the benefit system of taxation argue that taxation by the ability principle penalizes the affluent and financially successful person. Such a process, they contend, stifles and curtails further activities of an economic nature and tends to create an indolent society. They point to the extremely high rate of the upper level of income tax as having a negative effect on business and industrial expansion.

Education and certain other services of government do not lend themselves to the benefit principle of taxation. Every state has had or now has a compulsory school attendance law that requires all children of certain ages to spend a predetermined amount of time in formal education. What about those required to attend who do not have the financial ability to pay for such required services of government? Are the parents of six children to pay six times as much as the parents of one child? Is the adult without children to be exempt from school taxation altogether? Such questions have faced the states through the years; even today, the relative importance of this form of taxation varies considerably among the states.

Cost-Quality Relationship in Education

Economic, political, and educational leaders are concerned with the question of how the amount of money spent for education relates to the quality of the educational product. Various reform movements have sought more productivity from instructional staff, lower administration costs, better utilization of buildings, and other cost-saving remedies, with the anticipation that the quality of services would not be affected. It is difficult to obtain data and other available evidence in relation to such cost-quality relationships. The difficulty of solving the cost-quality problem in education is increased by the fact that the term *high quality* has not been defined in ways that are measurable and acceptable to all concerned. Is high-quality education something that can be measured by scores on achievement and other tests? What relation does it have to vocational training or to the kinds of attitudes and habits developed by students? Is a student's score of 95 on an examination compared with a score of 80 by another student a measure of a difference in quality or in quantity of education or some other factor? Does extending the school year provide for potentially greater quality of education, or is quantity the variable? These and many other similar questions make the resolution of this important problem difficult, if not impossible.

The goals of education have been under almost continuous critical evaluation, resulting in frequent restatements. Quality of education should be a measurement of the extent to which the recipients of the educational offering of the schools have attained the established goals. But therein lies the difficulty—the "goals" of education vary from place to place and from time to time; even if they are agreed on, there is no way to measure all of the changes in human behavior that are the products of formal education. Although advances in scholarship and academic achievement can be measured objectively, there have always been other goals of varying importance, for which there are only the crudest methods of determining their degree of inculcation in the lives of a school's clientele.

The cost-quality relationship, in reality a matter of the efficiency with which schools reach their objectives with the smallest outlay of money, is not unique to education. All institutions that are financed with public funds are, to some degree, concerned with maintaining maximum efficiency—if such can be attained. This must always be true with the institutions and agencies of government that are responsible for wise and defensible expenditures of the limited tax dollar. A lack of concern for efficiency tends to destroy public confidence in social and governmental institutions.

Studies show that communities that spend more tend to be more adaptable and tend to utilize improved methods more quickly. In addition, higher expenditure schools get a different behavior pattern in the schools; skills and knowledge are taught more in line with the best understanding of how human beings learn; more attention is given to the discovery and development of special aptitudes; and more attention is given to the positive unfolding in individual boys and girls of stronger patterns of behavior-citizenship, personality, character.[12]

The relation of cost and quality in education has been questioned more critically as a result of studies by Coleman[13] and Jencks.[14] The results of these studies seem to indicate that costs (as evidenced in such things as salaries and facilities) have only a minor effect on achievement of students when compared with the much larger effect of their intelligence and family background. The net effect of these studies has been to raise doubts and controversy concerning input–output relations in education. Perhaps Coons, Clune, and Sugarman best summarized the debate in the following:

> There are similar studies suggesting stronger positive consequences from dollar increments, and there are others suggesting only trivial consequences, but the basic lesson to be drawn from the experts at this point is the current inadequacy of social science to delineate with any clarity the relation between cost and quality. We are unwilling to postpone reform while we await the hoped-for refinements in methodology which will settle the issue. We regard the fierce resistance by rich districts to reform as adequate testimonial to the relevance of money. Whatever it is that money may be thought to contribute to the education of children, that commodity is something highly prized by those who enjoy the greatest measure of it. If money is inadequate to improve education, the residents of poor districts should at least have an equal opportunity to be disappointed by its failure.[15]

Economists refer to education as a labor-intensive activity. Since approximately three-fourths of the costs of education are required to pay the salaries of personnel, and since these salaries are not related to the degree of success achieved by the individuals receiving them, additional funds for education may be merely increases in salaries. This is particularly true in areas where teacher organizations have become powerful and effective in their bargaining with local boards of education.

There is a need for the public and the school personnel to recognize that there is a positive relationship between cost and quality in education. Coons, Clune, and Sugarman stated a practical and reasonable rationale concerning that point of view:

> The statutes creating district authority to tax and spend are the legal embodiment of the principle that money is quality in education. The power to raise dollars by taxation is the very source of education as far as the state is concerned. By regulating the rates of taxation, typically from a minimum to a maximum, the state is in effect stating that dollars count (at least within this range) and that the district has some freedom to choose better or worse education. If dollars are not assumed to buy education, whence the justification for the tax?[16]

It is apparent that the statistical evidence between spending and student outcome is difficult to measure because of the variables that determine student achievement. Money is only one element, for one must consider the characteristics of a family, the effectiveness of the school, the expertise of the teacher, the native intelligence of the child, and the multiple talents of diverse human beings. Although Hanushek stated that there is no strong or systematic relationship between school expenditures and student performance,[17] Hedges, Laine, and Greenwald maintained that relying on the data most often used, "We find that money does matter after all."[18]

Verstegen and King wrote that "a large and growing body of research—that has taken advantage of improvements in technology, better databases and advances in methodologies and measurements—provides further evidence that school inputs can and do make a difference in education and are positively associated with both enhanced student achievement and labor market earnings."[19] They continue, "There are clear relationships between funding and achievement."[20] Their basis for these conclusions was the work of several investigators who used different research technology, databases, and methodology. The researchers found:

- Teacher characteristics relate positively to student performance.
- There are significant relationships between school resources and student outcomes (Ferguson).
- Significant relationships exist between schooling inputs and students' success (Cooper and associates).
- A teacher's education links to positive student outcomes (Monk).
- Lower pupil–teacher ratios relate to higher student outcomes (Finn and Achilles).
- School revenue was found to account for one-third of the variations in proficiency test scores (Verstegan).
- The proportion of teachers with master's degrees and class size affect student learning (as measured by ACT scores), and since these variables cost money, that means that money matters (Ferguson and Ladd).
- The more money schools spend, the higher the achievement of students (Baker).
- There are significant relationships between spending on education and labor market outcomes (Card and Krueger; they used earnings as the outcome measures rather than test scores).[21]

Even though profound improvements have been made in recent research techniques, studies that investigate cost-quality relationships are still two-edged. Picus concluded, "There is still a great deal of debate as to whether or not money makes a difference in education. . . . Everyone agrees that high spending provides better opportunities for learning and seemingly higher student achievement, [but] statistical conformation . . . has been hard to develop."[22] Other variables exist as well. A 15-year analysis of studies done by the National Institute of Education noted that the place called school makes a difference if it has instructional leadership from the principal, a safe and secure environment, high expectations of students, a good monitoring system, and commitment to basic skills instruction. Family, money, leadership, teacher attributes, pedagogy, research methodology—all are important when attempting to unravel the variables in scientific research as it relates to cost-quality studies.

Summary

Economists regard education as an investment in human capital. Resource allocations to education are a responsibility of government at all levels. The scope of services provided is determined by the value of those services as compared to the value of other services at the same cost. Funding the rapidly increasing costs of education is a serious challenge to Americans in the twenty-first century. Education requires additional resources to accommodate population growth and the continual increase in spending per pupil. Funding is problematic because it is difficult to prove definitively that gains in output are commensurate with increases in financial inputs. It is problematic to define education output. Economists and politicians, from a broad ideological spectrum, value education. Not only does the individual benefit from an investment in an organization, but society as a whole benefits when goods and services are produced for all. When seeking financial support for schools, educators need insight to relate to various philosophies.

Education is recognized as an important stimulator of economic growth. Its sponsorship and financing is a public-sector responsibility. Its services should be provided equitably, but it cannot be provided with equality to all. Although expenditures for education continue to increase annually, the burden is eased by the fact that most school costs involve money, particularly in salaries, that is returned quickly to the private sector. The money is not removed from the marketplace.

Education provides many benefits to individuals and households—economic as well as social and political. Since it provides external benefits beyond those provided to its consumers, it must be financed by the ability principle rather than by the benefit principle. The relationship between cost and quality in education is high, but there is a difference of opinion among researchers in defining and measuring quality in education.

ASSIGNMENT PROJECTS

1. Provide a definition for each of the following terms: *human capital, virtuous circle, taxation, equity, adequacy, benefit principle, free rider, cost-quality relationship, diminishing marginal utility, value added, opportunity costs, labor intensive, positive externality, negative externality.*

2. Trace the development of the economic theory that education is an investment in human capital.

3. Prepare a paper to be presented to a state legislature to aid it in determining the extent of state resources that should be allocated to public education in comparison with those allocated to other services of state government.

4. Prepare a feature article for a local newspaper in support of an upcoming school election for an increase in the local tax levy. Show that education is an investment in, not a drain on, the local economy.

5. Choose a prominent economist and study his or her economic theories. Relate those theories to education and the role of government in education.

Computer simulations and questions, research exercises, and website addresses relevant to this chapter can be found at

www.ablongman.com/edleadership

SELECTED READINGS

Becker, G. S. *Human Capital.* New York: Columbia University Press, 1964.

Benson, Charles S. *The Economics of Public Education,* 3rd ed. Boston: Houghton Mifflin, 1978.

Berne, Robert, and Lawrence O. Picus, eds. *Outcome Equity in Education.* Fifteenth Annual Yearbook of the American Education Finance Association. Thousand Oaks, CA: Corwin, 1994.

Carnegie Forum on Education and the Economy. *A Nation Preparing Teachers for the 21st Century.* Washington, DC: Carnegie Forum on Education and the Economy, 1990.

Chubb, J. E., and T. M. Moe. *Politics, Markets, and America's Schools.* Washington, DC: Brookings Institution, 1990.

Friedman, Milton, and Rose Friedman. *Free to Choose: A Personal Statement.* New York: Harcourt Brace Jovanovich, 1980.

Galbraith, John Kenneth. *The Affluent Society,* 4th ed. Boston: Houghton Mifflin, 1984.

Garfield, Rulon R., Gene J. Garfield, and J. D. Willardson. *Policy and Politics in American Education.* Atlanta, GA: St. Barthelemy Press, Ltd., 2003.

Hanushek, Eric, et al. *Making Schools Work.* Washington, DC: Brookings Institution, 1994.

Keynes, John Maynard. *The Collected Writings of John Maynard Keynes.* 24 vols. New York: Macmillan, 1971.

Marcus, Laurence R., and Benjamin D. Stickney (with 16 other contributors). *Politics and Policy in the Age of Education.* Springfield, IL: Charles C. Thomas, 1990.

Marx, Karl. *Das Kapital,* ed. Frederick Engels. Chicago: Encyclopedia Britannica, 1952.

Marx, Karl, and Frederick Engels. *The Communist Manifesto,* trans. Samuel Moore. Chicago: Regnery, 1963.

Mill, John Stuart. *On Liberty.* London: Longmans, Green, 1913.

Mill, John Stuart. *Principles of Political Economy.* London: Colonial Press, 1900.

Mort, Paul R., Walter C. Reusser, and John W. Polley. *Public School Finance.* New York: McGraw-Hill, 1960.

Murphy, J., and K. Seashore Louis, eds. *Handbook of Research on Education Administration,* 2nd ed. San Francisco: Jossey-Bass, 1999.

Perkinson, Henry J. *The Imperfect Panacea: American Faith in Education, 1865–1990.* New York: McGraw-Hill, 1991.

Plecki, Margaret L., and David H. Monk, eds. *School Finance and Teacher Quality.* 2003 Yearbook of the American Education Finance Association. Larchmont, NY: Eye on Education, 2003.

Rouse, Cecilia Elena, and Michele McLaughlin. *Can the Invisible Hand Improve Education? A Review of Competition and School Efficiency.* National Research Council, National Academy of Sciences, 1999.

Smith, Adam. *An Inquiry into the Nature and Causes of the Wealth of Nations,* general eds. R. H. Campbell and A. S. Skinner, textual ed. W. B. Todd. New York: Oxford University Press, 1976.

Smith, Adam. *The Theory of Moral Sentiments.* London: Oxford Clarendon Press, 1976.

Sowell, Thomas. *Race and Economics.* New York: David McKay, 1975.

Statistical Abstract of the United States 2006. U.S. Department of Commerce, Economics and Statistics Administration, Bureau of the Census, 2006.

Stevens, Edward, Jr., and George H. Wood. *Justice, Ideology, and Education,* 2nd ed. New York: McGraw-Hill, 1992.

Underwood, Julie K., and Deborah A. Verstegen, eds. *The Impact of Litigation and Legislation on Public School Finance: Adequacy, Equity and Excellence.* New York: Harper & Row, 1990.

Werbane, Patricia H. *Adam Smith and His Legacy for Modern Capitalism.* New York: Oxford University Press, 1991.

World Bank. *World Development Report 1991: The Challenge of Development.* Oxford: The World Bank and Oxford University Press, 1991.

ENDNOTES

1. Dennis Romboy, "Human Capital Called Key to U.S. Success in Information Age," *Deseret News,* July 11, 2000, pp. D6 and D8.

2. Ibid.

3. Theodore W. Schultz, "The Human Capital Approach to Education," in Roe L. Johns et al., eds., *Economic Factors Affecting the Financing of Education* (Gainesville, FL: National Educational Finance Project, 1970), p. 31.

4. OECD, *2005 Education at a Glance: OECD Indicators,* www.oecd.org/document/34/0,2340,en_ 2649_201185_35289570_1_1_1_1,00.html.

5. Ibid.

6. Charles S. Benson, *The Economics of Public Education* (Boston: Houghton Mifflin, 1961), p. vii.

7. *The Unfinished Agenda: A New Vision for Child Development and Education* (New York: Research and Policy Committee, Council for Economic Development, 1991), pp. 43–44.

8. Habte Aklilu, *Education and Development—Views from the World Bank* (Washington, DC: World Bank, 1983), p. 8.

9. "Education and the Wealth of Nations," *The Economist,* March 29–April 4, 1997, p. 15.

10. William P. McLure, "Allocation of Resources," in Warren E. Gauerke and Jack R. Childress, eds., *The Theory and Practice of School Finance* (Chicago: Rand McNally, 1967), p. 78.

11. "Annual Cost of Inadequate Education is Hundreds of Billions of Dollars," October 24–25, 2005, www.schoolfunding.info/news/policy/10-31-05tcsymposium.php3.

12. Paul R. Mort and Walter C. Reusser, *Public School Finance,* 2nd ed. (New York: McGraw-Hill, 1951), pp. 140–141.

13. James S. Coleman et al., *Equality of Educational Opportunity* (Washington, DC: U.S. Government Printing Office, 1966).

14. Christopher Jencks et al., *Inequality: A Reassessment of the Effect of Family and Schooling in America* (New York: Basic Books, 1972).

15. John E. Coons et al., *Private Wealth and Public Education* (Cambridge, MA: Belknap Press of Harvard University Press, 1970), p. 36.

16. Ibid., p. 26.

17. E. A. Hanushek, "The Impact of Differential Expenditures on School Performance," *Educational Researcher,* Vol. 18, 1989, p. 47.

18. L. V. Hedges, R. D. Laine, and R. Greenwald, "Does Money Matter? A Meta Analysis of Studies of the Effects of Differential School Inputs on Student Outcomes," *Educational Researcher,* Vol. 23, 1994, p. 13.

19. Deborah Verstegen and Richard A. King, "The Relationship between School Spending and Student Achievement: A Review and Analysis of 35 Years of Production Function Research," *Journal of Educational Finance,* Vol. 24, Fall 1998, p. 243.

20. Ibid., p. 262.

21. Ibid., pp. 246–249.

22. Lawrence O. Picus, "Does Money Matter in Education? Policymaker's Guide," *Selected Papers in School Finance 1995, NCES* (Washington, DC: National Center for Educational Statistics, U.S. Office of Education, Office of Educational Research and Improvement, 1995), p. 31.

2 Financing Education Adequately

Americans should welcome a global society and economy in which nations and states and communities compete to develop human talent, primarily by getting more people better educated. But we must enter this competition and we must win it.

—Charles E. M. Kolb, 2007

No adequate substitutes have been coined to replace the clichés "Education in the United States is big business" and "Education is a major user of the nation's economic resources." Although the meanings of the statements are obvious, they fail to communicate their real significance. Relatively few people realize the enormity of educational operations in this country. As "big business," the field of formal education employs more people than any other industry in the United States.

Year after year student and community services offered by the public schools have continued to increase in spite of the rising costs of education. Most of the normal improvements in living discovered by scientific research, social conditions, and economic circumstances soon find a place in the curriculum of the schools. The school constantly receives added responsibilities for teaching new programs, improved techniques, and better processes. Seldom, if ever, are successful school services taken away and given to other agencies or institutions.

Society recognizes the fact that there are few, if any, institutions that are better prepared or equipped than the schools to render or provide for certain emerging services. The point is that such additional services require additional funds and the taxpaying public must accept financial responsibility for the added costs.

Societal Impact on Educational Needs

In fiscal year 2006, it is estimated that more than $800 billion was spent on public and private education from preprimary through graduate school. The revenues for public elementary and secondary schools totaled $416,839,227,000 in fiscal year 2004–05; spending per student, nationally, was $8,618. The average per-pupil expenditure among the states ranged from $5,245 in Utah to $15,073 in the District of Columbia (see Table 2.1). By far, the greatest part of education revenues came from state and local sources, which provided 91.5 percent of all revenues (see Figure 2.1).

TABLE 2.1 Current Expenditures per Student in Public K–12 Schools and Total ($000) by State

Rank 2003–04	Rank 2004–05	State	2004–05	Rank 2003–04	Rank 2004–05	State	2004–05
1.	1.	District of Columbia	15,073*	1.	1.	California	49,409,615
2.	2.	New Jersey	13,370*	2.	2.	New York	36,344,791*
3.	3.	New York	12,879*	3.	3.	Texas	31,310,388
4.	4.	Connecticut	11,893*	4.	4.	Illinois	20,117,054
5.	5.	Massachusetts	11,681*	5.	5.	New Jersey	18,614,364
6.	6.	Vermont	11,608*	6.	6.	Florida	18,504,396
7.	7.	Delaware	11,016*	7.	8.	Pennsylvania	17,495,394*
8.	9.	Rhode Island	10,641*	8.	7.	Ohio	17,648,889*
9.	8.	Maine	10,723*	9.	9.	Michigan	16,858,734*
10.	11.	Alaska	10,042*	10.	10.	Georgia	13,127,904*
11.	10.	Wyoming	10,198*	11.	11.	Massachusetts	11,395,704
12.	14.	Pennyslvania	9,638*	12.	12.	Virginia	10,333,248*
13.	15.	Wisconsin	9,619*	13.	13.	North Carolina	9,886,070
14.	16.	Illinois	9,591*	14.	14.	Indiana	8,904,028*
15.	12.	Maryland	9,762*	15.	15.	Wisconsin	8,478,671*
16.	13.	New Hampshire	9,642*	16.	16.	Maryland	8,452,000*
17.	17.	Ohio	9,557*	17.	17.	Washington	8,050,495
18.	18.	West Virginia	9,448*	18.	18.	Minnesota	7,748,711
19.	19.	Minnesota	9,249*	19.	19.	Connecticut	6,856,175
20.	20.	Michigan	8,909*	20.	21.	Colorado	6,392,168
21.	22.	Hawaii	8,622*	21.	20.	Missouri	6,648,451*
22.	21.	Indiana	8,723*	22.	22.	Tennessee	6,366,027
23.	25.	Colorado	8,337*	23.	23.	Louisiana	5,494,106
24.	23.	Virginia	8,577*	24.	25.	Arizona	5,398,853*
25.	24.	Georgia	8,451*	25.	27.	Alabama	5,034,347
26.	26.	New Mexico	8,236*	26.	24.	South Carolina	5,468,808
27.	31.	Oregon	7,842*	27.	26.	Kentucky	5,035,059
28.	28.	Montana	8,025*	28.	28.	Oregon	4,331,044
29.	32.	California	7,815	29.	29.	Oklahoma	3,944,107*
30.	29.	Kentucky	7,906*	30.	30.	Iowa	3,576,501
31.	30.	Washington	7,858*	31.	31.	Kansas	3,540,781
32.	34.	Nebraska	7,608*	32.	32.	Mississippi	3,129,764*
33.	36.	Kansas	7,558*	33.	33.	Arkansas	2,803,750*
34.	37.	Iowa	7,477*	34.	34.	New Mexico	2,676,121
35.	35.	Louisiana	7,589*	35.	35.	West Virginia	2,640,225
36.	40.	Texas	7,142*	36.	37.	Utah	2,591,596*
37.	33.	South Dakota	7,618*	37.	36.	Nevada	2,614,546
38.	39.	North Carolina	7,350*	38.	38.	Nebraska	2,164,975
39.	27.	South Carolina	8,161*	39.	39.	Maine	2,136,591
40.	38.	Missouri	7,451*	40.	40.	New Hampshire	1,994,498*
41.	41.	Florida	7,035*	41.	41.	Rhode Island	1,708,667*
42.	42.	North Dakota	7,033*	42.	42.	Idaho	1,685,569*
43.	43.	Alabama	6,886*	43.	43.	Hawaii	1,579,442
44.	44.	Tennessee	6,856*	44.	44.	Alaska	1,335,243*
45.	46.	Nevada	6,525*	45.	45.	Delaware	1,312,073*
46.	45.	Idaho	6,743*	46.	46.	Montana	1,177,310*
47.	47.	Mississippi	6,452*	47.	47.	Vermont	1,104,892
48.	49.	Arkansas	6,202*	48.	49.	South Dakota	926,510*
49.	48.	Oklahoma	6,269*	49.	48.	District of Columbia	939,166*
50.	50.	Arizona	5,474*	50.	50.	Wyoming	852,880*
51.	51.	Utah	5,245*	51.	51.	North Dakota	698,536
		U.S. and D.C.	**8,618***			**U.S. and D.C**	**416,839,227***

*Computed from NEA Research, Estimates databank. The figures are based on reports through August 2005.

30

**FIGURE 2.1   Percent Distribution of Revenue for Public Elementary
and Secondary Schools, by Source: School Year 2002–2003**

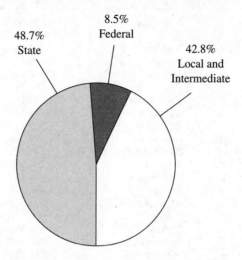

Note: Percentages may not sum to 100 due to rounding. Intermediate revenues were
combined with local revenues.

Source: U.S. Department of Education. National Center for Educational Statistics,
Common Core Data, "National Public Education Financial Survey," School year
2002–2003.

There are more than 3 million teachers and more than 3 million professionals,
administrators, and support staff in the elementary and secondary schools in the United
States. These numbers add up to make public elementary and secondary education
the primary activity of more than 55 million Americans. About one in every four is
involved in some aspect of education as student, teacher, administrator, counselor, aide,
or support staff in the more than 92,000 schools of America.[1]

Enrollment in elementary and secondary schools grew rapidly in the last half of the
twentieth century (see Figure 2.2). This enrollment rise was caused by what is known
as the "baby boom," a dramatic increase in births following World War II. After a modest decline in the 1970s and early 1980s, enrollment hit record levels in the mid-1990s.
Overall, school enrollment set new records every year until 2005, with an enrollment of
48,367,410 students, a 300,000-pupil increase from 2003–04 (see Table 2.2). In 2006,
the U.S. population reached 300 million people. In 2030, the population in the United
States will increase about 29.2 percent to an estimate of more than 350 million. The
school-age group of 5- to 17-year-olds is expected to increase in that period to about
60 million students.[2]

The greatest population increase will be in the West (45.8 percent) and South
(42.9 percent); the least will be in the Midwest (9.5) and the Northeast (7.6 percent)
(see Figure 2.3). Regionally, enrollment will follow the population increase in the

TABLE 2.2   Enrollment, Fall 2004–05 and 2003–04 (Revised)

Rank 2003–04	Rank 2004–05	State	2004–05	% Change from 2004	2003–04
1.	1.	California	6,322,142	0.4	6,298,769
2.	2.	Texas	4,383,871	1.7	4,311,502
3.	3.	New York	2,822,000	–0.1	2,826,116
4.	4.	Florida	2,630,229	1.5	2,591,033
5.	5.	Illinois	2,097,518	1.8	2,060,048
6.	6.	Ohio	1,846,763*	0.1	1,845,428
7.	7.	Pennsylvania	1,815,170	–0.3	1,821,146
8.	8.	Michigan	1,726,204*	0.7	1,715,048
9.	9.	Georgia	1,553,437	2.0	1,522,611
10.	10.	New Jersey	1,392,204	0.8	1,380,882
11.	11.	North Carolina	1,345,101	1.6	1,323,541
12.	12.	Virginia	1,204,808	1.0	1,192,539
13.	13.	Washington	1,024,495	0.3	1,021,497
14.	14.	Indiana	1,020,753	1.0	1,010,463
15.	16.	Massachusetts	975,574	–0,5	980,459
16.	15.	Arizona	986,221*	2.3	964,003*
17.	17.	Tennessee	928,572	0.9	919,896
18.	18.	Missouri	892,194*	–0,1	892,872
19.	19.	Wisconsin	881,480*	0.2	880,031
20.	20.	Maryland	865,836	–0.4	869,113
21.	21.	Minnesota	837,760	–0.6	842,428
22.	22.	Colorado	766,707	1.2	757,668
23.	23.	Alabama	731,085	0.2	729,339
24.	24.	Louisiana	724,002	–0.5	727,316
25.	25.	South Carolina	670,080*	–1.0	676,817
26.	26.	Kentucky	636,880	0.8	631,852
27.	27.	Oklahoma	629,134	0.5	625,826
28.	28.	Connecticut	576,474	0.0	576,205
29.	29.	Oregon	552,320	0.2	551,407
30.	31.	Mississippi	485,094*	–0.6	487,812*
31.	30.	Utah	494,100	1.5	486,938
32.	32.	Iowa	478,319	–0.6	481,226
33.	33.	Kansas	468,512	–0.3	469,825
34.	34.	Arkansas	452,057*	0.0	452,036
35.	35.	Nevada	400,671	4.0	385,414
36.	36.	New Mexico	324,924	0.7	322,657
37.	37.	Nebraska	284,559	0.1	284,169
38.	38	West Virginia	279,457	–0.4	280,561
39.	39.	Idaho	249,984*	0.5	248,743*
40.	40.	New Hampshire	206,852	–0.3	207,417
41.	41.	Maine	199,253	–1.5	202,210
42.	42.	Hawaii	183,185	–0.2	183,609
43.	43.	Rhode Island	160,574*	0.5	159,825*
44.	44.	Montana	146,705	–1.1	148,356
45.	45.	Alaska	132,970	–0.7	133,933
46.	46.	South Dakota	121,622	–2.3	124,469
47.	47.	Delaware	119,109	1.1	117,777
48.	48.	North Dakota	99,324	–1.8	101,137
49.	49.	Vermont	95,187	–2.9	98,051
50.	50.	Wyoming	83,633	–1.3	84,741
51.	51	District of Columbia	62,306	–4.3	65,099
		U.S. and D.C.	**48,367,410***	**0.6**	**48,070,309***

*Computed from NEA Research, Estimates databank. The figures are based on reports through August 2005.

FIGURE 2.2 Total Enrollment in Public Elementary and Secondary Schools: 1950–2005

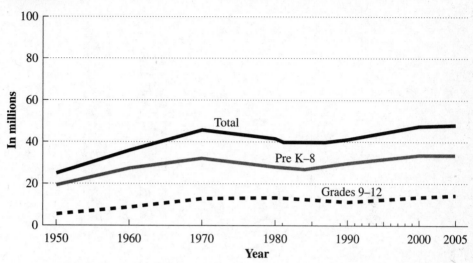

Source: U.S. Department of Education. National Center for Education Statistics, Statistics of State School Systems; Statistics of Public Elementary and Secondary School Systems; Statistics of Nonpublic Elementary and Secondary Schools; Projections of Education Statistics to 2007; Common Core of Data. National Center for Education Statistics (NCES). 1999. Digest of Education Statistics. 1998. NCES 1999-036. Washington, DC: U.S. Department of Education, Office of Educational Research and Improvement.

South and West. It is estimated that California will have nearly one million new pupils in 2008. With 25 children in a classroom, such growth will require hiring 40,000 new teachers and building 2,000 schools. The Clark County Nevada School District, one of the fast-growing school districts in the West, had to build 43 (more than one a month) new schools between January 2000 and June 2003. The district hired nearly 30,000 school personnel, 14,592 of whom were licensed teachers. A capital improvement campaign of $3.5 billion to build 88 new schools and improve existing ones was passed to provide the facilities needed to accommodate the growth.

The less than 10 percent growth in the Northeast and Midwest, while the South and West are approaching 50 percent growth, has staggering implications, including the impact on school finance. Increases in spending are related to several factors: (1) changing enrollments of students, (2) additional programs and services provided, (3) changing rates of inflation, and (4) inequities in the quantity and quality of services provided in the country's thousands of school districts.

Inequities in the amounts of revenue available per person to be educated and heavy property tax burdens on individual citizens have provided motivation for school finance reform in nearly every state. The population's increasing mobility also results in increased school costs, particularly for new school facilities. As families move, they leave

FIGURE 2.3   Interim Projections: Percent Change in Population by Region of the United States, 2000 to 2030

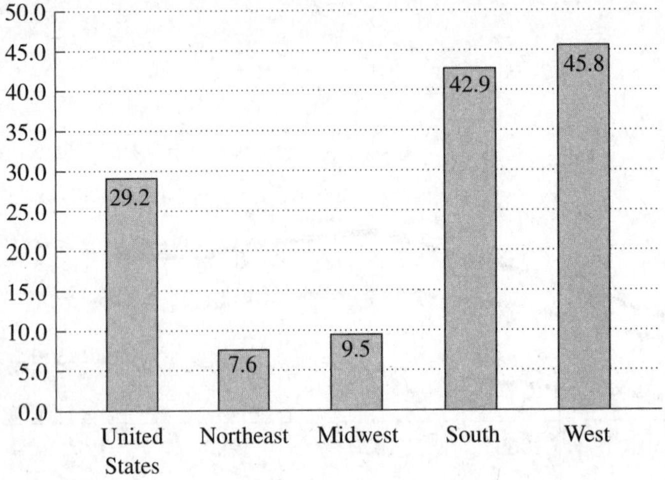

Source: U.S. Census Bureau, Population Division, Interim State Population Projections, 2005.

behind partially occupied school buildings and reduced pupil-teacher ratios. Families frequently find that the places to which they move have overcrowded classrooms and high pupil-teacher ratios.

Such imbalances naturally increase the total cost of education and change the responsibility of the various states and the nation in financing education adequately, and it is apparent the problems of financing education will continue to plague school boards and state legislatures in the future. In spite of the increasing needs of education in many states, there is public resistance to taxes. Schools of the twenty-first century will find little relief from these issues.

Education Deserves Higher Priority

Unfortunately, many of the citizens of this country have not given education the high priority it deserves and requires if the schools are to accomplish their objectives. Too few people realize the contribution that formal education has made to the social, political, and economic achievement of the United States. The historic report "A Nation at Risk," published in April 1983, stated, "We recommend that citizens across the nation hold educators and elected officials responsible for providing the leadership necessary to achieve these reforms and that citizens provide the support and stability required to bring about the reforms we propose."[3]

According to a report issued in 2005 by the Center on Education Policy, since the "A Nation at Risk" report was released, the nation has focused seriously on its schools. The authors stated that after this momentous report, a more balanced picture of education emerged. The report outlines some of the shortcomings of public education with the need to:

- Improve high school graduation rates.
- Reduce dropout rates.
- Close the achievement gaps for minority, low-income, disabled, and non-English speakers.
- Reduce funding inequities between school districts.
- Attract and retain qualified teachers.

"A Nation at Risk" maintained that in the past two decades the education system had made gains:

- More children are attending full-day kindergarten.
- High school students are taking a more challenging curriculum.
- More students with disabilities are being educated in regular classrooms.
- Student achievement has gone up in math and reading.
- Some achievement gaps are narrowing.
- Pupil-teacher ratios are falling.
- Students are safer in school.
- Public school teachers are better educated and more experienced than private school teachers.
- The percentage of high school graduates immediately enrolling in college has risen.[4]

School authorities continue to request the necessary funds to operate and maintain educational programs. Citizens of the United States need to react positively and give education the high priority that it requires. Groups who oppose taxes may injure the financing of public education. Although some taxpayer relief may be necessary and overdue, the field of education in particular stands to lose much—and the nation stands to lose more—if tax revolts have a harmful effect on the future of the public school system.

The Committee for Economic Development emphasized the need for the adequate funding of public education:

> We believe that education is an investment, not an expense. If we can ensure that all children are born healthy and develop the skills and knowledge they need to be productive, self-supporting adults, whatever is spent on their development and education will be returned many times over in higher productivity, incomes, and taxes and in lower costs for welfare, health care, crime, and a myriad of other economic and social problems.[5]

Many voices are calling for the states to meet the challenges facing education. In *Florida Today*, the views of the editors reflect the high priority of education in the 50 states:

> Education is the focus of a growing debate in homes, on the streets, at our workplaces and in the corridors of government. The questions being raised are not new, but in recent months have taken on increased urgency. They involve the methods and adequacy of school funding, the commitment of parents and public officials to education and possible solutions to a variety of education problems. The outcome of the debates is likely to shape the state's future for decades because the ramifications are far-reaching. Without a top-notch school system, Florida cannot hope to sustain its many industries. Without good public schools, this state cannot hope to prepare its young people to become happy, healthy, law abiding and productive citizens. That's why education is literally everyone's business and deserves a high priority in public policy.[6]

The Increasing Costs of Education

Education is most meaningful when it is fashioned in terms of goals or objectives, whether they are implied or formally stated in the literature. Education without purpose or philosophical commitment would have little value and would stimulate little, if any, support or dedication. The purposes of education have much to do with the cost of the program that is established and operated to achieve those objectives. To compare the problems of financing, a three Rs curriculum with those of financing a program constructed to achieve the far-reaching and comprehensive goals of present-day education is a futile exercise, guaranteed to result in frustration. As the schools reach out to supply new curricula and provide new methods of attaining increasingly complex and comprehensive goals for their clientele, the costs multiply, and taxpayers are forced to reach into their treasuries.

The revenues made available for financing public elementary, secondary, and postsecondary institutions from local, state, and federal sources have increased dramatically. Education problems do not belong to educators alone. Institutions and the family must share in preparing children for the future. When deciding how much should be spent for education, educators and legislators must agree on what the schools are expected to do. As the goals and objectives of education become more inclusive and more difficult to achieve, the taxpayers must face the stark fact that the costs will likewise increase.

Goals Have Increased

The persistent but irregular march of change and innovation in the public schools is shown by the many successive changes in the goals and objectives of education. Such redefinitions have usually come after serious study, based on changing needs. Not all resultant statements have made an indelible imprint on education in the United States, but a few have. Statements of the objectives of education were limited, easy to achieve, and correspondingly inexpensive. Goals of the schools became more comprehensive and costly as the schools improved and as public confidence in them increased. The Seven Cardinal Principles of Secondary Education, the Four Objectives of the Educational Policies Commission, and the Ten Imperative Needs of Youth are early examples of some of the important statements of what people have at different times viewed as the important goals of education. None of the statements in the past has promoted more than worthy objectives that educators could hope to accomplish. That changed with the passing of the No Child Left Behind Act of 2001, which prescribes accountability for teachers and students among other requirements.

Just as the costs of education have increased almost geometrically, so have the demands placed on schools. Each level of government, each important social organization, and almost every individual continues to increase the expectations with which the school is confronted and on which its achievements are evaluated.

Citizens of the United States continue to make large investments in the educational enterprise in spite of its alleged inadequacy in many states and school districts. The reasons for these perennial increases are often beyond the power of school boards or administrators to change. However justified these increasing costs become when viewed in proper perspective and in comparison with the alternatives, they tend to irritate the overburdened taxpayer, whose resistance often becomes a cumulative matter and often one of deep personal concern.

People Want Better Education

Data from the 2006 *Phi Delta Kappa/Gallup Poll of the Public's Attitudes Toward the Public Schools* emphasized that the number-one conclusion from the survey was that the public had a strong preference to seek improvement of education through the existing public school system—71 percent. In 2002, 27 percent preferred seeking an alternative system for reform, whereas in 2006, that percentage was reduced to 24 percent.[7]

The second most important conclusion, according to the PDK/Gallup Poll, was that public ratings of the local schools are near the top of their 38-year range—the length of time the poll has been conducted. Forty-nine percent of the respondents gave an A or a B ranking to the schools in their own communities. Parents of public school students expressed a stronger satisfaction: 56 percent gave an A or B; while parents gave the school their eldest child attended an A or B 64 percent of the time. PDK declared that "in stories reported about the public schools, declining public support for the schools is taken almost as a given. The grades assigned the schools in this poll since 1974 demonstrates clearly that such is not the case."[8]

The 2006 poll indicated that the significant generalization derived from responses to these questions over the years is that the closer respondents are to their public schools, the higher the grades they give them. People give the schools in their own communities much higher grades than they give the nation's schools. Only 21 percent of the nation's schools received an A or B grade from respondents.

The 27 percent difference (48% − 21%) from schools in one's own community is impressive. The 35 percent variation from public school parents, compared to what people in general think of the nation's schools, and the 43 percent (64% − 21%) contrast with the public school parents of schools where their eldest child attends, are even more striking.[9]

The poll asked, "What do you think are the biggest problems the public schools in your community must deal with?" The answer 24% of the time was "the lack of financial support/funding/money."[10] In the history of the 38 polls, that is the only question that has been asked every year. "Discipline was the problem the first 16 years. Drugs then took over and occupied the top position alone until financial support drew into a tie in 1991. Frequent changes occurred in the Nineties until lack of financial support came back to the top in 2000. It has held that position in each poll since."[11] The answer given in 2006 by 24 percent of the respondents was up from 20 percent in 2005 and 21 percent in 2004. In 2006, overcrowded schools were mentioned by 13 percent of the respondents (which has financial overtones), lack of discipline garnered 11 percent of the answers, and 8 percent listed use of drugs.

A Phi Delta Kappan Commission has stated, "The expenditure of government funds should reflect the needs, wants, and demands of the people."[12] But the justification for expenditure of public funds for education goes much deeper. Mass public education can be justified on the more basic grounds that it creates and perpetuates the culture, promotes social equality, and enhances economic development. Each of these alone may be ample reason for government to finance education, but to view them in combination leaves little doubt as to the importance of education. To gain and advance the accumulated culture and knowledge of humankind, create a respect for humanity, promote the attributes of citizenship, and inculcate ethical and moral character is fundamental. Education not only preserves the cultural heritage but it also exalts the status of humans and provides at least a minimum level of citizenship. The advantages of education cannot be quantified. The benefits of reading a book, appreciating a painting, playing a violin, speaking a foreign language, and understanding a theorem are priceless.

Demographic and Social Changes

The history of public education in the United States has been one of growth and expansion. Most of the serious problems of financing have concerned increasing enrollments, shortages of buildings and classrooms, inadequate facilities, and the need to employ greater numbers of teachers and other staff members. With such causal factors, taxpayers were generally able to understand the reasons for annual increases in their investment in education. Taxpayers did not, however, anticipate the expanding numbers of high-cost students with disadvantages, disabilities, and bilingual programs for minority groups that were beginning to be brought into the schools, thereby increasing the cost of education per student. For example, the proportion of minority students in elementary and secondary schools increased greatly between 1972 and 2004. Forty-three percent of public school students in 2004 were considered to be part of a racial or ethnic minority. In 1972, this number was 21 percent. In those 32 years the number of minority students more than doubled. The percentage for Whites decreased from 78 percent to 57 percent, whereas Hispanics increased from 6 percent to 19 percent, which resulted in the proportion of Hispanics in elementary and secondary schools increasing at a greater rate than the proportion of Blacks. In the West, the identified minority public school pupils exceeded the White pupils (see Figure 2.4).

FIGURE 2.4   Racial/Ethnic Distribution of Public School Students in Kindergarten through Grade 12: Fall 1972 and 2004

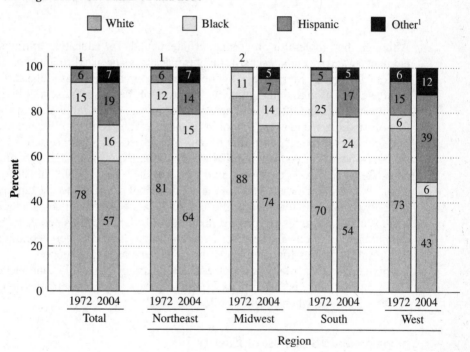

Rounds to zero.

[1]Included Asian/Pacific Islanders.

Note: Detail may not sum to totals because of rounding. Black includes African American, Hispanic includes Latino, and Pacific Islander includes Native Hawaiian. Race categories exclude Hispanic origin unless specified. Includes all public school students enrolled in kindergarten through 12th grade. Starting in 2003, the categories for race were changed on the Current Population Survey (CPS), allowing respondents to select more than one race. Respondents who selected more than one race were placed in the "Other" category for the purposes of this analysis. In 2004, some 2.4 percent of public school students were more than one race.

Source: U.S. Department of Commerce, Census Bureau, Current Population Survey (CPS), October Supplement, 1972 and 2004, previously unpublished tabulation (September 2005).

Similarly, taxpayers did not anticipate that more effective bargaining for higher salaries for all employees, the cost of new and expensive federal programs for exceptional and bilingual students, and the high cost of implementing desegregation programs in some schools would keep the total cost of education on a steep incline in spite of fluctuating enrollments. Nor did they expect the increases required by the No Child Left Behind Act.

Research literature and media accounts have been advising educators, policymakers, and the public that enrollment changes and increases are inevitable. Implications for the demand for public school teachers and other education personnel are obvious, and education expenditure decisions by state and local governments will need to accommodate expanding resource demands associated with changing enrollment growth and demographic changes.

Effects of Inflation

Although the problem of procuring sufficient funds for educating millions of public elementary and secondary school students has always been a difficult one, the inflation rates of the last quarter of the twentieth century greatly increased the difficulty. The erosive effect of high and continuous inflation of the dollar on school budgets needs few illustrations and little documentation, for it is an undesirable phenomenon that affects every citizen and every school in the nation. The problem of financing education, once considered the responsibility of only a few specialists with vested interests in the schools—boards of education, school administrators, state departments of education, and state legislatures—developed into a priority item for virtually all citizens.

Uncontrolled inflation causes the dollar cost of education to rise rapidly. Inflation not only reduces the real income of the individuals but it also increases their tax obligations under a progressive income tax system. Inflation causes people to cut back on the purchase of goods and services in an attempt to maintain their economic position. The result is serious for schools. At the same time as taxpayers press to reduce their tax burden, the costs of operating an educational program usually continue to increase. Predicting inflation is difficult, as Figure 2.5 shows. It is nevertheless an important factor to consider when providing adequate funds for education.

Scarcity and High Cost of Energy

Energy is a crucial factor in the increasing costs of education. Conservation is the key to survival when reviewed in the tumultuous world scene influenced by oil-producing countries. School programs are affected by the cost of gasoline and oil products necessary for the transportation of millions of students to and from school. The cost of a gallon of gasoline and diesel fuel doubled from 1999 to 2006, crimping many school transportation budgets. School districts are hit hard when heating fuel prices in the East and electrical energy prices soar. Some school districts in the western states have had increases of over 50 percent for heating costs, and California schools were "left in the dark" with the lack of electric power to fully meet their needs. Massive blackouts that paralyze the United States and Canada foretell future energy crises. In some cases,

FIGURE 2.5   Inflation Rates

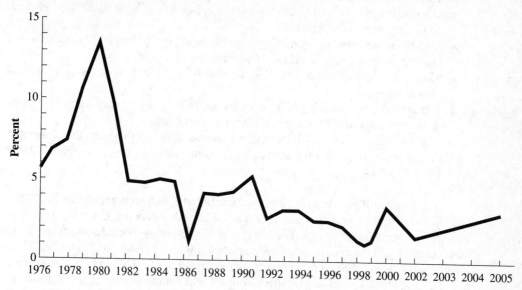

Source: Statistical Abstract of the United States, 2003, Bureau of Census, U.S. Department of Commerce, July 2003.

school districts were faced with paying extremely high premiums for power to keep schools open.

In general, schools should be well equipped to initiate and carry out their own conservation measures. Some of the lessons this nation has generally ignored about the wise use of limited energy resources can be practiced effectively in school operations. More energy-efficient construction and maintenance procedures can decrease energy expenditures without seriously diluting the overall school program.

Social Indicators

The United States is undergoing significant social changes, including dramatic alterations in the nature of the typical family. According to the U.S. Commerce Department's 2000 Census report:

- The increase of 32.7 million people in the United States between 1990 and 2000 is the largest 10-year population increase in U.S. history. For the first time in the twentieth century, all states gained population.
- Married-couple families dropped from 55 percent to 52 percent of all households—from 248.7 million in 1990 to 281.4 million in 2000 (still an increase of 32.7 million, and more than half of the total number of families).
- The nation's housing units numbered 115.9 million, an increase of 13.6 million from 1990.

- The average household size in 2000 was 2.59, down slightly from 2.63 in 1990.
- The number of nonfamily households rose at twice the rate of family households: 23 percent versus 11 percent.
- Families maintained by women with no husband present increased three times as fast as married-couple families: 21 percent versus 7 percent.
- More than 8 out of 10 of the nation's population (226.0 million) lived in metropolitan areas.
- The median age (meaning half are older and half younger) rose from 32.9 years in 1990 to 35.3 in 2000—the highest it has ever been.
- The number of males (138.1 million) edged closer to the number of females (143.4 million), raising the sex ratio (males per 100 females) from 95.1 in 1990 to 96.3 in 2000.

The number of people living alone in the United States grew rapidly in the 1990s, and for the first time, less than one-fourth of all households consisted of married couples with children under age 18. The number of single-person households amounted to 26 percent of all households, whereas households with married couples and children under age 18 dropped to 23.5 percent from 25.6 percent in 1990, and 45 percent four decades ago. Nuclear families (married couples with children under age 18) have accounted for fewer than 25 percent of households since 1997.

People ages 31 to 40, in 2006, are members of what often is called the "baby bust" generation. Their number fell 8 percent. The number of children ages 5 to 14 increased 17 percent between 1990 and 2000. In 2002, the United States birth rate fell to a record-low level since national data have been available. More than one-third of all births were to unmarried women. The average age for a woman to have her first child was 25.1 years—an all-time high. The rise reflects a drop in teen births and women delaying motherhood. Birth rates among teenagers were 43 births per 1,000 females from 15 to 19 years of age. The decline in the birth rate for younger teens, ages 15 to 17, is even more substantial, dropping 38 percent from 1990 to 2002. Among Black teens, the birth rate dropped by more than 40 percent, from 114.8 births per 1,000 women in 1991 to 66.6 per 1,000 in 2002. The rate for Black teens, ages 15 to 17, dropped by more than half, from 83.6 births per 1,000 women in 1991 to 40 per 1,000 in 2002.

In 1946, the baby boom began as families were reunited after World War II. The rise in birth continued for 18 years, until 1964. (In 2006, those children range in age from 60 down to 42). The 1960s created a new track for household change, with fewer children being born—creating the "baby bust." In the 1970s, women joined the labor force in heretofore-untold numbers, divorce rates increased rapidly, marriage rates fell, and married women postponed child bearing, thereby continuing the baby bust. The 1980s were a time of immigration from Asia and Latin America; the poor and the wealthy grew in number while the middle class shrank. In the 1990s, divorce rates declined and a "baby boomlet" (sometimes referred to as an echo baby boom) occurred. The 1990s concluded 18 years of continual economic expansion. High school graduates of 2000 had lived their entire lives in excellent economic times. Virtual full employment was the axiom for those who had graduated from high school at the beginning of the twenty-first century. The twenty-first century has been marked by immigration, much of which has been determined to be of an illegal nature.

Looking at the future of families today, Americans continue to pursue the same general goals as their grandparents, such as raising children and getting ahead. But the 1980s changed the rules of the game. One of those changes is that the proportion of couples in which the woman is chief breadwinner increased so markedly that nearly one in three working wives nationwide in 2000 was paid more than her husband, compared to one in five in 1980. The trend is particularly pronounced among the most highly educated women, nearly half of whom have incomes higher than their spouses.[13] Rising incomes of women are an outgrowth of social changes, including education. Other changes include the increasing tendency of women to work full time, not to take time from their jobs to raise children, and to take up occupations that were once dominated by men. By the 1990s, U.S. colleges and universities were graduating one-fifth more women than men.[14] Projections of the total population by age and sex, from 2010 to 2050, are shown on Table 2.3.

The roller coaster of change in household growth rates will continue for two reasons. First, the number of people in the baby boom, baby bust, and echo baby boom generations will vary as they move through the life cycle. Second, future young adults may delay having children. The late 1990s were the prime household formation years for both the youngest boomers and oldest busters, the larger halves of both generations. After 2000, growth slowed because the youngest baby busters—a very small group—formed new households, and the children of baby boomers will be just beginning to form new households (see Figure 2.6). According to the U.S. Census, the future population trend is one of an aging America. For example, in 2050, there will be more than 20 million inhabitants over 85 years of age (see Figure 2.7).

Coleman and associates have noted that higher educational achievement is attained by children from higher-income families, by children whose parents complete more years of school, by children who have fewer siblings, and by children whose parents have higher education expectations for them. In contrast, children from single-parent homes and from homes where both parents work achieve lower levels of education.[15] Another study noted that of 100 children born in 1986 (who, in 2006, were college age), 18 were illegitimate, 37 will have parents who are divorced, 9 will have parents who are separated, 2 will have one parent die before the child is age 18, and only 4 will be in the "typical" nuclear family—working father, homemaker mother, and two school-aged children.[16]

A 2001 Census Bureau study, authored by Jason Fields, stated that in the prototypical nuclear family—where mom, dad, and their biological children all live together—the percentage of children living in those traditional families rose from 51 percent in 1991 to 56 percent in 1996. As the total number of children increased, more of them were being born into traditional households. One reason for the increase is partly because couples married or began having children later in life and many of them are forming as traditional nuclear families. Present socioeconomic conditions are in flux and educators are hard-pressed to recognize their impact on individual students, classrooms, and schools.

TABLE 2.3   Projected Population of the United States, by Age and Sex: 2000 to 2050 (in thousands except as indicated)

Population or Percent, Sex, and Age	2010	2020	2030	2040	2050
Population					
Total					
Total	308,936	335,805	363,584	391,946	419,854
0–4	21,426	22,932	24,272	26,299	28,080
5–19	61,810	65,955	70,832	75,326	81,067
20–44	104,444	108,632	114,747	121,659	130,897
45–64	81,012	83,653	82,280	88,611	93,104
65–84	34,120	47,363	61,850	64,640	65,844
85+	6,123	7,269	9,603	15,409	20,861
Male					
Total	151,815	165,093	178,563	192,405	206,477
0–4	10,947	11,716	12,399	13,437	14,348
5–19	31,622	33,704	36,199	38,496	41,435
20–44	52,732	54,966	58,000	61,450	66,152
45–64	39,502	40,966	40,622	43,961	46,214
65–84	15,069	21,337	28,003	29,488	30,579
85+	1,942	2,403	3,340	5,573	7,749
Female					
Total	157,121	170,711	185,022	199,540	213,377
0–4	10,479	11,216	11,873	12,863	13,732
5–19	30,187	32,251	34,633	36,831	39,632
20–44	51,711	53,666	56,747	60,209	64,745
45–64	41,510	42,687	41,658	44,650	46,891
65–84	19,051	26,026	33,848	35,152	35,265
85+	4,182	4,866	6,263	9,836	13,112
Percent of Total					
Total					
Total	100.0	100.0	100.0	100.0	100.0
0–4	6.9	6.8	6.7	6.7	6.7
5–19	20.0	19.6	19.5	19.2	19.3
20–44	33.8	32.3	31.6	31.0	31.2
45–64	26.2	24.9	22.6	22.6	22.2
65–84	11.0	14.1	17.0	16.5	15.7
85+	2.0	2.2	2.6	3.9	5.0

Source: U.S. Census Bureau, 2004, "U.S. Interim Projections by Age, Sex, Race, and Hispanic Origin," www.census.gov/ipc/www/usinterimproj/.

FIGURE 2.6   The Pace of Growth and Households: 2000–2010

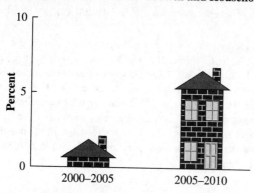

As two generations move through life, household growth will swing wildly (percent growth in number of U.S. households for five-year intervals, 2000–2010)

Source: American Demographics, 2000.

FIGURE 2.7   Projected Population Pyramid for United States: 2050

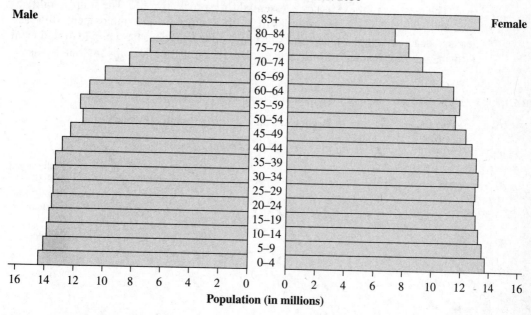

Source: U.S. Census Bureau, International Data Base. Updated April 2005. www.census.gov/cgi-bin/ipc/idbpyrs .pl?cty=US&out=s&ymax=250.

The Consequences of Not Educating People

Perhaps all people think of the high costs of educating the nation's citizens, but comparatively few give much thought to the higher cost of not educating them. Crime rates and costs related to public welfare or private charity are much greater among those who have an inadequate education. The Campaign for Educational Equity (CEE) declares:

> A one-year increase in average years of school for dropouts would reduce murder and assault by almost 30 percent, motor vehicle theft by 20 percent, arson by 13 percent, and burglary and larceny by about 6 percent. Direct costs to taxpayers of keeping a person incarcerated are many times the per-pupil cost of educating a student. Additional costs are incurred by the victims, and often by the prisoner's family. In the future, the costs of dealing with failing to educate the populace will undoubtedly be exponentially greater than would be the provision of additional finances for a quality education for all the people. Failure to provide educational opportunity results in some penalties to the students involved and is a costly injustice to society in general.[17]

Illiteracy

Often overlooked while examining adequacy in public school finance issues are the basic proficiencies in literacy, numeracy, problem solving, and high school completion. The mastery of these basics is essential for a productive life. The simple ability to read and calculate offers opportunities for further education and employment. Illiteracy leads to dead-end employment. Several special-interest groups have provided statistical information that seemed to inflate the percentages of illiterates in America by using

FIGURE 2.8   **National Assessment of Educational Progress (NAEP) Literacy Scale: 2000**

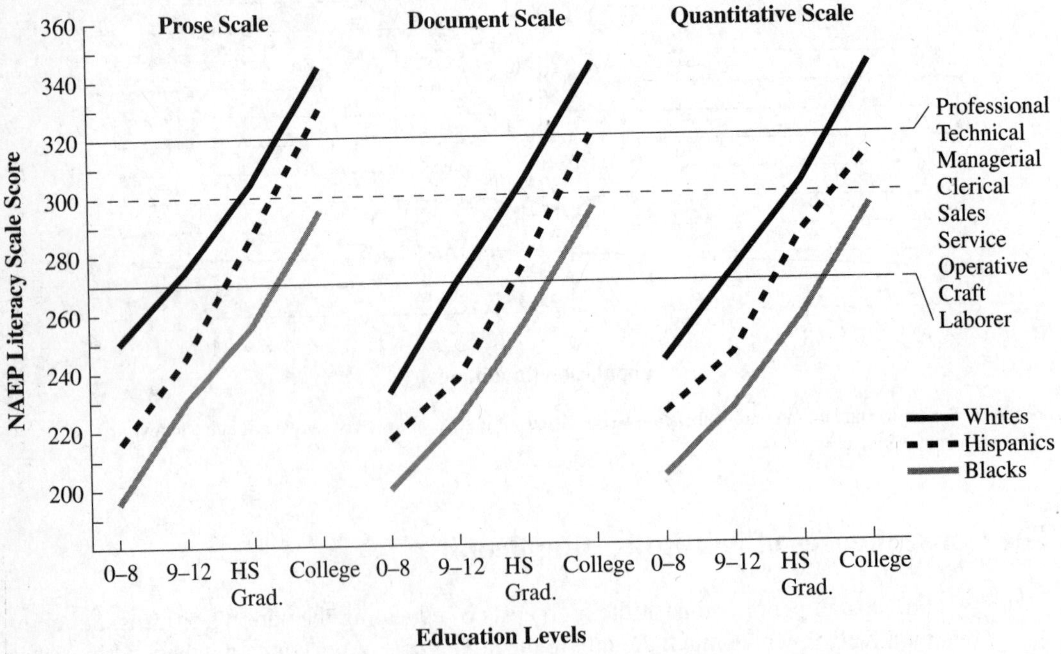

Source: www.nald.ca/www.nald.ca/fulltext/adlitus/Page137.htm.

devices to show that a person was illiterate if he or she could not distinguish between *infer* or *imply, while* and *when,* or *surprised* and *astonished.*

The U.S. Department of Education developed three scales to test literacy skills: prose, document, and quantitative. *Prose literacy* is the ability to understand and use information contained in various kinds of textual material. *Document literacy* reflects the knowledge and skills used to process information from documents. *Quantitative literacy* is the ability to perform numerical operations in everyday life.

The relationship among young adults of different ethnic groups as they relate to literacy skills is shown in Figure 2.8. For all ethnic groups, literacy development is clearly related to their level of education. However, for similar amounts of education, when compared to the average literacy skills of occupational groups (shown at the far right side), the ethnic groups differ greatly in the level of literacy skill achieved. Both Latino and Black high school graduates score well below the average skill level of clerical workers, whereas White high school graduates score above that level. With average scores slightly below 260 on each literacy scale, Black high school graduates score well below the average skill level of around 270 for laborers.

Reading Figure 2.9 from left to right shows that in the year 2000, there were over 17 million professional jobs, some 22 million clerical jobs, and just over 4 million

FIGURE 2.9   Prose, Document, and Quantitative Literacy Levels

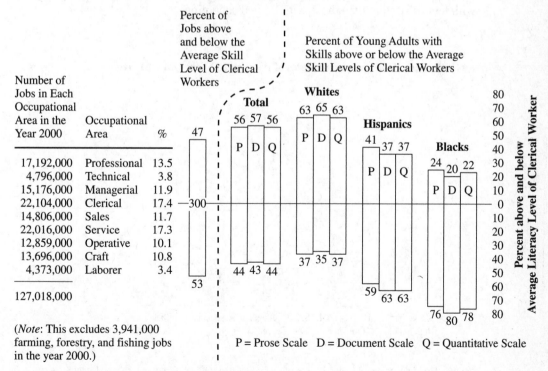

Source: www.nald.ca/www.nald.ca/fulltext/adlitus/Page136.htm

laborer jobs (the data exclude 3.9 million forestry jobs because there were no corresponding data on jobholders and their literacy skills for this category in the sources summarized). About 53 percent of jobs are fields with skill levels below that of the average clerical worker, whereas some 56 to 57 percent of young adults have skill levels in prose, document, and quantitative literacy above that level. However, while two-thirds or more of Whites and 37 to 41 percent of Hispanics possess skill levels above the average level of clerical workers, about one in five Blacks have literacy skills above the average for clerical workers. President George W. Bush, in support of the No Child Left Behind Act, declared, "Reading is the new civil right, the cornerstone of hope and opportunity in America."[18]

Unemployment

Unemployment is closely related to lack of adequate education. Figures show that it is much more of a problem to school dropouts and to those with a minimum education than to those who have attended schools and succeeded academically. Unemployment in 2006, for workers 25 years and older, was 6.2 percent among those who had not graduated from high school. High school graduates' unemployment was 4.0 percent. For those with associate degrees or some college, it was 3.5 percent. Unemployment was only 2.0 percent for college graduates (see Figure 2.10). Those with adequate education are usually able to adjust to new jobs and new occupations more easily and with less frustration than those with limited schooling.

FIGURE 2.10 Unemployment Rates of Persons 25 Years Old and Over

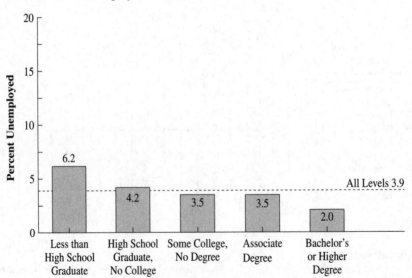

Source: U.S. Department of Labor, Bureau of Labor Statistics, Office of Employment and Unemployment Statistics, current population survey.

According to the National Committee for Support of the Public Schools, the great financial and social losses from unemployment can never be recovered:

> Economic losses from unemployment are never regained. The social costs of unemployment are even greater than the economic losses. The discouragement and frustration of able-bodied men and women, eager to work but unable to find employment, cannot be measured in dollars any more than can the distress of their families. Prolonged unemployment contributes to further unemployment, since human capital deteriorates when it is idle. Unemployment impairs the skills that workers have acquired. It also contributes to family disintegration, crime, and other social ills.[19]

Military Service Incapability

Undereducation saps the nation's defense potential. The United States is not interested in soldiers without high school diplomas. Modern warfare in an era of Patriot missiles, Stealth airplanes, and other sophisticated weapons could not endure a poor or inadequate education.[20] Figure 2.11 depicts strong evidence for the importance of education in job performance in the military. The figure shows three groups of military workers having reading grade levels of 4–6.9, 7–8.9, and 9–11.9 on the horizontal axis. There are two types of workers: supply specialists and automobile repairman (mechanic). The filled points show how well workers performed actual job sample tasks in a test situation. Proficiency increased across all three reading groups. The effects of both having higher levels of reading skill represents about a 20 percent increase in productivity due to having and using higher levels of reading ability.

FIGURE 2.11 Performance as a Function of Reading Ability

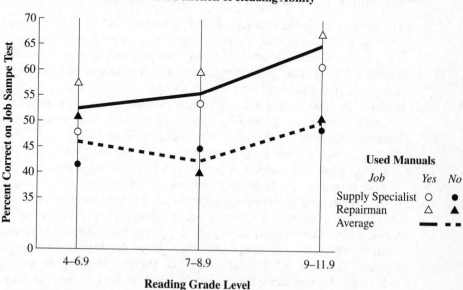

Source: www.nald.ca/www.nald.ca/fulltext/adlitus/Page140.htm.

Prison Incarceration

In 2006, the Bureau of Justice Statistics reported that there were nearly 2.2 million inmates locked up in jails and in state and federal prisons in the United States. The total direct justice expenditures reached $200 billion, growing from $36 billion in 1982. Prisons are largely populated with individuals who have little formal education; 41.2 percent of them are high school dropouts.[21] The District of Columbia, which has the highest high school dropout rate (10.6 percent) in the United States,[22] also has the highest prisoner incarceration rate (1,913 per 100,000 inhabitants).[23] Minnesota, which has the lowest prisoner incarceration rate (117 per 100,000 inhabitants),[24] has arguably the best record in the United States in high school achievement: 87.9 percent of its population 25 years old or over have high school diplomas or higher, and 93.3 percent of 18- to 24-year-olds are high school graduates.[25] The United States leads the world in the proportion of its citizens incarcerated. The Mississippi Department of Corrections found that a year in the maximum state prison costs more that $25,000 per inmate.[26] Public school district expenditures per student in 2006 were $8,618. If high school graduation rates could be increased by just 1 percent for all men ages 20 to 60, the United States would save up to $1.4 billion per year in reduced costs from crime, according to the CEE.[27]

Unless America continues its commitment to educational opportunities that provide constructive paths to responsible adult life experiences, it will "lock up" a growing share of the population. The focus should be on providing a good education rather than suffering from the lack of a good education.[28]

Inadequate Occupational Preparation

The media are replete with reports that applicants seeking occupational positions in business and industry lack adequate educational preparations. Business and industry have implemented basic education and retraining programs to overcome these inadequacies. This condition results in an obvious waste in time and cost for U.S. industry. The employment status of high school graduates is higher than that for dropouts. For example, in 2004, only 5.0 percent of the graduates were unemployed; for dropouts, 8.5 percent were unemployed—nearly twice as many. Similar employment benefits continue with ethnic and gender differences (see Table 2.4).

Education is an investment in human skills, involving both a cost and a return. In summarizing statistics on the employment benefits of education, the U.S. Department of Education notes the following: "Among the returns related to the labor market are better employment opportunities, jobs that are less sensitive to general economic conditions, better opportunities to participate in employer-provided training, and higher earnings. The immediate difficulty of making the transition from full-time school attendance to full-time work appears much greater for those who leave school before finishing high school."[29] "Education is the key to improving the quality of life for individuals, for improving the climate of economic development, and for maintaining and improving this nation's democracy and economic competitiveness."[30]

TABLE 2.4   Unemployment Rate of Persons 25 Years Old and Over, by Sex, Race/Ethnicity, and Educational Attainment: 2002, 2003, and 2004

Sex, Race/Ethnicity, and Educational Attainment	Unemployment Rate, 2002,[1] 25 Years Old and Over	Unemployment Rate, 2003,[1] 25 Years Old and Over	Unemployment Rate, 2004,[1] 25 Years Old and Over
All Persons			
All education levels	4.6	4.8	4.4
Less than high school completion	8.4	8.8	8.5
High school completion, no college	5.3	5.5	5.0
Some college, no degree	4.8	5.2	4.5
Associate's degree	4.0	4.0	3.7
Bachelor's or higher degree	2.9	3.1	2.7
Male			
All education levels	4.7	5.0	4.4
Less than high school completion	7.8	8.2	7.6
High school completion, no college	5.4	5.7	5.1
Some college, no degree	4.7	5.4	4.4
Associate's degree	4.3	4.4	4.0
Bachelor's or higher degree	3.0	3.2	2.7
Female			
All education levels	4.6	4.6	4.4
Less than high school completion	9.5	9.8	—
High school completion, no college	5.1	5.2	4.9
Some college, no degree	5.0	4.9	4.7
Associate's degree	3.7	3.7	3.4
Bachelor's or higher degree	2.8	2.9	2.7
White, Non-Hispanic			
All education levels	3.9	4.0	3.6
Less than high school completion	7.5	7.6	7.7
High school completion, no college	4.5	4.6	4.3
Some college, no degree	4.2	4.3	3.7
Associate's degree	3.5	3.5	3.3
Bachelor's or higher degree	2.7	2.8	2.5
Black, Non-Hispanic			
All education levels	7.7	8.3	8.1
Less than high school completion	—	—	—
High school completion, no college	8.8	9.4	8.7
Some college, no degree	6.9	8.6	8.4
Associate's degree	6.0	6.1	5.9
Bachelor's or higher degree	4.2	4.3	4.2

(continued)

TABLE 2.4   Continued

Sex, Race/Ethnicity, and Educational Attainment	Unemployment Rate, 2002,[1] 25 Years Old and Over	Unemployment Rate, 2003,[1] 25 Years Old and Over	Unemployment Rate, 2004,[1] 25 Years Old and Over
Hispanic Origin[2]			
All education levels	6.1	6.4	5.7
Less than high school completion	7.7	8.2	7.5
High school completion, no college	5.9	5.9	5.2
Some college, no degree	5.7	5.8	5.1
Associate's degree	5.0	5.3	4.2
Bachelor's or higher degree	3.4	4.1	3.5

[1]The unemployment rate is the percent of individuals in the labor force who are not working and who made specific efforts to find employment sometime during the prior 4 weeks. The labor force includes both employed and unemployed persons.
[2]Persons of Hispanic origin may be of any race.

Note: Some data have been revised from previously published figures.

Source: U.S. Department of Labor, Bureau of Labor Statistics, Office of Employment and Unemployment Statistics, Current Population Survey (CPS), March 2002, 2003, and 2004, unpublished tabulations. (This table was prepared in May 2005.)

Dependence on Public Relief

There appears to be a high positive relation between inadequate education and the need for financial assistance. A number of studies have shown that recipients of public assistance are likely to be individuals of low educational attainment.

A Chicago study of relief recipients showed that 50.7 percent of the sample could not pass reading and vocabulary tests at the fifth-grade achievement level. "The conclusion was that the problems of public welfare stem from unemployment and economic and technological displacement and, most important, from relief recipients' lack of basic educational skills which are essential to compete in our modern society."[31]

The Campaign for Educational Equity states:

America could save between $7.9B and $10.8B annually on Temporary Assistance for Needy Families (TANF), Food Stamps, and housing assistance by improving the educational attainment of those who currently do not complete high school. Single-mother high school graduates are 24 percent to 55 percent less likely to be on TANF than single-mother high school dropouts. If all single-mother dropouts earned a high school degree, there would be over 140,000 fewer recipients on Food Stamps, saving $353 million. If all single mother dropouts earned high school degrees and some also attained additional education, 63,000 fewer single-mother families would be on housing assistance, saving an additional $313 million annually. If one third of all Americans without a high school education went on to get more than a high school education, the savings would range from $3.8 billion to $6.7 billion for TANF, $3.7 billion for Food Stamps, and $0.4 billion for housing assistance.[32]

The U.S. Census Bureau has reported, "Close to half of all welfare mothers never finished high school." In its first survey of women collecting Aid to Families with Dependent Children (AFDC), it stated that 44 percent of welfare mothers, ages 15 to 44, "lack a high school diploma." Nearly half (48 percent) of AFDC mothers have never been married. It was noted that recipients of welfare are poorly educated. Some 85 percent of those not on welfare graduated from high school—a dramatic difference.[33]

There are many reasons why families may need public assistance. Lack of education shows up as a significant factor. Compounding the problem, those with less education need assistance for a longer period of time.

High Health Costs

The Center for Disease Control and Prevention (CDC) has conducted a major study about health and education in the United States. The CDC found that there was a correlation between health and education across the board for all races. "Americans who never graduated from high school are more likely to smoke, live a sedentary life and be overweight than more educated people." The study came to the following conclusions:

- Smoking, excess weight, and lack of exercise put people at risk for heart disease, stroke, diabetes, and cancer—which account for 70 percent of all deaths in the United States.
- People with fewer than 12 years of education are most likely to engage in those high-risk behaviors.
- For male Asians and Pacific Islanders, 34.4 percent of those with less than a high school diploma smoked, compared to 16.3 percent of those with more than 12 years of schooling.
- Among Black women lacking a high school diploma, 50.9 percent were overweight, compared to 28.9 percent of those with more than 12 years of schooling.
- For Asians and Pacific Islander women with fewer than 12 years of education, 17.6 percent smoked, compared to 6.4 percent of those with more than 12 years' education.[34]

The Campaign for Educational Equity declared:

High school dropouts have higher rates of cardiovascular illnesses, diabetes, and other ailments, and require an average of $35,000 in annual health-care costs, compared with $15,000 for college graduates. A 65-year-old person with a high school diploma typically enjoys better health status than a 45-year-old who dropped out in the 10th grade. Overall, high school dropouts live an average of nine fewer years than graduates . . . and the net present value of the drop in health-related costs due to an increase in attainment from 11th grade to high school graduation is approximately $83,000 per student. . . . Improving all

600,000 high school dropouts in 2004 by one grade would have been a $41.8 billion drop in health-related costs.[35]

Society Suffers the Effects of Poor Education

The individual who suffers the consequences of poor or inadequate education is not confined to a particular area, town, city, or state. The frustrations that unemployment, inadequate income, and substandard living conditions bring often produce high mobility rates among those who suffer them. The problems related to poor education in one locality then become the welfare or reeducation problems of another community. High mobility rates of people may quickly move the problems of the disadvantaged (higher welfare and law-enforcement costs, for example) from the source of their creation to a state or locality whose educational system is adequate or even superior. Thus, the effects of poor education are not localized. The problems of providing adequate and high-quality education are not only local but are also statewide and national in scope. No longer can states and districts have concern only for their own citizens.

The spiraling costs of education and the changing social climate of the country have combined to raise serious questions concerning public education. Have the increased costs resulted in proportionately increased productivity? Why has the public lost confidence in the schools? Why does the public not accept the arguments for increased costs of education as explained by the professionals? These are a few of the unanswered questions that have resulted in taxpayer revolts, student militancy, racial unrest in the schools, and a general deterioration in the traditional confidence that many citizens have shown in the nation's schools.

The Public Demands Improvement

The public demands improvement and increased efficiency in the operation of public schools. The cry of the people is couched under the broad umbrella of accountability. The accountability movement has gathered momentum; critics as well as friends of public education hold the schools firmly accountable for making output commensurate with input. Public sentiment virtually demands that the educational establishment produces valid information and proof that the schools are achieving their intended objectives and that in the process they are using tax revenues efficiently.

Plaintiffs in the courts of the several states question whether legislatures and other funding sources are providing adequate revenues for effective educational programs. This demand has led to numerous suits challenging school finance formulas. A major shift has occurred questioning the adequacy of funds that states are expending to meet education's needs (see Chapter 9).

Although actions toward accountability are desirable and should be encouraged, some potential dangers are inherent in rushing too quickly into the process. One danger is that taxpayers may expect the schools to be accountable, at the same time ignoring their own responsibility for providing adequate funds for achieving the comprehensive goals of education. Closely related is the possibility that some lawmaking bodies may, without fully understanding the ramifications, legislate school accountability laws. These could involve such questionable notions as requiring all pupils to take certain academic examinations to determine the degree of success or failure of the schools to achieve their purposes.

Equality Not Yet Attained

Equality of educational opportunity is sound philosophy. Providing such opportunities has its challenges and has often drawn attention from the courts. The U.S. Supreme Court in *San Antonio Independent School District* v. *Rodriguez* (1973)[36] ruled that education is not a fundamental right under the federal Constitution. That decision shifted court action to the several states, and education finance issues since have been adjudicated at that level rather than in federal courts (see Chapter 9). Many state courts have questioned the response of legislatures in providing appropriate educational opportunity for all students and have ruled that social injustices exist and equality has not yet been attained.

One of the primary problems in this regard—dealing fairly and objectively with social and racial injustices—must base its chances for solution on education. No other agency or institution has greater hope and greater responsibility than education for eradicating the hazards that prevent cultural and economic improvement. Just as the schools have justified national faith in them in their responsibility for dissolving the great problems created by differences in national origin of students, so are they now challenged by the tremendous problem of providing equality of educational opportunity. The price of such a worthy goal will be high in dollars and human effort, but it is a price that all thinking citizens will be willing to pay. If education fails in this, its most challenging charge, future generations may never receive the same chance or responsibility.

Underinvestment Is Poor Economy

The determination of the optimum amount of money the nation should invest in education is a difficult problem. Although numerous schools are without financial problems, there are also many that operate with inadequate laboratories, limited libraries, overcrowded classrooms, and poorly trained teachers. Of course, not all the limitations of poor schools are the result of insufficient financing. Adequate revenues provide the possibility of producing a good educational program but do not guarantee it. Inadequate revenues, however, will almost certainly guarantee a poor educational program. No prudent person would invest large sums of money in an enterprise and then forget it or refuse to use all possible means of protecting that investment. Sometimes adequate protection may involve spending additional funds. Such is the case with investment in education, for inadequate future expenditures may result in loss of all or a major part of the original investment.

Every economist and most intelligent citizens readily recognize the fallacy of assuming that economy requires spending the smallest amount of money possible in purchasing a good or service. Certainly, examples of underspending that have resulted in lack of protection of original investment are easy to discern in any area of business, industry, or education. For example, the school board that employs an unqualified or incompetent teacher at a low salary, or that refuses to keep its buildings and equipment in good repair with the excuse of saving money, will sooner or later recognize such actions as poor business and a violation of true economy. The educational system that provides only a small part of an optimum program for its students will at some time come to realize that the taxpayers' investment in human capital has not been protected adequately. This country must protect the value of its investment in the education of its citizens; this cannot be fully measured in standard dollars and cents. It must also protect the individual's indirect and intangible benefits that are a part of the educational process. Education, or the lack of it, has serious social consequences. Hodgkinson stated:

> In a state that retains a high percentage of its youth to high school graduation, almost every young person becomes a "net gain" to the state—with a high school diploma, there is a high probability of that person getting a job and repaying the state for the cost of his education. However in a state with a poor record of retention to high school graduation, many youth are a "net loss" to the state, in that without a high school diploma, the chances of that student getting work and thus repaying the state for that person's education, are very small indeed.[37]

A Question of Priorities

In the past, educators and economists have done remarkably well in convincing large numbers of taxpayers that education is an investment in people. But they have done less well in showing the investors how much they have earned on the added investments that education has required each year. In the current frenzy to try to place a dollar value on the student who submits to the educational process, it must be understood that cost-benefit studies have not been producing conclusive results concerning this complex problem and cannot be expected to do so.

All groups of people who are concerned with education appear to be demanding their own version of accountability—often with little regard for their own responsibility. But the principle of accountability applies to all segments of the school complex: administrators, students, teachers, boards of education, parents, and the legislative bodies. The public schools cannot prosper or achieve their intended place in the lives of their students if any one of these groups is not held accountable to play its part in the educational process. However, the important point as far as school finance is concerned is that the educational fraternity—administrators, teachers, and other staff members—must realize that the taxpaying community needs and demands more comprehensive and objective ways to measure output of education compared with input. Without such accountability, the economic theories and principles that are generally followed in financing education may be counterbalanced by the actions of skeptical taxpayers. Education will suffer irreparable damage if the public decreases its support because of insufficient evidence that schools are doing what they purport to do.

Many people believe that education is receiving its equitable share of the wealth of this country and that additional funds are not available. Others insist that the nation's priorities are inconsistent with its values and that there is little, if any, defense for the fact that more is spent on cosmetics, liquor, and tobacco than on education.

Summary

Most citizens of the United States recognize education as "big business." The taxpayers of the country often do not give it high enough priority so that it can receive the resources it requires.

There are numerous reasons for the greatly increasing costs of education year after year. These include (1) the nation's educational goals and objectives continue to increase, (2) communities are constantly demanding more and better services from the schools, (3) more programs and professional services are being provided for high-cost students such as those with disabilities, (4) inflation has increased, (5) the cost of treating students in alternative educational settings has vacillated, (6) energy costs have increased, and (7) changing social and demographic influences affect expenditures.

As expensive as public education may be, the cost to society of not educating people is much higher. The detrimental effect of illiteracy on employment, on military capability, and on the size of welfare and relief rolls is strong evidence of the costliness of permitting people to remain uneducated.

Financing education at less than an adequate level is poor economy. With such a large investment in buildings and facilities, the 50 states must provide enough revenue to protect that investment and to achieve the best possible education for all their youths, regardless of their place of residence, the wealth of their parents, or the wealth of their school district.

ASSIGNMENT PROJECTS

1. Provide a definition for each of the following terms: *adequacy, demographics, inflation, social indicators, current dollars, constant dollars, accountability, literacy, numeracy.*
2. Show by a review of some school districts that have experimented with an extension of their school year what the problems and the advantages of such extensions are.
3. What evidence can you find that increasing social problems are causing large increases in the annual costs of public elementary and secondary education?
4. Show how projected demographic and economic changes in a local area will affect the revenue and expenditures of the school district. Determine what school officials should do to prepare for such changes.
5. Study the shift in population within a state and report on the impact it has had on the finances of various local districts within the state.

Computer simulations and questions, research exercises, and website
addresses relevant to this chapter can be found at

www.ablongman.com/edleadership

SELECTED READINGS

Benson, Charles S. *The Economics of Public Education,* 3rd ed. Boston: Houghton Mifflin, 1978.

Berne, R., and L. O. Picus. *Outcome Equity in Education.* Thousand Oaks, CA: Corwin, 1994.

Card, David, and Alan B. Kruegar. "School Quality and Black-White Relative Earnings: A Direct Assessment," *Quarterly Journal of Economics,* 107, February 1992.

Carnegie Forum on Education and the Economy. *A Nation Preparing Teachers for the 21st Century.* Washington, DC: Carnegie Forum on Education and the Economy, 1990.

Galbraith, John Kenneth. *The Culture of Contentment.* Boston: Houghton Mifflin, 1992.

Hinrichs, William L., and Richard D. Laine. *Adequacy: Building Quality and Efficiency into the Cost of Education.* Springfield: Illinois Board of Education, 1996.

Kronick, Robert F., and Charles H. Hargis. *Dropouts: Who Drops Out and Why, and the Recommended Action.* Springfield, IL: Charles C. Thomas, 1990.

Marseth, Katherine K. *Cases in Educational Administration.* New York: Longman, 1997.

Monk, David H. *Educational Finance: An Economic Approach.* New York: McGraw-Hill, 1990.

Ogle, Laurence, Nabeel Alsalam, and Gayle Thompson Rogers. *The Condition of Education, 1991: Elementary and Secondary Education.* Washington, DC: National Center for Educational Statistics, U.S. Department of Education, 1991.

Reich, Robert B. *The Work of Nations.* New York: Alfred A. Knopf, 1991.

Thompson, David C., R. Craig Wood, and David S. Honeyman. *Fiscal Leadership for Schools, Concepts and Practices.* White Plains, NY, 1994.

Verstegen, D. A. *School Finance at a Glance.* Denver, CO: Education Commission of the States, 1990.

ENDNOTES

1. http://nces.ed.gov./ccd/pubs/npefs03/table_3.asp?popup=1.

2. NCES, Educational Statistics to 2007, p. 1.

3. The National Commission on Excellence in Education, *A Nation at Risk: The Imperative for Educational Reform* (Washington, DC: U.S. Printing Office), April 1983, p. 32.

4. www.schoolfunding.info/news/policy/8-29-05 latestgoodnews.php3.

5. *The Unfinished Agenda: A New Vision for Child Development and Education* (New York: Committee for Research and Policy, Committee for Economic Development, 1991), p, 15.

6. www.floridatoday.com/!NEWSROOM/special/education/stories/0519eeditorial.htm.

7. The 38th Annual Phi Delta Kappa/Gallup Poll of the Public's Attitudes Toward the Public Schools," *Phi Delta Kappan,* September 2006, www.pdkint.org/kappan/k0609pol.htm p. 3.

8. Ibid.

9. Ibid., p. 5.

10. Ibid., p. 7.

11. Ibid.

12. *Financing the Public Schools* (Bloomington, IN: Phi Delta Kappa Commission on Alternative Designs for Funding Education, 1973), p. 6.

13. Amy Goldstein [Washington Post], "Nearly 1 in 3 Wives Now Earning More than Husband," *Minneapolis Star Tribune,* February 29, 2000, p. A6.

14. Ibid.

15. Coleman et al., *Public and Private Schools and High School Achievement* (1981), provided by the United States Department of Education, 1986.

16. Harold Hodgkinson, *All One System: Demographics of Education, Kindergarten through Graduate School* (Washington, DC: Institute for Educational Leadership, 1985), p. 3.

17. Henry M. Levin, *The Social Costs of Inadequate Education* (New York: Teachers College, Columbia University, 2006), p. 2.

18. www.msnbc.com/msn/517502.asp.

19. *Changing Demands on Education and Their Fiscal Implications* (Washington, DC: National Committee for Support of the Public Schools), p. 11.

20. Speech given by Richard Cheney to U.S. Chamber of Commerce Convention, Washington, DC, April 29, 1991.

21. Postsecondary Education OPPORTUNITY, Number 89, November 1999, www.postsecondary.org/last12/8911Prisoner.pdf.

22. http://nces.ed.gov/pubs98/dropout/ch05t03a.html.

23. Postsecondary Education OPPORTUNITY, Number 89, November 1999.

24. Ibid.

25. http://nces.ed.gov/pubs98/98018/Tab1.prn, U.S. Department of Commerce, Bureau of the Census.

26. Report to the Legislature, The Joint Committee on Performance Evaluation and Expenditure Review, Mississippi Department of Corrections, 2002.

27. Levin, *The Social Costs,* p. 2.

28. Postsecondary Education OPPORTUNITY, Number 89.

29. *The Condition of Education, 1991: Volume 1, Elementary and Secondary Education* (Washington, DC: U.S. Department of Education, National Center for Education Statistics, 1991), p. 42.

30. Booth Gardner, "Directions for Education in America," *Journal of Education Finance,* Vol. 15, No. 4, Spring 1990, p. 602.

31. *Changing Demands on Education and Their Fiscal Implications* (Washington, DC: National Committee for Support of the Public Schools), pp. 49–50.

32. Levin, *The Social Costs,* p. 17.

33. Leslie Phillips, "Welfare Pit Deep for Uneducated," *USA Today,* March 3, 1995, p. 3A.

34. A. J. Hosteller, "CDC Study Finds High Health Cost of Poor Education," *Daily Herald* (Provo, UT), December 15, 1994, p. A15. Story from Associated Press.

35. Levin, *The Social Costs,* p. 16.

36. *San Antonio Independent School District* v. *Rodriguez,* 411 U.S. 1, 93 S.Ct. 1278 (1973), rehearing denied.

37. Hodgkinson, *All One System,* p. 11.

3

Financing Education Equitably

We ought to finance the education of every child in America equitably, with adjustments made only for the greater or lesser needs of certain children. And the funding should all come from the collective wealth of our society.

—Jonathan Kozol, 2007

Equally difficult and important as financing education adequately is the challenge of distributing and expending available revenues with fairness to schools and to students, regardless of their location within a state. This is the principle of *equity,* or fairness. *Equity* should not be considered synonymous with *equality* in this context.

Equality, as it relates to educational opportunity, is a fundamental principle in U.S. education. Democracy is best served by extending to all children not only the ability to read, write, numerate, and compute but also by providing an equal opportunity to attend schools that are adequate for the achievement of self-realization, economic sufficiency, civic responsibility, and satisfactory human relationships. Equality in this sense does not mean an identical education for all children, but rather the provision of certain minimum essentials, with no ceiling on opportunity. Spending the same number of dollars on each student is evidence of *equality,* but it may not be equitable—some students, such as those with special needs, require greater expenditures for their education than do other students.

The problem of equity as it applies to financing public education is often discussed in the literature. The following statements illustrate the concern with which writers discuss equity as it applies to the various school finance systems of the nation: "Equity in school finance systems is a complex concept." "Taxpayer 'equity' and 'social justice' are terms often used but seldom defined." "Equalization and equity in school finance have different meanings for different people." Natale noted, "Although it is rooted in numbers and complicated school financing formula, equalization is an emotional issue that evokes powerful images of disparity between educational haves and have-nots. At the heart of the controversy—often portrayed as a struggle between classes—is the issue of equal educational opportunity for all."[1]

Sue Books portrayed the problem of defining equity in these terms:

> Because little consensus exists, even among educational researchers, either about what *equity* means or about how it ought to be measured, it is difficult to answer the seemingly straightforward question: How equitable is school funding? It depends. Inequitable in the sense of unfair or in the sense of unequal? And unfair or unequal from whose perspective—public school students or the taxpayers who fund their education? Finally, inequitable with respect to what: funds allocated, dollars actually spent, the quality of education students receive, or the level of educational achievement they attain?[2]

Inequalities in Financing Education

As previously stated, education should be financed and operated equitably, but this cannot and should not be done with complete equality, because of the many differences in the abilities and needs of students. Benson and associates emphasized this point in the following:

> Obviously, providing equal dollar inputs for unequal students produces unequal results. Equal spending does not make education the "great equalizer of the conditions of men" as Horace Mann suggested. . . . If education is to facilitate the movement of the poor and disadvantaged into the mainstream of American social and economic life, if it is to afford everyone equal probability of success (however one defines it), then equal facilities, teaching skills, and curriculums are not the answers. Additional resources must be made available to students who enter and pass through the educational system with handicaps such as language barriers for which they are not responsible. We do not know how much more should be spent to make these additional resources available.[3]

This apparent dilemma has received considerable treatment by writers in the field, as well as in the formulas for financing education adopted by various states since the court ruling in *Serrano* v. *Priest* (1971)[4] and many legal cases since. A few of these rulings have been misinterpreted or overstated in their application. For example, in *Serrano,* the principle of fiscal neutrality was established—a child's education must not be affected by wealth, except the wealth of the state. This principle, made applicable as a standard for California by the court and applied in practice to some other states as well, did not mandate equal dollar expenditures per child in any state. It did not rule out expending more money for children with higher educational costs—such as those who are bilingual or from minority populations, those who have disabilities, and those who require compensatory measures. It did not exclude property taxes as a basis for local financial support of education. In short, it did not legislate equality in financing education.

Equity Issue Revisited

The equity issue that fomented a revolution in state spending on public schools during the 1970s resurfaced with greater impact during the 1980s. The next decade brought little relief. In August 2006, 40 of the 50 states have been or were involved in litigation at the highest state court, contesting some financial aspect of school funding.

The disparities in per-pupil spending are a continual concern. For example, at the time of the 1971 *Serrano* case, the ratio difference between the two districts involved was 6.2 to 1. However, some districts were as high as 50 to 1 in California when the case was brought to the courts. In general, states have attempted to alleviate the disparities. Without continual evaluation, margins soon spread. More recent data note that extremes still exist in these states:[5]

Texas	$2,112 to $19,333	9.2 to 1
North Dakota	$2,085 to $11,743	5.6 to 1
Ohio	$4,000 to $12,000	3.0 to 1
Virginia	$2,979 to $ 7,726	2.6 to 1

Results from Education Trust, an organization concerned with equity issues for minorities, described other discrepancies in funding as it relates to low-income school districts in various states even when state formulas have been designed to provide equity. The conclusions of the study indicate the following:

- In most states, districts with high numbers of low-income students receive substantially fewer state and local dollars per pupil than districts with few such students.
- The funding gap between high- and low-poverty districts has narrowed somewhat over the past several years in the nation as a whole, but it has increased significantly in nine states.
- In most states, districts with high numbers of minority students also receive substantially fewer state and local dollars per pupil than do their counterparts with few minority students.[6]

The report lists these states with the largest *funding gap* between expenditures per pupil in high-poverty districts and low-poverty districts:[7]

	High Poverty	*Low Poverty*	*Difference*
New York	$6,445	$8,598	$2,153
Illinois	$5,400	$7,450	$2,050
Montana	$4,826	$6,361	$1,535
Pennsylvania	$6,037	$7,285	$1,248
Michigan	$6,815	$7,917	$1,102
U.S. average	$5,846	$6,182	$ 336

Solving the equity dilemma is not an easy task; researchers have used various criteria to determine equity, but find it elusive. Some suggest that if per-pupil funding or expenditures are within 10 percent, then equity is within acceptable limits.

Equity in the support of the educational program does not always produce equal learning. Many factors other than money affect educational achievement. These include, but are not limited to, the quality of the family, the intelligence of the student, school leadership, time on task, school climate and culture, community attitudes, parental support, high expectations by the teacher, curriculum, and instructional strategies. Some districts, because of location, may attract and retain good teachers and administrators, which affects learning. Individual students may take better advantage of opportunities than other students.

Quality versus Fiscal Equity

Emphasis on excellence has resulted in differences of opinion about equity. Some believe additional resources should be targeted to guarantee quality. Those who espouse excellence as a priority see the main goals of financing education to be the attainment of quality. Others feel that states have yet to reach fiscal equity and that the priority still rests there. Those who promote equity based on quality emphasize that districts that do better on prescribed standards or outcomes should be rewarded monetarily—that the use of dollars should be refocused from attendance to competence. Grants should be given to those schools and districts that demonstrate excellence; state support should be differentiated according to the quality of instruction. Rewards should be given to districts that show improvement. Advocates of fiscal equity would rely on formula grants, cost reimbursement, general aid, and special support for students who are poor, are low achievers, and have special needs.

Equity: An Objective of School Finance Reform

Traditionally, each state has enjoyed almost complete freedom in the way it has allocated funds to local school districts. Some states chose to leave the financing of education almost completely to each local district; others used grants of varying kinds to alleviate local overburden; and still others used equalization programs of varying degrees of complexity.

Allocations of state money to local districts have usually been made on the basis of the number of pupils to be educated and in terms of the ability of the district to finance a minimum or foundation program. Equality of educational opportunity has been interpreted to mean providing the same amount of money for each pupil who is to be educated. Gradually, however, financing formulas have recognized that it costs more to educate some pupils than others. Among the earliest changes in this regard was providing more money per pupil for those who lived in rural areas where the unit cost of education was higher and where transportation was an important cost factor. Later, the provision of additional funds for educating exceptional children, especially the physically and mentally disabled, became acceptable and desirable. Today, one of the great needs is for special financial consideration for large city and metropolitan districts, where deprivation, tax overburden, and racial and ghetto area problems have increased the unit costs of education well beyond those in average districts.

Implementation of programs with unequal amounts of money per pupil is fertile ground for confrontation and litigation. In one form or another, the issue of equal protection of all citizens as provided by the Fourteenth Amendment has often been a matter of litigation. The Supreme Court required equal rights for the education of all citizens regardless of race, stating: "In these days, it is doubtful that any child may reasonably be expected to succeed in life if he is denied the opportunity of an education. Such an opportunity, where the state has undertaken to provide it, is a right which must be made available to all on equal terms."[8] Geographic discrimination was eliminated in the legislative reapportionment decision. The Court determined that lack of financial resources could not be used to deny criminals equal protection of the law. Courts have faced the issue of unequal protection of students because of unequal expenditures of money for children attending different school districts.

The main thrust of court decisions in this new century are still evaluating the equity or fairness issue with a new emphasis on adequacy. The school finance reforms in most of the 50 states seem to echo the words *sameness, standardization, fairness,* and *equity.* The new formulas generally emphasize two aspects of equity: fairness for the children who are being educated and fairness for the taxpayers who defray the costs of education.

Equity for Children

Equity for children concerns fairness in the amount of revenue and the services provided for children—the actual expenditures per child. To be completely fair, such equity would involve all funds expended, but common practice in comparing such expenditures usually includes only local and state revenues, disregarding federal finance programs. Such comparisons also usually include only current expenditures, ignoring the area of capital outlays.

Equity for children should be more concerned with equality of output than with equality of input in the educational process. Since the input is only a means to an end, equity should involve evenness of attainment of school objectives. There must be some accurate measurement of achievement, competencies developed, degree of fulfillment of requirements for graduation or grade advancement, attainment of positive attitudes and habits, and similar goals of an educational program.

At present, equity for children can best be measured in terms of comparing the expenditures per child. However, many studies have been conducted to show that even horizontal equity (equal treatment of equals) has many ramifications when attempting to use a simple allocation of providing districts with an equal amount of revenue for each child in the district. For example, even within a district, inequities are immediate in learning environments, support services, facilities, availability of books and supplies, and many other factors. Vertical equity (unequal treatment of unequals) complicates the fairness issue even further, and is more difficult to determine, since no one can define fairness with complete assurance when treating children with unequal characteristics. Equality in support of the educational program does not always produce equal learning, as indicated in the following statement by Lindley J. Stiles:

> Complicating theories and practices of educational finance even more is the fact that equal support does not produce equality in learning. So many factors bear upon how well any individual student will take advantage of educational opportunities that it is almost impossible to prove that equalizing school expenditures will make a difference, particularly for those who need help most. We know that the quality of education a school provides is not always related on a one-to-one ratio to per-pupil costs. Some school districts with modest

means—because of such factors as geographical location, community attitudes, philosophy of education, leadership, or personal policies—are able to attract and retain good teachers and administrators. The curriculum, instructional resources and strategies, as well as disciplinary standards of a school all contribute to educational productivity.[9]

The Weighted-Pupil Approach

A step toward meeting the challenge of vertical equity and the most common method used to improve the equity of school finance formulas, in allocating funds to local districts, is the use of *pupil weightings*. These are nothing more than cost differentials injected in the formula to compensate or allow for the additional cost of education of some students because of their innate characteristics, the types of educational programs they pursue, or other pertinent cost factors. Weightings (additional funds) for students who are bilingual, are from minorities, are learning disabled, and require compensatory measures are often used in recognition of their disadvantages and the higher cost of their education. For several years, some states have provided cost differentials for pupils in small and more costly schools—usually in sparsely populated and isolated areas. A few states provide density weighting or correction factors for pupils in large cities where the higher cost of educational and other government services is such that financial relief is required, in the interest of fairness to the pupils being educated as well as to the taxpayers bearing the cost. A number of other weightings are sometimes found in state formulas, such as those for secondary school students over those in elementary grades, although this practice is becoming less justified as the costs of elementary education move closer to those of secondary education. Some states also provide for weightings for teachers who have more academic preparation and experience (and who therefore are higher on the salary schedule), weightings for early education pupils (kindergarten and the first two or three years of elementary school), and weightings for higher-than-average-cost programs, such as vocational education and driver education.

The weighted-pupil approach adds objectivity and equity to the school finance system. Under this concept, all programs suffer or prosper comparably when funds are reduced or increased. This is particularly beneficial to high-cost programs, which are often the first ones to be cut back or deleted when school revenues are reduced.

A number of states and finance authorities have favored the weighted-pupil approach to equity in school finance—that substantially equal amounts of money per pupil be provided, taking into consideration the differences in costs of various school programs. Such an approach has several advantages over the use of the actual number of students attending school, including the following: (1) The costs of education are not the same for all students. (2) Many court decisions considered the unequal cost of education, as reflected in the cost per person being educated. (3) The principle tends to build fairness into a finance formula, for *all* classifications of pupils receive their proportionate share of revenue increases as well as decreases with changes in the school budget. (4) Several states have used this approach with success. (5) The principle tends to reduce the number of categorical grants that are required in the financing of educational programs. (6) Such an approach usually results in a simplification of the state's school finance formula. The weighted-pupil method serves as an excellent foundation structure compared to other formulas.

Equity at the School Level

As states continue to struggle with the complexities of bringing financial equity to local districts, some districts are being scrutinized to determine how individual schools within the district compare financially. Although the concern for a breakdown of school-level costs does not seem to be of vital interest to local districts, writers in the field of education finance are finding it a topic for research. "For the past several years, there has been considerable interest in measuring educational expenditures at the school level for the purpose of linking student costs to student results. This attention has developed as a variety of interested parties and issues have converged around the effort of improving the effectiveness and efficiency of schools."[10]

The appropriate data are not readily available, and attempting to follow the expenditures at the school level to the classroom and the child level is practically impossible. Even the first step of comparing the states is difficult because of the wide variety of funding patterns. "Researchers found a great deal of variability in the level of detail and type of school data collected by various states, which made it extremely difficult to compare the results of analyses of school-level resources across states."[11] "The key problem is that if the use of the data is limited and does not affect schools, or cannot be easily used by them, it is likely that schools will not take much care in providing data items for the data collection system."[12] In an attempt to design a workable model for such reporting, Hartman, Bolton, and Monk agree that if data have little meaning for administrators and even less for school principals, collecting and reporting would result in unrewarding efforts:

> Before committing significant funds, time and energy into program changes, a district will want to be confident that the analyses are valid and the improvements can be effectively implemented in their schools. At the same time a significant concern of this group is the burden of data collection and reporting that they would face under a school-level data system. The burden would consist of the time required of various personnel at the school and district level along with the expenses associated with changing and maintaining new data systems. This is particularly true if the main immediate beneficiaries of the data would be other groups. Therefore, if substantial administrative burden and expense are incurred to develop and maintain a school-level data system, there will need to be compensating benefits of an immediate and concrete nature in order for districts to participate willingly and conscientiously in such an effort. Otherwise, such a burden will be viewed as another unfunded mandate without a useful benefit to the mission of the school.[13]

Cohen and Goertz have noted that to produce sound and reliable data, the system must be applicable to all levels of education—including the classroom, the school, the district, and the state—and should play a role in the state's accountability system and policy-making environments.[14]

In 1970, Title I of the Elementary Secondary Education Act required districts to complete a rather detailed report showing that schools within school districts were *comparable*. The formula included expenditures in various maintenance and operation categories that demonstrated that the district was not *supplanting* district funds with federal Title I dollars and were *supplementing* specific programs with the revenues. In 1981, the reporting procedures were lessened because districts claimed that they were time consuming and showed a lack of trust. The local education agency's Title I schools can satisfy the comparability requirements using *either* of two tests: option 1, schools must have equal or lower student–instructional staff ratios; or option 2, equal or higher per-pupil expenditures than the corresponding averages for its non-Title I schools. These ratios or expenditures for each Title I school shall be considered "equivalent or comparable" to the averages for non-Title I schools if they are within 10 percent of those averages in each category.[15]

The concern for equity at the individual school level is valid but there are many factors that can influence the outcome of a study. In some respects, the same elements are part of the site-based versus central-control issue. For example, are large capital expenditures to be considered in a formula when awarding a budget to a site-based school? Likewise, are capital expenditures to be considered when determining the per-pupil expenditures at one school when compared to another within a district? Other areas that may skew results in a study are the following:

1. *Teacher length of service.* An experienced teacher at the top of the salary schedule may be making twice as much as a beginning teacher. A teacher receiving $50,000 per year with 30 students in a room would be an expense of $1,667 per pupil, whereas a class with a beginning teacher making $30,000 per year would be an expense of $1,000 for 30 students. This variable must be considered. The value of a teacher who has many years of experience versus the value of a new teacher with limited experience is a debate outside the purview of this text.

2. *Class size.* Unless every classroom is the same size, comparisons fall short. If the teacher making $50,000 per year has only 25 students, then the per-pupil cost is $2,000. A teacher with the same salary in another school with 35 students would have a per-pupil value of $1,430.

3. *School boundaries.* It is practically impossible to have every grade in each school each year with the same number of students. Without this control, class size can vary markedly. Boundaries might be altered each year to attempt to balance loads, or students might be shifted from one school to another—a decision that would need to be determined by school administrators.

4. *Maintenance costs.* Some buildings are considerably more expensive to maintain than others. One may have high energy costs compared to another. One may be an older building and need more repairs in a year's time. One plant may be utilized longer hours for community activities.

5. *Special program funds.* Programs for the gifted, state special education programs, and federal revenues are basically categorical in nature. Are these to be considered in comparing school revenues within a district? Some federal programs require that funds be supplemental to local sources and cannot supplant district revenues.

6. *Auxiliary personnel.* Are principals, assistant principals, media specialists, secretaries, counselors, custodians, and other auxiliary personnel serving the same number of staff and pupils? Are they on the same salary level? These two areas would influence the per-pupil costs at the local school level.

7. *Comparing schools.* Are all grade levels comparable? Should the high school and junior high students receive greater financial support than elementary students?

Table 3.1 compares per-pupil costs in 12 elementary schools in a district that demonstrates the complexities of equalizing expenditures at the local level. Note that Table 3.1 covers only a few of the costs that a comprehensive study should entail. For example, federal programs (such as Title I) and categorical state programs (such as gifted and talented, at-risk students, and other similar programs) are not included in this table. The *significant* difference is that per-pupil expenditures are influenced by two major categories: teacher salaries and enrollment. Schools with experienced staffs with higher salaries for teachers and administrative personnel are going to produce greater per-pupil costs. That being equal ($37,848 as shown in the next to last column of Table 3.1), lower enrollment is the greatest factor influencing differences in per-pupil expenditures. Utility and custodial costs are greatly influenced by the size, age, and utilization of the building, which makes comparisons difficult. In general, with the various influences on the per-pupil expenditures at the local school level, there appears to be little impact on the teaching/learning process.

Most local districts are willing to accept that there are differences in teachers' salaries, energy costs, administrative costs, and maintenance costs. They therefore attempt to make equitable provisions by allotting funds to individual schools in categories such as supplies, materials, media, textbooks, and equipment on a per-pupil basis.

Comparative budget figures are important for administrators to monitor and to develop strategies for savings. However, with all the ramifications associated with determining local-level financing of public schools, unless mandated, it appears there will be limited interest from local districts to become involved.

Equity for Taxpayers

Equity for taxpayers is more difficult to achieve in a finance formula than is commonly believed. States vary in their assessing practices and in the ways they levy taxes on property. A tax levy may be based on a *rate,* a *percent of market value,* mills (.001) or *dollars per $100* ($/per $100 assessed valuation [AV]), or *dollars per $1,000* ($/per $1,000 assessed valuation). The tables and text of this book are shown in mills. The reader can easily convert mills by studying the following:

Assessed Value of Property	Tax Levy	Revenue Generated
$100,000	20 mills (.020)	$2,000
$100,000	$2/per $100 AV	$2,000
$100,000	$20/per $1,000 AV	$2,000

TABLE 3.1 A Comparison of Selected Per-Pupil Costs in 12 Elementary Schools (A–L) in a Local School District

Teachers (FTE)[1]	Enrollment	Average Teacher Salary	Teacher Per-Pupil Costs	Administration Costs[2]	Media Costs	Custodial Costs	Utility Costs[3]	Total Per-Pupil Costs	Teachers' Salaries Averaged	Teacher Per-Pupil Costs
A–27.8	860*	$39,088	$1,209	$151	$76	$ 83	$ 88	$1,607	$37,848	$1,233*
B–18.5	520	40,471*	1,440*	187	89	90	93	1,899*	37,848	1,347*
C–23.0	670	37,358	1,282	143*	55	89	109	1,678	37,848	1,299
D–19.5	560	37,031	1,289	176	83	108*	107	1,763	37,848	1,318
E–24.7	748	37,568	1,240	168	91	73	63*	1,635	37,848	1,250
F–28.0	790	38,779	1,374	154	93	84	82	1,787	37,848	1,341
G–17.5	510	38,332	1,315	198	63*	81*	115*	1,772	37,848	1,299
H–19.5	565	35,102*	1,211	169	80	93	90	1,643	37,848	1,306
I–17.0	519	37,070	1,214	191	82	93	92	1,672	37,848	1,240
J–21.0	620	39,607	1,342	176	71	88	72	1,749	37,848	1,282
K–17.0	506*	38,538	1,295	201*	95*	90	85	1,766	37,848	1,272
L–17.5	530	35,235	1,163*	193	69	88	93	1,606*	37,848	1,250
Average	**616**	**$37,848**	**$1,281**	**$176**	**$79**	**$88**	**$ 91**	**$1,715**		**$1,286**

*High and low schools

Differences between high and low schools | $5,369 | $277 | $58 | $32 | $27 | $52 | $293 | | $114

Note: The district provides each school $75 per pupil for capital expenses, which include supplies, textbooks, and equipment. The district provides $40 per pupil for library books, supplies, and travel.

[1]FTE = Full-time equivalent
[2]Includes principal, secretarial, and clerical personnel
[3]Includes natural gas, electricity, phone, and waste expenses

Theoretically, taxes should be paid according to the ability of taxpayers to pay, or according to the burden the tax imposes on them. Consider the question of taxpayer equity for the following mythical taxpayers under the conditions of ownership of real property, income, wealth, and taxpaying ability, as indicated in the following examples:

Taxpayer	Annual Income	Total Wealth	Real Property	Ownership (real property)	Tax (mills)	Total Taxes
A	$80,000	$500,000	$100,000	$100,000	20	$2,000
B	50,000	400,000	100,000	80,000	20	2,000
C	25,000	200,000	100,000	60,000	20	2,000
D	20,000	100,000	100,000	40,000	20	2,000
E	16,000	40,000	100,000	20,000	20	2,000

Tax Amount as Percent of Income, Wealth, and Owned Property

Taxpayer	Property Owned	Income	Wealth
A	2.0	2.5	0.4
B	2.5	4.0	0.5
C	3.3	8.0	1.0
D	5.0	10.0	2.0
E	10.0	12.5	5.0

This example illustrates some of the inequities that may exist in the taxation pattern in a typical school district, where local taxes for public education are determined by a fixed tax rate levied on the assessed value of real property. Assessed value ranges from actual market value to a percentage of market value established by a taxing entity. A state may have an assessed value at 20 percent. Thus, a home and property with a market value of $100,000 would have an assessed valuation of $20,000. In the example, all five individuals would pay taxes on $100,000 of real property at the rate of $2 per $100 of assessed valuation. Some would argue that there is complete taxpayer equity, since all five pay 2 percent of the total value of the property being taxed. However, it becomes obvious that equity is lacking when the amount of taxes paid is measured as a percentage of each individual's actual ownership in the property, or of annual income, or of the total wealth of each. Local taxes are usually not equitable on the basis that most states levy property taxes—without regard to the degree or amount of ownership the taxpayer has in the parcel of land being taxed. Berne and Stiefel referred to the fallacy of equating equity with equal tax rates in the following:

> There are multiple formulations of taxpayer equity in school finance. . . . On the one hand, there are cases where taxpayer equity is equated with an ambiguous formulation such as "equal tax rates," a formulation that is equitable only by definition. On the other hand, less ambiguous formulations such as "equal yield for equal effort" are utilized without reference

to other equally plausible ones. A useful distinction that has been introduced into the school finance literature is between ex ante and ex post taxpayer equity. . . .

Ex ante taxpayer equity is generally evaluated by examining the characteristics of a school finance plan, while ex post equity involves an assessment of the actual spending patterns that result from school districts' response to a school finance plan.[16]

In the example, only A has complete ownership of the property being taxed; the other four taxpayers owe varying amounts on loans or mortgages that affect their ability to pay taxes. In terms of the value of the property being taxed, without regard to the extent of actual ownership of each, there appears to be fairness in the taxes to be collected from each of the five taxpayers. Considering the degree of ownership of each, the range of the percent of taxes to ownership goes from 2 percent to 10 percent. In terms of annual income, A pays 2.5 percent in property taxes, whereas E pays 12.5 percent; if wealth is used as the base of ability to pay, A is required to pay only 0.4 percent in taxes, whereas E must pay 5 percent.

Unequal Assessments

Other practices in the process of taxing real property add to the unfairness of this method of obtaining local revenue for public schools. One of these is unequal rates of assessment of like parcels of property found in taxing jurisdictions. Such unfairness can be seen in the following example, which uses the same individuals as in the previous one. The only difference is that varying rates of assessment have been used to determine the assessed valuation of the property being taxed.

Taxpayer	Market Value of Property	Assessed Valuation	Tax Rate (in mills)	Taxes Paid	Taxes as a Percent of Real Value
A	$100,000	$100,000	20	$2,000	2.0
B	100,000	80,000	20	1,600	1.6
C	100,000	60,000	20	1,200	1.2
D	100,000	40,000	20	800	0.8
E	100,000	20,000	20	400	0.4

In the above example, A's property was assessed at 100 percent of its real or market value. At the other end of the scale, E's property was assessed at only 20 percent of its real value. Under this arrangement, A paid 2 percent of the total value of the property in taxes, while E paid only 0.4 percent. This example shows extreme differences, but many states, particularly those that use local or politically appointed assessors, are not able to assess all similar parcels of property at the same rate, thus leading to unfairness in local taxation practices.

Assessing or reassessing the current value of property is not an easy task, though most states have strong tax commissions that use objective standards and more sophisticated technology than was previously available to assist in updating records more rapidly. Without current figures, if property values increase because of inflation or other economic factors and the assessments are not brought up to date over a three- to five-year period, the actual percentage of market value decreases, causing inequities. Those who have just purchased property, had property reassessed, or had a newly constructed home put on the tax rolls suffer; those who have owned property for a period of time benefit. For example, a taxpayer whose home was assessed four years ago at $100,000 and who lives in an area where inflation is 4 percent per year now has a home with a value of over $116,000. Without reassessment, the present assessed valuation is only 17 percent of market value instead of 20.

Inequity is a factor in a deflated economy as well. Where unemployment is prevalent and property values decrease, without reassessment, property owners may pay too much tax. A property that was valued at $200,000 and now has a market value of $180,000 has lost 10 percent of its value. If the property has an assessed value of 50 percent of market value and the tax rate is 20 mills, the tax should reduce from $2,000 to $1,800. When tax hearings are held, if adjustments have not been made, the homeowner should contest the amount. Extending this example as it relates to the total taxing entity demonstrates how such a factor can influence the tax base of the local school district.

General Classifications of Taxes

Generally, taxes may be classified as proportional, progressive, or regressive. The *proportional* tax requires that the same percentage of each person's total taxable income, regardless of income size, be paid in taxes. A tax is *progressive* if the percentage of the total taxable income required for taxes increases as the taxable income becomes higher. A *regressive* tax finds higher incomes paying lower percentages of the total taxable incomes for taxes than do lower incomes.

The following example compares three individuals who pay different tax amounts on their income, according to measures of taxation commonly used. The example illustrates proportional, regressive, and progressive taxation of income but does not show all the possibilities of a regressive or progressive tax.

Taxpayer	Annual Income	Taxes Paid	Taxes as a Percent of Income
Proportional Taxation			
A	$100,000	$5,000	5.0
B	60,000	3,000	5.0
C	20,000	1,000	5.0
Regressive Taxation			
A	$100,000	$5,000	5.0
B	60,000	3,600	6.0
C	20,000	1,400	7.0

	Progressive Taxation		
A	$100,000	$5,000	5.0
B	60,000	2,400	4.0
C	20,000	600	3.0

Since taxation theory is based on the premise that taxes paid should be related to the burden each taxpayer bears, it is reasonable to argue that taxes should increase proportionately faster than income—assuming that income is the measure of fiscal capacity being used. In the example, it is reasonable to expect A to pay a much higher tax than either B or C, since A's income is much greater. Although A has five times the income, he or she pays more than eight times the taxes paid by C. In terms of the burden caused by such progressivity of taxes, A "suffers" less than C because of the much larger amount of money at his or her disposal after taxes. The problem for tax authorities is not whether A, B, and C should pay the same tax rate; rather, it is how much greater the tax rate of A should be than that of B and C, and how much greater the tax rate of B should be than that of C. They must decide the degree of progressiveness that is most desirable and that produces the greatest equity in the burden borne by taxpayers with high incomes, wealth, or property ownership, whichever form is used to determine fiscal capacity in that taxing district. Here, the important question of values comes into operation. It must be determined what portion of taxes should be paid by each level of income or wealth, without partiality and without undue burden or hardship on any classification of tax-paying ability.

Measures of School District Wealth

Currently there is general agreement that the valuation of real property, regardless of its percent of market value, is not the best possible measure of local fiscal capacity to support public education. Although such a measure has been standard for determining school district wealth in most state school finance programs, its appropriateness is now being questioned by many students of school finance. Some relatively new measures are being considered and tried as possible alternatives (singly or in combination) to property values in determining school district wealth or taxpaying ability. What, then, is the ideal measure of fiscal capacity as far as equity to children and equity to taxpayers are concerned? There is no easy answer to that question.

Assessed Valuation per Pupil

One way to address the issue of wealth of an area as it applies to funding local schools is simply to divide the number of students into the total assessed valuation of property. Figure 3.1 compares the wealth in seven districts based on the number of students enrolled. In District 1, for example, there are only 852 students in an area that boasts $96,000,000 in assessed valuation, which converts to $112,676.05 per pupil in average

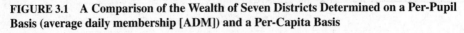

FIGURE 3.1 **A Comparison of the Wealth of Seven Districts Determined on a Per-Pupil Basis (average daily membership [ADM]) and a Per-Capita Basis**

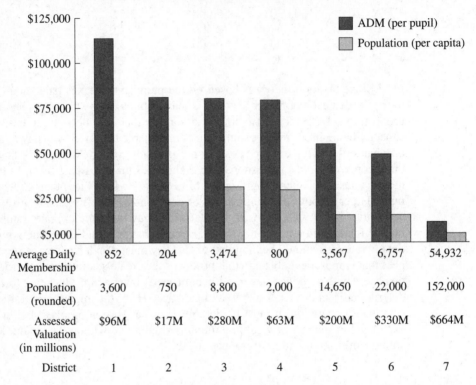

	District 1	District 2	District 3	District 4	District 5	District 6	District 7
Average Daily Membership	852	204	3,474	800	3,567	6,757	54,932
Population (rounded)	3,600	750	8,800	2,000	14,650	22,000	152,000
Assessed Valuation (in millions)	$96M	$17M	$280M	$63M	$200M	$330M	$664M
District	1	2	3	4	5	6	7

daily membership (ADM). Compare that to District 6, which has an assessed value of $330,000,000 divided by 6,757 pupils. The result is $48,838.24 per average daily membership, or only 43 percent of that of District 1.

The principal objection to using assessed valuation of real property per pupil in determining the comparative wealth of districts is that property is no longer a fair or accurate measure of the wealth of people or of school districts. Too many people have invested their wealth in assets that are not readily available for taxation. In spite of that fact, many states still use that method of determining local fiscal capacity. That this method causes inequality in expenditures per child was noted by McMahon:

> It is the theme of this paper that both the inequality in expenditure per child and tax inequity are aggravated by a common key factor—the narrow definition of wealth based only on property wealth that is still used in most states to measure both local ability-to-pay and local effort. . . . Wealth in Elizabethan times consisted almost exclusively of land and buildings, but in modern industrialized societies other forms of capital and the incomes they yield have become much more important.[17]

It is argued, too, that since all taxes must be paid out of income—past, present, or future—taxes and measures of wealth should bear some relation to income. Assessed valuation of real property per pupil favors districts with greater educational needs and discriminates against those that have other needs not related to the number of school pupils to be educated. Increases in the book value of property do not increase the taxpaying ability of the owner of property unless it is sold. For example, a farmer whose property increases from $150,000 to $175,000 in one year does not have increased ability to increase products or crops on the land and thus to pay higher taxes, barring other improvements. However, with real property tax laws, the farm land now presumably (and legally) generates more taxes because of the increased value. The only practicable way in which that farmer can profit from the increased book value of a farm is to sell it at a higher price than could have been demanded before the increase in its value.

Assessed Valuation per Capita

The assessed valuation of real property per capita indicates the wealth of an area in relation to raising funds for any or all purposes. Although not as common a measurement of fiscal capacity as assessed valuation per pupil, it is used in a number of states, particularly for noneducation purposes. Using the same two districts shown in Figure 3.1 to compare the assessed valuation based on per-capita data, the results are as follows: District 1 has an assessed value of $96,000,000 divided by a population of 3,600, with a net result of $26,667 per capita. District 6 has an assessed valuation of $330,000,000 divided by a population of 22,000 resulting in $15,000 per capita. Be apprised that if taxing districts within a state are not uniform in the percent at which property is assessed, then comparisons are useless.

Statistical Approaches to Equalization

Several states have considered moving to a per-capita measure, and some states have used both in educational formulas. Various statistical approaches have been used to analyze fiscal equalization, including the Pearson coefficient of correlation and the Spearman rank order correlation, both of which can determine the relationship between per-pupil wealth and per-pupil expenditure. Also, the Lorenz curve, Gini coefficient, Verstegen index, Theil index, McCloone index, and Atkinson index have been used to measure the extent of fiscal equalization in some states.

Over the past several years, publishers of *Education Week,* in their yearly *Quality Counts* edition, have graded states on their equity in spending for education. The major variables in its comparison are:

1. A *state equalization effort,* which is a sophisticated multivariate approach for measuring the extent a state's finance program provides local districts a certain funding level when applying the same tax rate
2. A *wealth-neutrality score,* which measures the extent to which education funding is related to property wealth
3. The *McLoone index,* which measures the gap between what the bottom half of districts spend per student and what they *would* spend if they spent as much as the district in the middle of the funding pack[18]

TABLE 3.2 A Comparison of State Per-Pupil Expenditures (with Adjusted Regional Cost Differences) with Ranking of the States on Spending on K–12 Education, and a Grading on Equity Provided in Relation to Available Resources

	Per-Pupil Expenditures (PPE), Adjusted for Regional Cost Differences (2003)			Percent of Total Taxable Resources Spent on Education (2003)		Spending Index (2003)		Overall Grade for Resources: Equity	
	State Average	Rank	Percent of U.S. Average		Rank		Rank		
Alabama	$7,058	41	75.0	3.49	35	90.8	37	C+	78
Alaska	$7,791	29	82.8	3.81	23	87.6	41	D+	67
Arizona	$6,331	50	67.2	3.55	32	73.4	50	D+	69
Arkansas	$7,439	39	79.0	3.87	17	90.5	38	B–	81
California	$6,765	43	71.9	3.57	31	85.6	43	B–	81
Colorado	$7,490	37	79.6	3.13	44	93.6	29	C–	72
Connecticut	$9,605	6	102.0	3.86	18	100.0	6	C	76
Delaware	$9,472	8	100.6	2.17	50	100.0	1	B–	81
District of Columbia	$11,031	1	117.2	NA	NA	100.0	1	NA	
Florida	$6,729	45	71.5	3.07	45	84.7	45	B–	81
Georgia	$8,346	20	88.7	3.85	19	98.4	14	C	75
Hawaii	$8,123	25	86.3	4.09	10	100.0	1	NA	
Idaho	$6,609	48	70.2	3.8	24	83.3	47	F	59
Illinois	$8,030	28	85.3	3.51	34	92.5	31	D+	68
Indiana	$8,620	18	91.6	3.43	38	97.5	17	B–	80
Iowa	$8,586	19	91.2	3.83	22	97.9	15	B+	89
Kansas	$8,334	21	88.5	3.97	14	97.1	18	C+	78
Kentucky	$7,451	38	79.1	3.32	40	92.2	32	C	76
Louisiana	$7,746	32	82.3	3.34	39	94.6	26	B	83
Maine	$9,521	7	101.1	4.82	3	99.1	11	C–	70
Maryland	$8,968	13	95.3	3.79	25	99.9	10	C–	72
Massachusetts	$8,921	14	94.8	3.73	28	98.5	13	C–	72
Michigan	$8,646	17	91.8	4.6	4	96.8	21	C–	71
Minnesota	$8,270	22	87.8	3.74	27	95.9	24	B	83
Mississippi	$6,646	47	70.6	3.84	21	83.7	46	C–	72

Missouri	$7,741	33	82.2	29	3.64	39	90.0	C	73
Montana	$8,249	23	87.6	12	4.03	34	91.7	D–	62
Nebraska	$9,117	12	96.8	33	3.55	19	97.0	C+	77
Nevada	$6,394	49	67.9	47	2.89	48	82.8	A–	92
New Hampshire	$8,186	24	87.0	20	3.85	25	95.1	D	63
New Jersey	$10,908	2	115.9	5	4.59	7	100.0	C–	72
New Mexico	$7,668	34	81.5	13	4.00	42	86.4	B+	88
New York	$10,665	3	113.3	7	4.21	5	100.0	C	74
North Carolina	$7,153	40	76.0	49	2.69	36	90.9	C–	71
North Dakota	$8,056	27	85.6	41	3.24	28	94.1	D–	62
Ohio	$8,735	16	92.8	6	4.26	20	96.8	C	74
Oklahoma	$6,756	44	71.8	30	3.59	49	82.0	B–	80
Oregon	$7,753	31	82.4	36	3.49	33	91.7	C–	72
Pennsylvania	$8,777	15	93.2	16	3.9	22	96.4	C–	72
Rhode Island	$9,386	10	99.7	9	4.14	16	97.9	D	66
South Carolina	$7,776	30	82.6	11	4.04	27	94.1	C	76
South Dakota	$7,663	35	81.4	46	2.97	35	90.9	C+	78
Tennessee	$6,704	46	71.2	48	2.71	44	84.9	C	73
Texas	$7,570	36	80.4	26	3.79	30	92.7	C–	72
Utah	$5,067	51	53.8	37	3.45	51	66.6	B+	87
Vermont	$10,571	4	112.3	1	5.21	12	99.0	F	59
Virginia	$8,071	26	85.7	43	3.16	23	96.4	D+	67
Washington	$6,985	42	74.2	42	3.23	40	88.0	C	74
West Virginia	$9,286	11	98.6	2	4.88	8	100.0	B	85
Wisconsin	$9,414	9	100.0	8	4.2	9	99.9	B–	82
Wyoming	$9,811	5	104.2	15	3.94	1	100.0	C+	79
U.S.	**$8,041**	—	**100.0**	—	**3.69**	—	**93.2**	—	—

Source: Education Week, Quality Counts 2006 edition, Editorial Projects in Education, January 5, 2006.

The sources of data are from multiple agencies and span several years. The ranking of states for both adequacy and equity shown in Table 3.2 is an example of a more sophisticated approach to providing a comparison of per-pupil expenditures made available from state resources as reported by *Education Week.* The publishers gave a score to each state based on the criteria and assigned a letter grade for the states' efforts in the areas of adequacy and equity. The data are used here to demonstrate one approach in attempting to evaluate adequacy and equity. A full analysis of the study is necessary to appreciate the effort made by the publishers to provide some meaningful comparisons. By going to the source, the student of school finance will understand the complexities in such an undertaking and will reaffirm the elusive nature of determining equity between states and, by extension, between districts within a state.[19]

The literature is full of examples of complicated plans that attempt to meet the need of being "fair and equitable" to both students and taxpayers. In many approaches these two factors are given various weighting. Limitations that exist in presenting the data are as follows: (1) The availability of the information from the states is not always comparable. (2) The data are three to five years out of date by the time of publication. (3) There is so much discrepancy in equity among districts within states that national comparisons seem insignificant. (4) School budgets are only one of the many factors legislators must consider in allocating money, and many find the various formulas too complicated to incorporate into the system even though some have great merit.

Income Tax

It does not seem reasonable to compare the abilities of districts or states to finance education by comparing their share of potential assets or taxes that are not available for use by the districts or states being compared. Income has therefore not been used as a measure of the fiscal capacity of school districts, because school districts by and large do not have access to local income taxes. Few people, however, deny its place as a determinant, in whole or in part, of ability to pay taxes for the financing of education. In recent years, local governments in a few states have introduced income tax capability to school districts.

Johns summarized a point of view concerning the use of tax measures that are not available for local use:

> If the foundation program equalization model is used, the measure of local taxpaying ability should include only the local tax sources to which the school district has access. This is, if the only local tax revenue available to the district is the property tax, then the measure of local taxpaying ability should be based entirely on the equalized value of taxable property. However, if a local district can levy a local sales tax, or a local income tax, or some other local tax, then that local nonproperty tax source can equitably be included in the measure of local taxpaying ability.[20]

There is no general rule or standard correlation between the income of a person and the property tax obligations. For example, generally high values of large agricultural areas of land often do not translate into high incomes for the owners of that land.

Some states utilize income taxes that are available to local school districts. They use taxable income in addition to assessed valuations of property in determining their state allocations to local districts. A few states use income figures along with property values in their school finance formulas. A number of other states are moving in the direction of utilizing income as an addition to their other measures of fiscal capacity.

The importance of utilizing income as a measure of school district wealth for the purpose of allocating state funds to local school districts include:

- The relationship between fiscal capacity and income is apparent.
- Income is an excellent variable for determining fiscal capacity.
- All taxes are paid out of income.

Wealth Tax

Fairness of taxation is increased when more kinds of wealth are included. The use of a wealth tax as an alternative revenue source to the property tax has often been considered by tax authorities who recognize the unfairness and limitations of the traditional property tax in determining the fiscal capacity of school districts.

A wealth tax, as the term implies, is based on the net worth of an individual or a household. By definition, this means all assets minus all liabilities. In contrast, a property tax is a tax on the gross value of a particular kind of property, regardless of the equity the taxpayer has in the object being taxed or in other forms of wealth he or she owns.

A wealth tax would eliminate discrimination against the person who pays full property taxes but who has only limited or incomplete ownership in the property being taxed. It measures *total* ability to pay. It has the advantage over an income tax, in that the latter taxes only annual increases in ability to pay, without regard to accumulated ability. For example, under an income tax, taxpayers A and B may have the same income per year, but A may derive income from interest on property owned, whereas B may get income from personal services without the added property values that A has. In the event of total loss of income, A has assets in the form of property to rely on; B has nothing to replace loss of income. Thus, even though their incomes are identical, their ability to pay taxes is not the same.

There are certain disadvantages that would affect the use of a wealth tax. Some of the most obvious are the following: (1) It is administratively difficult to determine the total wealth of an individual or household; it is almost impossible for taxing authorities to learn of all the individual pieces and the value of all the items of wealth that are owned by an individual or a household, particularly if the people involved are uncooperative. (2) There is the question of privacy and people's dislike of having government representatives aware of their financial affairs—even among honest people. (3) The cost, timing, and actual process of assessment would undoubtedly create major problems. Although experience with a wealth tax is very limited in the United States, certain European countries have applied such a tax with reasonable success.

Historical Influences on Equity

In the early history of public education, the states seemed content to accept responsibility for education but were reluctant to assume major responsibility for financing it.

Local school districts—usually of small size and often with limited resources—bore the responsibility of financing education for many years without state assistance. It is true that the states generally provided ways of legalizing local school property taxes, but grants, equalization funds, and a general state-local "partnership" arrangement received little attention until the middle of the twentieth century.

This system of operating an educational program was generally satisfactory and workable in most school districts during the time when there was extreme local pride in the public schools and limited competition for the property tax dollar. This was true, perhaps, because of satisfaction with limited curricula, low costs, and little state control or interference. But its obvious weakness soon rose to the surface, and demands for change and for some form of state financial support began to be heard in legislative halls. Even though citizens continued to hold fast to their historic conviction that public schools should function as locally controlled institutions, they began to advocate the idea of some form of state support for financing education in order to equalize educational opportunity and equalize the burden of paying for continuously expanding school programs.

Much of the early inequality and inequity in financing education was caused by the fact that school districts varied greatly in size and in wealth, from large city districts to ones that operated only one- or two-room schools. The taxable property base per person to be educated varied tremendously from one district to another, resulting in similarly large variations in property tax levies.

Local District Funding

Full local district funding was the first of all school finance plans. Over the years, it has proven to be the least desirable and the least effective in producing equality of educational opportunity among the districts within a state. Its operation as the sole producer of school revenue terminated near the turn of the twentieth century, with the beginning of state grants and other allocations to local districts. Its almost exclusive use in the years preceding the use of flat grants and foundation programs preceded any modern-day philosophy of equal educational opportunity or equal sharing of the burden of taxation. The place of a child's birth determined to a large degree the quality and the quantity of education he or she received. A person's place of residence and the extent to which he or she invested in real property were major factors in the calculation of his or her burden in financing education.

As the costs of education increased and as competition for the revenues generated by a local property tax became greater, it was logical and necessary for local districts to obtain some financial assistance from state government. This support emerged principally as flat grants and categorical aids until the theory of foundation programs and equalization was developed and implemented.

Although state financial support for education is largely a twentieth-century development, Mort reported that about one-fourth of public school revenue in 1890 came from state sources. He did not differentiate between the funds derived from federal land grants and those obtained from strictly state sources.

Flat Grants

In the early attempts of states to assist local districts in financing their schools, flat grants were used extensively. These grants were usually funds per pupil, funds per teacher, or percentage grants. They were provided as a form of relief to local taxpayers, with no real intent of providing equalization. Their effect on local districts was usually nonequalizing, except with the use of percentage grants, which do not change the ratio of tax effort among districts either toward or away from equalization of tax effort. Model 3.1 shows the effect of a flat grant of $800 per pupil on three districts based on the following data:

District	State Funds per Pupil	Local Funds per Pupil	Total Funds per Pupil	Mills Tax Levy
L	$800	$2,400	$3,200	60
M	800	2,400	3,200	30
H	800	2,400	3,200	15

In Model 3.1, a flat grant of $800 per pupil leaves each district with the need to provide the additional $2,400 by a local property tax levy varying from 60 mills in District L to 15 mills in District H. Since the state is providing one-fourth of the revenue of each district, the grant has the same effect as any percentage grant—the ratio of highest tax levy to lowest tax levy remains the same as without the grant (in this example 4:1), and no equalization is effected. If examples are used with varying

MODEL 3.1　State Flat Grants

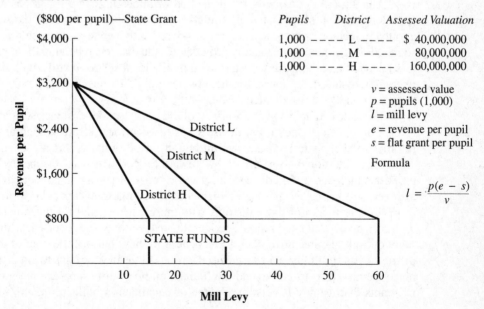

($800 per pupil)—State Grant

Pupils	District	Assessed Valuation
1,000 ----	L ----	$ 40,000,000
1,000 ----	M ----	80,000,000
1,000 ----	H ----	160,000,000

v = assessed value
p = pupils (1,000)
l = mill levy
e = revenue per pupil
s = flat grant per pupil

Formula

$$l = \frac{p(e - s)}{v}$$

numbers of weighted pupil (or other base on which the grant is made), the effect of the grant is usually nonequalizing.

Even though flat grants do not usually accomplish the purpose for which they are intended, they obviously reduce the burden on taxpayers in all districts and are therefore a first step in replacing the outmoded system of complete local financing. For example, in the model, District L has had its tax burden lessened by 20 mills, District M has had its tax burden lessened by 10 mills, and District H has been able to reduce its tax by 5 mills. In terms of percentage decrease, each has reduced its required mill levy by 25 percent.

Even though flat grants are generally not equalizing to local school districts, they are still being used in some state school finance formulas, usually in combination with other equalizing state allocations. Tradition continues to play an important role in financing education, even though there are far better methods of allocating state funds to local districts.

Flat grants were first provided by states to local districts on an incidental and haphazard basis. Gradually, however, the states developed theories and guidelines for such appropriations.

Equalizing Grants

Most states now use an equalizing grant in allocating some or all of their state money to local districts. Such grants are made in terms of tax-raising ability of the local districts. Some states use combinations of grants—equalizing, percentage, flat, and variations of these—but the trend is toward allotting a higher percentage of all state funds on an equalization basis.

Although the equalizing-grant method of allocating state funds has been used for a long time in some states, it is relatively new in others. Most of the state funds allotted to local districts take the form of nonrestrictive general-purpose grants. Some standards or guidelines are usually provided for the districts receiving these grants, but it is intended that their use be determined by the local school boards, with little or no restriction by the state. States, for the most part, put the onus on the receiving districts for proper and wise use of such funds.

The states do not want to absorb all of the yearly school cost increases at the state level. Consequently, they often devise ways to keep local effort as high as possible, in order to keep state increases within bounds. Traditionally, this has been done by "reward for additional tax effort" or by "reward for performance." Cubberley's finance proposals included a kind of reward for effort; not only was this nonequalizing but it also actually increased the degree of inequality in many instances. His plan was to provide more funds for those districts with more teachers and for those with schools with enriched or extended school services. Since the more wealthy districts already had more of both, the incentive plan was a benefit to them but of little help to the poorer districts. As a result, the states have used various kinds of programs to aid districts that make the tax effort to go beyond the foundation program—supplementary or leeway programs that usually have some degree of equalization built into them. Most state school finance plans are not set up in pristine simplicity; they often combine several kinds of state aid in varying mixes.

Programs beyond the foundation must be supported solely by the local district. Utah requires the local overage (called *recapture*) of a required foundation program levy—if a district has such—to revert to the Uniform School Fund to be used to help finance the program in other districts.

The Equalization Principle

The work of Strayer and Haig in introducing the foundation program principle of financing education was a major breakthrough in school finance theory. It now seems unfortunate that such a simple and defensible principle should not have been discovered and applied much earlier in school finance history. Its relatively late appearance in the late 1920s was followed by an even slower rate of adoption by the states. For years, knowledgeable people had observed and deplored the disparities, the inequities, and the injustices that existed in the United States in terms of unequal wealth, unequal incomes, and unequal opportunities. Similar inequities in educational opportunities and in sharing the costs of education seem to have been accepted with the same feelings of frustration and inability to change the existing situation.

The birth of the foundation program concept provided a means of removing some of the disparities in school revenues and expenditures. But changes come slowly, and some states were reluctant to apply the principle to their school finance program to any great degree. The principle is not perfect and has many limitations, but its application would have eliminated or at least reduced much of the unfairness of revenue distribution that still exists in many states. Improved finance formulas involving extensions and improvements of Strayer-Haig-Mort foundation programs have been visible and available, yet their utilization has been sporadic or nonexistent. Adoption of the foundation concept may be a first step to the even more effective program of power or open-end equalization now being advocated in the field of school finance theory.

Improving State Equalization Practices

The theory of the foundation program to achieve equalization of educational opportunity is relatively simple, but its practical application is often complex, usually unnecessarily so. The formula that each state uses involves three essential conditions:

1. Calculation of the "monetary need" of each school district necessary to obtain a state-guaranteed minimum program, measured objectively in terms of the number of weighted pupils (and other measures of need)—to be financed at the level of support that the state will guarantee.
2. Determination of the amount of local school revenue that can be expected with a state-established uniform tax rate levied against the equalized assessed valuation of all taxable property within the district.

3. Determination of the state allocation by finding the difference between the district's established need and the revenue obtainable from its required local tax effort.

Complications arise in applying the theory in practice, for a number of reasons:

1. Not all pupils require the same number of dollars of expenditure, even under a commitment to the principle of equality of opportunity. Children who have special needs are more expensive to educate than others, and children who attend very small schools and those who attend very large ones are more expensive than those in medium-sized ones.
2. Wide variations may exist in the assessment practices in the districts of a state, even when all are presumed to be assessed at uniform rates.
3. The quality of the teaching staffs may vary considerably, as determined by educational preparation and experience, thus varying the costs of instruction among the districts.
4. The dollars provided do not purchase the same amount or quality of goods and services in all districts, thus favoring some districts and penalizing others.
5. Some states operate many different kinds of school districts with different taxing responsibilities and restrictions.

The net result of these and other differences among districts is that finance formulas usually include provisions to try to offset inequalities. Weightings for school size differentials, such as sparsity and density factors, special consideration for exceptional children, allowances for transportation costs, and provision for additional funds for experienced teachers, are among the most common adjustments in formulas. Such adjustments add to their complexity but also increase their validity and effectiveness.

Foundation Program Variations

The foundation program concept can be applied with a number of variations: with or without local options to go above the state guaranteed minimum program, with or without state matching of local optional revenues, or in combination with flat grants and/or categorical allocations. Some of these possibilities are illustrated in the following simplified models.

Model 3.2 consists of two parts. The vertical columns marked *a* for each of the three districts illustrate a foundation program constructed with the mill levy necessary to produce the state program. In the richest district, the per-pupil revenues are reached with no surplus being generated. The three columns marked *b* illustrate the same program with a required levy high enough to give the wealthiest district a surplus, which may or may not be recaptured by the state, depending on the philosophy of the particular state using the program.

This model is a mandatory foundation program comparing the three districts L, M, and H, which have assessed valuations of $40,000,000, $80,000,000, and $160,000,000, respectively; each district has 1,000 weighted pupil units. In the part *a* example, a required mill levy of 20 mills is applied, with no surplus above the foundation program. There is no provision in this model for board or voted options to go above

MODEL 3.2   Foundation Program (without local options)

a - - - - Local levy of 20 mills
b - - - - Local levy of 25 mills (with surplus in wealthy district)

v = assessed value of taxable property
l = mandated tax levy
e = revenue per weighted-pupil unit
p = number of weighted-pupil units
s = state allocation per weighted pupil

$$s = \frac{ep - vl}{p}$$

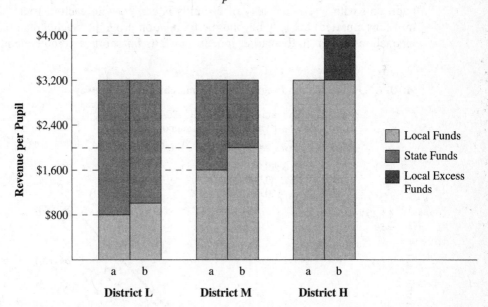

the mandated program. Hence, it is an unequalized minimum as well as maximum program. It illustrates the application of a simple form of foundation program where equality of educational opportunity, as measured by equal dollars of total revenue per weighted pupil, is achieved; at the same time, local property taxpayers share the burden equitably. In its simplest form (without local capability of supplementing the program) it makes "perfect" equalization of a minimum-maximum program; it provides no opportunity for districts to enrich the state-mandated program. It is usually unsatisfactory unless accompanied by provisions for local extension of the program beyond the foundation level, unless it is equalized at a high enough level to provide adequate funds for all districts.

Columns b illustrate the use of the foundation program concept when the required local levy produces more revenue in some districts than the state-guaranteed level per weighted-pupil unit (WPU). The surplus may be left with the local district or it can be used (recaptured) by the state to help equalize the costs in other districts. The argument in favor of its being kept where it is produced is that since it is coming from a so-called wealthy district, the taxpayers there are already providing proportionately higher percentages than in poorer districts to the state coffers through sales taxes, income taxes, and the like. On the other side of the argument is the observation that even with state recapture, the local district taxpayers are paying the same property tax rate as is being paid by those in all other districts. Columns *b* in Model 3.2 illustrate a foundation program (without state recapture of surplus local funds raised by a 25-mill local levy). Columns *b* with recapture become the same as columns *a*, except that equalization has been effected in all three districts—but with a 5-mill higher local levy being required.

Model 3.3 illustrates a foundation program with board leeway options not supported with state funds. It assumes the same three districts as before. This model shows that the equalizing effect of a foundation program guaranteeing $3,200 per weighted-pupil unit with a required levy of 20 mills is eroded with each district using a 10-mill (unsupported) tax levy beyond the foundation program. Such a plan reduces the inequalities shown in the earlier models but falls far short of complete equalization.

MODEL 3.3   Foundation Program with Unmatched Board Leeway

Foundation Program—$3,200/WPU—20-mill levy
Board Leeway—10 mills—no state support

District	Assessed Valuation	Weighted-Pupil Units
L	$ 40,000,000	1,000
M	80,000,000	1,000
H	160,000,000	1,000

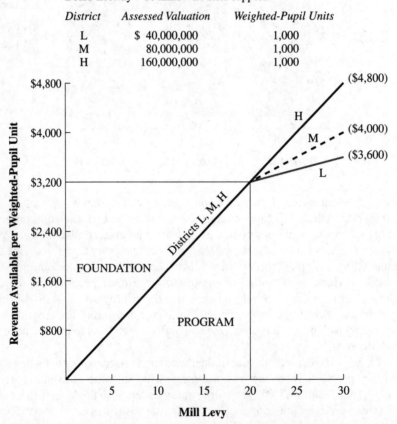

The lower the base of the foundation program and the greater the leeway above it, the greater are the inequalities that result from the use of this model. Ten additional mills produce $400 per WPU for district L, $800 for district M, and $1,600 for district H.

All the school finance models used in this text are shown in their simplest form. It should be noted that differences in the numbers of weighted-pupil units, differences in local levies to be made, differences in the amount of state funds to be provided, and the possibility of numerous combinations of these programs would increase the inequities shown in these models.

Model 3.4 shows the effect of flat grant and foundation programs, with or without school board and voted options. Several states have used different methods and

MODEL 3.4 Combination Flat Grant, Foundation Program, and Unmatched Board Leeway

Flat Grant—$800/WPU
Foundation—$3,200/WPU—20-mill levy
Leeway—10-mill levy—no state support

District	Assessed Valuation	Weighted-Pupil Units
L	$ 40,000,000	1,000
M	80,000,000	1,000
H	160,000,000	1,000

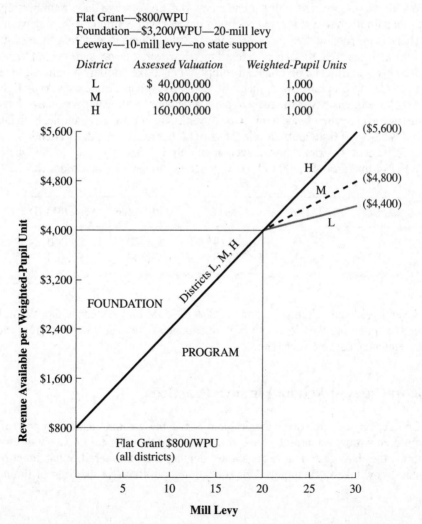

procedures to go above the state-guaranteed program. The kind and number of combinations of such programs are almost unlimited. Various states have used different combinations to suit their own school finance philosophy.

It should be emphasized that whatever system or process a state may use in financing education, the state should support the program to a greater extent in poor districts than in wealthy ones. When a state provides unsupported board options and taxpayer-voted options that go above the state program, such a process simply widens the gap between the wealthy and poor districts and thus produces a nonequalizing effect in the finance program.

The Impact of Average Daily Attendance on Equity

Whether to use average daily attendance (ADA) or average daily membership (ADM) as an administrative student accounting process will continue to be a debatable issue. There is much evidence supporting the fact that attendance with a time-on-task relationship has a great influence on learning. However, the way states count their students can have an influence on financial equity. When a fixed dollar amount is established in a foundation program, some inequities can arise when a state uses ADA figures over ADM. Formulas based on average daily attendance will usually penalize larger urban districts where attendance tends to be lower. In the following example, both Districts A and B have 1,500 students enrolled. District A has an average daily attendance of 1,425, or 95 percent; District B has an average of only 1,275, or 85 percent. For District A, the WPU shrinks from $3,200 to $3,040, whereas in District B, it erodes to $2,720.

District	ADM	ADA	WPU Value	Actual WPU
A	1,500	1,425 (95%)	$3,200	$3,040
B	1,500	1,275 (85%)	$3,200	$2,720

Several years ago, Utah shifted from ADA to ADM in two steps without a "hold harmless" stipulation. Districts with high attendance figures suffered, whereas those with low attendance were rewarded.

Confusion in Current School Finance Practices

Court cases have not solved the problem of providing equal financial opportunity for all children within a state; they have simply opened the door for debate and reform. Certainly they have raised more questions than they have answered. What direction should states now take in financing their educational programs in the light of limitations on property tax as a source of locally provided revenue for schools? How can other taxes be used to replace or reduce property taxes? To what extent do court decisions mandate standardization and uniformity of school programs? What are the ramifications of the reshaping of the federal income tax law for local and state funding?

As a result of this confusion in school finance, some states and school districts continue to use educational finance practices that have been determined to be ineffective and obsolete:

1. Some states still require local school districts to rely almost completely on a local property tax as the source of funds for education in spite of the unfairness and regressiveness of such a means.
2. In spite of sound theories of equalization that have evolved during the last half-century from the thinking of numerous school finance specialists such as Strayer, Haig, Updegraff, and Mort, some of the 50 states have not yet incorporated these principles in their school finance programs.
3. Although it can be documented that education is really an investment in people, many legislative bodies give the impression that the cost of education threatens the economic capability of those who provide its funds.
4. Many different groups of people are denied equity by the failure of state and local governments to provide sufficient funds to educate them. Students who are disabled and/or gifted, aspire to vocational training, or are not of the dominant culture may not always have a reasonable chance to reach their potential as citizens.
5. Even though pride in "free education" seems to be a sincere expression on the part of nearly all citizens, in practice such a designation is almost a mockery in many places. Numerous fees and incidental charges in many schools discriminate against children of low-income families and relegate them to second-class citizenship.

Summary

Equity in school finance refers to fairness in the expenditures per pupil and fairness in the treatment of taxpayers. In this context, equity and equality, although often used synonymously, do not mean the same. Fairness is more important in financing education than evenness or sameness, because students have wide differences in their abilities, needs, and educational desires. The school finance reforms emphasize equity of educational input; it is impossible to measure accurately equity of output.

Even though real property taxes are usually paid at the same tax rate in a given district, they are not always equitable, because of different rates of assessment as compared to market values, different degrees of ownership of the property being taxed, and differences in the income or the wealth of taxpayers—even though their property taxes may be relatively similar. Income and wealth have some advantages over property assessments in formulas for determining the fiscal capacity of school districts.

It is much easier to treat equals equally—the horizontal component of equity—than to treat unequals unequally—the vertical component of equity. No one has determined exactly how unequally those with unequal needs or abilities should be treated. Since the cost of education varies with the abilities and the needs of students, the use of weighting factors adds some measure of fairness to finance formulas. The use of assessed valuation of property per pupil is more equitable than assessed valuation of property per capita for the operation of school finance programs. Wealth and income are gaining some support as bases for determining fiscal capacity.

The equity issue at the local school level has become a topic for researchers in the field of education finance. Critics are anticipating that it in some way may relate to accountability. The complexities in comparing one state to another is difficult because data of this nature are not required of local districts. It is important for administrators to monitor the budget figures. However, unless mandated, there appears to be limited interest in collecting and providing local-level finance information.

Taxes are classified into three general types: proportional (the same percentage of income spent for taxes for all levels of income), progressive (higher percent of income for taxes for higher levels of income), and regressive (lower percent of income for taxes for higher incomes). It is generally agreed that reasonable progressive taxes are the most equitable and regressive taxes the least equitable.

In the early history of the United States, many of the individual states were slow in accepting responsibility for financing their public schools. Consequently, full local district funding was the first of all school finance systems. Because of the extreme differences in the size and wealth of local districts, local financing proved to be a very unfair and discriminatory method of financing education.

Early efforts of the states to aid local districts in financing education came principally in the form of flat grants. These, too, proved to be nonequalizing. Gradually, however, the states moved to equalizing grants and to the equalization principle in supporting local districts.

Some states and school districts continue to use obsolete and unfair educational finance practices in spite of the relationship between equal protection and equalization in school finance. Such practices are being challenged in state courts.

ASSIGNMENT PROJECTS

1. Provide a definition for each of the following terms: *equity, weighted-pupil, assessed value, market value, proportional tax, regressive tax, progressive tax, flat grants, foundation program, ADA, ADM, mill, mill levy, wealth tax, minimum program, equalization.*
2. Compare various definitions found in the literature of *equality* and *equity* in school finance programs or formulas.
3. Discuss the problems and ramifications involved in improving school finance formulas in order to provide greater equity for taxpayers.

4. According to the literature, what are the apparent trends in the measurement of school district wealth? What are the problems involved in applying these measures to school finance formulas?

5. Some states express their tax rates in mills; others express them in dollars per hundred dollars of assessed valuation. For example, in some states, the tax rate for school purposes might be expressed as 50.5 mills; in others, it would be expressed as $5.05 per $100 of assessed valuation (AV). It could also be expressed as $50.50 per $1,000 of assessed valuation. Express the following as indicated:

a. 156.25 mills as dollars
b. $0.375 as mills
c. $17.51 as mills
d. 57.3 mills as dollars per $100 (AV)
e. $3.60 per $150 (AV) as mills

f. .78 mills as dollars
g. .78 mills as dollars per $100 (AV)
h. .78 mills as dollars per $1,000 (AV)
i. 2,341.5 mills as dollars
j. $5,491.54 as mills

Flat Grants

6. With the help of the following information, answer the questions concerning the effect of flat grants on the two districts.

District	Assessed Valuation	Paid by State	Budget Needs	Mill Levy	Number of Students
A	$6,000,000	nil	$240,000	_____ (1)	360
B	5,000,000	nil	100,000	_____ (2)	150

a. Would a grant of $24,000 by the state to each district be equalizing in its effect on the two districts? Yes____ No____ (3)

b. Would a state grant of $100 per student be equalizing in its effect on the two districts? Yes____ No____ (4)

District	Assessed Valuation	Paid by State	Budget Needs	Mill Levy	Number of Teachers
C	$ 8,000,000	nil	$400,000	_____ (5)	50
D	10,000,000	nil	300,000	_____ (6)	40

c. Would a grant of $40,000 be equalizing in its effect on the two districts? Yes____ No____ (7)

d. Would a state grant of $500 per teacher be equalizing in its effect on the two districts? Yes____ No____ (8)

Foundation Programs

7. Determine the state funds that would be paid in the following equalization program: District A has an assessed valuation of $10,580,000. Its budget needs for this part of the program are $495,000. The required local levy is $1.56 per $100 of assessed valuation.

   a. Under an equalized program, the state would pay the district $_____

   b. What are the three parts of any state foundation program?

8. Assuming a certain state has a fixed dollar amount of money to allocate to the following three districts on a proportionate share basis, which district would probably prefer to have the state use each of the three methods of allocation?

	District A	District B	District C
Pupils on census list	2,000	2,500	3,000
Pupils in ADM	1,860	2,140	2,000
Pupils in ADA	1,548	2,052	1,820

   a. (Census) _____   b. (ADM) _____   c. (ADA) _____

   d. What is the advantage of using ADA in allocating state money to local school districts?

   e. What is the advantage of using ADM in allocating state money to local school districts?

   f. What would be the advantage of using aggregate days attendance in allocating state money to local school districts?

Computer simulations and questions, research exercises, and website addresses relevant to this chapter can be found at

www.ablongman.com/edleadership

SELECTED READINGS

Burtless, Gary. *Does Money Matter? The Effect of School Resources on Student Achievement and Adult Success.* Washington, DC: Brookings Institution Press, 1996.

Carnegie Forum on Education and the Economy. *A Nation Preparing Teachers for the 21st Century.* Washington, DC: Carnegie Forum on Education and the Economy, 1990.

Coleman, J. S. *Equality of Educational Opportunity.* Washington, DC: U.S. Government Printing Office, 1966.

Cubberley, Ellwood P. *School Funds and Their Apportionment.* New York: Teachers College, Columbia University, 1905.

General Accounting Office. *School Finance: State Efforts to Reduce Funding Gaps between Poor and Wealthy Districts.* Washington, DC: General Accounting Office, 1997.

Guthrie, James W., Springer, Matthew G., Rolle, R. Anthony, and Houck, Eric A. *Modern Education Finance and Policy.* Peabody College Education Leadership Series. Boston: Allyn & Bacon, 2007.

Honeyman, D. S., D. C. Thompson, and R. C. Wood. *Financing Rural and Small Schools: Issues of Adequacy and Equity.* Gainesville: University of Florida Press, 1989.

Jencks, C., M. S. Smith, H. Acland, M. J. Bane, D. Cohen, H. Gintis, B. Heyna, and S. Michaelson. *Inequality: A Reassessment of the Effect of Family and Schooling in America.* New York: Harper & Row, 1972.

Kozol, Jonathan. *Savage Inequalities.* New York: Harper Perennial, 1991.

Kronick, Robert F., and Charles H. Hargis. *Dropouts: Who Drops Out and Why, and the Recommended Action.* Springfield, IL: Charles C. Thomas, 1990.

Ladd, Helen R., Rosemary Chalk, and Janet Hansen. *Equity and Adequacy in Education and Finance Issues and Perspectives.* Washington, DC: National Academy Press, 1999.

Naisbett, John, and Patricia Aburdene. *Megatrends 2000.* New York: Avon, 1990.

Odden, Allan R., and Lawrence O. Picus. *School Finance: A Policy Perspective.* New York: McGraw-Hill, 2000.

Picus, Lawrence O., and James L. Wattenbarger. *Where Does the Money Go? Resource Allocation in Elementary and Secondary Schools. Sixteenth Annual Yearbook of the American Educational Finance Association.* Thousand Oaks, CA: Corwin Press, 1996.

Pole, J. R. *The Pursuit of Equality in American History.* Berkeley: University of California Press, 1978.

"Quality Counts 2000." *Education Week,* January 13, 2000.

School Finance Trends in U.S. Education Spending. Washington, DC: U.S. General Accounting Office, September 1995.

Thomas, Gloria Jean, David J. Sperry, and F. Del Wasden. *The Law and Teacher Employment.* New York: West Publishing, 1991.

Thompson, David C., R. Craig Wood, and David S. Honeyman. *Fiscal Leadership for Schools, Concepts and Practices.* White Plains, NY: Addison-Wesley, 1994.

Toward High and Rigorous Standards for the Teaching Profession, 3rd ed. Washington, DC: National Board for Professional Teaching Standards, 1991.

The Unfinished Agenda: A New Vision for Child Development and Education. New York: Committee for Economic Development, 1991.

Verstegen, D. A. *School Finance at a Glance.* Denver, CO: Education Commission of the States, 1990.

ENDNOTES

1. JoAnna Natale, "Just Desserts," *The American School Board Journal,* Vol. 177, No. 3, March 1990.

2. Sue Books, "School Funding: Justice v. Equity," *Equity and Excellence in Education,* December 1999, p. 54.

3. Charles S. Benson et al., *Planning for Educational Reform* (New York: Dodd, Mead, 1974), p. 8.

4. *Serrano* v. *Priest* (1), 96 Cal. Rptr. 601, 487 P.2d 1241 (Calif. 1971).

5. See Deborah A. Verstegen, "Equal Education Under the Law: School Finance Reform and the Courts," *The Journal of Law and Politics,* Summer 1998, University of Virginia, pp. 555–559.

6. "The Funding Gap: Low-Income and Minority Students Receive Fewer Dollars," *The Education Trust, Inc.,* 1725 K Street, N.W., Washington, DC. www.edtrust.org, pp. 1, 2.

7. Ibid.

8. *Brown* v. *Board of Education,* 347 U.S. 483, 74 S.Ct. 686 (1954).

9. Lindley J. Stiles, "Editor's Introduction," to Charles S. Benson et al., *Planning for Educational Reform* (New York: Dodd, Mead, 1974), p. v.

10. William T. Hartman, Denny G. Bolton, and David H. Monk, "A Synthesis of Two Approaches to School-Level Financial Data: The Accounting and Resource Cost Model Approaches," *Selected Papers in School Finance, 2000–2001,* National Center for Education Statistics, U.S. Department of Education, NCES 2001-378, p. 81.

11. Carolyn Busch and Allen Odden, "Introduction to the Special Issue—Improving Education Policy with School-Level Data: A Synthesis of Multiple Perspectives," *Journal of Education Finance,* Winter 1997, p. 238.

12. Ibid., p. 237.

13. Hartman et al., "A Synthesis of Two Approaches," p. 86.

14. Busch and Odden, quoting Goertz, p. 237.

15. Title I Comparability Report, Title I Regulations, Utah State Office of Education, August 2003.

16. Robert Berne and Leanna Stiefel, "Taxpayer Equity in School Finance Reform: The School Finance and the Public Finance Perspectives," *Journal of Education Finance,* Vol. 5, No. 1, Summer 1979, p. 37.

17. Walter W. McMahon, "A Broader Measure of Wealth and Effort for Educational Equality and Tax Equity," *Journal of Education Finance,* Vol. 4, No. 1, Summer 1978, pp. 65–66.

18. "Quality Counts 2003," *Education Week,* January 2006.

19. Ibid. www.edweek.org/sreports/qc03/reports/resources-t1.cfm.

20. Roe L. Johns, "Improving the Equity of School Finance Programs," *Journal of Education Finance,* Vol. 1, No. 4, Spring 1976, p. 547.

4

Patterns for School Finance Systems

Public education is an essential ingredient of an effective democracy; in reality it has been a shining success. We cannot allow the critics to destroy public confidence in our system of tax-supported education.

—Don Thomas, 2007

Important events in the United States have increased the need for, and helped accelerate the implementation of, plans for greater equality of educational opportunity and equal protection for school-age citizens. Patterns of school finance systems vary from state to state and from school district to school district. Every state has different formulas and procedures for financing education. Each state, however, has a system in which the local district, the state government, and the federal system share in the support of education. Generally, property taxes are a major part of local districts' revenues, whereas sales and income taxes are the major source of state funds. However, in 2006, ten states cut or considered cutting the local property tax. This shifts more of the responsibility of funding public schools to the state level. States are raising other taxes, especially the sales tax, to replace lost property tax revenues usually available to local districts. Industrialization increased the discrepancies in the financial ability of school districts and states to finance education. The amount of money particular schools receive "vary dramatically, depending on property values, not just from state to state but from district to district, and from year to year."[1]

Developing Patterns

School finance scholars are presenting evidence that state school finance programs do not produce the equal educational opportunity they were devised to provide. The courts have varied interpretations of what conditions are acceptable in school finance formulas, depending on the divergent tenets of the several states' constitutions. Flat grants, percentage grants, foundation programs with or without local options, power equalization, full state funding, or any combination of these methods are being used throughout the 50 states.

95

Cubberley stated years ago, "All the children of the state are equally important and are entitled to the same advantage."[2] That is a verbalization of certain tenets of school finance philosophy and theory that had been sponsored by such theorists as Updegraff and Morrison. Some of their ideas of how to provide equality of educational opportunity—which were not popular when introduced, nor given an opportunity for practical development—were gradually recognized as potentially valuable. Morrison's ideas concerning greater state control and virtual elimination of local districts now seemed logical to many who favored full state funding of public education.

More than half a century of state effort to equalize educational opportunity and school tax burdens by state-local partnership finance formulas have not achieved its goals. The reason that all states could attain this objective is if they collected and controlled the disposition of all school funds.

Basically there are three different degrees of state participation possible for financing and operating public schools:

1. *State operation* of public schools, with substantial reductions in the administrative and operational responsibilities of local school boards
2. Complete *state support,* with elimination of locally raised funds but with state basic programs increased to adequate levels
3. The *foundation program* approach, with state funds added to local tax funds to produce a state-guaranteed level of school support

Determining the Best Finance Plan

Many plans are available to states for the allocation of funds to local districts. Various combinations of equalizing grants, adaptations of the foundation program principle, and varying degrees of power equalization may be employed to utilize the advantages and eliminate the disadvantages of each. The state may use categorical or special-purpose funding to encourage the introduction or stimulation of innovative programs. It may use instructional programs or units as the basis for determining the size of state allocations to local districts, or it may set up state standards or guidelines and use state committees to negotiate with local districts for budget plans that meet the unique needs of districts. Thus, the number of potential state financing patterns is almost unlimited.

A state may be making excellent strides in improving its system of financing the foundation program. However, through politics and pressure groups influencing legislators, many special categorical programs emerge that tend to skew the equity aspects of a state's basic program. California is an example of this phenomenon, providing over 50 categorical programs funded from state sources. It has been estimated that the various states use nearly 400 kinds of aid to local districts, including the minimum program, transportation, salary-schedule allowances, and others.

The choice of financing programs is great, but at this point in school finance reform there is no perfect system for distributing state funds to local school districts. Each plan has limitations and falls short of equalizing financial resources to the complete satisfaction of all the people concerned. Some systems are better than others, and some states make greater efforts to improve than others. Given the inequities that exist in almost every state plan, there is no room for complacency in viewing school finance reform in any state. Certainly, there is little justification for maintaining or preserving traditional methods until a panacean formula is discovered.

No one way is generally accepted as the best, in terms of its popularity over all other plans, for organizing the state-local partnership for financing education. Programs now in existence vary from Hawaii's one-district system, where the district covers the entire state and is the sole taxing and financing unit for the operation of all its public schools, to programs in which state-level allocations to local districts involve only a relatively small part of the total funds available to local districts. All other states come somewhere in between these two extremes.

It is safe to assume that school financing plans of the future will emphasize greater state involvement and proportionately less local responsibility. Since the property tax is the realistic source of local revenue and since its utilization has reached most extreme proportions, it is evident that state tax sources will have to be increased to meet the surging costs of education. Of the big revenue producers, the sales tax and income tax are used mostly by state government. These taxes are probably destined to bear the brunt of the tax increases that appear to be necessary now and in the future to finance the high-quality education programs that nearly all citizens demand.

Model 4.1 is an illustration of two plans for full state funding of education, with minor adjustments that could be used. Columns *a* illustrate full state funding without allowance for local options. All districts would receive the same number of dollars per weighted-pupil unit. Its disadvantage is that the state legislature would determine by itself the maximum number of dollars per pupil to be provided. Local needs, local desires, and local initiative would be ignored under this type of financing.

Columns *b* provide almost full state funding, with limited local options to go beyond the state-sponsored program. Although this plan purports to provide for local preferences, it is nonequalizing and favors wealthier districts, as do all finance plans where local effort is not state supported.

The plan, shown in columns *a,* provides exactly the same amount of revenue per weighted-pupil unit in each district. This has some serious limitations:

1. It makes the state-determined program a minimum as well as a maximum program.
2. It provides no way for a school district to enrich its program beyond that which the state mandates.
3. It removes fiscal responsibility from the control of local school boards.
4. It may tend to jeopardize local school programs when the state's revenue will not support full state funding at a desirable level.

When the columns *b* model is used, the result is nonequalization among districts of varying taxable wealth per weighted pupil. Thus, when all three districts use the maximum 10-mill levy, the net effect is that District L has available only $360 per mill per weighted-pupil unit, whereas District H has $480 per mill per weighted-pupil unit. By the use of nonsupported local optional levies, the equalization accomplished

MODEL 4.1   Full State Funding versus Almost Full State Funding with Local Option

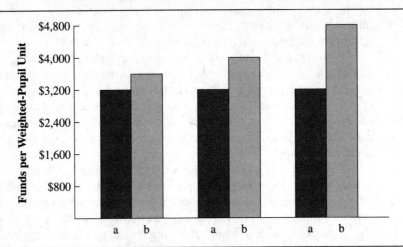

Full State Funding

Districts	Assessed Valuation	State Funds per WPU	Required Local Levy
L	$40,000,000	$3,200	Nil
M	80,000,000	3,200	Nil
H	160,000,000	3,200	Nil

Almost Full State Funding with Minimum Local Options

Additional Local Levy	# WPUs	Local Funds per WPU	Total Funds per WPU	Total Funds per M per WPU
District L—10 mills	1,000	$ 400	$3,600	$360
District M—10 mills	1,000	$ 800	4,000	400
District H—10 mills	1,000	$1,600	4,800	480

with full state funding has been neutralized to some degree. Of course, if the state provides funds for nearly all the cost of school district programs, with only minimal local optional levies, the latter may not seriously upset the overall equalization that the program produces.

Full State Funding

Full state funding under any plan raises some questions about an attendant increase in state control of local schools and a corresponding decrease in the power and authority of local school boards. Some feel that recent increases in state support of local school revenues have already reduced the role of local school boards in administering schools to an undesirable and irreversible point. Others suggest that the high degree of local control of half a century ago may not be possible or desirable in today's world.

As the name implies, full state funding places the burden for providing a good public school program completely on the state itself. There is little promise that the typical legislature, in the face of extreme pressure for state funds from all state institutions, would year after year provide the money necessary for the high-level educational program desired by the citizens of its various school districts. Determining the amount of money necessary for education could very well become an "average practice" minimum program, completely lacking in local incentives.

Full state funding is an acceptable plan for districts that would be "leveled up" to expenditure levels or standards above their previous position. But "leveling down" or forcing some districts to remain at their current expenditure level could result. It is doubtful that leveling down or maintaining the status quo could be operable in any state. Hence, the state itself would be forced to find a system or rationale for providing funds above the established amount for expensive or high-expenditure school districts.

Probably the most negative aspects of full state funding are twofold. First, the state would exercise the power to determine the amount of revenue in every district with little regard for the educational needs or desires of the local citizenry. Second, there is no way to determine, on a rational and objective basis, which districts should be given the funds necessary to explore innovative practices or encouraged to become exemplary. Since local districts would make no tax effort on their own to finance education, the state would lack a legal framework or device with which to determine which schools or in what amount state funds should be allocated to "deserving" districts.

It is likely that full state funding would lead to the extended use of sales and income taxes, with less emphasis on the property tax. There is much to be said in favor of this change, but the plan tends to discourage, if not obliterate, local initiative and special tax effort to provide better schools than those legislated by the state. Thus far, the states have found no satisfactory substitute for the incentive grants that have been used to provide better programs in districts where there is no expressed desire to extend local effort to obtain such excellence.

District Power Equalization

An alternative to full state funding is *district power equalization (DPE)*. Various terms have been used to describe the concept, including *equalized percentage matching* and *open-end equalization*. *Power* is perhaps a more appropriate term to use than the others because the principle literally provides a poor school district with the power to obtain as much revenue per student as more wealthy districts making the same local tax effort. By definition, *DPE* means that each local district mill levy should produce the same number of dollars of total school revenue per mill per weighted student in every district, and the last mill to be levied should produce the same total funds as the first one. This concept was advocated in 1922 by Updegraff but found little support until the early

1970s. Its later popularity came largely as a result of the lack of support for full state funding as a means of providing equal protection as mandated by court decisions and recommended by several school finance studies.

Burke summarized the philosophy concerning extension and improvement of the foundation program concept in the following:

> A given unit of tax effort in a locality with low fiscal ability is made to produce the same number of dollars of revenue per pupil as would result from the same effort in a district with average or above-average fiscal capacity. Thus, the level of the state-supported equalization program rises with local tax effort in the ready and willing local units and with the success of the state and/or local leadership in overcoming nonfiscal limitations in others.[3]

Some states require state equalization at the same rate for the entire educational program as is determined in the foundation program. The local district determines the limits of the local effort, and the state maintains financial responsibility for the entire program. This open-end equalization program is often referred to as *equalized percentage matching (EPM)*. It is sometimes viewed as a means of opening a state's financial coffers to every local district. It is extremely effective in obliterating financial advantages for one district over another in providing for high-quality education rather than simply a minimum or foundation program.

Model 4.2 illustrates district power equalization with full state support for each mill of tax levy. Model 4.2a shows the same principle, but with all levies above those

MODEL 4.2   District Power Equalization; 4.2a Reduced Percentage Power Equalization (dashed lines)

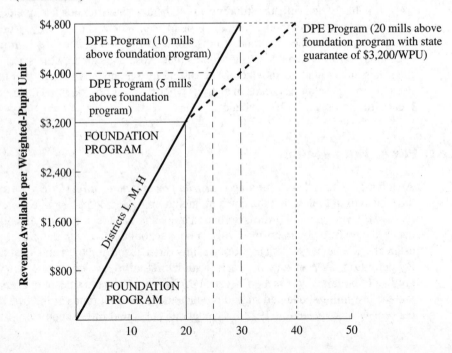

of the foundation program supported by the state at a fractional part of the original amount. This, of course, flattens the graph line (see model), thereby decreasing the state percentage and increasing the local percentage of revenue produced. The program remains equitable, however, so long as the level is kept above the amount the wealthiest district could produce locally or if all surpluses were recaptured by the state.

It should be noted that the steeper the line in a DPE formula graph, the greater the so-called raid on the state treasury and the less the effort required at the local level. Increased costs by this process would probably cause a state to flatten the DPE line and thereby increase the local district's share of the cost of the educational program. By this process the state should be able to control the degree of depletion of its treasury this program would bring.

Following is a simplified example of how an equalized percentage or power equalization program might function. Note that four mythical districts of widely varying assessments of taxable property per weighted-pupil unit (WPU) are compared in the calculation of a foundation program with an equalization program of $2,000 per weighted-pupil unit with a required local levy of 10 mills.

Foundation Program

| District | Assessed Value/WPU | Mill Levy | Guaranteed Amount/WPU | Revenue/WPU | | Local/State Ratio |
				Local	State	
A	$100,000	10	$2,000	$1,000	$1,000	1:1
B	80,000	10	2,000	800	1,200	2:3
C	20,000	10	2,000	200	1,800	1:9
D	10,000	10	2,000	100	1,900	1:19

Program above the Foundation

| District | Assessed Value/WPU | Mill Levy | Guaranteed Amount/WPU | Revenue/WPU | | Local/State Ratio |
				Local	State	
A	$100,000	2	$400	$200	$200	1:1
B	80,000	2	400	160	240	2:3
C	20,000	2	400	40	360	1:9
D	10,000	2	400	20	380	1:19

District A has its local revenue matched by the state on a 1:1 basis, District B on a 2:3 basis, District C on a 1:9 basis, and District D on a 1:19 basis. This, of course, is a simple foundation program. If each district goes 2 mills above the foundation program on a DPE basis, District A gets a $2,400 per WPU, with $1,200 local and $1,200 state revenue; District B has the same program, with $960 local and $1,440 state revenue; District C has $240 local and $2,160 state revenue; and District D has $120 local and $2,280 state money. Thus, a power equalization program requires the state to continue its degree of partnership with each district for the full program. By this process, financially weak districts (such as District D in the preceding example) are able to offer as good a program (in terms of cost) as wealthier ones. This is the essence of the philosophy of equality of educational opportunity.

At first glance, it may seem that this creates a standard program for every district within a state. Such is not the case, however, for each local district would have the right and the responsibility, within state limits, to determine what the local tax rate would be over and above the mandated foundation program levy. In this way, local control is assured and state partnership responsibility is mandated. To illustrate this optional program, suppose that District A elected to levy 1 mill above the mandated foundation program, District B decided on a 2-mill increase, District C a 4-mill program, and District D a 5-mill increase. The result of this would be as follows:

Optional Program above Foundation Program

District	Increased Tax Levy	Guaranteed Amount per WPU	Local Revenue	State Revenue	Local/State Ratio	Total WPU
A	1 mills	$200	$100	$100	1:1	$2,200
B	2 mills	400	160	240	2:3	2,400
C	4 mills	800	80	720	1:9	2,800
D	5 mills	1,000	50	950	1:19	3,000

It can be seen that equal levies bring equal dollars in all districts, but each district is free to choose the level at which its program will be supported. This preserves the element of local control in decision making, but at the same time it requires the state to support the entire program to whatever level the law permits local districts to operate.

The merits of district power equalization are readily discernible. Local control of the extent to which the educational program goes above the state minimum rests with each individual school board, but the state cannot escape its proportionate financial responsibility. Districts are motivated to make adequate tax effort, for if they spend less, they lose more. Complete equalization is possible in spending as well as in tax effort. If there is a high enough ceiling on local tax options, the inequalities encountered between wealthy and poor districts, which are obvious in a typical foundation program with unsupported local options, disappear. The only restriction to an adequately financed program thus becomes the willingness or unwillingness of the people at the local level to tax themselves within reasonable limits. With the state matching the local district on a predetermined basis in terms of local ability, the previously unrealistic tax requirements for a quality education program in a poor district are reduced greatly or even eliminated.

Figure 4.1 is an example of the limited power equalization concept. Of the 40 districts shown, 4 provide 100 percent of the basic program. Note that only 32 percent (the state average) of the total maintenance and operation basic program is provided from local property tax when all districts assess a required 20 mills. The 68 percent state guarantee of $3,200 per weighted-pupil unit comes from state resources. The limits are controlled by the $3,200 guarantee.

In Figure 4.1, District 17 is used to further clarify the concept. There are 14,500 students in average daily membership with various weighting factors that provide the

FIGURE 4.1   Limited Power Equalization—Percent of Local Revenue Raised toward the Basic Maintenance and Operation State-Guaranteed Program of $3,200 per WPU When a Minimum of 20 Local Mills Is Required

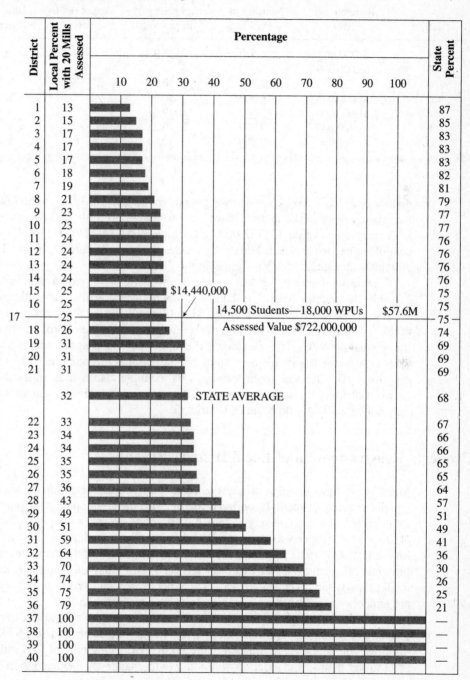

District	Local Percent with 20 Mills Assessed	Percentage	State Percent
1	13		87
2	15		85
3	17		83
4	17		83
5	17		83
6	18		82
7	19		81
8	21		79
9	23		77
10	23		77
11	24		76
12	24		76
13	24		76
14	24		76
15	25	$14,440,000	75
16	25		75
17	25	14,500 Students—18,000 WPUs $57.6M	75
18	26	Assessed Value $722,000,000	74
19	31		69
20	31		69
21	31		69
	32	STATE AVERAGE	68
22	33		67
23	34		66
24	34		66
25	35		65
26	35		65
27	36		64
28	43		57
29	49		51
30	51		49
31	59		41
32	64		36
33	70		30
34	74		26
35	75		25
36	79		21
37	100		—
38	100		—
39	100		—
40	100		—

TABLE 4.1   Revenue Raised in Local Districts with a Voted Leeway and No State Support

District	Revenue per Mill	Number of WPUs	Revenue per Mill per WPU	Mills Approved by Voters	Total Revenue per WPU
A	$ 200,000	1,600	$125.00	10	$1,250.00
B	$3,000,000	35,000	$ 85.71	4	$ 342.84
C	$ 375,000	7,500	$ 50.00	3	$ 150.00
D	$ 480,000	16,000	$ 30.00	7	$ 210.00
E	$1,600,000	82,000	$ 19.51	9	$ 175.59
F	$ 400,000	39,000	$ 10.26	10	$ 102.60
G	$ 600,000	20,000	$ 30.00	0	$ 0

district with 18,000 WPUs. The state guarantees $3,200 per WPU, or $57,600,000 for the basic program. The district is required to assess 20 mills (.020) against property with an assessed value of $722,000,000, which raises $14,440,000 locally, or 25 percent of the needed revenue. The state provides the other 75 percent, or $43,160,000, to guarantee an equalized dollar figure for the district.

Table 4.1 demonstrates how a specific program, in this case a *local voted leeway,* can shift the delicate balance of equity without power equalization participation from the state. Note that 1 mill (.001) raises $125.00 per WPU in District A, whereas in District F it raises only $10.26 because of the low assessed value of property in relation to the number of WPUs. If the average expenditure per WPU in the state is $3,000, then District A is able to provide over 40 percent additional revenue per WPU when voters approve a 10-mill local voted leeway. This example also demonstrates the inequity between districts if one is able to pass a local leeway while voters in another district may not be willing to do so, as in District G.

Property Reassessment and Local District Revenues

Many states have found it difficult to raise their finance programs beyond the state equalization requirement. It is often difficult to get the voting public to approve leeway or override levies in the face of already high property taxes. This is particularly difficult at times when property assessments have just been increased, a practice that is mandatory at stated intervals in several states. Those who do not understand the equalization principle often have the idea that property assessment increases automatically result in local property tax revenue increases. They thereby assume that local leeway increases are unnecessary under those conditions and vote against them.

District 17 in Figure 4.1 will be used in a further example: If, after a reappraisal of property, the assessed value increased by 10 percent (or to approximately $790 million), 20 mills would raise $15.9 million, which provides a "windfall" of $1.5 million to the state rather than to the local district and would change the percentage of local contributions from 25 percent to 27.5 percent and decrease the state contribution to 72.5 percent. Of course, if the program is not state supported, increases in assessment bring commensurate increases in local revenue.

The state would participate in a leeway to the same degree as in the basic equalization program, if it were involved in a power equalization program. The amount of total funds available to the district would be the same—regardless of the extent of property assessment increase. On the other hand, if the override or leeway portion is not state supported, increased assessments do bring additional local tax revenues. When the state-supported foundation program and a nonsupported leeway program are considered together, the percent of total budget increase in a "poor" district is considerably less than in a "rich" district.

Computerization has made it possible for counties and states to reevaluate property on a yearly basis. For many years, the reassessment was a continual job, and some properties may have gone for years without updated values. Extremes were very noticeable when, in some cases, properties were not reassessed for over 20 years. To control local districts from gaining a "windfall," legislators often reduce the required mill levy in a power equalization program and limit increases in voted leeway and capital outlay budgets. In some cases, it might be a percentage cap in relation to the previous year's revenue or require a "truth in taxation" hearing to provide the public the opportunity to express concerns over tax increases brought about by increased property values. Basically, the state has three options to raise property tax revenue: the tax rate, the assessed value of property, and setting the mill levy required of each district to provide its part toward the minimum program.

Equalization of Services

One idea on future state financing of education, whether through complete state financing or some degree of state-local partnership, involves state equalization of services rather than of dollars. One of the chief problems in state allocation of funds revolves around the incontrovertible fact that equal dollars provided to unlike districts result in unequal units of service. Similar amounts of money never result in equal purchases of instructional services, since some districts must pay much higher salaries than others. The costs of school buses, gasoline, or any other required services or supplies vary considerably in all the districts of all the states. The fairest measure of equalization, then, would be the program that equalizes the required school services in all school districts. Such a principle needs no justification, but much more research and experience will be required before it replaces present-day equalization of dollars among the school districts of any state.

Emphasis on Weighting Factors

Determining the funds necessary to operate a school program, regardless of the process or formula used, is a function of the "need" of the school district. Need is related first of all to the number of pupils to be educated. There are many other determinants of need, but the number of pupils in average daily attendance (ADA) or the number of students in average daily membership (ADM) forms the basic unit of measurement. Established number reported (ENR) is used in national reports. Although schools have used, and continue to use, the idea of providing equal dollars for all children in the state as the measure of equality of educational opportunity, such a concept is really not valid. Equal dollars per student do not produce equal products or equal results. Further, unequal educational opportunities are certain to result when funding does not consider such common variables as physical and mental disabilities, socioeconomic backgrounds, language deficiencies, and many other diverse characteristics of students.

In addition to differing student characteristics, the cost of an educational program is related to such existing variables as the size of the school district and the size of the school attendance area, for the cost of educating 25,000 pupils is not necessarily exactly 100 times that of educating 250 pupils. Similarly, the cost of operating a high school of 500 pupils may not be the same as that of financing 500 elementary pupils. Schools with a high percentage of pupils with disadvantages cost more than those with a lower percentage. Sparsity factors make the cost of education in small rural communities higher than in average-sized towns. On the other hand, the unique problems of large cities and metropolitan areas make the cost of education proportionately higher, even though some might expect economies of scale to apply.

Weighting factors are perhaps the best measures of the amount of additional resources and services needed to provide all students, regardless of their personal or environmental disabilities, with reasonably equal educational programs. Fortunately, there are relatively few citizens who continue to challenge the humanistic view that children who have physical or mental challenges, or who attend school in exceedingly small or extremely large and disadvantaged schools, should benefit from educational programs that are more costly than "normal" ones. With the No Child Left Behind law, states may consider adding a weighting factor for those students who are not able to meet the achievement standards required.

The weighted-pupil concept is not new. Mort and Reusser pointed out the long tradition of this fundamental principle over 50 years ago: "The weighted-pupil unit (or its mathematical equivalent—the weighted-classroom unit) is the most systematically refined of all measures of educational need and has been in practical use for a quarter of a century in state-aid laws, in expenditure comparisons of various types of districts, and in comparisons of ability to support schools."[4]

The many inequalities that exist force states to recognize that the number of pupils by itself does not indicate the operational need of school districts. Disparity in fiscal needs arises from the composition of the pupil populations. That being true, it becomes necessary for weighting to be made if fairness and equality of educational opportunity are to be achieved.

Weightings would lose their importance and become superfluous if the schools to be served had the same proportions of variables that appear to require weightings. If 40 percent of the pupils in every school district are secondary school pupils, there would be little need for weighting this factor. If every district had 10 percent of its pupils in small or isolated school attendance areas, there would be little need for weightings here. However, these factors are never constant from district to district. Weighting tends to put the extra costs incurred in providing maximum quality education for pupils with special or more than average problems where they belong—on the state.

Principal Types of Weightings

In any consideration of the number of pupils as a determinant of the money needs of a district, several important weightings could be considered: (1) the sparsity or isolation of pupils in rural areas, (2) the density of pupils in heavily populated metropolitan areas, (3) the grade levels of pupils, and (4) the degree of disadvantage certain classes of pupils may suffer, such as those who require special education services. Consideration should also be given to the training and experience of the professional staff members of each district. To consider all pupils to be of equal worth or cost is no more erroneous than to consider all teachers to be of equal worth or cost to a school system.

Sparsity Factors

The need to provide additional funds to help finance the small schools that operate in nearly every state has long been recognized and accepted. Bass noted:

> Small rural school districts face a wide variety of problems, from difficulty in hiring and retraining quality teachers to the inability to field competitive athletic teams because of the limited number of students. But by far the most critical and pervasive problems deal with costs and revenues. Small schools, if they are to provide educational programs similar in breadth and quality to those of larger schools, will inevitably incur higher per-pupil costs due to limited enrollment, small pupil-teacher ratios, higher utility and other operational costs per pupil, and other factors that limit economies of scale.[5]

State legislatures, mostly rurally dominated until recently, have usually made provisions for the protection of small and expensive schools and districts. The methods used may vary from state to state, but the end results are much the same. Typically, the process used involves weighting such pupils in the finance formula so as to require the state to pay its proportionate share of the higher costs involved in the education of pupils in small groups. At the same time, some states give the state board of education the responsibility of determining when such privilege may be rescinded or withdrawn, as when some small schools might reasonably be expected to be consolidated or reorganized into larger and more efficient units. Sparsity weighting factors are difficult to construct.

In an effort to reduce the inequalities of schools with small enrollments, Utah uses a model formula that provides extra revenue for necessarily existent small schools. The state has one school of three persons in a remote area on the Utah-Nevada border, another of five on the Utah-Idaho border, and nearly 100 other small schools scattered across the state. This condition is not unique; many states with a large land area and small populations have small and remote schools. The concept that the formula reflects is since additional per-pupil costs exist in schools with fewer students, to provide them an adequate education it is more equitable to contribute extra resources per pupil than in a normal-sized school.

Based on the weighted-pupil unit and average daily membership, the formula covers the various school levels—elementary through a six-year secondary program. At the elementary level, a school with an enrollment of 1 to 10 in average daily membership receives 30 added WPUs, increasing to 54.8057 additional WPUs for a 50-student school. At this point, the scale lessens as average daily membership draws closer in size to a normal school and the extra WPUs end at 160 students (see Table 4.2). The WPUs per ADM is shown on the right side of the table. In a school with 2 students, the per-pupil WPUs would be 15 ($15 \times 2 = 30$; for 3 students, $10 \times 3 = 30$; for 4 students, $7.5 \times 4 = 30$; and so on). At the 159-student level, it would be $0.01069 \times 159 = 1.6996$ additional WPUs, which is reflected on the left side of the table and used in computations; at 160 pupils, it is $0.00625 \times 160 = 1$. The small school has reached the size of a normal school, hence only 1 additional WPU is provided.

The same principle applies at the secondary level in one- or two-year schools, as well as three-, four-, and six-year schools. The corresponding numbers in Table 4.2 show the additional WPUs generated for each of the schools at the various levels. Each of the secondary schools increase their WPUs as the student numbers increase, which encourages schools to consolidate smaller schools. At a certain point, the additional WPUs decrease as they approach the size of a normal school. For a one- or two-year high school, the optimum WPU level is at 100 students, who generate 119.1384 additional WPUs in average daily membership; the additional WPUs cease at 300 students. For three-year secondary schools, the apex is at 142 students, who produce 114.5469 additional WPUs, which cease at 450 students. A four-year secondary school tops at 171 students at 140.69901 additional WPUs and ends at 550. The six-year secondary school yields 150.4232 at 192 students and ends at 600 students (see Figure 4.2). This may appear to be unnecessary manipulation to approach equity. In a state with small schools it is an important factor in providing an adequate education in small and remote areas.

Density Factors

The sparsity factor has long been accepted and applied in finance parlance and in practice, but allocation of additional funds per pupil to large city school districts is relatively new and has had only limited application. Municipal overburden, large numbers of disadvantaged and exceptional children, the practical problems and additional costs needed for racial integration, and the higher salaries and operational costs resulting from strong union organizations are all a part of the finance problem of large urban areas. The best answer to this complex problem appears to be weighting of pupils. This would guarantee that the state would share in paying for these additional expenses, which are largely beyond the control of the districts involved.

There is an understandable reluctance on the part of people, even many of those who are knowledgeable in school finance matters, to recognize and solve this problem. For many years, the city school districts enjoyed financial and cultural advantages over their rural counterparts. Less reluctance to exploit the property tax, better-prepared teachers and administrators, more cultural opportunities to abet the school program,

TABLE 4.2 Necessarily Existent Small Schools

	Weighted Pupil Units					WPUs/ADM				
ADM	6-Yr. Sec.	4-Yr. Sec.	3-Yr. Sec.	1- or 2-Yr. Sec.	Elem.	6-Yr. Sec.	4-Yr. Sec.	3-Yr. Sec.	1- or 2-Yr. Sec.	Elem.
1	30.0000	30.0000	30.0000	30.0000	30.0000	30.00000	30.00000	30.00000	30.00000	30.00000
2	30.0000	30.0000	30.0000	30.0000	30.0000	15.00000	15.00000	15.00000	15.00000	15.00000
3	30.0000	30.0000	30.0000	30.0000	30.0000	10.00000	10.00000	10.00000	10.00000	10.00000
4	30.0000	30.0000	30.0000	30.0000	30.0000	7.50000	7.50000	7.50000	7.50000	7.50000
5	30.0000	30.0000	30.0000	30.0000	30.0000	6.00000	6.00000	6.00000	6.00000	6.00000
6	30.0000	30.0000	30.0000	30.0000	30.0000	5.00000	5.00000	5.00000	5.00000	5.00000
7	30.0000	30.0000	30.0000	30.0000	30.0000	4.28571	4.28571	4.28571	4.28571	4.28571
8	30.0000	30.0000	30.0000	30.0000	30.0000	3.75000	3.75000	3.75000	3.75000	3.75000
9	30.0000	30.0000	30.0000	30.0000	30.0000	3.33333	3.33333	3.33333	3.33333	3.33333
10	30.0000	30.0000	30.0000	30.0000	30.0000	3.00000	3.00000	3.00000	3.00000	3.00000
20	54.3168	55.0927	59.1034	56.2480	43.0594	2.71584	2.75464	2.95517	2.81240	2.15297
30	70.7077	71.2559	75.7042	74.8348	50.2153	2.35692	2.37520	2.52347	2.49449	1.67384
40	84.1603	84.3296	88.8065	87.2609	53.7624	2.10401	2.10824	2.22016	2.18152	1.34406
50	95.4590	95.1459	99.3597	96.9447	**54.8057**	1.90918	1.90292	1.98719	1.93889	1.09611
100	131.5347	127.9862	128.2964	118.6364	39.2204	1.31535	1.27986	1.28296	1.18636	0.39220
110	135.9124	131.6283	130.8270	**119.1384**	33.6986	1.23557	1.19662	1.18934	1.08308	0.30635
142	145.5437	138.8279	**134.0254**	114.5469	13.4291	1.02496	0.97766	0.94384	0.80667	0.09457
150	147.0642	139.7315	133.8461	112.1111	7.9612	0.98043	0.93154	0.89231	0.74741	0.05307
160	148.5350	140.4302	133.1553	108.4257	**1.0000**	0.92834	0.87769	0.83222	0.67766	0.00625
171	149.6426	**140.6901**	131.8466	103.5998		0.87510	0.82275	0.77103	0.60585	
192	**150.4232**	139.8658	127.9338	92.3232		0.78345	0.72847	0.66632	0.48085	
200	150.3029	139.1414	126.0068	87.3668		0.75151	0.69571	0.63003	0.43683	
250	145.1713	130.3762	109.5269	49.1519		0.58069	0.52150	0.43811	0.19661	
300	133.9787	115.8863	87.2031	**1.0000**		0.44660	0.38629	0.29068	0.00333	
350	118.2511	97.2908	60.8835			0.33786	0.27797	0.17395		
400	99.0728	75.7405	31.8815			0.24768	0.18935	0.07970		
450	77.2547	52.0959	**1.0000**			0.17168	0.11577	0.00222		
500	53.4264	27.0246				0.10685	0.05405			
550	28.0905	**1.0000**				0.05107	0.00182			
600	**1.0000**					0.00167				

Note: For publishing purposes, the increments are in units of tens or more. On the Allyn and Bacon Educational Administration Supersite (www.ablongman.com/edleadership), the entire table in single digits can be found.

Source: Utah State Office of Education (USOE), Finance and Statistics, 2007. www.USOE.K12.ut.us./data.

FIGURE 4.2 Necessarily Existent Small Schools

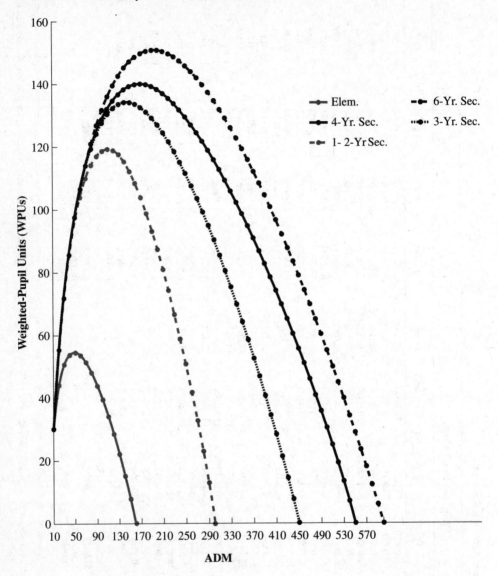

and less citizen resistance to accept change and innovation all added their part to the natural advantage that city schools enjoyed over rural schools. Hence, the city schools provided much of the leadership for improving the curriculum and increasing the monies available for education.

The problem today is not the same and neither is its solution. The cities have been losing many upper- and middle-class citizens to suburbia, at the same time as less affluent and less well-educated citizens move to the cities to obtain employment. The tax base has thus been weakened while the problems of city school systems are increasing. The problems attending migration of people to and from the core of large cities, such as lower taxpaying ability, increased competition for the tax dollar to provide better police protection, greater social problems in the ghettos, and additional services required of government have placed the cities at a financial disadvantage for the first time in the nation's history.

Grade-Level Weighting

Traditionally, weightings for secondary pupils as compared with elementary pupils were widely accepted and implemented. The pupil-teacher ratio was lower, the average salary of teachers was higher, the cost of instructional materials and equipment was higher, and the student activities and out-of-school programs were more extensive and expensive for the secondary level. The validity of the assumption that secondary school pupils should have a weighting when compared with elementary pupils is questioned by some. The chief argument favoring the weighting is that pupil-teacher ratios are lower in secondary schools, thereby increasing the cost per pupil. There are, however, a number of arguments that build a strong rationale against such weighting: (1) There is little difference in salaries between the two levels in most states, since salary schedules make no differentiation. (2) With the emphasis on the use of computer laboratories, instructional media, and improved libraries for elementary schools, the differences in costs have largely disappeared. (3) Activities and field trips are no longer restricted or limited to secondary schools.

Special Education Weightings

Some aspects of the school's program will be more expensive than others—vocational education, compensatory education, and education for students who are physically or mentally disabled, for example. If one accepts the thesis that public education of the kind and extent that will allow all students to develop to their maximum potential should be provided, one must accept the corollary that these pupils or their programs must receive a weighting in the school finance plan. Programs in these areas were stalemated or nonexistent until states and school districts gave them weighting commensurate with their needs. Here again, the weightings may take many forms, such as special appropriations or grants and weightings of the individual students in such programs.

Following is a weighting approach that might be utilized to develop a finance structure for special education students:

Communicative disorder	1.1
Visually impaired	1.6
Other health impaired	1.8
Bilingual	2.0
Intellectually disabled	2.4

Learning disabled	2.4
Severely intellectually disabled	2.6
Hearing impaired—hard of hearing	2.7
Hearing impaired—deaf	2.9
Behavior disordered	2.9
Orthopedically disabled	2.9
Multiple disabilities	3.4

Students of school finance need to be aware of difficulties in defining special education categories and the significant task that legislators have in financing programs adequately. As a safeguard to state treasuries, *prevalence* limits may need to be applied, capping totals that would be available for each category. For example, in the area of learning disabled noted previously, a percentage of the total of student population could be applied at both the state and local district levels. In such a formula, if a percentage of .03 were established in a district of 10,000 students, the state through the legislature would provide funding for up to 300 students who are learning disabled. Although the financing structure is dependent on some type of special education identification, any form of labeling of students is unfortunate. Such designations should be handled with caution.

Teacher Qualification Considerations

Universal high-quality education is being stressed everywhere; it seems to be one of the absorbing concerns of the professional educator at the moment. The number of salary schedules throughout the country strongly implies that increased academic preparation and increased experience in the field improve the teacher and thereby improve the quality of instruction.

The finance problem enunciated by this dilemma can be seen very easily. The foundation program provides money for teachers and other operational costs in terms of the number of weighted pupils to be educated and also for other specialized employees or services. But the teacher requirement places the school district in a precarious position. If, in the employment of professional personnel, the superintendent strives to improve the quality of instruction, he or she will usually recommend hiring the teachers with the most training and experience—with attendant higher salaries. This leaves little or no state-equalized foundation program funds for operational costs. These would then have to be paid with local funds. If, however, a less qualified teacher is employed, funds from the foundation program can be used for other expenses, but this does little to improve the quality of the instructional program. The net result is that the wealthy districts employ the personnel they think will do most to improve the quality of instruction, but the poorer districts are forced to employ those with least demands on the salary schedule, regardless of other factors.

State foundation programs should include weightings that consider the qualifications of the professional employees, so that the state will pay its proportionate share of the cost of employing a better-qualified staff. Otherwise, the onus for improving instruction by employing better-trained and more experienced teachers rests strictly on the local district. If it is to the advantage of the local school district to employ personnel with more training and experience, it is also to the advantage of the state to help see that this is possible financially.

The average teacher index is calculated by placing each teacher's name in the proper training and experience slot on an index salary schedule, adding the index figures for all teachers, and dividing that total by the number of teachers. In the following example, District A (which obviously has a predominantly young faculty with limited teaching experience), with an average index of 1.20, is entitled to an additional 20 percent of its total of 80 teacher-earned classroom units. District B would receive 35 percent of 80 as additional units; and District C would receive 55 percent. The calculations for the foundation program would then be as follows:

Experienced Teacher Weighting Program

District A

1. Minimum program need—$(100 + 16)(15,000)$ = \$1,740,000
2. Local tax effort—$(40,000,000)(0.015)$ = 600,000
3. State allocation—(step 1 minus step 2) = 1,140,000

District B

1. Minimum program need—$(100 + 28)(15,000)$ = \$1,920,000
2. Local tax effort—$(40,000,000)(0.015)$ = 600,000
3. State allocation—(step 1 minus step 2) = 1,320,000

District C

1. Minimum program need—$(100 + 44)(15,000)$ = \$2,160,000
2. Local tax effort—$(40,000,000)(0.015)$ = 600,000
3. State allocation—(step 1 minus step 2) = 1,560,000

District C, with its more experienced and therefore more expensive staff of teachers, would receive considerably more state money than District A or District B. The state thereby shares the additional costs of experienced teachers. Under such an arrangement, no district would be forced to employ inexperienced teachers simply because they cost less. Teachers with greater experience and more extensive training would then be able to compete for positions with current-year college graduates and others with limited experience and training.

The arguments favoring weighting teacher qualifications in the foundation program do not go uncontested. Rural and urban districts and less wealthy districts are often forced, economically, to hire less qualified personnel. To the extent that this is true, such allowances for training and experience may reduce instead of induce equalization. For example, the only means the poor districts would have of competing with wealthier ones in hiring the best-qualified teachers would necessarily come through greater local tax effort. With teacher-qualification weighting, however, the possibility of poor districts increasing the qualifications of their teachers becomes a reality. Further, states may need to consider additional weightings to provide higher salaries for "highly qualified" teachers as defined by the No Child Left Behind law. Concern over what the wealthy districts can do in this matter should be of little consequence, for most of the costs of such improvement in the more or less impoverished districts would come from all the taxpayers of the state rather than only from those who live in the school district.

Miscellaneous Weighting Factors

Many other weighting factors can reasonably be expected in state foundation programs. Notable examples include provision of funds for transportation, administrative and other professional nonteaching personnel, and capital outlay or debt service. The incidence of such factors is low, and there is little state acceptance of these in foundation programs. Though some of these are covered by special grants or appropriations, there is concern that they have a nonequalizing effect that erodes the foundation concept. After the courts have ruled and states have developed an equalization plan, legislators have circumvented the funding formulas by utilizing the categorical approach.

Greater interest and more state support needs to be developed in the weighting concept. Two areas that could receive immediate attention for stronger and more equalized support are capital outlay and debt service expenditures.

Summary

In this century, various patterns of financing education are emerging. Full state funding of public education has been advocated by some writers for several years. Such a plan raises some important questions about increased state control and the problem of financing districts that desire to maintain special higher-cost programs.

District power equalization involves the principle of state-local partnership, where each local district mill levy would produce the same number of dollars of revenue per mill per weighted student (state and local) in every district. Its main disadvantage is the fear that such a principle might open the doors of the state treasury.

Property reassessment upward does not necessarily increase the total revenues made available to school districts. Typically, it increases the local district's share and decreases the state's share of funds—provided the program includes some form of equalization.

The use of weightings is increasing in school finance formulas. Special-interest groups have had an impact, and legislators have circumvented equalization plans by adding categorical programs to basic finance programs. The use of weighted pupils is gradually replacing the use of the actual number of pupils in determining the financial needs of a school district. Sparsity and density factors are also being used more extensively in determining the budgetary needs of local education agencies. States will continue to refine and expand weighting factors in school finance programs.

ASSIGNMENT PROJECTS

1. Provide a definition for each of the following terms: *full state funding, nearly full state funding, district power equalization, equalized percentage matching, sparsity, density, weighting factor, WPU, ADM, ADA.*
2. Using the following information about two school districts, solve the indicated problems.

District	Assessed Valuation	Weighted Pupil Unit
A	$100,000,000	2,000
B	$ 45,000,000	900

Foundation Program		Board Leeway	Voted Leeway
State Guarantee	$1,800/WPU	$1,000/WPU	$400/WPU
Required Levy	20 Mills	$1.40/$100 AV	$10/$1,000 AV

	Need (in $) a	Local Effort b	State Allocation c	Total b + c
District A				
Foundation Program	$_____	$_____	$_____	$_____
Board Leeway	$_____	$_____	$_____	$_____
Voted Leeway	$_____	$_____	$_____	$_____
Total All Three Programs	$_____	$_____	$_____	$_____
District B				
Foundation Program	$_____	$_____	$_____	$_____
Board Leeway	$_____	$_____	$_____	$_____
Voted Leeway	$_____	$_____	$_____	$_____
Total All Three Programs	$_____	$_____	$_____	$_____

Power Equalization

3. From the previous problem, calculate the following:

	District A	District B
Ratio of state revenue to local revenue (Foundation program)	_____:_____	_____:_____

Under the power equalization principle, how much money would the state provide for each of these districts using all three programs?

District A—$_____ state money

District B—$_____ state money

Total WPU value from
all sources

District A—$_____

District B—$_____

Computer simulations and questions, research exercises, and website addresses relevant to this chapter can be found at

www.ablongman.com/edleadership

SELECTED READINGS

Benson, Charles S., Paul M. Goldfinger, E. Gareth Hoach-lander, and Jessica S. Pers. *Planning for Educational Reform: Financial and Social Alternatives.* New York: Dodd, Mead, 1974.

Berne, Robert, and Lawrence O. Picus. *Outcome Equity in Education.* Thousands Oaks, CA: Corwin Press, 1994.

Carnegie Forum on Education and the Economy. *A Nation Preparing Teachers for the 21st Century.* Washington, DC: Carnegie Forum on Education and the Economy, 1990.

Chambers, Jay, Thomas Parrish, and Cassanddra Guarino, eds. *Funding Special Education.* Thousand Oaks, CA: Corwin Press, 1999.

Chubb, J. E., and T. M. Moe. *Politics, Markets, and America's Schools.* Washington, DC: Brookings Institution, 1990.

Cubberley, Ellwood P. *School Funds and Their Apportionment.* New York: Teachers College, Columbia University, 1906.

Cubberly, Ellwood P. *The History of Education.* Boston: Houghton Mifflin, 1920.

Hartman, William T., and William Lloyd Boyd. *Resource Allocation and Productivity in Education: Theory and Practice.* Westport, CT: Greenwood, 1998.

Honeyman, D. S., D.C. Thompson, and R. C. Wood. *Financing Rural and Small Schools: Issues of Adequacy and Equity.* Gainesville: University of Florida Press, 1989.

Johns, Roe L., and Edgar L. Morphet. *The Economics and Financing of Education,* 2nd ed. Englewood Cliffs, NJ: Prentice-Hall, 1969.

Kozol, Jonathon. *Savage Inequalities.* New York: Harper Perennial, 1991.

Mueller, Van D., and Mary P. McKeown. *The Fiscal, Legal and Political Aspects of Elementary and Secondary Education. Sixth Annual Yearbook of the American Education Finance Association.* Cambridge, MA: Ballinger, 1986.

Strayer, George D., and Robert M. Haig. *The Financing of Education in the State of New York.* New York: Macmillan, 1923.

Thomas, Gloria Jean, David J. Sperry, and F. Del Wasden. *The Law and Teacher Employment.* New York: West Publishing, 1991.

Updegraff, Harlan. *Rural School Survey of New York State: Financial Support.* Ithaca, NY: Author, 1922.

ENDNOTES

1. www.edweek.org/context/topics/issuespage
   .cfm?id=22.
2. Ellwood P. Cubberley, *School Funds and Their Apportionment* (New York: Teachers College, Columbia University, 1906), p. 17.
3. Arvid J. Burke, "Financing of Elementary and Secondary Schools," in Warren E. Gauerke and Jack A. Childress, eds., *Theory and Practice of School Finance* (Chicago: Rand McNally, 1967), p. 127.
4. Paul R. Mort and Walter C. Reusser, *Public School Finance,* 2nd ed. (New York: McGraw-Hill, 1951), p. 491.
5. Gerald R. Bass, "Isolation/Sparsity," *Journal of Education Finance,* Fall 1990, p. 180.

5 Sources of Revenue

Equal opportunity for quality schools requires enhanced, stable and adequate revenue streams particularly for the many children in poverty. This lack of funding for those who need it most is a moral imperative.

—Deborah Verstegen, 2007

Profits are realized only in the private sector of the economy. Since the public sector requires financial resources to perform its various functions and provide necessary services for society, some satisfactory system of diverting funds from the competitive and profit-making sector to public institutions must be arranged. The most successful system yet devised for that purpose is taxation. By such a process, resources are transferred with relatively little difficulty from where they are produced to where they are needed. Although the tax system in the United States has its critics and its areas of unfairness, it does provide for the orderly transfer of private monies to public purposes.

Economists often refer to the affluence of the private economy, but similar references to the financial status of the public sector are seldom made. The latter is always dependent on the former for its degree of affluence, and even its survival. Periodically, people in the private sector indicate their dissatisfaction with the performance or the products of public institutions and withdraw a portion or all of their financial support from the "offenders." Because of taxpayer revolts against taxes, court or legislative action, or even voter indifference, the financial well-being of public institutions is determined by the attitude of those who provide its financial support through a system of taxation.

The Taxation System

The term *tax* serves as a firm reminder to people that they have been given personal and mandatory responsibility to divert a certain amount of their wealth—past, present, or future—to become part of the revenue required by institutions and units of government performing public services. A direct relation may or may not exist between the amount of tax paid and observable benefits to the individual taxpayer.

Taxes are a function of three variables: (1) the tax base (value of the objects or items to be taxed); (2) the assessment practices being followed (the percentage of market value applied to the object being taxed); and (3) the tax levy (the rate applied to the assessed value of an object or item to determine the amount of tax obligation). Tax rates mean little until they are related to assessment practices and values or compared with them. When comparing taxes and tax effort where there are differing assessment practices, one must convert assessed value into market or sale value of the property in question.

A county in Pennsylvania draws attention to the misleading practice of determining a true tax effort. Reassessments had not occurred for over 50 years and new homeowners were paying an exorbitantly high percentage of property tax. By court order the county was mandated to upgrade the assessments and change the tax rate. At the time, homes were assessed at 3.3 percent of market value. To raise needed revenue, school districts coped by imposing extremely high tax rates, such as $450 per $1,000, which raised about $3,000 on a $200,000 home with an assessed value of only $6,600 ($200,000 × .033 = $6,600 ÷ 1000 = 6.6 × $450 = tax rate = $2,970). New assessments were more balanced, basing them on 100 percent of market value and a rate of $15.00 per $1,000, raising $3,000 on a $200,000 home ($200,000 ÷ 1,000 = 200 × $15.00 = $3,000). This presents a more realistic picture of the community—one with a reasonable tax base in an affluent area.[1]

The tax system, even though it has existed and operated for a long time in each state, does not provide an easy answer to the question of how much or what percentage of government revenue should be allotted to each of the institutions or agencies it sponsors. What formula or what device should be used to allocate private funds to the publicly sponsored organizations in order to bring maximum benefits to society? No one claims to have found the answer to this question.

Although the public sector obtains most of the revenue it uses by taxation, several other minor sources are used to supplement tax funds. The sale of government services or products, the sale of government-owned property—including land and such other assets as surplus equipment (licenses, fines, forfeitures, incomes from investment, special fees, gifts, business partnerships, and transfer funds from other levels and agencies of government)—are among the other sources of such funds.

Education—Financed by Government

Education is a beneficial service (nonmaterial good) that should be made available to all eligible citizens of a country regardless of their degree of affluence. Under such a system, it is necessary for education to be financed by government with its capability of collecting resources from the private sector and distributing them equitably among institutions in the public sector. In spite of the fact that education produces externalities and large-scale spillovers that benefit the larger society, historically, it has been financed largely at the local school district level. In the opinion of many, this fact creates one of the more difficult problems with which educators must concern themselves—providing equitable school programs and creating equitable tax burdens within the framework of the property tax system.

Rate Bills Are Obsolete

Early in its history, the United States proved to the satisfaction of its citizens that rate bills (the requirement that each pupil pay a fee), tuition charges, and the like would not provide universal and equal education for its children and youths. Discrimination against the poor and against large families destroyed the supporting philosophy for this method of financing education. The only defensible alternative was the development of a tax system with a supporting rationale. It was slow in its implementation; states gradually adopted their own unique systems of taxation. Although these were satisfactory for a long period of time, local dependence on property taxes to the omission of other forms of taxation has been widely criticized.

Taxes Are Often Unpopular

It has been said that the only good tax is the one paid by someone else. Dislike for paying taxes that increase year after year is a normal reaction for people for many reasons: (1) If the tax rate is high, paying taxes may seriously curtail other activities and reduce the quantity and quality of other economic goods and services then available to the taxpayer. (2) The complex society of interrelated institutions makes it increasingly more difficult for a taxpayer to see and understand the personal benefits resulting from tax dollars. (3) The increased services that are required as the population increases and social institutions become more complex are not understood or favored by many people. (4) If tax rates get too high, individual assets decrease. There is a point when taxes decrease revenue because it seems futile to earn more, as too much is taken in taxes. (5) When increased taxes are being considered, much misleading information concerning taxation is often issued by those who favor increased taxes as well as by those who oppose them. (6) The average taxpayer thinks of the "cost" of education rather than the "investment" in human capital that results from taxation for that purpose.

Characteristics of a Good Tax System

Most school finance and tax authorities agree on many of the most important guidelines that should be followed in establishing or evaluating a good tax system. It is extremely difficult to achieve complete or even satisfactory implementation of these general principles, however. Consequently, no taxing unit—local, state, or federal—has yet produced a taxation program that meets universal acceptance by all its taxpaying clientele. Nonetheless, certain basic principles and theories of taxation are generally accepted as appropriate characteristics of a viable tax system at any level of government.

Tax Systems Should Be Coordinated

Even though there is usually very little planned coordination in the tax programs of the three levels of government, none of the three can be evaluated realistically without simultaneous consideration of the other two. Individuals tend to measure their tax "burden" by the total taxes they are required to pay rather than those they are required to pay to any one level of government. It is important, then, that the total number of tax systems operable in any community or geographic unit be coordinated and interrelated in a defensible and balanced program. Any duplication of taxation structure should be minimal. Equity and balance should exist among the various forms of taxes that are an integral part of the total system.

All Citizens Owe Taxes

The benefits of government services are shared by all the nation's citizens in varying degrees, depending on their needs. Protection from fire and acts of violence, and also many other aspects of the police power exercised by government, are the inherent right of all individuals, businesses, and other organizations. Financial support for these services is therefore required from all who receive the benefits or who stand to receive them.

A good tax system provides that every person and every business be required to pay some tax to government. It is a distinct violation of good taxation theory to use tax laws that have gaping loopholes whereby many citizens or businesses can escape paying their share of the tax burden. Such unfair exclusions make those who contribute pay more than their fair share of the costs of government services.

Justice and Economic Neutrality

As a matter of simple fairness, a good tax system distributes the burden it creates among all its citizens in an equitable manner. Admittedly, what is equitable is often a question of the frame of reference of the person or organization making the determination. Generally, however, it can be shown that a reasonable progressive income tax is the most equitable single tax. Income is the best of all the measures of taxpaying ability; progressive tax rates make the tax fair, for even though higher incomes require higher taxes, the burden to the taxpayer is not greater. In spite of the advantages of the income tax, no economist or tax authority would favor using it to the exclusion of all others. A single tax, regardless of its basic fairness, can never be fair for all citizens of a taxing unit. Taxation theory requires diversification with a broad tax base—such as income, sales, and property—so that an individual's "escape" from a particular kind of tax does not mean complete exemption from paying a tax of any kind.

Diversification of taxes is important, but simplicity is equally necessary in any good tax system. Taxpayers cannot be expected to support intricate and complicated tax laws they cannot understand. In theory, taxpayers should be able to calculate their own taxes with a minimum of help or instruction.

The maintenance of economic neutrality among taxpayers must not be disturbed by patterns of taxation. Citizens and business should be left in the same relative position to one another after paying taxes as they were before. Persons with greater income before taxes are paid should still have greater unspent income after taxes are deducted than those with lower incomes. It is important that special taxes that affect certain individuals or businesses be minimized in comparison with broadly based taxes.

Adequacy of Yield

Maintenance of the extensive services of government requires large amounts of tax revenue. It is therefore important that taxes be applied to productive sources. There is no point in complicating the system by the addition of taxes that have little individual potential for yielding revenue in substantial amounts. Nuisance taxes that provide only minimum revenue should be avoided as much as possible in the taxing system of any level of government.

Progressive versus Regressive Taxes

The proportional, progressive, and regressive features of taxes should be considered in devising or improving a tax system. Taxes should involve, at best, the defensible characteristic of being progressive; at worst, they should be proportional. Ideally, they should never be regressive, but in practice they often contain regressive features. All taxing devices should be constructed to reduce their regressive features as much as possible. High incomes should never pay lower rates than lower incomes, if it is assumed that the taxing system should be based on the ability-to-pay principle.

Tax Erosion Should Be Minimized

Tax erosion possibilities and provisions should be minimized or eliminated for every tax. For example, the deserving veteran and the worthy widow or homesteader may well deserve pecuniary benefits from government, but they should be provided by government in some form other than exclusion from paying property taxes. Erosion of the tax base, regardless of the worthiness of the cause, entails more problems than it solves. Special pleadings and other avenues of escape from paying taxes should be reduced to a more reasonable base by tighter laws and better enforcement practices. Estimates by some tax authorities of the amount of such tax base erosion have amounted to as high as one-fourth of the total real property value in the United States. The effect of such tax losses on schools and other government institutions that depend on tax revenues for their operation is obviously great.

A tax system should avoid or minimize preferential tax treatment sometimes offered to attract individuals or businesses to a state or community. Obviously, the tax system should not be oppressive to the point where it discourages new industry.

Taxpayer Convenience Is Important

It is generally believed that taxes should be direct rather than indirect. Taxpayers should know when they are paying a tax and should be able to do so as conveniently as possible. Paying hidden or indirect taxes, standing in long lines to pay taxes, and hearing about others who have escaped similar tax payments are examples of practices that demoralize many otherwise conscientious taxpayers. Fairness and courtesy in collecting taxes and in dealing with tax problems must characterize any successful taxation structure.

Collection Costs Should Be Low

To the extent possible, the taxes that are used should have a relatively low collection and administrative cost. Government institutions are interested in the amount of net revenue available to them rather than the gross amount of dollars collected. For example, the high cost of locating, assessing, and eventually collecting personal property taxes has been such that most of the states have either minimized or eliminated this potentially excellent source of tax revenue except in cases where the personal property can be easily identified. An example of identifiable personal property are vehicles and boats. In order for them to be used, they must be licensed. Before licensure, a personal property tax must be paid. Such a system provides considerable revenue to government.

Taxes and Services Should Be Visible

A common complaint of taxpayers is that they cannot see what value they are receiving for the taxes they pay. Too often, they appear to take the services of government for granted. It is a proper function of government and its institutions to make taxpayers aware that their payments are contributing to the important services of government that they have demanded. Theoretically, this makes them demand fewer of such services and increases their demand for operational efficiency.

Tax Shifting Should Be Minimized

The tax system of any unit of government should be such that tax-shifting possibilities are minimized. To the casual observer, it would seem that taxes are paid by the person on whom they are imposed and that it would be an easy matter to add taxes on any group in society or drop them. This would mean that if property owners or wage earners were not being taxed to their fair share of the burdens of government services, the correction could be made by additional taxes on property in the first case or by increased income taxes for the wage earners.

Shifting taxes to the point that the impact of a tax (point of tax imposition) is different from the incidence of that tax (person who finally pays the tax) makes taxation extremely delicate and difficult to regulate. In far too many instances, it may result in overtaxation of some groups and undertaxation of those groups who can successfully shift some or all of their tax burdens to others.

Earmarked Taxes Should Be Minimized

Dedicating tax revenues to a particular purpose should be avoided as much as possible. Such earmarking makes for too much rigidity in the budget practices of the receiving institution. Under such regulations, the minimum expenditure tends to become the maximum, thus depriving administrative boards of the flexibility so necessary in publicly controlled organizations. On the other hand, designating the use of some taxes based on the benefit principle is justifiable, as when a gasoline or motor fuels tax is earmarked for the maintenance of streets and highways.

Tax Structure Should Avoid Restrictions

Taxes sometimes have effects that may seriously change the economic practices of the individuals who pay them. The intent of taxation is to divert private funds into the public sector to produce necessary goods and services; it is not its purpose to alter the behavioral patterns of taxpayers.

Excessive taxes on certain commodities or services may destroy producers' competitive potential in the market or reduce their economic productivity. This violates a fundamental concept of taxation, for the tax on a desirable economic good should never be such that its more favored competitor has free access to a noncompetitive market.

The taxing pattern should not unduly restrict an individual in determining economic behavior in earning a living or in choosing the goods or services desired to satisfy needs or wants. Nor should the taxing system create a desire to restrict production of economic goods and services by individuals or organizations. In short, the taxing pattern should have the least possible negative effect on the living style of its contributors and the greatest possible positive effect in developing and achieving the goals of the agencies and institutions it is constructed to serve.

Criteria for Evaluating Tax Structure

McCann and Delon emphasized certain criteria for evaluating a tax system and the governmental structure necessary to administer it.[2] The characteristics they rated important in any tax system include efficiency, equity, adequacy, and adaptability. By *efficiency,* they referred to the structure for fiscal administration, which is best when operated with the least economic and social costs and the highest order of services for the money spent. They used the term *equity* to mean that the structure should provide the highest degree of fairness in the treatment of the individual citizen. The criterion of *adequacy* indicates that the system ought to provide enough funds to support the level of public service that is adopted for the particular government agency in question. By *adaptability,* they reasoned that any system that provides for the administration of a program of school finance ought to be adaptable to (1) changing economic conditions, (2) modified social demands for education, and (3) significant changes in education.

Taxpayers themselves are constantly evaluating the tax system to which they are responsible. They do not usually formally rate all the individual segments of the structure, but they have a practical way of making their opinions known concerning the total tax pattern. School administrators know all too well what will happen to their appeals for increased taxes when the public feels that taxes are already high enough. Citizen evaluation of the taxes required for government services often results in lost elections for bond and even current expenditure levy questions. Taxation cannot be pushed to a point beyond the limit of taxpayer acceptance. Benson referred to the "normal" as well as the "absolute" limits of taxation in the following:

> During any period of relative stability in a society, certain "normal" levels of taxation are extremely difficult to breach. Such conventional levels of taxation should never be confused with absolute limits. For any major tax instrument an absolute limit to yield does not in the practical sense exist. In a major social upheaval, such as a war, the conventional limits of

taxation are likely to be discarded. After the period of upheaval has passed, the volume of nonemergency public services is more likely to expand and absorb the revenue than are tax rates to fall to their former levels.[3]

Taxes for Education

Some of the principal taxes used to transfer funds to the public sector include property, personal income, corporation income, sales, severance, and sumptuary taxes. Most of these are used to some degree in financing education in all of the 50 states. Others that are being considered but have not yet received general acceptance include site-value and value-added taxes. In many states, one popular revenue source that has the effect of transferring funds to the public sector is a lottery. Of course, there is continuing debate as to whether the concept is truly a tax or not. Many states still use the property tax and the sales tax as their most reliable and lucrative sources of revenue.

Property Tax

A property (*ad valorem*) tax is levied against the owner of real or personal property. *Real property* is not readily movable; it includes land, buildings, and improvements. It is usually classified as residential, industrial, agricultural, commercial, or unused (vacant). *Personal property* is movable; it consists of tangibles—such as machinery, livestock, crops, automobiles, and recreational vehicles—or intangibles—such as money, stocks, and bonds.

Property taxes were the first kind of school taxes, and they still constitute almost the complete local tax revenue for schools. Property tax rates are usually expressed in mills per dollar of assessed valuation or dollars per hundred dollars of assessed valuation, though some states use a *tax rate* on market value. Facility in changing or interpreting different ways of stating tax rates is a valuable skill for anyone interested in comparing district budgets and taxing procedures in different states.

Historical Use

The states have based their local school revenue systems on a property tax. This policy seems to have been justified in its early history, for property ownership was considered to be a good measure of the wealth of people—especially before the advent of industrialization. For a long time, the property tax seemed to be reasonably satisfactory, and severe critics of it were relatively few. The property tax at the local level has proved to be a good and reliable source of revenue for operating schools and providing many other services of government.

The following characteristics are generally accepted as desirable traits of the property tax:

- Operates as a direct tax, with most people understanding its purpose
- Is easily collected by the regular machinery of state and county government

- Is regulated and controlled by local boards of education according to the provisions of state law
- Is almost impossible to avoid paying
- Is highly productive—mainstay of local governments for generations
- Is highly visible—provides direct linkage between services provided by local government and the cost of those services

Assessment Practices

Widespread unfairness exists in the assessment practices and in the adequacy of property tax administration in the various states. Unequal assessment practices are often found among the parcels of property within any one school district. It may be argued that such a condition simply means that a higher tax rate must be used to get the desired amount of revenue, but such an argument is of little value because the general public resists increased tax levy rates and state laws often prohibit them. Thus, a school board often finds itself powerless to overcome the revenue problems caused by underassessment.

The application of the *foundation program* concept of allocating state funds to local districts has created another problem involving underassessment. Fractional assessment was originally only a problem of inadequate revenue to the district concerned. Now, however, in financing the foundation program, underassessment becomes an advantage to that district because the decreased revenue from its own property taxation will be offset by the addition of an equal increase in state funds. This places a premium on underassessment and certainly is not fair to other districts that are fully assessed.

Assessment practices vary widely. Some states assess real property according to its classification or type, and some assess personal property at a different rate from real property. Tax authorities argue for assessment of property at 100 percent of its market value. It is difficult for assessors to keep assessment increases in line with changes in market value.

Present problems of property assessment are largely the result of the predominantly political system under which taxation laws have been made and administered. Elected county, town, or township assessors, often not particularly well qualified for their responsibilities, face the difficult problems of raising assessments because of inflation or actual improvements in the property, keeping assessments fair and equitable among all property owners, deciding on the relative worth of different kinds of property, and other equally difficult problems. Assessors, under this obsolete system of tax administration, have to weigh the value of fairness and equity against their desire to be reelected to their positions. Some states have developed strong tax commissions in an attempt to alleviate this problem. To develop statewide consistency using objective criteria, officials of state tax commissions audit various assessor practices. In Utah, for instance, the state is divided into five regions. Every five years, one region is scheduled to be evaluated—usually resulting in an increase of the assessed value of property and a possible increase in taxes paid or, more probably, a lowering of the tax levy. Through this procedure, more professional assessments are made.

In addition to the problem of fractional assessment, determining whether to use classified property assessments still remains in question. Should property used for one purpose be assessed differently from property used for another purpose? If so, how should relative rates be determined? What should be the relative assessment value placed on residential property as compared with income property? What is the proper relation of assessment to be applied to a corner business lot as compared to a similar lot in the middle of the block? These and many other unresolved assessment problems make the property tax system less equitable than would be expected.

Unfairness of the Property Tax

Even though the property tax has served the schools well for many years, it has always been under some criticism. Some features that were generally accepted as advantages early in its existence now seem to have changed to disadvantages. It is not the fair or equitable measure of taxpaying ability that it was years ago. People may now be inclined to invest their surplus earnings in personal property, some of which can escape taxation. The owner of land and buildings fares less well than a counterpart who puts wealth into more intangible assets that are less likely to be included in the normal taxation process. This makes the property tax somewhat regressive—which counters the ability-to-pay principle on which sound tax systems for financing education are based. Some states are reducing regressivity by using tax credit plans that provide property tax relief to low-income families, particularly to elderly people.

The finance problems encountered by most urban centers illustrate some of the deficiencies of the property tax. The typical city's tax base is eroded to a serious degree by the departure of the middle class, by pressure for desegregation, by old industries leaving and new ones becoming reluctant to locate there, and by the high percentage of tax-exempt property—the property of government, churches, schools, and welfare organizations. To complicate the condition further, cities have higher percentages of high-cost students to educate—disabled, disadvantaged, and minorities. They suffer, too, from pressures for higher salaries by strong unions, higher costs for building sites and construction, and higher costs for noneducational services, commonly referred to as *municipal overburden.*

The property tax is unfair to the person who must pay taxes on the full value of property of which he or she does not have complete ownership. This disparity is shown in a simple example. A and B both have tax responsibility for $50,000 worth of property, for which they each owe $2,000 in taxes. A owns the property; B is purchasing the property and has only $10,000 of equity in it. A pays only 4 percent of property wealth in taxes, whereas B pays 20 percent of equity in taxes. If wealth instead of property were the base of the tax, B would owe only $400 in taxes as compared to the $2,000 owed by A.

Other Criticisms of the Property Tax

Another serious defect of the property tax system arises from the limitations that states sometimes place on it. This has been achieved by state-imposed tax rate restrictions—legislated to protect beleaguered taxpayers. Many school districts are still struggling to raise adequate local revenues with state limitations on tax levies. In some states, the state legislature has imposed a tax rate limit, which can be increased to a higher limit only by a favorable vote of the people in the district. The practical effect is that few school districts are able to exceed the limit under which the school board is required to operate. Since all taxes are paid from income, the critics of the property tax and other taxes wonder why there should be any other tax than one on income. The local school board, however, is virtually powerless to control an income tax, but a property tax is comparatively easy for it to administer. Its use as a source of local revenue for schools has been alternately praised and condemned.

The condemnation of the property tax has reached new heights as a result of court decisions in some states, adverse opinions of the tax by many governmental leaders, the negative vote of people in referenda in some states, and actions by state legislators. Michigan, for example, abolished the property tax without knowing how schools were to be funded until future legislative sessions. The revolt has been directed particularly against the abuses and unfairness of the property tax. Described by many as the most oppressive and inequitable tax of all, it has lost much of its traditional popularity as a source of revenue for schools. Many segments of society—taxpayers, educators, and economists—have added their protests to its use and particularly to its extension.

Although the courts have not declared the property tax unconstitutional, they have said that disparities and inequalities exist. Thus, the structure of school finance laws is changing, and the years ahead are likely to see other modifications in the use and administration of the property tax.

Circuit Breakers

A plan used to protect certain classes of individuals from excessive property tax burden is the *circuit breaker.* It is designed to assure that the property taxes of people with low incomes will not exceed a stated portion or percentage of their annual income, regardless of the value of their property or the tax in effect in their taxing unit.

Circuit breaker plans in the various states are somewhat complicated. They may include relief for persons age 65 years and older, widows and widowers, and persons with limited income. The income of an individual may be the basis for determining tax relief, whereas some states require the total income of all persons living at a residence to determine qualification for the benefit.

To demonstrate a simplified illustration of the circuit breaker principle, a person with an annual taxable income of $15,000 who owns property with a market value of $120,000 may be assessed a tax of $625. Through a circuit breaker, the value of the property may be reduced, or the tax burden may be cut by a percentage. By decreasing the tax 40 percent, the required payment would be $375, resulting in a $250 savings.

So that local property taxes are not eroded, which would affect school revenues, taxpayers may pay their taxes to the local entity and be reimbursed through the state. Or, in some cases, the county may lower the tax and seek reimbursement from the state. As the legislature provides the legislation for the circuit breaker, the state becomes responsible for providing the lost revenue to the local taxing agency, rather than shifting the burden to the local entity (in the case of this text, the local schools).

Determination of "income" and how to apply the circuit breaker principle to welfare recipients and renters is a difficult problem for states that use this method of providing property tax relief.

Personal Property Taxes

The real property tax with all its objectionable features remains the primary source of the local school finance structure, but the personal property tax is an enigma in local tax theory and practice. On the surface, the personal property tax has many attractive characteristics and is used quite successfully in some states.

Today, much of the wealth of people is invested in personal property holdings such as stocks, bonds, mutual funds, and savings accounts. This vast pool of wealth is a potentially lucrative source of revenue to help defray the costs of government, but the problem of assessing such property and recording it on the proper tax rolls has not been solved. Lack of information or evidence of ownership and almost complete reliance on owners to report the extent of their personal property assets—as well as ideological differences, that such a tax amounts to double taxation on what one has already earned—have served to defeat this form of taxation. This measure of the wealth and taxpaying ability of people is therefore minimized as a source of public school or other government revenue.

Income Tax

The personal income tax is usually a progressive tax levied on the income of a person received during the period of one year. It is the basis of the federal financial structure, but it is also used to a lesser degree by nearly all of the states. The relationship of income taxation and the ability-to-pay principle was pointed out by the National Education Association in the following:

> Long after Adam Smith's time, there developed in economics the principle that as more and more of any good is purchased, its utility to the consumer becomes less and less. The first pair of shoes, for example, is a necessity, the second very important, the third important, the fourth useful perhaps, and the fifth, sixth, and the like, successively less desirable. Application of this theory proved useful in explaining the fact that as the supply of a commodity increases, the price at which it is sold decreases. Then, as often happens, this principle, formulated for use in one area of human thought, was extended to others. It came to be believed that the law of declining utility also applied to money. Once that was accepted, the extension to taxation was thought to be clear. The rate, it was said, should increase in some ratio to the declining utility of the dollars of increased income. Thus the theory of ability to pay was born.[4]

Income taxes should include taxes on personal and on corporation incomes. The rationale justifying taxes on corporations is that otherwise individuals and organizations would incorporate to avoid taxation. "Corporation income taxation has been justified on the ability to pay, privilege or benefit, cost of service, state partnership, and control theories."[5] It is used in nearly all the states. It is responsive to economic and income changes, but it is sometimes complex in form and difficult to administer.

The real value of the personal income tax (and by implication the corporate tax as well) was emphasized in the following: "A personal income tax is the essential added ingredient to erase the regressive effects of property and sales taxes. Moreover, the income tax is far more sensitive to economic growth than are property or sales taxes and therefore can help solve the state-local fiscal crisis."[6]

There is a continual cry for a revamping and overhaul of income tax laws at both the national and state levels. Kotlikoff described the dilemma:

> We seemingly cannot decide whether our taxes are too high or too low, too progressive or too regressive, too replete with loopholes or too devoid of incentives. In addition, we seem unable to make up our minds whom—business or individuals—or what—income or consumption—we want to tax. And we cannot decide whether to tax all components of a given tax base, such as income from dividends and income from capital gains, at the same rate.[7]

Sales Tax

A sales tax is a levy imposed on the sale value of certain goods and services. It is generally imposed at the retail operation, rather than the wholesale. Sales tax rates are usually at the same level for all transactions, but if food and other necessities are subject to a sales tax, the tax becomes regressive. The sales tax is used most often at the state level of government, although it is sometimes used at the county and city levels. It produces large amounts of revenue, but its use without exclusion of necessary goods and services tends to overburden poor families.

The sales tax could become a fairer and more effective tax with certain improvements: (1) Auditors need to be sufficient in number and well trained, since they have much to do with the honesty and the efficiency of administration of the tax. (2) There should be strict enforcement by the states of tax collections and reporting. (3) Exemptions should be restricted to items of food and necessities. (4) A service or use tax should be included. (5) Loopholes in taxes on goods purchased in other states and on casual sales between individuals (such as on used cars) should be eliminated. (6) Tax collection should be simplified in those states that provide for more than one agency of government to collect tax revenues.

The value of the sales tax as a source of state revenue is indicated in the following:

> The general sales tax is the largest single state tax source, accounting for almost one-third of all state tax revenue. It is a broad-based tax and fairly sensitive to economic growth. But in one respect it is too broad based, for in most states it taxes food. Since low-income families spend a larger proportion of their budget on food than do high-income families, the tax on food introduces a strong element of regressivity.[8]

With the growth of e-commerce, the sales tax may be altered extensively. The federal government has passed legislation exempting such items sold over the Internet from sales tax. The position of those who favor this exemption maintain that since the

Internet is the future, it should not be burdened with taxation. They also maintain that the Internet is now overtaxed. The federal government presently claims an excise tax on "telecommunication services," and some state and local governments impose a fee and tax on Internet providers. The Supreme Court ruled that states cannot impose sales tax on some products from out-of-state catalog and mail-order houses. Internet providers have taken the position that this prohibition has been passed on to them.

Those who favor taxing sales on the Internet stress that it is unfair for businesses in a community to be required to pay sales tax while those who sell the same items over the Internet are exempted from paying sales tax. Opponents of the exemption declare that the affluent may have greater access to Internet purchases, making e-commerce regressive in nature. Some argue that it may be the end of Main Street businesses or that these businesses will overwhelm state legislatures with a plea to "level the playing field" by enacting legislation that would create a confrontation between the statutes of the states and federal legislation that create the exemption. Senate Bill 150—Internet Tax Non-discrimination Act of 2003—extended the legislation by making "permanent the moratorium on taxes on Internet access and multiple and discriminatory taxes on electronic commerce imposed by the Internet Tax Freedom Act."[9]

There is great diversity in the approach states take in applying sales tax to various commodities and the percent they charge. Not only is there an inconsistency between states, but amounts charged may vary in counties and cities within a state. In an attempt to rectify this position, legislative representatives in 42 states and the District of Columbia (other states are expected to join) have created a consortium to design plans to "simplify and modernize sales and use tax collection and administration," define "taxable goods," and determine ways that states may collect sales tax on phone orders, catalog sales, and Internet purchases.[10] The project originally proposed that "sellers who do not have a presence or 'nexus' are not required to collect sales and use taxes."[11] That stance was modified in 2005 with the caveat that sellers who do not have a presence or nexus "are not required to collect sales and use taxes unless Congress chooses to require collection from all sellers *for all types of commerce.*"[12] The goal of the Streamlined Sales Tax Project is to provide states with a tax system that has these key features:

- Uniform definitions within tax laws
- Rate simplification
- State-level tax administration of all state and local sales and use taxes
- Uniform sourcing rules
- Simplified exemption administration for use- and entity-based exemptions
- Uniform audit procedures
- State funding of the system

State legislators must approve the various sections of the plan. In 2006, 41 of the states "moved forward and enacted all or part of the conforming legislation"[13] The potential revenue from e-commerce sales is great. One study estimates that the loss in 2006 was $45.2 billion, and projected that in 2011 it could reach $55 billion *on Internet sales alone.*[14] These revenue losses have a major impact on many state budgets and in turn local education agencies.

Sumptuary Tax

A *sumptuary tax* is sometimes imposed by government, with the primary purpose of helping to regulate or control a certain activity or practice not deemed to be in the public interest. In this kind of tax, the collection of revenue is only a secondary purpose of the tax. For that reason, this revenue is usually comparatively small, and there is little room for expansion or extension of the tax. Such taxes provide a division of interest, as indicated by Corbally:

> In general, *sumptuary taxation* receives little support from tax theorists. The fact that sumptuary taxes do, in fact, produce revenue often leads to a situation in which a governmental unit in need of funds is tacitly encouraging an activity which tax legislation sought to discourage. Liquor taxes, for example, have the intent of "punishing" the user of an "immoral" commodity and yet the revenue from these taxes often becomes such an important source of funds that a government unit establishes attractive establishments for the retail sale of the heavily taxed product.[15]

The last decade saw the tobacco industry involved in several lawsuits, with individuals winning large sums of money with claims that smoking caused illness and death. Various states have participated in lawsuits that have caused the tobacco companies to pay large compensation for health care costs. In Maryland, the legislature allotted money to purchase textbooks for students in private schools from their $4.4 billion share of the cigarette settlement. Demonstrating the sumptuary principle, federal taxes have been increased on tobacco products with the intent of paying for programs that warn the young, in particular, of the harmful effects of using tobacco products.

Taxing goods and services that are generally held to be against the public interest is usually justifiable, but it can be overdone. Sumptuary taxes should be used with caution and wisdom, to minimize the negative effects of taxing any particular segment of society for the benefit of another. Such controversial forms of taxation become highly discriminatory if used too extensively. Governmental control of socially unacceptable practices usually requires more than excessively high taxation to curb such activities.

Severance Tax

A *severance tax* is defined by the Department of Commerce as "taxes imposed distinctively on removal of natural products—e.g., oil, gas, other minerals, timber, fish, etc.—from land or water and measured by value or quantity of products removed or sold."[16] The tax is imposed at the time the mineral or other product is extracted (severed) from the earth. Levies are made for the privilege of removing a given commodity from the

TABLE 5.1   Severance Tax Revenue per Capita and as a Percent of State Tax Collections: 2004 (revised January 2006)

State	Revenue in Millions	Per Capita	Percent
Alaska	$ 646.9	$1,059.87	50.2
Wyoming	683.2	1,350.21	45.4
New Mexico	587.6	308.79	14.7
North Dakota	175.6	276.14	14.3
Oklahoma	655.1	185.88	10.2
Texas	1,896.8	84.41	6.2
Louisiana	476.6	105.75	5.9
West Virginia	204.1	112.59	5.4
Montana	83.5	90.08	5.1
Kentucky	187.1	45.17	2.2
Kansas	98.1	35.90	1.9
Alabama	113.6	25.12	1.6
Colorado	115.9	25.18	1.6
Utah	47.8	20.66	1.1
United States	$593,488.9	21.71	1.1

Source: U.S. Census Bureau, State Tax Collections 2005, www.census.gov.

ground or from water. These levies are sometimes called *production, conservation,* or *mine* (or *mining*) *occupation* taxes. The concept originated as a way to collect revenues in lieu of property taxes, because it was difficult to determine an appropriate assessed valuation for mineral lands, water, and the commodities produced from them. The justification for assessing a severance tax is that the mineral or resource is irreplaceable, and through a severance tax the state can, to some degree, advance its human resources with the loss from the natural resources. Also, some believe that charging a tax to extract natural resources may deter exploitive use of them and therefore enhance conservation and rational resource development.

A number of states have severance taxes on coal, oil, gas, oil shale, refined petroleum, liquid hydrocarbons, and minerals. The use of severance tax is varied. In 2006, the Bureau of the Census reported that 33 states imposed the tax with only 14 producing more that 1.0 percent of total tax revenue. Alaska receives 50.2 percent of their tax revenue from severance taxes. Although the revenue is significant in several states, the overall impact is only 1.1 percent of total tax revenue reported in all states[17] (see Table 5.1).

Excessive reliance on severance tax can cause serious fiscal problems in certain states. The fluctuation of oil prices, for example, has at times greatly impacted tax revenues in Alaska, Oklahoma, Texas, and Louisiana, demonstrating the value of a broad tax base. In 2006, the state of Alaska faced financial difficulty when a break occurred in the Alaska oil pipeline. Severance tax revenues diminished, which caused some anxiety among state leaders to fund public services.

Potential New Taxes

The pressure that some courts applied on the states to achieve equity in financing education will likely be followed by similar legal pressure to provide equity in other functions of government. With the accompanying acceleration of criticism of the property tax will come increased emphasis on attempts to discover and use other kinds of taxes. This will require revision and upgrading of the taxing pattern of the states and local school districts. As the states assume more of the responsibility of financing education, the principal base for the taxing structure increases, and as limitations on property taxes are imposed, the importance of finding new revenue sources for financing education is going to become even more critical in the next decade.

Site-Value Tax

Recommendations for improving or replacing the present property tax system have taken many different forms. Some economists advocate a site-value (or land) tax. This is a tax on the actual value of the land, whether improved or not. As the land appreciates in value from investments or changes of any nature, the value of the tax revenue produced increases proportionately. Some other countries are using such a tax, and the plan has gained some support in this country, where this idea of property tax reform is old but untried.

Value-Added Tax

Another tax proposal that has received considerable support is a national value-added tax—popularly referred to as VAT. In its simplest form, it is a tax on the value of goods at each transaction level from production to consumption. The price of an economic good rises at every stage of its production and development. The farmer tilling the soil, sowing the seeds, harvesting the crop, delivering it to the miller, and the baker converting the grain into bread to be marketed is a process that involves numerous steps. A tax could be levied on the value added to the good or service at each stage of its production. Thus, a value-added tax is in reality a multiple sales tax.

Congress has proposed a value-added tax a number of times, but no law has ever been passed to utilize such a tax in this country. Its proponents point to its wide acceptance in the industrialized nations of Europe and the fact that it would be a single-rate tax with few exemptions. They admit that passage of such a tax would require reductions in other taxes in order to reduce the burden on taxpayers. Opponents of such a tax say that it would be regressive and would create a tax burden on poorer people if necessities, especially food items, were to be included. They say that in order to make the tax less regressive there would need to be so many exemptions that the tax would be difficult to administer. To offset its alleged unfairness, proposals have been made to give tax rebates to the poor who would be adversely affected. Some economists believe that a VAT would decrease spending and thus release more money for savings and investments. Others say that it would result in serious inflationary trends and would probably result in higher wages in the labor market.

Lotteries

One system of raising funds for state governments that began in 1964 in New Hampshire is the lottery. In 2006, lotteries were being used in 42 states and the District of Columbia. Lottery revenues have increased from $5.5 billion in 1983, to $20 billion in 1990, to $52.6 billion in 2005. As the interest in lotteries expands, so does the debate as to whether lotteries are an appropriate way for government to raise revenue.

Thomas Jefferson called the lottery a "wonderful thing, it lays taxation only on the willing." Lotteries were used to support colonial soldiers and to build Harvard, Princeton, Yale, Dartmouth, Columbia, and William and Mary.[18] They have been used from time immemorial; the Bible describes property distributions made by the process. The term comes from the Germanic word *hleut,* which describes a dish or pebble that was cast to divide property, settle uncertainties, or decide disputes.[19] The concept has grown in popularity because legislators are looking for tax alternatives, and lotteries are popular with the public. People like to participate because there is always a hope that they can strike it rich. Tickets are inexpensive and the poor feel happy about giving money to the government if they stand a chance of reaping a large reward. This attitude is one of the major problems of the lottery as a revenue source. Although the question remains as to whether a lottery is a tax, the end result is that it is regressive in nature—those who can afford it least are paying the most as a percentage of income.

Basically, lotteries for schools are not as great a revenue source as publicity would suggest. In most states, contributions to state treasuries are less than 2 percent with no state generating more than 5 percent. (The North American Association of State and Provincial Lotteries indicates that lotteries, on average, provide only one-half of 1 percent of state budgets.)[20] Note in Table 5.2 that the percent spent per dollar raised ranges from 46.1 in California to 82.3 in South Dakota. Inversely, California shows a profit of 53.9 percent, whereas in South Dakota it is only 17.7 percent. Although 25 states have earmarked lottery revenues in part or in total for education, 8 states and the District of Columbia support the general fund that may be used for education purposes. When the general distributions are made, they are often reduced in proportion to increases that may come from the lottery, leaving education with no greater funding than before the lottery. Voters in Oklahoma passed the Oklahoma Education Act by a large margin in November 2004. The act was specific in identifying that the funds were to "support improvements and enhancements for education purposes and programs, furthermore, net proceeds will be used to *supplement* rather than replace existing funds for education."[21]

The governor of North Carolina signed into law the State Lottery Act (H.1023) in August 2005 with 100 percent of the proceeds earmarked for education. The first allotment from revenues were distributed in June 2006.[22] At this writing, the following

TABLE 5.2 State Lottery Sales and Profits in Millions

Lottery Jurisdiction	Population (millions)	FY '05 Sales (millions)	FY '05 Profit (millions)	% Spent per Dollar Raised	FY '05 Sales per Capita	Use of Revenues
Arizona	5.83	$397.56	$116.80	70.6%	$68.19	Education
California	35.89	$3,333.60	$1,795.30	46.1%	$92.88	Education
Colorado	4.60	$416.97	$103.74	75.1%	$90.65	Parks, recreation, conservation
Connecticut	3.50	$932.93	$268.52	71.2%	$266.55	General fund
Delaware	0.83	$689.29	$234.00	66.1%	$830.47	General fund
District of Columbia	0.55	$233.43	$71.05	69.6%	$424.42	General fund
Florida	18.40	$3,470.73	$1,103.63	68.2%	$188.63	Education
Georgia	8.91	$2,922.33	$802.24	72.5%	$327.98	Education
Idaho	1.39	$113.50	$26.00	77.1%	$81.65	Public schools and buildings
Illinois	12.71	$1,806.75	$614.00	66.0%	$142.15	Common school fund
Indiana	6.08	$739.63	$189.04	74.4%	$121.65	Education, pensions, capital
Iowa	2.95	$210.67	$51.09	75.7%	$71.41	General fund, economic development
Kansas	2.74	$206.72	$62.28	69.9%	$75.45	Economic development
Kentucky	4.15	$707.26	$158.19	77.6%	$170.42	Education
Louisiana	4.52	$307.01	$108.92	64.5%	$67.92	General fund
Maine	1.32	$209.29	$50.33	76.0%	$158.55	General fund
Maryland	5.60	$1,485.73	$477.10	67.9%	$265.31	General fund
Massachusetts	6.43	$4,484.72	$936.13	79.1%	$697.47	Local governments
Michigan	10.11	$2,069.49	$667.58	67.7%	$204.70	Education
Minnesota	5.14	$408.57	$106.18	74.0%	$79.49	General fund, environment
Missouri	5.75	$785.59	$218.64	72.2%	$136.62	Public education, general fund
Montana	0.93	$33.81	$6.22	81.6%	$36.35	Education
Nebraska	1.75	$100.66	$23.86	76.3%	$57.52	Education, environment
New Hampshire	1.30	$227.98	$69.30	69.6%	$175.37	Education
New Jersey	8.70	$2,273.81	$804.42	64.6%	$261.36	Education and institutions
New Mexico	1.90	$139.27	$32.23	76.9%	$73.30	Education

State					Purpose
New York	19.23	$6,270.49	$2,062.70	67.1%	$326.08	Education
North Dakota	0.63	$19.15	$6.46	66.3%	$30.40	General fund
Ohio	11.44	$2,159.10	$645.10	70.1%	$188.73	Education
Oklahoma*						Education
Oregon	3.62	$943.11	$415.48	55.9%	$260.53	Public education, economic development
Pennsylvania	12.41	$2,644.86	$852.56	67.8%	$213.12	Age related services
Rhode Island	1.08	$1,636.84	$307.55	81.2%	$1,515.59	General fund
South Carolina	4.20	$956.95	$277.50	71.0%	$227.85	Education
South Dakota	0.77	$675.58	$119.32	82.3%	$877.38	General fund
Tennessee	5.96	$844.32	$227.42	73.1%	$141.66	Education
Texas	22.91	$3,662.46	$1,076.82	70.6%	$159.86	General fund
Vermont	0.62	$92.59	$20.35	78.0%	$149.34	General fund, education
Virginia	7.46	$1,333.94	$423.52	68.3%	$178.81	General fund, education
Washington	6.20	$457.62	$115.60	74.7%	$73.81	General fund, education
West Virginia	1.82	$1,399.07	$563.32	59.7%	$768.72	Education, aging, tourism
Wisconsin	5.51	$451.87	$128.54	71.6%	$82.01	Property tax relief
TOTAL U.S. ($US)	**265.84**	**$52,255.25**	**$16,339.03**	**68.7%**	**$196.57**	

*Oklahoma's lottery was approved but had no sales in 2005.

Source: North American Association of State and Provincial Lotteries (NASPL), www.naspl.org.

states do not have a lottery: Alabama, Alaska, Arkansas, Hawaii, Mississippi, Nevada, Utah, and Wyoming.

Summing up the pros and cons of the lottery, Thomas and Webb offered the following:

> In each area where the lottery has been legalized, or is being considered, similar arguments pro and con have been proposed. The primary arguments supporting the lottery are: that it is a rather painless way to increase revenues; that the lottery is not a tax, or if it is a tax, it should be considered a "voluntary tax"; that the desire to gamble is inherent to man and that it is socially more desirable for gambling to be offered by the government than by organized crime. . . .
>
> Those who oppose the lottery contend that it is capable of increasing state revenues by only a small percent; that it is more costly to administer than other taxes; that it will not reduce the present level of taxation; that it is a regressive form of taxation; and that it does not substantially compete with illegal games. It also is argued that although people may have a strong desire to gamble, such activity undermines the moral fiber of society, and that government is obliged, at the very least, not to encourage gambling, either through sponsorship and solicitation, or by making it convenient.[23]

Private Foundations

In an effort to meet the demands of tighter budgets, school districts are reaching out to the private sector to develop new revenue sources. Some districts have established private foundations for the purpose of raising funds for local schools. Only a few foundations existed prior to 1980. The greatest effort came from districts in California that were impacted when a property tax rollback initiative was passed by the voters. Districts sought funds from outside sources and school district foundations were developed. To provide tax benefits for donors, most foundations have been established as nonprofit corporations under Internal Revenue Service section (501 c). In so doing, they are required to become separate entities with separate boards and out of the jurisdiction of local boards of education. True to a purpose, most of the foundations provide support to education endeavors.

In 2006, there were over 500 education foundations in California with most participating in the California Consortium of Education Foundations, which was established as a nonprofit organization "dedicated to strengthening public education by facilitating the creation, growth, and effectiveness of local education foundations and by advocating for public education."[24] Foundations for K–12 now exist in most states with varying success. Usually, the effort is at a school district level with emphasis on providing revenue for specific projects established as priorities. With the broad growth and the need for consulting assistance, a U.S. education grant was awarded to the National Center for Public and Private School Foundations (NCPPSF) to establish a website as an information support system. The NCPPSF merged with the Association of Education Foundations and became the National School Foundation Association (NSFA) with the mission of "encouraging K–12 school and school foundation personnel in the very important process of establishing, developing and maintaining school foundations."[25] The NSFA noted that \$31.6 billion was donated to education in 2003—the second largest category of charitable giving in the United States, with religion being the first.[26]

In one state, the legislature has provided a minimal amount of matching money in its Incentive for Excellence program, which provides funds for districts that are able to match the revenue from the private sector with the following guidelines:

- A school district shall use its allocation to promote a strong partnership between public education and private enterprise, to seek additional financial support from the business community, and to enhance its educational excellence.
- School districts are encouraged under this program to develop projects that rely on matching private and public monies to promote educational excellence.
- Districts are required to designate district leadership, and organize an ongoing structure such as an advisory board or education foundation.[27]

The foundation programs raise some school finance issues: (1) What role should school officials play in the foundation and in the determination of how money should be expended? (2) Will states reduce their aid to school systems that have successful foundations? (3) Since affluent school systems are more likely to have successful foundations, will private money damage efforts to make the quality of education more uniform among rich and poor communities?[28]

School-Business Partnerships

The thrust for school-business partnerships is closely related to the foundation movement. The natural evolvement of seeking revenues extended to asking business and industry leaders for contributions to assist schools in meeting budget needs and extending programs. Simultaneously, the business-education relationship was emerging on its own as business executives felt an urgency to coordinate efforts with educators to meet the needs of developing a work force that could compete in a global marketplace. Partnerships can vary greatly in scope and are as diverse as the companies involved. Following are types of partnerships and their level of impact on the educational system:

1. *Partnerships in special services.* Focuses on student support activities and on programs that encompass fund-raising, scholarships, and donation of equipment
2. *Partnerships in classrooms.* Involves activities such as mentoring, tutoring of students, and extracurricular activities
3. *Partnerships in professional development.* Sponsors conferences, workshops, and in-service training
4. *Partnerships in management.* Provides management support and business expertise in strategic planning, goal setting, and school building improvement
5. *Partnerships in systemic educational improvement.* Involves community compacts, alliance consortia, and technical assistance
6. *Partnerships in policy.* Involves national or state task forces, private industry councils, school boards, and city councils[29]

Business and industry interests are not completely altruistic. They have an agenda. However, the concept that makes the partnership function is that educators are striving for the same goal—to produce students who are prepared for the future. Concerns are that the schools are not teaching relevant subject matter for jobs that require special training and skills. Critics claim that education is not staying in touch with societal and workplace needs. They assert that students are being trained with twentieth-century methods that will not meet the demands of a world economy.

The literature contains many examples of companies that have been generous with both money and in-kind contributions to schools. Although much of the annual support has gone to higher education, the trend is changing as business leaders are recognizing the necessity of supporting education programs that start at an earlier age.

There are some concerns in the education arena that the schools are willing to accept assistance in areas that may not be in the best interest of students. Channel 1 is an example of this. The debate is whether taking valuable classroom time for a short news program that also provides the producers a captive audience for commercials is a worthwhile trade-off for television sets in each classroom.

A spokesperson for the National Association of Partners in Education stated that solutions need to be locally based; there is not one solution that is going to be applicable to every community. Therefore, the partnerships need to be at the local district level where those who live in the community can work toward defining and solving the problems.[30] This raises some concerns. After reviewing various partnership studies, Pautler noted that many districts in the United States are in rural areas far from major businesses and such partnerships may be difficult to arrange.[31]

As school administrators look to business and industry as an additional funding source to supplement the education budget, business and industrial leaders who support education with corporate dollars will be expecting educators to produce a student who is literate, prepared, and already employable when graduating from high school. Accountability and results are expected when business and industry "foot the bill."

Summary

Taxation is a system of transferring money from the private sector to the public sector of the economy. The public institutions of the nation are almost completely dependent on this method of obtaining funds for their operation. Taxation is fairer and more dependable for financing education than the previously used rate bills, tuition charges, and student fees.

A good tax system should include the following features: (1) There should be coordination among all levels of government with little or no duplication of taxes. (2) All citizens should pay some tax. (3) Taxpayers should be left in the same relative financial position with each other after taxes are paid. (4) The tax should bring a reasonable yield, not be merely a nuisance tax. (5) Tax erosion should be minimal, regardless of the benefits government owes to deserving citizens. (6) Tax collection should be simple and convenient for taxpayers and of little cost to the collectors. (7) The tax should be levied on the person or household who pays it—the shifting of the tax should be minimized. (8) The payment of the tax should not cause a major change in the economic practice or vocation of the taxpayer.

The property tax is becoming less and less fair as people increasingly invest their surplus monies in other forms of wealth. The unfairness of a property tax is evident in many ways, such as unequal assessment practices, taxation without relationship to net ownership of the property being taxed, unequal tax bases per pupil to be educated in various kinds of school districts, and lack of a direct relationship between the taxes owed and the amount of wealth or income of the person or household being taxed. Taxpayer resistance to property taxes has increased greatly.

Circuit breakers were adopted by most states to relieve elderly and low-income people of part of their property tax burden. Legal steps were taken in a number of states to restrict the use of the property tax, and some states passed legislation restricting government expenditures.

Personal property taxes are difficult to collect, and their use has proven to be somewhat ineffective. Income taxes are probably the most equitable of all taxes, but their use at the local level is limited for two major reasons: (1) They are already used to a high degree by the federal government and to a limited degree by most states. (2) It is relatively easy for resisting taxpayers to find loopholes to avoid such taxes.

The income tax is probably the fairest of all taxes. In practice, it is less than ideal as a revenue-collecting measure. It is usually a progressive tax and should include personal and corporate income. There is a continual cry for overhaul of the income tax laws.

Sales taxes are effective at the state level but are not readily manageable at the local level, especially in small school districts. Sales taxes are regressive when food items and other necessities are taxed, since low-income families generally spend a higher percentage of their income on necessities than the more affluent do. E-commerce has spurred a sales tax debate.

Potential new taxes include site-value and value-added taxes, which have a history of successful use in some foreign countries. Congress has attempted unsuccessfully to introduce the use of some new kinds of taxes several times in the last few years.

Although the concept is very old, lotteries have become popular in some states as a source of revenue for the schools. Since lotteries generate only a small percentage of total state allocations, school administrators need to be concerned about relying on this source because of the uncertainty of receipts. The debate will continue on whether a lottery is truly a tax. In any case, it is regressive in nature, since many buyers of tickets are among the members of society who can least afford them. The pros and cons will continue to be debated as more states consider the possibilities of instituting lotteries to raise money for state budgets.

Private foundations may be a source of revenue for school districts. However, the collaborative effort of the private and public sectors working for education may have a greater impact than the actual funds raised through foundations.

School-business partnerships have continued to increase in numbers, as business and industry leaders have become more concerned with developing a work force that can compete in a global marketplace. The collaborative efforts will require revenues from business and industry and accountability from educators.

ASSIGNMENT PROJECTS

1. Provide a definition for each of the following terms: *rate bills, fees, tuition, tax erosion, tax shifting, ad valorem, real property, personal property, income tax, sales tax, sumptuary tax, severance tax, site-value tax, value-added tax, lottery, tax rate, tax base.*

2. For taxation purposes, property is usually assessed at a fractional part of its sale (market) value. Revenues are determined by applying tax rates against these assessed values. Since states use different percentages of sale value in calculating assessed value, comparisons ation of sale values and true tax rates.

〈 rate) = (sale value) (true tax rate)
AV) (tr) = (SV) (ttr)

,000 and assessed at $40,000 has a tax rate (sometimes it would have a true tax rate of 16 mills.

operty is 25 percent of its sale   3. ___ percent
s true tax rate is what percent of

12,675 under a fractional prac-   4. _____
lue of the property?

7,424 and the sale value of all   5. ___/$100 (AV)
be assessed at 60 percent), what
0 of assessed valuation?

tax rate in mills?   6. _____ mills

(handwritten note: Due Feb 21 #34156 2.)

Mr. Smith has a house assessed at $51,000 (60 percent of sale value). His tax is $3.50 per $100 of AV. Mrs. Jones has a house assessed at $35,550 (45 percent of sale value). Her tax rate is 36.2 mills. From the following information, answer the following:

Who pays the greater tax?   7. _____

How much greater?   8. _____

Using the tax rate and the assessment practices of Mr. Smith's dis-   9. _____
trict, how much tax would Mrs. Jones pay?

Ms. Brown has a house assessed at $55,800 (62 percent of sale value). Her tax rate is $3.25 per $100 of assessed valuation. Mr. Barnes has a house assessed at $42,720 (48 percent of sale value). His tax rate is $32.75 per $1,000 (AV).

Who pays the greater tax?   10. _____

How much greater?   11. _____

Using the tax rate and the assessment practices of Ms. Brown's   12. _____
district, how much tax would Mr. Barnes pay?

School District A has an assessed valuation of taxable property of $49,410,000. It has 5,400 public school pupils. School District B has an assessed valuation of taxable property of $86,260,000 and 9,500 public school pupils.

Which district has the greater ability to support its schools?   **13.** _____

In problem 13, how much greater?   **14.** _____

Jane Miller has a house assessed at $45,000 (45 percent of its sale value). Her tax rate is $4.20 per $100 of AV. Tom Gale has a house assessed at $55,000 (50 percent of sale value). His tax rate is 35.25 mills.

Who pays the greater tax?   **15.** _____

How much greater?   **16.** _____

If both houses were taxed on full sale value with a true tax rate of   **17.** _____
23.3 mills, who would pay the greater tax?

How much greater?   **18.** _____

Computer simulations and questions, research exercises, and website addresses relevant to this chapter can be found at

www.ablongman.com/edleadership

SELECTED READINGS

Benson, Charles S. *The Economics of Public Education,* 3rd ed. Boston: Houghton Mifflin, 1978.

Borg, Mary O., Paul M. Mason, and Stephen L. Schapiro. *The Economic Consequences of State Lotteries.* New York: Praeger, 1991.

Expenditures versus Expenses, Developments in School Finance: 2004 (Washington, DC: National Center for Educational Statistics, 2005).

Friedman, Milton. *Capitalism and Freedom.* Chicago: University of Chicago Press, 1962.

Goodman, J. L., and J. B. Ittner. "The Accuracy of Homeowners' Estimates of House Value." *Journal of Housing Economics,* 1992.

Jacobsen, Stephen, Kenneth Leithwood, and David H. Monk. *Leadership and Policy in Schools.* Amsterdam: Sweet & Zeitlinger, March 2002.

Jones, Thomas H., and John L. Amafalitano. *Lotteries: America's Gamble: Public School Finance and State Lotteries.* Lancaster, PA: Technomic Publishing, 1994.

Peckman, Joseph A. *Tax Reform, the Rich and the Poor,* 2nd ed. Washington, DC: Brookings Institution, 1989.

Salmon, Richard G., and S. Kern Alexander. *The Historical Reliance of Public Education upon the Property Tax: Current Problem and Future Role.* Cambridge, MA: Lincoln Institute of Land Policy, 1983.

Spring, Joel. *Conflicts of Interest,* 3rd ed. New York: McGraw-Hill, 1998.

Staff of the Committee on Education, The Florida Senate. *A Review of Lottery Funding for Education,* December 1996.

ENDNOTES

1. Delaware County Assessors Office, Delaware, Pennsylvania, July 2003.
2. Lloyd E. McCann and Floyd G. Delon, "Governmental Structure for School Finance," in Warren E. Gauerke and Jack A. Childress, eds., *Theory and Practice of School Finance* (Chicago: Rand McNally, 1967), pp. 90–93.
3. Charles S. Benson, *Perspectives on the Economics of Education: Readings in School Finance and Business Management* (Boston: Houghton Mifflin, 1963), p. 160.
4. *Taxes Contribute to Progress* (Washington, DC: National Education Association Committee on Education Finance, 1960), p. 18.
5. Ibid., p. 19.
6. *Productivity in Education: Measuring and Financing* (Washington, DC: National Education Association Committee on Educational Finance, 1972), p. 146.
7. Laurence J. Kotlikoff, "The Economic Impact of Replacing Federal Income Taxes with a Sales Tax," *Policy Analysis,* No. 193, April 15, 1993, Cato Institute, Washington, DC, p. 8.
8. *Productivity in Education,* pp. 145–146.
9. United States Senate Bill 150—Internet Tax Non-Discrimination Act of 2003.
10. "Streamlined Sales Tax Project," www/streamlinedsalestax.org/oprules.html, July 10, 2003.
11. Ibid.
12. Ibid. Updated May 2006.
13. Ibid.
14. Institute for State Studies, www.statestudies.org/summary.html, July 10, 2003.
15. John E. Corbally, Jr., *School Finance* (Boston: Allyn and Bacon, 1962), p. 14.
16. State Government Tax Collections, U.S. Department of Commerce, Bureau of the Census, November 1992, p. 48.
17. U.S. Department of Commerce, Bureau of Census, www.census.gov. See also: Judy Zell, "State Energy Revenues Gushing," for the National Conference of State Legislatures, www.ncsl.org/programs.
18. Richard L. Worsnop, "Lucrative Lure of Lotteries and Gambling," *Congressional Quarterly's Editorial Research Reports,* October 19, 1990, p. 637.
19. Stephen B. Thomas and L. Dean Webb, "The Use and Abuse of Lotteries as a Revenue Source," *Journal of Education Finance,* Vol. 9, No. 3, Winter 1984, p. 289.
20. "Did You Know," North American Association of State and Provincial Lotteries (NASLP), www.naspl.org. Assisted by Tom Tulloch, NASPL, Director of Administration, May 2006.
21. Oklahoma Education Act, November 2004.
22. "North Carolina Education Lottery," State of North Carolina, 2005, http://lottery.nc.gov/, June 2006.
23. Stephen B. Thomas and L. Dean Webb.
24. "About CCEF," California Consortium of Education Foundations, Stanford, CA, www.ccefink.org, May 2006.
25. National School Foundation Association, www.schoolfoundations.org, May 2006.
26. Ibid.
27. *Utah School Finance Reference Manual, 1994–95,* Utah State Office of Education, Salt Lake City, p. 68.
28. Thomas Toch, "Time for Private Foundations for Public Schools," *Education Weekly,* Vol. II, No. 9, November 1982, p. 15.
29. Husein M. Toubat, "Marketing Education to Business," Business Partnerships, *Thrust for Educational Leadership,* April 1994, p. 29. Quoting from "The Fourth R: Workforce Readiness," National Alliance of Business publication.
30. Charlene Mariner Solomon, "New Partners in Business," *Personnel Journal,* April 1991, p. 59.
31. Albert J. Pautler, reviewing "Three Books on Partnership in Practice," *Phi Delta Kappan,* June 1990, p. 818.

6

Eroding Local Control

Many states are taking responsibility for funding education.
Local districts are being transformed. Educational policy makers
need to determine what, in the long run, is best for students.

—Marilyn Hirth, 2007

Local control of schools has been a hallmark of the American system of public education throughout the history of the nation. Although the ultimate responsibility for the education process rests with the state, local communities have been the ultimate caretakers and have resisted any infringements on that trust. Many factors have been slowly impacting a change in the authority of local boards of education, and the power and influence once prevalent is waning. State control has been influenced by a need for states to become more involved in equalizing funding formulas, and the demand for more accountability by the public at both the state and federal level have diminished the authority of local boards.

Diminishing Local Control

Citizens of the United States view the gradual change from local to state control of the public schools with some degree of alarm, yet they know that such a change is inevitable. They see local control as a frontier where people in small towns and neighborhoods can make their voices heard in determining who shall be educated and by what process. They feel threatened by nationwide trends toward centralization and standardization. They value their importance as citizens in the selection of school board members, in voting for or against levies and bond issues, and in their right to evaluate the accomplishments of their schools.

At the same time, Americans feel a degree of helplessness and inability to influence state legislatures; they envision the federal government as being far beyond their horizon of influence. Consequently, they tend to hold firmly to their commitment to local control of education. They accept its accomplishments with pride when it excels and fault themselves and their community when it falls short or fails to compare favorably with schools elsewhere. In their pride for school and community, they often lose sight of the high price that must be paid for maintaining small districts and small attendance areas. In their minds, it is a price worth paying. They tend to evaluate the schools' successes and failures in terms of what the situation was when they were in school and often have closed minds with regard to the potential virtues of school reorganization and consolidation.

As states are playing a greater role in financing public schools, they are assuming firmer control. The adage "He who holds the purse strings holds the power" is apparent as state governments continue to provide a large part of budgets for operating public schools. The state share of revenues for public elementary and secondary schools grew steadily for many decades but this trend began to reverse in the late 1980s. In 1995, revenues at both the state and local levels were within a few percentage points, at 46.8 provided by the states and 46.4 percent from local sources. In 1996 through 1999, the states showed a continual increase, leveling at 48.7 percent, but the local contribution dropped to 44.2 percent. The federal revenues ranged between 6.6 to 7.1 percent for this period, and in 2003, increased to 8.5 percent.

Federal and state revenues increased at a faster rate than all local revenues (both property tax revenue and other local revenue). Thus, the proportion of total revenue for public elementary and secondary education from local sources declined, from 47 percent in 1989 to 43 percent in 2002–03. The proportion of total public school revenue from property taxes declined in both the Midwest and Northeast from 1989–90 to 2002–03, whereas the proportion grew in the South and West.

The Midwest experienced the largest decreases in the proportion of total revenue from local sources. Local funding there dropped from 55 percent of all revenue for public elementary and secondary education in 1989–90 to 43 percent in 2002–03. Declines in the proportion of property tax revenue accounted for most of this decrease. The Northeast also experienced declines in the proportion of revenue from local sources. In both regions, there were increases in the proportion of total revenue from federal and state sources. The South and West during this period experienced little change (less than 1 percentage point) in the proportion of total revenue from local sources. However, the proportion of funding from property tax revenues in the South increased from 27 percent in 1989 to 31 percent in 2002–03, and it increased from 24 to 25 percent in the West. In both the South and the West, the proportion of revenue from state sources decreased and the proportion from federal sources increased[1] (see Figure 6.1).

The education and equal protection clauses of the various state constitutions have had an influence on how education is funded and have placed more responsibility on state legislators to provide additional financial aid to local education agencies. Courts in many states have had an impact when they have instructed state leaders to provide more equitable financing for local districts from state resources. These and other factors are reasons why state governments are generally considered to be the institutions that will be required to meet the expanding financial needs of the schools in the future.

FIGURE 6.1   Change in Revenue Sources: Percentage Distribution of Total Revenues for Public Elementary and Secondary Schools, by Region and Revenue Source: 1989–90 to 2002–2003

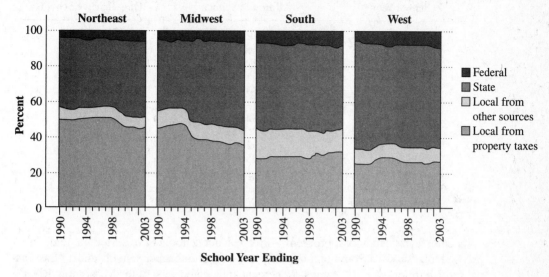

Note: Detail may not sum to totals because of rounding. Other local government revenue includes revenue from such sources as local nonproperty taxes, investments, and revenue from student activities, textbook sales, transportation and tuition fees, and food services.

Source: U.S. Department of Education, National Center for Education Statistics, The NCES Common Core of Data (CCD), "National Public Education Financial Survey," 1989–90 to 2000–03, previously unpublished tabulation (July 2005).

Decreasing Rural Influence on Education

In recorded U.S. legislative history, legislators representing rural areas dominated the lawmaking bodies of the states. Disproportionate representation in at least one branch of the legislature was usually given to small towns, counties, and sparsely populated areas, as compared with the representation given to large towns, cities, and metropolitan areas. Since property taxes bore a major portion of school costs, rural legislators and rural school board members tended to be reluctant to provide the funds necessary for optimum school programs. When the U.S. Supreme Court issued a ruling that reapportionment of the membership of state legislatures must meet a "one man–one vote standard," it reduced the relative legislative power of rural areas and increased that of cities.

Also, as the United States became less of an agrarian society, and people moved from rural areas, the number of one-teacher schools decreased significantly over the years (see Table 6.1). The diminution of the number of one-teacher schools illustrates the debility of rural America. In 2004, 80 percent of all inhabitants lived in urban metropolitan areas.

As educators and researchers increasingly turn their attention to the benefits of small schools—such as cooperative learning, small teacher-pupil ratios, nurturing

TABLE 6.1   Decrease in Number of One-Teacher Schools

School Year	All Public Schools	One-Teacher Schools
1947–48	172,244	75,096
1953–54	136,512	42,865
1957–58	120,953	25,341
1963–64	104,015	9,895
1973–74	90,976	1,365
1982–83	84,740	798
1988–89	82,081	583
1994–95	86,221	458
1999–2000	92,012	423
2003–2004	95,726	376

Source: Digest of Education Statistics, U.S. Department of Education, National Center for Education Statistics, Office of Educational Research and Improvement (NCES 2000333), June 2005.

students, fewer behavioral problems—one-teacher schools have shrunk in numbers. A close look "shows a South that has all but lost its one-teacher schools and an East that is soon to follow suit. . . . Almost 90 percent are located west of the Mississippi River"[2] (see Figure 6.2).

FIGURE 6.2   One-Teacher Schools

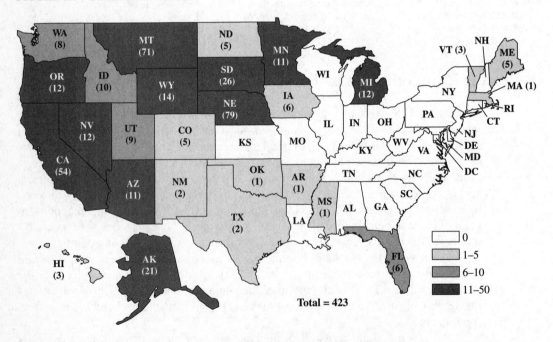

Source: U.S. Department of Education, National Center for Education Statistics, 2006.

Decreasing Urban Economic Advantages

Although cities have gained in their representation in legislative bodies, they have lost their economic advantage in the operation of schools. When property taxes were the main source of school revenue and state allocations were minimal, city school districts usually enjoyed certain revenue advantages. City school boards tended to be less vocal in their opposition to property tax increases for education than their rural counterparts. As a consequence, city schools generally outdid their rural neighbors in providing good education. City schools became the leaders in administrative efficiency and in student achievement.

In recent years, however, the pattern has changed. Radical changes in the socio-economic makeup of larger cities with consistent emigration of the more affluent to suburbia, and the impact of immigration and other social factors, have resulted in cities losing much of their previous financial advantage. Legislative bodies that once faced the formidable problem of financing small rural schools equitably now face a similar problem in providing adequate and equitable revenue for urban districts.

School Districts: Basic Administrative Units

The local school district is the basic administrative unit for the operation of public schools in this country. Each district has a governing board, usually referred to as the *school board,* and a chief administrative officer, usually called the *superintendent of schools.* The size, characteristics, and authority of school districts vary greatly from state to state and even within the same state. In most of the states, the more than 15,000 school districts (including county and other special districts) operate as independent governmental units. In some of the states, however, school districts are dependent on some other unit of government for certain aspects of their operation—usually budgetary operations.

The number of school districts in the country reached the staggering total of 127,649 in 1932. Fortunately, much progress has been made in reducing the number since that time. As might be expected, reorganization of school districts proceeded at a snail's pace at first. However, improvements in the laws providing for such mergers did much to accelerate the process. There were 117,108 school districts in 1940, 83,178 in 1950, 40,520 in 1960, and only 17,995 in 1970—a reduction of about 100,000 school districts in a 30-year period. In 2005, there were 14,383 school districts in the United States. Texas continues to have more than 1,000 independent school districts; 10 other states still have more than 500 (see Figure 6.3).

In the past, most of the problems of school district reorganization were concerned with combining small districts into larger ones to improve the educational opportunities for children and at the same time provide a broad tax base, reduce variations in the taxpaying ability of districts, and provide some degree of stabilization, equity, and satisfactory management of funds. Recently, however, the problem of decreasing the sizes of some large metropolitan districts or reorganizing them by allowing other public-sector agencies, such as universities, and private for-profit companies to sponsor public

FIGURE 6.3 Number of Basic Administrative Units: 2005

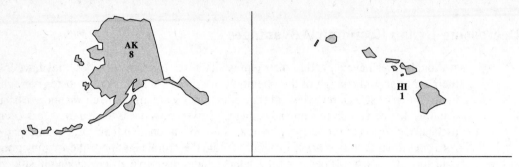

*1.	Hawaii	1	21.	South Dakota	172	36.	Massachusetts	350
2.	Nevada	17	22.	Kentucky	176	37.	Iowa	370
3.	Delaware	19	23.	Colorado	178	38.	Wisconsin	437
4.	Maryland	24		New Hampshire	178	39.	Montana	438
5.	Rhode Island	38	25.	Georgia	180	40.	Pennsylvania	501
6.	Utah	40	26.	Oregon	199	41.	Nebraska	518
7.	Wyoming	48	27.	North Dakota	213	42.	Missouri	524
8.	Alaska	53	28.	Maine	283	43.	Oklahoma	541
9.	West Virginia	55	29.	Indiana	294	44.	Michigan	553
10.	Florida	67	30.	Washington	296	45.	New Jersey	598
11.	Louisiana	68	31.	Vermont	299	46.	Ohio	613
12.	New Mexico	89	32.	Kansas	302	47.	New York	726
	South Carolina	89	33.	Arkansas	309	48.	Illinois	887
14.	Idaho	114	34.	Arizona	313	40.	California	989
15.	North Carolina	117	35.	Minnesota	348	50.	Texas	1,040
16.	Alabama	130						
17.	Virginia	134						
18.	Tennessee	136						
19.	Mississippi	152						
20.	Connecticut	166						

* District of Columbia also has
1 school district.

United States 14,383

Source: http://nces.ed.gov/programs/digest/d05/tablesat05_086.asp. (This table was prepared in August 2005.)

schools has emerged. Such competition could bring diversity within urban schools and pressure ineffective schools to change.

The traditional argument that large school districts allow greater economy in the operation of schools can easily be overemphasized. Quite often, the funds saved in some aspects of the programs are spent to enrich or extend educational services—one of the main reasons for combining the districts in the first place. The argument that reorganization will save educational dollars, which may appeal to some taxpayers as a possibility for tax relief or reduction, often falls of its own weight. Instead of saving school tax money, reorganization usually results in a better school program, with little if any reduction in cost. However, reduction in the number of school districts will usually result in some subtle, but important and relevant, improvements in financing education:

1. The range in local ability to pay for education in the wealthiest as compared with the poorest district (as measured by the assessed value of taxable property per pupil to be educated) will be reduced.
2. State support formulas can be simplified, and greater equality of educational opportunity for all school pupils can result as the number and kinds of administrative units are reduced.
3. Larger school districts make possible greater efficiency in the expenditure of funds (but do not guarantee it) in nearly all categories of the maintenance and operation of schools, but particularly in administration, instruction of pupils, and purchase of supplies and equipment.

Each state has been free to determine the kind and number of local school units or districts that can be operated within its own boundaries. The number of such districts within a state varies from 1,040 in Texas to 1 in Hawaii.

The arguments concerning relative costs and quality of education in large, medium, and small school districts are still being debated in some parts of this country. Most informed students of educational administration recognize some relation between the costs of education and the organizational pattern of school districts the state operates. Further, large school districts are under considerable scrutiny because many feel they have, in fact, become too big, too bureaucratic, too unwieldy, too unmanageable, and too far removed from the classroom.

The optimum size of a district has long been an issue in the education world. It is not in this context that discussion of the issue is included but the size of school districts do have a financial impact and needs to be considered when financial decisions are being made.[3]

The following are some principles concerning the size of school districts that should be considered as a result of the experience of the states over the years:

1. Maintaining a small school district with only one or two small attendance areas is questionable in terms of the aims and objectives of present-day education. This does not rule out the obvious fact that some small schools and districts will always be needed in sparsely populated areas of this country.
2. Small school districts are comparatively inefficient and often represent a waste of tax funds.

3. Large school districts and attendance areas operating with adequate revenue provide the potential for an efficient and effective school system with a high-quality educational product, but do not and cannot guarantee it.
4. Although the admitted advantages of large school districts over smaller ones are important and can usually be documented, decisions over such matters may be made on the basis of the emotions of the people involved rather than the educational benefits that the pupils will derive.
5. Some districts and attendance areas are too large and unmanageable. The problem of decentralization must be faced in some districts at the same time that centralization is being emphasized in others.

Some principles concerning small schools include:

1. Schools that are too small suffer from curriculum limitations, even if the wealth of the district makes it financially possible to employ proportionately more and better-trained school staff members.
2. Small rural schools are sometimes unable to attract the best teachers, regardless of the wealth or the available revenues in those districts.
3. Small schools suffer from lack of special services, such as health, psychological, and counseling programs. No amount of revenue can provide these services if there are not enough pupils to warrant them.
4. Small attendance areas may be comparatively inefficient and often represent a waste of tax funds.

Over the past several decades, the trend to consolidate small schools has brought a large decline in the total number of public schools in the United States. In 1930, there were more than 262,000 public schools, compared with around 94,000 in 2004. This number has grown especially in recent years, with an increase of about 10,500 schools between 1994 and 2004. Such growth has raised an issue about the advantages and disadvantages of small and large schools. More than one in ten of the nation's high schools have enrollments of 1,500 or more, according to the National Center for Education Statistics. A school that has an operating unit cost per student caused by underutilization of staff and curriculum, which exceeds the average operating unit per student cost in the state, is considered too small. Bigger schools, some educators maintain, have not necessarily made for better achievement.

Lunenburg and Ornstein maintained that, in the future, "emphasis will be placed on smaller schools because they are cheaper than larger schools." They also say that "smaller schools usually mean not only more efficient use of space but also fewer administrators, which results in lower costs."[4] They contend that a "school is too large when a loss of personal or school identity among students occurs" and when "students are unable to fully participate in social and athletic activities or have difficulty interacting among themselves or feel they do not belong to the student body or school in general. There is a sense of aimlessness, isolation even despair among a large number of students which in turn causes other social and psychological problems (such as delinquency, drugs and cults) which are more overt in nature."[5] Financially, the advantages of reorganization of school districts outweigh the disadvantages, but there is great resistance from the public when states attempt to impose consolidation on local entities.

The Administration of Local School Districts

Local boards of education are finding their authority waning and being eroded on several fronts. Twenty-four states have provisions for local school districts to be "taken over" by the state, with 18 implementing this provision as a way of improving low-performing districts. The No Child Left Behind Act includes options for the state to take over schools that fail to meet adequate yearly progress.[6] Mayors of some metropolitan areas (Boston, Chicago, and New York) have brought the local school district under city control. One of the top campaign issues of the elected mayor of Los Angeles was the "takeover" of the Los Angeles Unified School District to "wrest control from the district's elected school board."[7] His "Taking Back Our Schools" proposal covers 26 other cities. Mayors of those cities would serve as a council of mayors with votes apportioned by population.[8] The California legislature passed a bill allowing Los Angeles's mayor to take over the city's school district. However, the school board unilaterally appointed a new superintendent and brought suit challenging the law, maintaining that the state constitution requires a separation of power between city officials and school districts. The court ruled in favor of the board on state constitutional grounds.

A consortium of educators and political leaders has proposed a varied approach to *weighting* factors in funding programs that would determine how revenues were expended at the local district level. Claiming a 100 percent solution, the ad hoc committee states, "The key change from traditional group approaches is that money is allocated to schools not based on staffing levels or programs, or just the number of students, but on the characteristics of the student attending the school." Opponents indicate that the plan undermines local school district decision making.[9] Recent activity from business and government officials in another effort has brought momentum to a design (First Class Education) that states as its goal: "By the end of 2008 . . . change the law in each of the 50 states and the District of Columbia to require that at least 65% of whatever taxpayers spend on K–12 education actually makes its way to the classroom."[10] Some states have enacted such legislation and others are considering it. The specific proposal requires the following:

1. The goal is for each school district in a state to spend at least 65% of its operating classroom instruction as defined by the National Center for Educational Statistics.
2. If a school district is currently spending less than 65% on classroom instruction, it must increase that amount by 2% or more per year until the 65% goal is reached.
3. If a school district felt special circumstances prevented it from reaching either the increase or the 65% goal, it could ask the State Superintendent of Public Instruction (the state's highest-ranking elected education official) for a renewable one-year waiver.
4. The State Superintendent would have the sole authority to grant-in-full, grant-in-part, or reject the school district's one-year waiver request.
5. The State Legislatures will be specifically left the task to set penalties to encourage compliance to the measure.[11]

The National Center for Education Statistics defines instruction in the classroom as classroom teachers and personnel, general instruction supplies, instruction aides, and activities such as field trips, athletics, music, and arts. It also includes special needs instruction and tuition paid to out-of-state districts and private institutions for special needs students. Outside the classroom includes administration, plant operations and maintenance, food services, transportation, instructional staff support (including media personnel/librarians), and student support such as nurses, therapists, and counselors. Labeled the 65% Solution, proponents claim that the approach will be a more efficient expenditure of school revenues and will increase spending for instruction without raising taxes. Opponents describe the plan as simplistic and one that will result in loss of local control, and believe that the definitions are nebulous and the reporting is not always consistent.[12]

It may be understandable that after Hurricane Katrina struck the New Orleans area that chaos in opening and operating schools normally would be a challenge. However, even before the destruction, the legislature was preparing to turn operation of many of the schools in New Orleans over to the Board of Elementary and Secondary Education. Legislation in November 2005 "gave final approval to strip the Orleans Parish School Board of its authority over all but 13 campuses," losing control of 102 schools.[13]

The role of local school boards in controlling and administering the operation and financing of schools has changed in the last few years. Accountability requirements, failing schools, mandated legislation at both the state and federal levels, court decisions, levy limitations, and other related activities have been factors in eroding and usurping the powers and duties of local school boards.

The politics of education has shifted with a rotation about a state-federal axis rather than a local-state axis. Thus, in the opinion of many, the traditional philosophy and practice of localism has become suspect and is in need of change. In an interview with the authors, Ernest T. Boyer observed, "I think for the first time America is more preoccupied with national results than local school control." Now, reinforced by the accountability emphasis in the No Child Left Behind law, Chester Finn, a proponent for less local control, asserted that there already has been a change in practice but theory has yet to be altered. He stated:

> So deeply ingrained in our consciousness is the idea of "local control of education" that few Americans even think about it anymore. Like "separation of church and state," "civilian control of the military," and "equality of opportunity," the phrase rolls off the tongue without even engaging the mind. To suggest that it may be obsolete or harmful is like hinting that Mom's apple pie is laced with arsenic.
>
> The time has come, however, to subject "local control" as we know it to closer scrutiny. It is one of those 19th century school-governance and finance arrangements that may not serve the country well at the dawn of the . . . millennium. It is enshrined in neither the Ten Commandments nor the Constitution. It could, therefore, be changed. Indeed, it has already been changing in practice even though we have not yet revamped the theory.[14]

Finn stressed that the governance of schools is antiquated and ought to be abolished. "Boards are not just superfluous, they are also dysfunctional."[15] Taking issue with that point of view, Thomas Shannon, Executive Director of the National School Boards Association, stressed a more traditional concept of local control and expressed the importance of the local board of education:

> Local school-board governance consists of several indispensable functions. The board translates federal law and integrates state mandates into local policy action; tests proposed education initiatives against the back drop of community need and sentiment; evaluates on behalf of the entire community the educational program; monitors the work of the superintendent and administrative staff who implement board policy; serves as the final appellate body short of the court system on appeals of citizens and school employees from administrative decisions; cooperatively deals (both as a board and as individual board members) with citizens in school matters in the tradition of responsive, responsible representative governance; and interacts with federal, state, and other local-government entities to ensure that the schools are given the attention they deserve. Each of these functions is so critical that they have given rise to the rubric, "If community school boards didn't exist, we should have to invent them."[16]

Shannon contested that "state legislatures have in fact adopted many oppressive statutes over the years that ruin the type of local school environment needed for innovation [and that] micromanagement by statute hinders local initiative and stifles local imagination by undercutting boards' authority to act as local policymakers."[17]

Fuhrman and Elmore[18] did extensive research on understanding local control and the degree of change required to conform with new state policies and the capacity to make the required changes. They concluded, among other findings, that "districts often leverage state policies by using local influence networks to reinforce local political agenda and to engage in local policy entrepreneurship. The result is often that the local effects of state policy are greater than those one would predict on the basis of state capacity and that localities often gain influence rather than lose it." Following are other conclusions from the study:

> Conventional notions of state and local control in education need to be modified in light of experience and research related to recent state-level reform. The most important modification is to move away from simple zero-sum conceptions of state-local relations, in which each increment of state policy results in an equal and opposite decrease in local control, and toward a conception that allows for the possibility that both state and local control can increase as a result of state policymaking and that recognizes that the exact effect of changes in state policy on state-local relationships is more a function of how states and localities mobilize and use political influence than of state control of local decision.
>
> New conceptions of state-local relations must take account of a range of factors not included in the zero-sum model. Among these factors are the following:
>
> ■ The volume of state policymaking is not a good indicator of the degree of state control. Rather, the content of state policy, the capacity of states to implement that policy, the degree of variability in local district capacity, and the degree of mobilization of state and local public and professional opinion are key factors in sorting out the relative influence of states and localities.
> ■ Examining the relationship between states and districts is not, by itself, a particularly useful way to characterize state-local relations. Districts are, in fact, multilevel systems,

and state influence depends on how state and local priorities are orchestrated around schools and classrooms.[19]

Some of the typical problems faced by local boards of education—including problems related to separation of church and state, providing equal educational opportunities for all students, including minority groups, and control of dissidents and incorrigibles—have been accentuated by a society that is constantly demanding additional services from government. On the other hand, boards of education find themselves subservient to new directives and the new rationale of the state and federal governments that attend the programs to alleviate poverty, extend educational opportunity, and push forward the frontier of knowledge. All these conditions, plus the proposal that seems to be gaining momentum that the states administer the collection and allocation of all funds for education, may seriously curtail the importance of local boards of education and the need for them.

Local Control by Contract

In recent developments, some local boards of education have been willing to turn the operation of the schools over to private, for-profit companies. Such an approach is being seen by some critics as boards absolving themselves of responsibility and further eroding local control. The concept of *privatization* is causing much debate in educational administration. Private companies are edging into the more than $440 billion business of secondary and elementary education with the intent of producing revenue for stockholders. Where entrepreneurs are promising to reach achievement goals, provide better maintenance of schools, and operate school lunch programs and transportation services for less and with more efficiency is causing some school boards to explore and adopt the private management of public schools approach.

Areas such as school lunch, maintenance, and transportation have been operated by private sources for some time, but in the field of instruction and management of the schools, the concept has developed only in recent years. The Consortium for Policy Research in Education issued a brief, stating:

> Contracting with for-profit firms is one of the new organizational arrangements to emerge in public education. . . . What is happening now is different: school districts are contracting for *regular* educational services, the very services they are organized to provide . . . . Private contracting is not an abdication of public responsibility; it is a *management mechanism* through which school districts may, or may not, better attain their traditional goals. By contracting, school districts simply decide to *buy* rather than *make*.[20]

Advocates of privatization see the virtue in government and business combining efforts. "They argue that government's oversight function and its responsiveness to the needs of citizens can be retained while exploiting business' ability to cut through bureaucracy, reduce costs, and maximize achievement."[21] Education management organizations (EMOs) are usually awarded contracts on the basis that they will improve student achievement in a cost-effective manner. The companies operate on the assumption that, through increasing the number of students served and utilizing proven curriculum materials, administrative costs can be reduced to the extent that investors will be rewarded. Proponents of the concept believe that the production of innovative ideas and competition will, in the long run, benefit public schools.

A brief from the Education Commission of the States (ECS) summarizes the debate for advocates of privatization in the following:

> Proponents believe that private companies can achieve economies of scale and greater efficiencies in operation of public schools, and then devote the money obtained through these gains to improve teaching and learning. Supporters further assert that privatizing K–12 public education services frees schools from the constraints of a public bureaucracy and thus allows them to be more innovative. According to supporters, it increases the variety of schools within a community, which, when combined with providing parents the opportunity to choose the most appropriate school for their children, forces schools to improve the quality of education services that they provide or risk losing students. Furthermore, low-performing schools with declining enrollments will be forced to close, thus increasing the overall quality of public education in a community.[22]

The ECS describes the critics' view of privatization in this description:

> Opponents believe that private companies operating public schools will make decisions based on increasing profits as opposed to improving teaching and learning. Critics also fear that in order to achieve cost savings, private companies will reduce staff or hire cheaper personnel. In addition, opponents feel that the distribution of taxpayer money to private companies is a misuse of public funds. From their perspective, while privatizing education services may help struggling schools stay afloat, it may also create private education monopolies with little or no accountability to the general public. Other critics assert that allowing private companies to provide education services diminishes a school's ability to pass on civic values and democracy and replaces it with a system focused on individual needs where teaching is product and parents are the consumers.[23]

Heidi Steffens and Peter Cookson described the *nuances* of business operating public schools:

> School design and curricula are only the starting points of the complex and nuanced task of creating a successful school. There's the matter of finding the right leadership and faculty, and nurturing their understanding of teaching and learning and their relationship with each other, their [students and students'] families, and communities. And once a thriving school climate is established, it requires cultivation and support.
> Public education is a social commitment that transcends individual interest and corporate gain. It is highly probable that schools designed to meet this responsibility are inherently unprofitable. This does not mean the commitment should be abandoned. It means that, as a human service, education is grounded in a belief in human dignity that transcends the values and behaviors associated with markets. It means public education cannot be squeezed to fit the market model and still meet the needs of a just society.[24]

The ramifications for school finance may be negligible at this time, and school budgets may not change much. However, the distribution of revenues from a private operation may be considerably different from those presently being made by public school administrators. Private management issues will continue to grow as long as school systems are having difficulties meeting community demands for achievement growth and other standards. If private, for-profit companies are successful in meeting goals, and if schools or districts are more efficiently operated with the same or even, in some cases, less per-pupil costs, then school administrators need to analyze procedures used by these companies and learn from them. "Though ambivalence toward private management of public schools may be acceptable for now, administrators should not only keep informed about private management, but consider its role in a changing society and a changing public school system."[25] Policy making in relation to the for-profit sector will be among the most important challenges education policy makers face in the years ahead."[26]

Local Control Not Guaranteed

State responsibility for education is guaranteed by the Tenth Amendment to the United States Constitution and many state constitutions. Local control of schools has long been taken for granted, but there is no guarantee of the extent or the duration of such authority. Since power comes to local districts by delegation from the states, it can be withdrawn at any time at the option of the delegating unit. Consequently, local school districts in each state have always operated at the pleasure of the state's legislature, operating within the limits established by the state constitution. As the states have gradually assumed more and more responsibility for financing education, the role of the local school district in its own governance has decreased commensurately. There is no indication that this trend is about to be reversed.

The great mobility of people has had much to do with the "insolvable" problems of financing education. As the little red schoolhouse has faded out of the picture, the extreme pride of citizens in a particular school has decreased. Average citizens want good schools wherever they go—to a different district or to a different state. The effects of good and of poor education diffuse among the towns and cities of the land. It thus becomes evident that good education is a state responsibility and cannot safely be left to local communities working alone.

Local Fiscal Control

The question of the degree or extent of power that local districts should have in the control of their own fiscal operations is controversial and unsettled. If the state provides most of the local school revenue, should it exercise more authority over local school districts than when it provides less? Do the advantages of local districts' control over their own fiscal operations counterbalance the disadvantages? These and other similar questions need to be answered in the states as they continue to increase their proportionate share of public school revenues. Although local districts have traditionally provided more than have the states toward the costs of education, that pattern has changed over the years (see Figure 6.4).

FIGURE 6.4   Sources of Revenue for Public Elementary and Secondary Schools: 2005

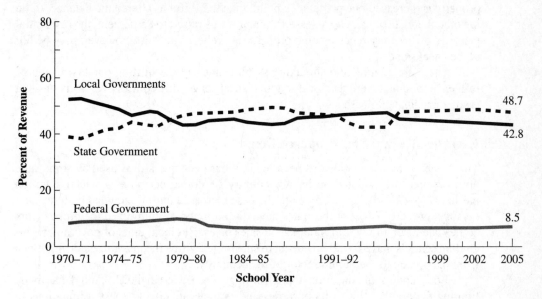

Source: *Digest of Education Statistics, 2005.* Common Core of Data surveys.

Local Control and Tax Shifting

As previously noted in this book, minimal tax shifting is one of the characteristics of a good tax system. The effect is often most detrimental to local school districts, which may have some influence but little control over decisions made at the state level. Economic factors have an impact on what legislators are willing and able to do in meeting the many fiscal responsibilities they face. Meeting the demands of the various public agencies and the myriad political pressures makes designing an equitable budget a complex matter for states, and actions taken often erode local tax revenues.

At times, court decisions, legislation, or legal rulings (such as tax commission edicts) may change the focus of one tax structure that may influence another. For example, when redevelopment agencies were established in states and the federal government made revenue available for projects, it had a rather dramatic effect on counties and local school districts by removing some properties from tax rolls. Redevelopment projects, on the other hand, have generally had a very positive impact on city and county governments, which benefit from new businesses generating additional sales tax dollars. To make up revenue for those affected by the loss of property taxes—public schools, in particular—some other source needs to be tapped, which may mean an increase in property tax for residential and business owners, or an increase in income tax.

The balance of assessing business and residential property is a delicate one that must be addressed by lawmakers. In some instances, business owners are taxed at a higher rate than homeowners. If political pressure from business owners results in a change—for example, from 80 percent of market value to 75 percent—then some adjustments would need to be made to meet budgetary needs. If, as a result, the residential property is increased one percentage point, then the shift has altered the balance. If, on the other hand, the business-assessed valuation was raised to 85 percent, the residential property owner may receive some property tax relief. The shift, however, may be felt at the checkstand.

There are complexities in taxing systems and in how shifting one taxing source influences another. At times, local school districts have little control over decisions that erode their financial base.

Excessive Reliance on Property Taxes

The property tax has not always been local; it has been and still is used by some state governments. It originated during the country's colonial period as a selective tax on particular kinds and classes of wealth. Its base increased until it included both real and personal property. Most of the states have discontinued or minimized the property tax at the state level, in favor of income and sales taxes. But local units of government, including schools, have found no adequate substitute for this means of transferring funds from the private to the public sector of the economy.

Local control of education, though strongly embedded in the U.S. mind, has many limiting factors that thwart its purposes and mitigate its effectiveness. Limitations in providing equality of educational opportunity from local tax sources alone are evident in every state. Obtaining adequate local funds for education is complicated by at least two facts: (1) Taxes on property is the major source of local revenue. (2) Competition for the local tax dollar is becoming increasingly more severe. Walker analyzed the use of the property tax in the following: "It has substantial vertical equity, meaning that it redistributes wealth from the rich to the poor through the schooling process. In addition, the tax tends to increase application of resources to high return human investments, such as education. The list could be extended, but perhaps it is sufficient to state that the prospects for reform of the tax are much greater than the prospects for elimination."[27]

One of the most obvious weaknesses of local control of fiscal operations is that in nearly all states local school districts vary greatly in their access to taxable resources. They must, of course, depend almost completely on property tax revenues for financing education. In poorer districts—those with a low assessed valuation per pupil to be educated—local tax requirements place heavy burdens on some property taxpayers, with the result that citizen pressure to hold down tax rates may result in a level of revenue inadequate for a good school program. Local school systems tend to become conservative and often refuse to inaugurate or operate high-cost programs, regardless of their potential value or the unmet needs of students.

A big problem each state faces in providing equal educational opportunity for all its citizens involves the extreme differences among districts in their ability to pay for education, as measured by the assessed valuation of taxable property per student to be educated. The difference of per-pupil expenditures between rich and poor districts is still extreme in several states.

The negative effects of inadequate support for schools are most pronounced for families of low income. Affluent families can provide alternatives to a poorly supported school, such as sending their children to more adequately financed public schools, sending them to private schools, employing tutors, or purchasing additional supplies and equipment. Such alternatives are rarely available to low-income families.

Municipal Overburden

Municipal overburden results from the fact that public schools and city governments must use the same property tax base to obtain the relatively large revenues required for their operation. The budgets of cities include large sums of noneducational public services, such as police and fire protection and health services. The high percent of total city property taxes required to finance these services (as compared to the percent required in small-city and rural areas) affects the property taxing power of city school districts for education.

Most large-city school districts must provide education for students who require additional funding—those from minority groups, those with disabilities or disadvantages, and those whose parents migrated there in the hope of finding more satisfactory social and educational programs. The situation became more complicated and the tax burdens more accentuated as affluent inner-city residents moved to the suburbs and were replaced by less affluent citizens who moved there in search of employment. Erosion of the tax base thus accompanied the increase in the need for government services, including education. The high cost of these additional city social and educational services resulted in a higher burden on property taxpayers.

Cities, of course, have made attempts to overcome their problems of overburden. Some have overassessed certain types of property; some have adopted income taxes to be calculated at the place of employment rather than residence in order to involve suburban residents in paying part of city government costs; and some have appealed to the state and federal governments for financial assistance. A few states have attempted to alleviate this condition by giving big-city school districts additional student weightings or a density factor in their school finance formulas.

A number of contributing factors relate directly to the overwhelming financial problems now in evidence in urban school districts in all parts of this country. Consider the following:

1. Conditions related to student militancy, student mobility, and integration problems have reversed the traditional trend for candidates for teaching positions to go to the cities, where salaries were more favorable, working conditions were better, and individual initiative could more easily be directed to innovation and experimentation.

2. Problems involving the education of the socially and culturally different and the physically and mentally disabled are accentuated in city districts. Cities must deal with many of these problems, whereas rural school districts, because of lack of numbers, very often minimize them. The inequality thus engendered is accentuated by the great expense of these programs.

3. Increases in city property values have not kept pace with the rapidly accelerating increases in school expenditures. The movement of large numbers of middle- and higher-income people from the core city to the suburbs has curtailed building needs, so property valuations have not risen in cities to the same extent that they have elsewhere.

4. The relative taxpaying potential of city school districts has been reduced by the migration of large numbers of low-income families to the cities. Large demand for compensatory education programs, great need for welfare programs, and the high cost of educating deprived citizens—now in a majority in many cities—have combined to downgrade the educational program.

Developers of school financing programs have long recognized the fact that small schools are generally more expensive per pupil than larger ones. To compensate for this, school finance formulas have usually included provisions for sparsity factors, which have been accepted as a necessary and fair requirement. Only recently, however, has serious consideration been given to the higher costs of education per pupil in large cities. The density factor in determining costs has not yet been accepted to the same degree as its older counterpart, the sparsity factor.

Local Nonproperty Taxes

Some tax and finance authorities have looked with much hope and expectancy at local nonproperty taxes, viewing them as a strong potential supplement to property taxes. Local sales taxes, income or earnings taxes, and others have been used in some communities for school purposes. Unfortunately, the revenues obtained and the inconvenience of collection, plus taxpayer resistance, have made these taxes of doubtful value in many school districts, especially in small cities or communities. Some larger city school districts have, however, used local nonproperty taxes satisfactorily.

Local nonproperty taxes have become somewhat popular, especially in urban centers where the total populations are large enough to make such taxation practicable. Tax authorities who had expected good results from such taxes were disappointed in their applications and their ineffectiveness in smaller districts. Fiscally independent districts have benefited little from such taxes. Some districts, however, have received substantial amounts of money from tax sharing with the state or county in the application of some forms of nonproperty taxation—the sales tax, for example. Up to this time, revenues from nonproperty taxes have been small in comparison with the total costs of education, but the trend may change in the next decade. Michigan has altered local property taxes and increased the state sales tax, and has imposed a tax rate on nonhomestead and business properties to fund schools.

It appears that local nonproperty taxes will be reserved, for the most part, as sources of state revenue. At present, nonproperty taxes do not seem to have an encouraging future as a source of local school revenues.

Advantages of Local Control

The local community and the local school district in the United States are far more influential in their relations to their own educational programs than are their counterparts in other countries. Educational philosophy generally supports the belief that a large degree of local control not only stimulates local interest and support but also more easily permits innovations and improvements. The idea of strong national administrative control of education is repugnant to most citizens.

In certain ways, the local districts have an advantage over the states and the federal government in obtaining additional funds for education. Those who have observed the long history of federal aid attempts point to the many years of indecision and frustration caused by the bitter debates involving racial discrimination, separation of church and state, political jealousies, and the ever-present fear of federal control. Action at the federal level to shore up the finances of school districts continues to be a controversial issue. Substantially increased funds at the state level is a reality.

Property taxes remain the mainstay of local source revenues. According to Augenblick:

> The viability of education finance depends on diverse sources of revenue. Any attempt to eliminate a revenue source (such as the property tax), no matter how well intended, poses a threat to the education system. Rather than doing away with property taxes, policymakers should improve assessment practices, collection systems, and the tax rate setting process. In this way, the equity of a state's school finance system can be balanced against the assurance that adequate revenues will be available to support the education system.[28]

Fiscal Independence of School Districts

The question of whether the local school board should have autonomy within the law in the use of local tax sources and revenues is relevant in a discussion of local responsibility for education. Many in the fields of economics and political science argue in favor of the fiscally dependent district—a system that places the local district board of education under some degree of jurisdiction by the city or county government. Usually, this involves city or county approval of the school district's annual budget. Under this arrangement, city or county officials make final decisions for school budgetary requests, which are based on deliberations of the board of education without the understanding or active participation of the municipal authorities involved. As a group, educators almost universally favor fiscal independence for school boards.

Trends in Local Taxation Practices

Many people hope for relief for local property taxpayers, with an increase in the state and federal revenues for education. Current trends follow:

1. Property tax administration will be improved; even though taxpayer resistance against such taxes may increase, the property tax will continue to be an important source of funds for the operation of public schools. Professionally trained career assessors, sophisticated computer assistance, realistic laws concerning property tax administration, the establishment of larger taxing districts to encourage specialization in tax administration, adequate and efficient state supervision of the program, and more effective communication between those who administer the tax program and those who pay the taxes—all are reasonable improvements that logically can be expected in the future.

2. Competition among local agencies for the tax dollar will continue to increase; schools will succeed in this arena only if they are able to be more sophisticated competing in the political arena.

3. The urban communities will continue to suffer from revenue shortfall unless given equitable treatment in local, state, and federal allocation of funds.

4. Efforts will be made to make the property tax less regressive and to relieve those who suffer economically from too much emphasis on this kind of taxation. Property taxpayers have justifiable cause for complaint in states that leave the financial responsibility of education almost completely up to the individual local districts.

Measures of Local Taxpaying Ability

The ability of a local school district to pay the costs of education without state or federal support is a function of two variables: the value of taxable property, the number of pupils to be educated, and the willingness of taxpayers to support the desired program. This is usually expressed as the assessed valuation of taxable property per person in average daily attendance or in average daily membership in school.

For nearly a century, scholars and practitioners of school finance have been studying how to measure the comparative abilities of local units of government to finance education and to provide other services. State equalization programs—particularly those involving power equalization—must use some valid and reliable measure of local fiscal ability if state and federal allocations of funds to local districts are to be justified.

Scholars have conducted extensive research in an attempt to refine the measurement of local fiscal ability. There seems to be little justification for using a theoretically computed index of ability, but there is a strong rationale for using the ability as measured by the tax structure and current system. Little is to be gained in comparing the abilities of school districts in terms of potential taxes and revenue that are not available to those districts. These are measures that may have real value in determining a state's ability to support education, since the state legislative body can make them available by statute, but their value in comparing local districts is limited and questionable.

Local, State, and Federal Tax Responsibility

A difficult problem arises in coordinating the taxing system of the three levels of government—federal, state, and local. No one has yet determined the ideal, or even the most practical, combination of taxing powers and authority of these levels of government that will produce maximum social and cultural benefits with maximum taxpayer equity and minimum taxpayer burden and inconvenience. To a very great extent, these three units of government operate their tax patterns in isolation from each other. Ideally, their taxing systems should be coordinated. The elements of taxation that are usurped to some degree by any one unit of government would seemingly be sources beyond the powers of the other two units to use. But adequate funds must be provided regardless of source if good education is to be provided for all our citizens.

In most states, the local school districts have traditionally had to raise the major part of the tax revenues required to finance their public schools. The states have assumed important but varying degrees of responsibility for financing education, and the federal government has participated. The National Education Association has stated, "Public education in the United States is a *joint* enterprise of federal, state, and local government. . . . Federal funds represent a modest supplement directed principally at special populations . . . states and school districts give substance to public education."[29] The principal responsibility for financing education rests with the states and their local units.

Summary

Because of the continual increases in funds allocated to public education by most of the states, local control of education is slowly decreasing. This is a source of some concern to many people who view education as a frontier where people at the local level can exercise some degree of authority in decision making in matters that directly affect them.

Rural areas of the country no longer have the strong influence on legislation they once enjoyed. On the other hand, urban areas have lost the financial advantage they once had over rural areas. City school districts suffer financially because of higher costs and the need to provide social and welfare services that are minimized in most rural areas.

Although much has been done to decrease the extremely large number of school districts that once existed in the United States, some states still operate far too many small districts. Just as many school districts are too small for efficient operation, many city districts are too large. Most states have been able to provide for the financial needs of small districts and are working toward a satisfactory solution for the municipal overburden of large cities.

Historically, there has been a fervor to maintain local control of education, but greater open debate and controversy regarding the effectiveness and usefulness of local boards have emerged and they are experiencing an eroding of authority. Business and political leaders are developing programs mandating more control over local school districts. Mayors of some large cities have gained control over schools in their jurisdiction and are usurping power from the school board. Some states have passed legislation requiring districts to expend at least 65 percent of revenue on a defined operating budget and have taken over the supervision of school districts. Accountability requirements, failing schools, mandated legislation, and other factors have diminished the administrative authority of some local school districts and will affect others in the future.

A good tax system has a minimum of tax shifting. The results are often detrimental to local school districts that have limited control over such matters. Court decisions, legislative action, or legal rulings may change the tax structure that can cause a local school district to lose revenue for the instructional program as well as capital outlay and debt service obligations. The process is complex, and local boards of education may have little control over factors that erode their financial base.

Mobility of the population is significant, and people want good schools throughout the nation, but the public may not be willing to pay for them. Recent developments have some local boards looking to private, for-profit companies to operate schools. Critics indicate that this approach will erode local control.

The states have always assumed general responsibility for education, but many of them have left the major financial obligation and control with local districts. The real property tax has been the major source of local funds for education since the early history of the nation. States have recently begun to place limits on such taxes and, in a few instances, have placed limits on annual expenditure increases for public education.

Local nonproperty taxes are not as effective or productive as they appear to be in theory, yet some states are branching to other sources. Education finance will need to depend on diverse sources of income in the future.

A relatively few school districts are still dependent on some other unit of government for approval of some aspect of their financing. The disadvantages of such a relationship far outweigh the advantages. Dependent school districts are much more likely to become involved in local government politics than are independent districts.

Certain trends are discernible in local taxation practices. Better property tax administration, continued competition for the tax dollar among various agencies and institutions of government, a continuation of the problems created by municipal overburden, more state support for education, and continued resistance to taxes are among the most evident.

ASSIGNMENT PROJECTS

1. Provide a definition for each of the following terms: *school district, school board, administrator, privatization, fiscal independence, consolidation, reorganization, tax shifting.*

2. Summarize the arguments for and against local control of public education.

3. Reducing the number of school districts in a state will generally reduce the difference in ability to support education between the "wealthiest" district and the "poorest" district in terms of assessed valuation per pupil to be educated. Construct a problem in a state (real or mythical) and show that this statement is true or false.

4. Interview the business administrator at a local district. Determine the revenue generated at the local level, the assistance from the state, and the implication the ratio has on local control of the district.

5. Write a paper presenting the pros and cons of the concept of municipal overburden payments to urban school districts.

6. Research and report on the advantages and disadvantages of consolidating school districts within a state.

7. Write a paper outlining the pros or cons of privatizing various elements of public education.

> Computer simulations and questions, research exercises, and website
> addresses relevant to this chapter can be found at
>
> **www.ablongman.com/edleadership**

SELECTED READINGS

Alexander, Kern, and Richard G. Salmon. *Public School Finance.* Boston: Allyn and Bacon, 1995.

Goertz, Margaret, and Allan Odden, eds. *School Based Financing.* Thousand Oaks, CA: Corwin Press, 1999.

Honeyman, D. S., D. C. Thompson, and R. C. Wood. *Financing Rural and Small Schools: Issues of Adequacy and Equity.* Gainesville: University of Florida Press, 1989.

Leithwood, Kenneth, ed. *Effective School District Leadership.* Albany: State University of New York Press, 1995.

School Finance Trends in U.S. Education Spending. Washington, DC: U.S. General Accounting Office, September 1995.

Theobald, Neil D., and Betty Malen, eds. *Balancing Local Control and State Responsibility for K–12 Education. 2000 Yearbook of the American Education Finance Association.* Larchmont, NY: Eye on Education, 2000.

Thomas, Gloria Jean, David J. Sperry, and F. Del Wasden. *The Law and Teacher Employment.* New York: West Publishing, 1991.

Thompson, David C., R. Craig Wood, and David S. Honeyman. *Fiscal Leadership for Schools, Concepts and Practices.* White Plains, NY: Addison-Wesley, 1994.

Verstegen, D. A. *School Finance at a Glance.* Denver, CO: Education Commission of the States, 1990.

ENDNOTES

1. "Context of Elementary and Secondary Education 2006, Changes in Sources of Public School Revenue," National Center for Education Statistics: http://nces.ed.gov/programs/coe/2002/section6/indicator44.asp.
2. Allison Shelley, "Vanishing Heritage," *Education Week,* May 28, 2003, p. 24.
3. Alan Richard, "Cortines' Plan for L. A. Would Cut or Restructure 800 Jobs," *Education Week,* March 22, 2000, p. 3.
4. Fred C. Lunenburg and Allan C. Ornstein, *Educational Administration Concepts and Practices,* 3rd ed. (Belmont, CA: Wadsworth, 1999), p. 373.
5. Ibid., p. 364.
6. Elizabeth Thurston, "Who Controls Urban Schools?" Access, www.schoolfunding.info/news, April 26, 2006.
7. John Rubin and Duke Helfand, "Details of Schools Takeover Emerge," *Los Angeles Times,* Latimes.com, April 13, 2006.
8. Thurston, "Who Controls Urban Schools?"
9. David Hoff, "Call for 'Weighted' Student Funding Gets Bipartisan Stamp of Approval," *Education Week,* July 12, 2006, pp. 1, 30.
10. "First Class Education—FAQ," www.firstclasseducation.org/faqs/asp, July 2006, pp. 1–5.
11. Ibid.
12. Gwendolyn Santiago and Tom Canby, "Is the 65% Solution the Silver Bullet for Education?" *School Business Affairs,* February 2006, p. 33. See also *School Business Affairs* articles, February 2006, pp. 29–34, and "65% of What," National School Plant Management Association, Lexington, KY.
13. Laura Maggi, "State to Run Orleans Schools," *The Times-Picayune,* November 23, 2005. See also Catherine Gewertz, "Dual Orleans Systems Grow in Storm's Wake," *Education Week,* June 7, 2006, pp. 1 and 20–21.
14. Chester E. Finn, Jr., "Reinventing Local Control," *Education Week,* Vol. 10, No. 18, January 23, 1991, p. 40.

15. Ibid.
16. Thomas Shannon, "Local Control and Organiza-rats," *Education Week,* Vol. 10, No. 21, February 13, 1991.
17. Ibid., p. 32.
18. Susan M. Fuhrman and Richard F. Elmore, "Understanding Local Control," *Educational Evaluation and Policy Analysis,* Spring 1990, p. 94.
19. Ibid., pp. 93–94.
20. Jane Hannaway, *Contracting as a Mechanism for Managing Education Services,* CPRE Policy Briefs, Reporting of issues in education reform, Graduate School of Education, University of Pennsylvania, November 28, 1999, p. 1.
21. "Education Inc., Perspectives on Private Management of Public Schools," A Special Commentary Report, *Education Week,* June 22, 1994, p. 41.
22. "Privatization," Education Commission of the States, Denver, CO, ecs@ecs.org, 2006. p. 1.

23. Ibid., pp. 1–2.
24. Heidi Steffens and Peter W. Cookson Jr., "Limitations of the Market Model," *Education Week,* August 7, 2002, p. 48.
25. Ibid.
26. John M. McLaughlin, "The Private Management of Public Schools," *Principal,* March 1994, p. 19.
27. Billy D. Walker, "The Local Property Tax for Public Schools: Some Historical Perspectives," *Journal of Education Finance,* Vol. 9, No. 3, Winter 1984, p. 288.
28. John Augenblick, "The Importance of Property Taxes to the Future of School Finance," *Journal of Education Finance,* Vol. 9, No. 3, Winter 1984, p. 393.
29. *Estimate of School Statistics 1990–91* (Washington, DC: National Education Association Data-Search, 1991), p. 5.

7 Education:
A State Function

America has a superbly successful public school system, due in large measure, to local and state leadership where elected officials are constantly "in tune" with their neighborhood schools. Responsibility for education is a primary role for the state level of government in America's federal system. The state ensures that every child is learning in a safe and secure climate where children are prized and nurtured toward success.

—Patti Harrington, 2007

Education appears to have been considered important in colonial times largely because of its presumed preventive effect in fortifying people to resist evil. Important as that purpose may have been, the rationale for the establishment and operation of schools has changed considerably since that era.

Establishing and operating a system of public schools has been recognized as a function of government rather than of private enterprise since the settlement of the first Europeans in what is now the United States. These early colonists recognized the importance of education in building and maintaining a democratic government and properly developing individuals and organizations to serve it. The general tone toward schools and education was succinctly expressed in the statement the Continental Congress included in the Northwest Ordinance of 1787: "Schools and the means of education shall forever be encouraged." The spirit of that declaration continues to be a part of the national ideal.

The present relation of government to education has evolved over two centuries. For the most part, the practical "partnership" of federal, state, and local levels of government has worked well. Each state has been responsible for its own system of education, with power to delegate whatever degree of control it chose to local districts of the kind and number it desired. As a result, there have been 50 versions of how education should function in as many states. The federal government over the years has assumed very little real authority over education.

Changes and innovations are an integral part of the continuing development of the nation's educational system. The need for improvement of education is becoming more observable year after year. But how shall the course of the three-level governmental relation to education be determined? Is the stage being set for more state and less local responsibility for financing education? Have the traditional arguments favoring local control become obsolete? Has the federal government become more involved in public education, requiring mandates for more accountability usurping state and local responsibilities?

Early Development of State Responsibility

The word *education* is conspicuous by its absence in the United States Constitution. The writers of that document avoided any specific designation of responsibility for the pattern that formal education should take in this country. The reasons for such an important omission are presumed to have been as follows: (1) The original 13 colonies had already established their own patterns of school organization and had recognized and accepted their individual obligations for education, at least to some degree, by action and legislation during the colonial period. (2) Many of the leaders of government presumed that a controversy over educational responsibility might lead to an impasse, or at least add greatly to the already overwhelming problems about which there was great dissension. (3) Government leaders viewed education as an activity to be handled by state governments and therefore adopted the Tenth Amendment to the U.S. Constitution, which left many powers to the states, thereby instituting the principle of federalism.

The Constitution should be interpreted and evaluated in terms of the unique conditions under which it was adopted. The United States of America was born as a legal entity after a period of stress that resulted in the American Revolution. The colonies won that bitter conflict after almost superhuman effort and sacrifice on the part of many, but not all, of their citizens. The founding fathers, recognizing their break with the philosophy of government of that day, were vitally concerned with how to establish perpetuity of government. They felt a need to avoid endowing the federal government with powers that might at some time overbalance the powers of the state governments. This they hoped to achieve by delegating certain powers to the federal government while strengthening the structure and framework of the individual states. As new states entered the Union, the enabling legislation usually required the states to assume educational responsibility in their constitutions.

It should not be assumed that early Americans were indifferent to education or had little interest in it. The establishment of Harvard in 1636, the Laws of 1642 and 1647, and the Ordinances of 1785 and 1787 (passed by the Continental Congress under the Articles of Confederation, which makes federal aid to education predate the Constitution), are examples of their actions to provide for some important aspects of an educational program. Education had been at a low ebb during the Revolution. It was provided mostly by private schools, with only local community support and with little or no cooperation among schools. The real battle for free public schools under colonial or state supervision had not yet begun.

Undoubtedly, the framers of the Constitution believed that the governmental framework they were creating implied provision for education. James Madison proposed the establishment of a university; Thomas Jefferson advocated appropriations of public lands for education; and George Washington pressed hard for a national university. With such support for specific aspects of education by these and other leaders of that time, few historians believe that education was not considered by the founding fathers.

In the minds of many interpreters of the Constitution, Article I, Section 8 gives Congress the authority to provide educational support. "The Congress shall have power to lay and collect taxes . . . to pay the debts and provide for the common defense and general welfare of the United States." Education is part of the general welfare of the nation.

A need to expand aspects of the Constitution were evident as soon as it was adopted. It was apparent immediately that it did not protect individual rights to the extent expected or desired. Consequently, the first 10 amendments were adopted in 1791 as the Bill of Rights. These, especially the Tenth Amendment, form much of the legal basis for the nation's present system of education. The Tenth Amendment provides that "the powers not delegated to the United States by the Constitution, nor prohibited by it to the States, are reserved to the States respectively, or to the people." Thus, education has been and continues to be primarily a function of state government. This responsibility is further documented by state constitutional provisions acknowledging and accepting this power, plus numerous court decisions supporting the states' leadership in education.

Development of Decentralized Educational Systems

State school systems developed from local units. State responsibility for education was accepted in theory, but little leadership at this level was in evidence until the early nineteenth century, when a few educational leaders, particularly Horace Mann and Henry Barnard, began their historic efforts to develop a state foundation for education.

The typical citizen tends to think of the state school systems as having existed as they now are from the beginning of the nation, but U.S. patterns of education, including financial formulas and schemes, are the products of more than two centuries of development under a grass-roots process of building—a process that was often erratic. However, appreciation for these systems, with all their limitations, comes quickly to the conscientious student of educational history. Those who understand the contributions of such men as Washington, Jefferson, Franklin, Paine, Barnard, and Mann must share some degree of pride in our systems of education, which have made such rich contributions to this country.

The story of the development of the 50-state school system is one of diversity, struggle, and dedication to the idea of a decentralized system of education, without a national system, a minister of education, or any national control. It seems, then, that the omission of specific educational provisions from the Constitution has proved to have been wisdom on the part of those who were responsible. Sound philosophy espousing decentralization, a willingness to involve people at the local and state levels, and national patience have proved to be better developers of our state school systems than anything that could possibly have been planned by the foresight of earnest educational and governmental leaders more than two centuries ago. From this process there emerged the best organizational pattern of education the world has yet produced.

Development of School Finance Policies

The history of financing public school education in the United States is an interesting one. Actually, it is 50 separate stories of various forms of informal local and state action. In the early part of the nation's history, most of the costs of school operation were defrayed with nonmonetary services, provided by school patrons to the school itself or to the teacher. Fuel, custodial services, room and board for the teacher, and similar services were provided in lieu of salaries, insurance, and benefits.

As the schools grew in size and complexity, so did the methods of financing them. These finance systems, and even the processes used to develop them, represent diversity and lack of standardization in the fullest meaning of those terms. Too often, the states profited little by the experiences of other states. Much too often, the states seem to have regarded variety as virtue and following the leader as vice. The lessons learned in one state seldom reduced the learning period required by taxpayers and professional leaders in another. This problem was solved in some small measure by the establishment of the Education Commission of the States as well as the creation of educational organizations such as the National School Boards Association, the Council of Chief State School Officers, the American Association of School Administrators, the National Association of Elementary School Principals, the National Secondary School Principals Association, and other similar alliances.

Land Grants and Other Nontax Funds

It is difficult to determine the exact beginning of state support for public education. Paul Mort reported that by 1890 the existing states provided about $34 million—almost 24 percent of that year's total school revenue. Since some of that state revenue was obtained from land given to the states by the federal government in the famous Northwest Ordinance of 1787, Mort included federal funds in the category of state funds. The states generally provided means of legalizing local school taxes in their early statehood years, but equalization and sound theories and practices of state-local partnership in financing education were developments of the twentieth century. When the twentieth century began, only 17.2 percent of public school district revenues came from state sources. When the twenty-first century began, around 48 percent came from state sources, an increase of nearly 300 percent.

In the early history of the colonies, land grants for the establishment and support of schools were common, especially in Massachusetts. As an example, from the early pioneer work in the field of land grants by Massachusetts, the state of Maine was created. Other more or less popular sources of the limited funds used to establish and maintain schools in the colonies included gifts, rate bills, and lotteries. Before taxation became the accepted method of financing schools, most of the known ways of collecting money were used in one or more of the 13 colonies to obtain school funds. The early settlers brought with them the traditions of their European homelands, which had little relation to practical methods of financing decentralized schools as they began to emerge in the United States. Thus, there followed a long period of conflict over how to solve this important problem.

In the early United States, with its seemingly unlimited expanse of land and other valuable resources, it was natural that the granting of lands should become a significant reality in financing education. This policy was implemented by the Northwest Ordinance of 1785 and 1787 (see Figure 7.1), which was enacted by the Continental Congress primarily to stimulate migration to the West and secondarily to foster education. This law provided for a survey of western lands by establishing townships with 36 sections. Each section contained 640 acres. Usually, a settler homesteaded 80 acres, constructed a home between 40-acre parcels, and called one portion the "north forty" and the other portion the "south forty." Section 16 of every township was reserved for education. Its purpose was in the now famous statement, "Religion, morality,

FIGURE 7.1   The Ordinance of 1785

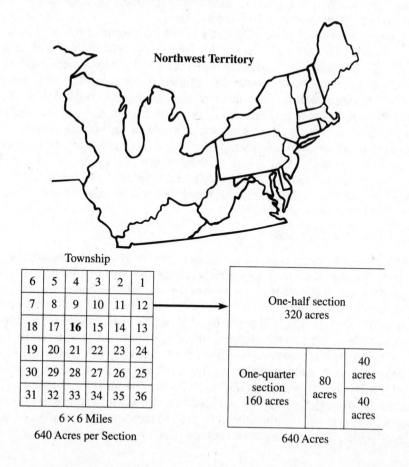

and knowledge being necessary to good government and the happiness of mankind, schools, and the means of education shall be forever encouraged."

The land grants of 1787 became effective with the admission of Ohio to the Union in 1802. When California became a state in 1850, the grant included two sections per township. Arizona, New Mexico, and Utah received four sections per township on becoming states in the latter part of the nineteenth and early part of the twentieth centuries.

The effect of the land grants on education was monumental. However, the lands were mismanaged in some of the states; the funds obtained from the rent or sale of the land were sometimes squandered. As a consequence of such mismanagement and inefficiency in many of the states, the potentially large revenues from this source were never fully realized.

The land-grant states relied to a great extent on the land grants to supply school funds until the end of the nineteenth century. The size of the grant was great, even in terms of the enormous expanses of unsettled territory of that day. For example, 12 states received the sixteenth section per township; 14 states received sections 16 and 36; and 3 states received sections 2, 16, 32, and 36 per township. Kentucky, Maine, Texas, Vermont, West Virginia, Oklahoma (which when settled was *Indian land*), and the 13 original states received no federal lands.

Since the original grant of land, the federal government has granted additional lands to some of the states, including salt lands, swamp lands, and internal improvement lands. Altogether, the land grants have been estimated to be more than 154 million acres, which is a land mass greater than Illinois, Indiana, and Ohio combined, and a value of billions of dollars—not including statehood grants to Alaska and Hawaii. In spite of the inefficient management of some of these lands, the funds derived provided many of the states with the means required to establish and operate schools while their state and local tax structures were being developed. They antedated state property taxes and thus became the revenue source for state improvement programs in extending the quantity and improving the quality of school services during the early development of state school systems, especially in the midwestern and western states.

Early Taxation Patterns

The taxation patterns for education in the newly formed United States were largely permissive, creating a situation that generally favored the city school districts, which were progressive, and penalized the rural areas of the country, which were more tax resistant. The taxing policies of the several states emerged gradually from the patterns that had been used in the New England states. By 1890, all the states then in the Union had tax-supported public educational systems. About one-fourth of them provided more than half of their public school costs from state funds, and only 11 states provided less than 15 percent of their public school costs. The states not only felt certain responsibilities to help build sound educational programs but they were also concerned with the settlement of the West. Hence, the first quarter of the nineteenth century saw the real beginning of a taxing pattern for the support of public education. By then, most of the nontax sources—gifts, lotteries, bequests, and rate bills—were beginning to vanish from the scene. Some of these practices have resurfaced and are evident today, especially lotter-ies. Other nontax sources—such as education foundations, and partnerships, gifts, and benefits—are becoming more prevalent. Taxation, however, still remains the primary source of state and school finance revenue.

Developmental Stages of School Finance

The development of public school finance theory and practice can be divided into six stages or periods. Admittedly, the periods overlap, and no specific dates divide them. Although theories have developed logically, their acceptance and use by the states have often been sporadic or almost nonexistent. Examples may be found of states that even now are in each one of the six stages of development. Of course, the size of a state, its educational finance needs and traditions, and its educational leadership may have equipped it for easier and freer transition and movement, compared with other states, into a modern and realistic stage of school finance theory and practice. Although states have continually pushed forward the frontier of educational finance theory, some are still trying to operate with outdated financing practices.

The six stages of development of state-local relations (disregarding the federal level for the moment) are (1) the period of local district financial responsibility, with little or no assistance from the state; (2) the period of emerging state responsibility, with the use of flat grants, subventions, and other nonequalizing state allocations to local districts; (3) the emergence of the Strayer-Haig concept of a foundation pro-gram; (4) the period of refinement of the foundation program concept; (5) "power" or "open-end" (shared costs) equalization practices; and (6) the shift of emphasis and influence.

Period One: Emphasis on Local Responsibility

Since schools were first established in the United States on a local basis, it was natural for school finance to be a local community or church problem. The original colonies used rate bills or tuition charges—a procedure that they brought from their European homelands—but some of the New England towns began very early in their history to use property taxes to help finance education. Massachusetts and Connecticut were the leaders in this field, and each used this practice to some extent during the latter half of the seventeenth century. Tax support was used to a limited extent in the original south-ern states and in some mid-Atlantic states for the support of pauper schools.

The permissive property tax laws that existed when the colonies became states gradually became mandatory toward the end of the eighteenth century and the early part of the nineteenth. As the westward movement of settlers accelerated and the number of local school districts began to multiply, the popularity and acceptability of the local property tax as the mainstay of the school financing program increased. By 1890, with the closing of the frontier, all of the states were using property taxes, supplemented in many instances with revenue from the land grants and from other sources.

The gross weaknesses and limitations of financing education at the local level are all too evident. Extremely wide differences in local taxpaying ability to meet the costs of education in hundreds of school districts (in a few instances, more than a thousand) in a state make a mockery of the theory of equality of educational opportunity for all school pupils, unless the state does something to help financially weak districts. Since each district is almost completely on its own as far as finances are concerned, the place of each pupil's residence becomes the all-important determinant of the quantity and quality of education available. Local initiative and local ability, important as they are in the philosophy of decentralization in education, should never be allowed to become the determinants of the caliber of education that the citizens in any community receive.

The weakness of complete local financing of education becomes more evident as the property tax becomes less and less based on the ability-to-pay principle of taxation. It is evident that the greater the number of school districts in a state, the greater the likelihood of wide disparities in wealth, so states with hundreds of school districts can least afford to confine themselves to this obsolete approach to the school finance problem.

In the early twentieth century, as rural communities and neighborhoods grew into larger ones, without accompanying expansion of taxable wealth, the need for state support of education became more evident. States were slow to move in this direction, however, until the Depression of the 1930s showed the hopelessness of financing education by complete reliance on local property taxes.

Some forms of state support had existed for some time before the Depression. The early work of Ellwood P. Cubberley in 1905 was the beginning of an era of study and experimentation in devising state plans that might assure equality of educational opportunity for all and at the same time improve school programs and equalize the tax burden.

Period Two: Early Grants and Allocations

About the turn of the [twentieth] century public schools in most population centers acquired their present structure—12 grades and a nine-month school term—and came to represent a greater cost to local taxpayers. As States legislated local programs of this scope, the issue of inequality in local wealth surfaced. Rural communities in particular found it increasingly difficult to impose tax rates stiff enough to meet the State mandated programs. Cities with their concentration of valuable properties could and did provide high level educational programs with moderate tax effort.[1]

From the very beginning of public financing of schools, a few states recognized and implemented their responsibilities in the matter. A number of reasons may be given for this early development: (1) The extreme inequalities that local property taxation generated among local school districts were soon obvious. (2) The funds that the sale and rental of the public lands provided were intended to find their way into the treasuries of local districts where control of education existed. (3) Many leaders in the educational movement recognized that the responsibility for education that the Tenth Amendment thrust on the states encompassed financial responsibility as much as any other kind.

Cubberley was the pioneer and foremost figure in the serious consideration of state apportionments of funds to local school districts. Some of the principal tenets of his philosophy of school finance are expressed in the following:

> Theoretically all the children of the state are equally important and are entitled to have the same advantages; practically this can never be quite true. The duty of the state is to secure for all as high a minimum of good instruction as is possible, but not to reduce all to this minimum; to equalize the advantages to all as nearly as can be done with the resources at hand; to place premium on those local efforts which will enable communities to rise above the legal minimum as far as possible; and to encourage communities to extend their educational energies to new and desirable undertakings.[2]

Cubberley's study of state allocations of funds to local districts—including flat grants, percentage grants, and others—showed that such allocations did not reduce inequalities and may even under certain circumstances have increased them. He saw little evidence that state fund allocations had reduced the wide range in the quality of education produced in school districts or the great disparity in ability to finance their programs. He made the first scientific study of the problem.

Cubberley was dedicated to the principle of equality of educational opportunity for all. Most of his ideas of how to provide such equality were far ahead of the practices of his time, even though most of them have been revised and improved in recent years. Noteworthy among the ideas and principles that Cubberley espoused were:

1. The belief that education was indeed a financial responsibility of the states, which they could not and should not ignore.
2. The firm conviction that state financial support was in addition to local effort, not intended as justifiable tax relief to local districts.
3. The awareness that existing methods of allocating state monies not only did not equalize the financial ability among local districts but may actually have increased financial inequalities among districts.
4. The need to increase the number of educational programs offered in the schools with attendant increases in state money for those districts with such extensions. This was Cubberley's widely known version of reward for effort.
5. The wisdom of using aggregate days attendance over census, enrollment, average daily attendance, or any other measure used in determining the amount of state funds to local districts. This would encourage the extension of the school year and would penalize those districts that shortened the total length of their school year.
6. The need to distribute some part of the state funds on the basis of the number of teachers employed in a district. This would aid the rural districts, which usually had a low pupil-teacher ratio.

Most of the Cubberley-inspired theories of school finance have become discredited and outmoded. It is easy to show that he was right in condemning flat grants, percentage grants, and subventions as nonequalizing. It is likewise easy, however, to show that his reward-for-effort principle was also nonequalizing. The wealthy districts already were employing more teachers, conducting more and better school programs, and holding more days of school per year than the poorer ones were. Thus, his reward for effort was applicable in the wealthier districts and much less applicable in the less wealthy ones.

Some states still use a few of the features of Cubberley's finance proposals. Fortunately, a number of these practices are in combination with other, more equalizing methods of allocating state funds. Although some nonequalizing grants may have justification in school finance formulas, they are not justified if used alone. They represent progress beyond local effort alone, but they are glaring examples of some of the inconsistencies so readily discernible in the Cubberley concept.

It must be emphasized that there are some potential dangers involved in allocating state funds to local districts, regardless of how this is accomplished. Two principal risks are (1) the state could increase its control over local districts as it increases its financial support and (2) state monies may be used to supplant rather than supplement local monies for education.

The first of these two considerations requires little discussion, for the state already exercises plenary power over its school districts. The degree of state authority and power over education is entirely a legislative matter that the will of each successive session of each state's legislative assembly controls and regulates. The extent of such control need not be in direct relation to the fiscal policies of the state as far as education is concerned, and it has not been so.

The purpose of state financial support of education is not to replace or reduce local effort unless that effort has been considered unduly burdensome to local taxpayers. Its purpose has been to supplement local tax revenues in order to provide an acceptable school program. The obvious answer to this problem is to require minimum school district levies before state funds are forthcoming.

Period Three: Emergence of the Foundation Program Concept

Modern school finance theory had its origin in the monumental work of George D. Strayer and Robert M. Haig. The real theory of equalization with its foundation program concept began with the findings of the Educational Finance Inquiry Commission of the schools of New York in 1923. The equalization of educational opportunity through the inception of a foundation or of a minimum program came as a direct result of the Strayer-Haig intensive studies of school finance programs built around the Cubberley philosophy and practiced in several states in the United States, particularly New York.

The Strayer-Haig studies discovered that in the school finance program of the state of New York, built as it was primarily around the distribution of state funds on a per-teacher quota basis, favored "the very rich and the very poor localities at the expense of those which are moderately well off." From this and other discoveries of deficiencies in the state finance plans of that era, Strayer and Haig advocated their *foundation,* or minimum program, concept. Their plan centered on several fundamental factors or standards:

1. A foundation program should be devised around the rich district idea—each local district would levy the amount of local tax that was required in the richest district of the state to provide a foundation, or minimum, program. The rich district would receive no state funds; the other districts would receive state funds necessary to provide the foundation program.
2. All foundation programs should guarantee equality of educational opportunity up to a specified point, but all local districts should have the discretionary right to go beyond that point and provide a better program through tax-levy increases.
3. The program should be organized and administered to encourage local initiative and efficiency.
4. The features of the program should be defined in the law and should be objective and apply to all school districts of the state.
5. Foundation programs should be constructed, after thorough study and careful planning, around the needs and resources of each individual state.
6. The cost of the foundation program should include a major part of the total cost of public education in that state.
7. The program should be organized so that no district receives additional funds because it is underassessed for property taxation purposes at the local level; uniform property assessment is essential in all foundation programs.
8. The plan should encourage the reorganization of school districts into a reasonable number and the consolidation of attendance areas wherever practicable, but provision must be made to avoid penalizing necessary small schools.
9. The foundation program should be a minimum and not a maximum program; local initiative and increased expenditures above the foundation program must be practicable in all the districts of a state.

The Strayer-Haig concept of equalization is summarized in the following brief statement:

> The Strayer-Haig approach became the model for numerous State adaptations. Compromises with the strict application of the equalization objective were made in most States to accommodate: (a) the long-standing tradition of flat grants; (b) the reluctance of State officials to increase State taxes to fully finance an equalization plan; and (c) the desire of some localities to finance truly superior public schools. In most States the foundation plan ended up providing the poorest district with a basic educational program at a level well below that which many school districts willingly supported. Wealthy districts were left ample local tax leeway to exceed the minimum foundation plan level without unduly straining local resources. Retention of flat grants as part of most State school financing plans left the wealthiest communities free to forge ahead.[3]

Period Four: Refinement of the Foundation Program Concept

The foundation program concept opened the gates for widespread experimentation and refinement of this method of approaching equal educational opportunity. In the state of New York, Paul Mort, working with Strayer and Haig, developed a program providing a degree of equalization plus the use of flat grants. The question of whether to take "surplus" monies from wealthy districts to help the states obtain equalization revenue was often debated and "settled" in various states. The question of the reasonableness of continuing the Cubberley concept of payment for effort was likewise debated by the individuals and commissions that were facing the problem of improving state finance programs. Wide differences in interpretation of the foundation program concept were developed and experimented with during this period.

Some important changes followed experimentation with the Strayer-Haig concept of equalization:

1. There began an early movement away from the levy of a statewide property tax, the proceeds of which were to be distributed to schools on a school population or average daily attendance basis.
2. Fiscal independence of school districts was attained in most sections of the country.
3. The change from state property taxation to local property taxation brought intricate problems of obtaining fair and equitable property assessments.
4. The Depression years saw the establishment of laws in most states limiting the taxing power of school districts.
5. Beginning efforts have been made in the use of local nonproperty taxes. These, however, have been insignificant except in a few large local districts.
6. The Cubberley emphasis on improvements and reward for effort with state funds was undercut by the Mort emphasis on equalization.

Mort found that this concept of equalization was incompatible with Cubberley's emphasis on reward for effort:

> The conclusion follows that these two purposes (equalization and reward for effort) that have controlled attempts to build state aid systems since the work of Cubberley two decades ago are found to be incompatible. We are, therefore, faced with the necessity of choosing one or the other. It is a choice between meeting the demands of a principle that cannot be met without state aid—the equalization of educational opportunity—and the use of one of many methods for meeting another principle.[4]

The Advisory Commission on Intergovernmental Relations noted some of the ways in which the Mort program improved on the Strayer-Haig theories:

> Perfecting amendments to the basic Strayer-Haig equalization thesis were developed as States enacted their foundation plans. For example, Paul Mort and other practitioners showed that educational costs differ for elementary and secondary pupils and that the unit of need in the foundation plan should be appropriately weighted to reflect these differences. . . . The physically and mentally handicapped children became the subject of special solicitude.[5]

Modern school finance theories were spawned and developed by a relatively few well-known leaders in the field, such as Cubberley, Strayer, and Mort. Their contributions are known to all who read the literature of school finance. But historians generally seem to have forgotten or minimized the importance of others' contributions to the field. This apparent oversight may have been due to the unpopularity or lack of acceptance of their ideas at the time of their introduction.

Two school finance pioneers of the early part of the twentieth century whose contributions to the field were important but who have not always occupied their rightful positions in school finance history were Henry C. Morrison and Harlan Updegraff. Their theories, while not particularly popular in their own time, are relevant in today's finance reform movement with its emphasis on increased state support for education and district power equalization.

Henry C. Morrison emphasized that the methods of financing education in the early 1900s were unsatisfactory. Local school districts, by their organizational structure, were perpetuating unequal educational opportunities for the school children of each state. The allotment of state funds or grants to districts for special purposes was not bringing the kind or amount of equalization its advocates expected. Morrison favored a new and different approach to the problem. He theorized that if the state were one large district, it could not only equalize the tax burden but it could also distribute the funds derived without complicated formulas such as were being used. Some of his main ideas—use of the income tax, full state funding, and considering the state as one large district—are much more acceptable today than they were in Morrison's own time. For example, several states now use the income tax to relieve the unfair and regressive property tax from some of its traditional burdens, and Hawaii has become a one-district state under many of the conditions Morrison advocated.

The unpopularity of Morrison's view resulted from his lack of support of a philosophy of local control of education and his willingness to replace "popular" property taxes with "unpopular" income taxes. Changes in two conditions have brought a degree of popularity to Morrison's ideas: (1) Local control has lost some of its traditional glamour. (2) The property tax—even though still necessary at the local level—has sunk to the bottom of desirability as a major source of school revenue.

Harlan Updegraff in 1922 developed a formula that would combine equalization and reward for effort without the objectionable features of the Cubberley plan. This was simply allowing the state to provide funds for program improvement (as well as for equalization), with each local district free to determine what the improvement program should be. (Updegraff's work in New York preceded the work of Strayer-Haig, but his contribution to the philosophy of school finance is more related to this period than to that of Cubberley.)

As indicated elsewhere in this text, the states have moved somewhat blindly from one form of state and local financing of education to another. The foundation program was accepted as the best method of leveling the inequalities that seemed to persist among the districts within every state. But even the foundation program has not proved to be a panacea. The high costs of compensatory education, the financial problems that result from municipal overburden, the unfairness among districts that varying policies and degrees of property underassessment create, and the inability of poor districts to go very much beyond the minimum program are evidence of the need for improving the minimum, or foundation, program concept in its current form.

Period Five: Power Equalization

The foundation program concept was an improvement over the older methods of distributing state funds to local school districts. In spite of that, however, school districts of differing financial capacities continue to have unequal abilities to exceed the foundation program. Thus, in the less wealthy districts, the foundation program has been not only a "minimum" but also a near "maximum" program, for tax levies above the foundation, or base, without state help remit such small amounts of revenue that they discourage local effort to exceed the base program.

The predominant theme in school finance practice for the first half of the twentieth century was *equalization of educational opportunity*. The wealth of the state was to be taxed to educate all the children of the state regardless of where they lived or the taxpaying ability of their parents or their school district. Various devices and formulas have been tried and notable improvements made. Equalization meant that the state and local districts were exercising a degree of partnership in establishing and paying for a basic program of education for every school-age child in the state.

In the mid-twentieth century, Paul Mort and others advocated a new concept of equalization—a "new look" in incentive financing. Their proposal guaranteed a foundation program at state and local expense for all districts and also encouraged local initiative for a better educational program by continuing to maintain a high degree of state-local partnership for whatever level above the foundation program the local district cares to go. Wisconsin used a variation of this concept between 1949 and 1969. Rhode Island, Alaska, New York, Maryland, Michigan, and a few other states initiated similar plans.

This open-end (shared cost or power) equalization plan for state and local financing of education is not really a new idea; in the early 1920s, Updegraff proposed such a plan, but it was too far ahead of the financial practices of the time. Although it has experienced limited adoption, it has resulted in a wider acceptance of state financial responsibility for education. It tends to be more acceptable in states that supply a high percentage of the total public education at state expense. In those states that exert only a minimum effort to finance education, the plan is ahead of their financial philosophy and therefore acceptance has been slow.

In its simplest terms, the open-end, or shared-cost, equalization plan proposes that a foundation program be established, with determination of the percentage of this program to be paid by each individual district and by the state. This percentage of state funds would be high for poor districts and low for wealthier ones. Once that determination has been made for each district, the same partnership ratio would be maintained to pay the total cost of the school program in each district. Each local board of education would still determine the levy to be made, thus preserving local control of education. There would be many variations and applications of this basic principle, but the fundamental premise of the program remains the same: state partnership throughout the complete finance program and thus a guarantee of a sound educational program for every district within the borders of every state.

Almost submerged and forgotten until recently, is this far-reaching policy, first enunciated by Harlan Updegraff, of an equalized matching formula that would combine equalization and reward for effort. In contrast to Cubberley, Updegraff would have the state help to provide the finances for improved programs but leave the expenditure decisions to the local school boards. Under the guidance and initiative of Paul Mort, this principle has been activated in a few of the states, but its use is not yet widespread.

The equalized percentage matching (EPM) concept was given strong support by the decisions in court cases of the 1970s, beginning with *Serrano* v. *Priest* (1971).[6] It lost support, however, with the Supreme Court's reversal of *San Antonio Independent School District* v. *Rodriguez* (1973)[7] when the principle of equalized percentage matching was not required in Texas and, by inference, in other states, depending on state constitutions. The majority opinion of the court stated that education was not a federal constitutional right; the responsibility for education should be left to lawmakers at the state level, through the democratic processes that elect them. However, the ruling does not disallow the equalized percentage matching concept. It is still valid, even if not required. Justice Powell, in speaking for the court, called on the states to not place a judicial imprimatur on the status quo and stated that the need for school finance reform was evident.

Opponents of EPM fear that it may deplete state treasuries. Such reasoning remains the chief deterrent to adoption of this principle, since it shifts the authority for using state money for education from the state to the local district. Local control of the educational program rest with each individual school board. The concept is that the state must match what the local district decides; therefore, the state cannot escape its proportionate financial responsibility. Another concern of those who question the EPM principle are variable taxing distinctions. Generally, the property tax is a local tax. Most states depend on the sales tax as their major source of revenue. Some states use the income tax, others the lottery, and still others the severance tax. When a state has an economic downturn, sales taxes, income taxes, and perhaps lottery and severance revenues diminish dramatically. The local districts can still tax property and may do so to such an extent that the state, because of its falling revenue sources, is not able to match what the local districts are entitled to under the EPM formula. Some states, including Michigan, repealed their EPM finance programs because the states believed that the EPM procedure had drained their already overburdened state treasuries.

Using the EPM principle, districts are encouraged to make adequate tax effort, for if they spend less, they lose more. Equalization is achieved in spending as well as in taxing. Payment by the state is in inverse ratio to the wealth of the district. If there were a ceiling placed by the state on how much the local districts can tax, the inequalities between wealthy and poor districts are lessened and the state treasury is less at the mercy of the school districts in determining how much state money will be required to fund the education program. Flexibility at the state level to amend its matching requirement during recessions help a state to control its own resources.

Period Six: Shift of Emphasis and Influence

Elements of the previous five developmental periods are still prevalent in the sixth as only limited progress has been made in attaining some of the requirements for equity and adequacy. State finance programs for schools have continued to be challenged in relation to state constitutions. Rudimentary power equalization concepts are not being adopted, and a climate that encourages accountability in deference to concentrating on fine-tuning equity for taxpayers and students has become a priority. Influences during this period are attributed to a greater influence from agents, such as the courts, legislatures at both state and federal levels, parents, business leaders, and others who demand more accountability, which takes on various forms. A greater voice in matters of choice available for students has added a new dimension on the financial structure in the past decade. The period can be identified further in terms of taxpayer revolt, fears of war and terrorism, natural disasters, and shifting economic factors.

The *Serrano* and *Rodriguez* decisions were the hallmark of court cases in Period Five. Many cases followed in ensuing years and had a major impact on school finance. Kentucky, Texas, New York, Ohio, Wisconsin, Arizona, and South Carolina represent the impact the courts had during the past two decades. Forty of the fifty states had litigation proceedings that had implications for financing public schools (see Chapter 9). Responding to court outcomes and the pressure of possible action, state legislatures were forced to meet mandates that judges interpreted as being required in their own state constitution. Difficult decisions based on defining nebulous terms needed to be addressed. Constitutions call for providing students an "adequate," "thorough," and/or "efficient" education. Legislation to meet these criteria were often threatened with a governor veto or was not adequate enough to pass court scrutiny.

Pressure for greater accountability for student learning and teacher competency evolved from various sources during the last part of the twentieth century. The "A Nation at Risk" report stimulated a great deal of activity after stressing that our public schools were not producing the product that was needed to compete in a world economic setting. Goals were established at the federal level through two administrations, and the controversial No Child Left Behind Act mandated testing of students (outcomes) and hiring and maintaining qualified teachers in the classroom. Concurrently, states required teachers to pass competency tests for certification and demanded more testing of students. Standards for high school students were generated with no diploma awarded if standards were not met. Elementary students in some areas were no longer simply "passed on" to the next grade if certain requirements, mainly determined by testing, were not met.

New players in education finance entered the arena and had a significant impact on the public schools. Private businesses were awarded contracts to manage public schools and operate private schools that competed for money from school districts. The proliferation of alternative education opportunities became available for parents and students. Forces from local and national entities brought about the charter school movement, which was stimulated by federal dollars and escalated the choice movement. Economists became more involved in defining the mission of education in terms of value-added measurements as financial accountability models. Researchers showed interest in identifying student progress in relation to actual per-pupil expenditures at the school level. School administrators reported little desire in providing such data.

The economic factors through this period played an important role in establishing priorities in the school setting. A war, terrorist attacks, natural disasters, fluctuating prices in energy, and other such influences made it necessary for states and local districts to rethink the safety of schools and the implications on budgets. Even so, the challenge of maintaining the focus on the schools' task of improving teaching and improving student progress remained a stated goal.

Period Six is an amalgam of complexities that reflect the era. As with the previous five, there are transitions and concepts that overlap. These various influences have all led to financial consequences for the public schools. The period will be identified as one where student outcomes are to be part of the policy design in financing public schools. This period has a uniqueness but it also has characteristics that will flow into a seventh period where results will be defined by policymakers and educational leaders in two or three decades.

The Varying State Programs

Much progress has been made regarding state school finance policies. Currently, the states have used a number of different school finance plans. The most common system is the *foundation approach,* which may be considered a *minimum foundation program.* The basic concept of this foundation plan is much like a foundation for a building—that is, the state agrees to guarantee a minimal annual expenditure per student for all school districts in the state, regardless of local district wealth. Above the guarantee (or foundation), one district can build an extensive school system while a poorer district can construct only a modest program. The poorer school districts in states with lower per-student resources often rely on the courts to ameliorate inequitable polarity between rich districts and poor ones when this method is used (see Chapter 9).

An adjustment to the minimum foundation approach is the *modified foundation program.* Rather than allowing rich districts to build elaborate school systems while poor districts construct meager programs, other resources are given to the impecunious districts. There are usually two procedures that states use to provide for a more equitable school finance design. One method is to take money from the richer districts and transfer those funds to the poorer districts. In order to achieve this form of equity, states may use what has been called the "Robin Hood" approach or the "leveling down" method. States that believe that educational finance is the responsibility of school districts, not the state, take a portion of the richer districts' school resources and distribute the monies to poorer districts (customarily called *recapture*). For example, assuming there are 100 districts in a state, with a uniform tax levy, the funds generated in the top 50 districts would be shared with 50 poorer districts. This "leveling down" makes for an unimpressive and middling school strategy.

A second method is commonly called the "leveling up" plan. Assuming a uniform tax levy—such as in the "Robin Hood" approach—disparate districts in wealth generate vast differences in resources. Rather than taking significant monies from all the richer districts, the state would be required to appropriate additional *state funds* (usually from sales tax, income tax, lottery, or severance revenues) to the poorer districts. A few of the richer districts would contribute to the plan; the money from the richer districts would also commonly be called *recapture.* The science of the plan is arithmetic and the administration of it is ministerial in nature. The art of the plan is designing it so that just a few of the richer districts have sufficient funds to meet their resource needs from the uniform tax levy. Financial resources in the poorer districts, using this approach, would nearly reach the resources available in financially dominant districts. Even so, less affluent districts often litigate the support that the state or the richer districts provide because the effort is insufficient or may not meet the requirements of the state constitution and statutes.

The oldest, simplest, and most unequal method of providing state support to local school districts is the *flat grant.* The usual flat grant *modus operandi* is for the state merely to multiply the number of students in attendance (ADA) or membership (ADM) by a fixed amount. It may not take into consideration the wealth of the district nor the needs of the students. Another type of flat grant provides discretionary funding using criteria based on certain eligibility.

Some states have adopted the *district power equalization (DPE)* plan using the equalized percentage matching (EPM) principle. This is a more recent plan, in which the state pays a percentage of the local schools current expenditures in inverse ratio to the wealth of the district. Implementation of this method is to determine an optimum amount per student that the state guarantees. State support becomes the difference between what the district raises per student and what the state guarantees per student. In full state funding or nearly full state funding, the procedure is handled at the state level. In states where local districts have the authority to determine tax levy, which the state must match, a shared-cost philosophy is used, with the state providing proportionate financing through a statewide uniform tax. Such a design develops upper and lower limits and the state may only have the resources to provide a less than adequate statewide school program. Equalized percentage matching has most of the elements that are needed for an equitable plan for both students and taxpayers.

Still other states amalgamate portions of these methodologies into their school finance process. Some may have a minimum foundation program and add to that an element of EPM, which makes a modified foundation paradigm. Others add a flat grant to a minimum foundation program, which may have a modified foundation design. Most states use some equalization factors, or formula funding, to ensure a somewhat comparable educational opportunity.

Describing the complex school finance systems of the states is an exhaustive process. There are as many finance programs as there are states. However, some commonality exists in a type of basic or foundation program, a relationship between state and local contributions, and a design for categorical programs. Changes occur often as legislatures meet and courts influence interpretations of various state constitutions. Following are brief descriptions of seven state finance programs that will serve as examples of the diversity in plans.

Students of school finance need to be cautioned that the cursory coverage of these state plans are meant to demonstrate the approach states are taking to provide equity for students in the maintenance and operation aspects of the budget. Other areas that make each state education funding plan complex are transportation, school lunch, federal programs, capital outlay, debt services, specifics in special education, and others.

California

The California school finance law has been greatly influenced by the *Serrano* v. *Priest* case (1971), Proposition 13 (1978), and Proposition 98 (1988). The *Serrano* v. *Priest* court case held that the school finance system, with its uneven tax burden and disparate spending patterns, was unconstitutional. "The California Supreme Court determined that the school finance system must be equitable for both students and taxpayers. The revenue limit scheme formed in 1972 was an attempt to freeze all districts' income at their then-current level of spending for general purposes."[8] Proposition 13 changed the nature of financing education in California. Prior to its passage, two-thirds of the revenue for education came from local sources; now about one-fourth does. Proposition 13 prevented local school districts from increasing property taxes, so the state became involved in distributing property taxes to schools and replacing revenue that was lost when those taxes were slashed statewide. Presently, "if the income from property taxes within a county rises, any increase that goes to schools will be matched by a decrease in the amount of state aid. Rising property taxes mean a lessened burden on the state's budget, not an overall increase in a district's revenue limit. School districts have no control over either the level of their revenue limit or the combination of local and state taxes that funds it."[9] Only the legislature can change the revenue limits of each district. Proposition 98 guarantees a minimum funding level, basically assuring that state support is the greater of the previous year's expenditure per pupil, adjusted for inflation and growth in average daily attendance or a specified percentage of state general fund revenues.

The California finance program is based on the distribution of funds for *general purpose* and *special purpose* (categorical aid) programs. Approximately 60 percent of district revenue is for the general purpose area, whereas the other roughly 40 percent provides for the categorical part of the yearly budget.

> The amount of general purpose funding a school district receives per student (using ADA—Average Daily Attendance) is called its "revenue limit." It is a combination of local property taxes and states taxes. Each of the nearly 1,000 school districts in California has its own revenue limit, based on its type (elementary, high, or unified), size (small or large), historical spending patterns, and a multitude of other variables which, together, make for a complicated and lengthy [formula].[10]

Basically, the plan calls for local support from property taxes and some local miscellaneous funds that are part of the effort toward the *revenue limit* established for the district. If the local funds do not provide the required limit, an allocation from the state makes up the difference. If a local district produces more revenue than required for the revenue limit, it is classified as a *basic aid district*. In California, the district is allowed to keep the overage, unlike some states that recapture the excess dollars. About

70 districts each year are designated as basic aid. As the local property tax revenue may change each year, a district status as basic aid may also change. "Basic aid is the minimum general purpose aid guaranteed by the state's constitution for each school district in California. The amount is $120 per student (using ADA) or $2,400 per district, whichever number is greater."[11]

More than 50 special programs are supported through the general fund and are restricted, or earmarked, in terms of dollars and number of students served. These funds are special purpose, or categorical.[12] Money is distributed to districts meeting regulated qualifications. Funding is determined each legislative session, allowing some flexibility in providing for more than the basic program. "School districts are responsible for managing the money they receive within both state and federal guidelines. In turn, the policies, employee union agreements, and practices of the local school district determine the amount of financial and operating discretion an individual school has."[13]

Special education is the largest categorical program, with about 10 percent of the students qualifying for special education services. The special education funding formula is complex, with state and federal dollars assuming most of the costs. Funding and services for special education are administered through Special Education Local Planning Areas (SELPAs), "which operate somewhat separately from the regular school district."[14]

There is a minimum funding level guarantee for all children attending school in the state. The California Constitution mandates that schools are free and that students must attend from ages 6 to 16 or until they receive a diploma or equivalent. More than 6 million students attend public schools in California. In fiscal year 2006, K–12 schools in California received more that $60 billion in revenue—approximately 60 percent from state sources, about 28 percent local, and 12 percent federal.[15]

Connecticut

The state goal for Connecticut is to provide excellence and equity in public school programs.[16] The State Board of Education, under Section 10–4 of the Connecticut General Statutes, is charged with:

> general supervision and control of the educational interests of the state, which interests shall include preschool, elementary and secondary education, special education, vocational education and adult education; shall provide leadership and otherwise promote the improvement of education in the state. . . . This charge includes implementing the Connecticut General Statutes and federal legislation relating to education. The State Board of Education has direct responsibility for the Department of Education, the Regional Vocational-Technical Schools, and the state's vocational rehabilitation services.[17]

This proviso of funding education is met through a cost-sharing method. Until 1977, the state distributed aid primarily on a flat per-pupil basis; every town received the same amount of aid per pupil served. At that time, the Connecticut State Supreme Court confirmed in *Horton* v. *Meskill* that the state had the responsibility of public education and that each child had an equal opportunity to receive a suitable educational experience. The ruling brought about major school finance reform. It included an equalization funding formula known as the guaranteed tax base (GTB). The GTB was later replaced by the education cost sharing (ECS) grant, which is designed to equalize each town's ability to finance a state-established minimum expenditure requirement (MER). Expenditures that are considered in the MER formula are those tied directly to educational programs made at the town level. Debt service and transportation are not included. In general terms, the ECS formula is not complex. For each town, the state pays a percentage of the total amount the town is required to spend under the MER program.

ECS Base Formula for 2005–06

Foundation $5,891	×	Need Students Resident • Poverty weighting • Mastery weighting • Other minor weighting	=	Base Aid Ratio (100% minus wealth as a percentage of state guaranteed wealth level)	=	ECS Base Aid

MER Calculation for 2005–06

2005–06 MER	=	2004–05 MER	+	2005–06 New Aid	–	2005–06 Resident Student Adjustment

The foundation, which is a *per weighted student* amount, began at $3,918 in 1989–90 and increased 7 percent annually. In 1995–96, the foundation was raised to $5,711, in part to accommodate the consolidation of special education into the ECS funding formula. From 2000 to 2007, the foundation was raised to $5,891, which was an increase of 4 percent. However, the foundation growth on a net current expenditure per pupil (NCEP) basis increased 44 percent from $7,424 to $10,682.

To raise local revenues for education, towns depend primarily on property taxes. The wealth of towns—the value of taxable property—varies widely. One factor in the court case was based on the property wealth per pupil in the state. The highest town was $170,000 and the lowest was $20,000, or 8½ times less than the highest town. The poorest towns were spending 35 percent less than the wealthiest towns but had tax rates 2½ times higher. Due to this wide variation in local taxable property wealth, Connecticut now provides more aid to "poor" towns to help equalize the ability of such towns to finance education. In addition, almost all other state education aid grants, competitive as well as noncompetitive, have an equalization component. Equalization is a goal for Connecticut in its education cost sharing program, which is designed to equalize programs and reduce disparities in per-pupil expenditures. Funds are distributed in accordance with an equalizing formula establishing a minimum spending level in each town. Tax rates are targeted for equalization as well. Categorical programs are available and cover various priorities that are evaluated each year to determine funding. In 2005–06, the local share of expenditures for public elementary and secondary education in Connecticut was 53.5 percent ($4.6 billion). The state share was 40.6 percent ($3.5 billion) and the federal and *other* share was 5.9 percent ($750 million).[18]

Florida

The Florida legislature enacted the Florida Education Finance Program (FEFP) in 1973. It is a weighting formula designed to provide funding on an equalized basis to local education agencies. The formula "recognizes" (1) varying local property tax bases; (2) varying education program costs; (3) varying costs of living; and (4) varying costs for equivalent educational programs due to sparsity and dispersion of student population."[19] The state policy indicates that the equalized funding objective is "to guarantee to each student in the Florida public education system the availability of programs and services appropriate to his or her educational needs which are substantially equal to those available to any similar student notwithstanding geographic differences and varying local economic factors." The primary funding for the operation of the schools in Florida is through the FEFP.[20]

> FEFP funds are primarily generated by multiplying the number of full-time equivalent (FTE) students in each of the funded educational programs by cost factors to obtain weighted FTEs. Weighted FTEs are then multiplied by a base student allocation and by a district cost differential in a major calculation to determine the base funding from state and local FEFP funds. Program cost factors are determined by the Legislature and represent relative cost differences among the FEFP programs. In addition to the base funding allocation, two major allocations within the FEFP are the Supplemental Academic Instruction Allocation and Exceptional Student Education Guaranteed Allocation.[21]

Factors that are considered in the distribution of funds to local districts in the weighted program are shown in Figure 7.2.

FIGURE 7.2   Florida Education Finance Program (FEFP)

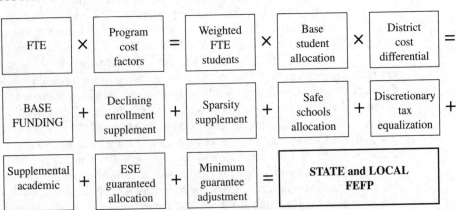

Source: www.firn.edu/doe/bin00042/home0042.htm, 2005–2006.

Funding for the FEFP is provided through the General Revenue Fund, which is appropriated by the state legislature. The predominant source is generated from sales tax. A small percentage of funds come from the Principal State School Trust Fund and from the Florida lottery. In the 2005–06 school year, two programs were funded with lottery revenue: the District Discretionary Lottery Fund at $146.2 million and the School Recognition Program at $117.2 million. Lottery funds provided $169 million for capital outlay and debt service projects.[22] The percent of state revenue spent to operate schools in Florida is about 45.01, with local support through the Required Local Effort at 44.7 percent and 10.42 percent from federal sources.

Local revenue is derived almost entirely from property taxes. The 67 counties constitute the school districts:

> Each school board participating in the state allocation of funds for the current operation of schools must levy the millage set for its required local effort from property taxes . . . . Each district's share of the state total of required local effort is determined by a statutory procedure which is initiated by certification of the property tax valuations of each district by the Department of Revenue. . . . The Commissioner of Education certifies each district's required local effort millage rate. These rates are primarily determined by dividing the dollar amount of required local effort by 95 percent of the aggregate taxable value for school purposes of all districts. Certifications vary due to the use of assessment ratios designed to equalized the effect on the FEFP of differing levels of property appraisal in the counties. Millage rates are also adjusted because required local effort may not exceed 90 percent of a district's total FEFP entitlement.[23] [See Figure 7.3.]

The FEFP in fiscal 2006 was supplemented with categorical programs. The major allocations included instructional materials, student transportation, public school technology, Florida Teachers Lead Program, teacher training, and class size reduction. The categories may change each year at the discretion of the legislature.

The average mills required from local districts for the operation of schools (FEFP) for the 2005–06 school year was 5.239. "Budgeted revenues from local taxes are determined by applying millage levies to 95 percent of the taxable value of property."[24] Additional levies at the local level may be assessed by board action or may be done so by qualified electors (bonds or voted leeway) with restrictions placed on the levies by the legislature.

Hawaii

Hawaii is the only state in the Union that uses full-state funding for financing education. The state constitution centralizes the school system for all aspects of education, including maintenance and operation, facilities, and transportation. The Hawaii State Board of Education is responsible for the development of advisory budgets, which are submitted to the governor's office for review. The state legislature reviews the budgets and appropriates the funds with the approving signature of the governor. The board of education distributes the funds to the schools. The legislature and governor exercise their control over education by incorporating statutory provisions for specific expenditure items. Therefore, the number and type of teaching and administrative positions,

FIGURE 7.3   Factors Determining the Allocation of Funds from State and Local Sources in Support of Public Schools in Florida

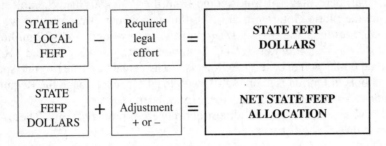

The TOTAL STATE ALLOCATION for the support of public school education is derived from the NET STATE FEFP ALLOCATION in the following manner:

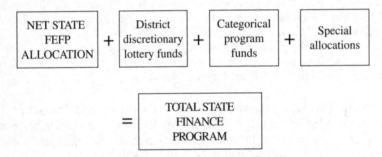

Source: www.firn.edu/doe/bin00042/home0042.htm, 2005–2006.

discretionary funds for individual schools, and program support are preempted by the appropriations system.

The process for distributing funds to local schools in Hawaii was influenced greatly when the legislature passed the Reinventing Education Act of 2004 (REACH—Act 51). The act represented a comprehensive effort to improve public education with emphasis on empowerment, accountability, and streamlining. The *empowerment* section of the act focuses on a weighted student formula at the *school level,* which includes a set amount of funds for basic needs, a specific dollar amount to educate each student enrolled, and additional money to educate students with special needs who require more resources. Under the new design, principals have a greater role in budget decisions, as do individual school community councils.[25] *Accountability* in the act requires "a working group [to] design performance based contracts for principals that will include rewards, assistance, and sanctions."[26] Teachers have an incentive (yearly bonus and fee reimbursement) to meet the standards of the National Board Certification program. The state board of education is required to hold community meetings throughout the state, and a yearly school report card at both the state and local school level is mandated. *Streamlining,* among other aspects, includes "cutting through bureaucratic red tape to get the job done faster," which includes transferring some state agencies to the department of education and establishing a school calendar for all schools in the state.[27]

In fiscal 2005, the source of revenue in the general fund was as follows: general excise and use tax, 47.5 percent; individual income tax, 30.74 percent; nontax revenue, 11 percent; tobacco and liquor taxes, 2.85 percent; corporate income tax, 1.9 percent; and other sources, 5.93 percent. The general fund was 49 percent of fiscal year 2005 operating appropriations, and other means of income to the state were from special funds, 20 percent; federal funds, 18 percent; and other sources, 13 percent. Twenty percent of the state budget was allocated for the K–12 education program, making Hawaii one of the lowest among the states in its support of education when percentage of the state budget was considered. Property taxes are used by the county governments to provide *noneducational* services.[28]

Louisiana

A salient feature of the Louisiana public education finance system is the minimum foundation program (MFP). Its goal is to ensure a basic minimum education program for all its public elementary and secondary schools. The MFP represents a philosophical change from a categorical resource-driven distribution to one based on students and characteristics of students with the flexibility to meet particular students' needs as determined by local school districts.

The funding formula for the school finance program is based on the state representative tax system (RTS), a calculation that measures taxpayers' capacities and efforts established by the state Advisory Commission of Intergovernmental Relations.

Louisiana has 68 local school systems. For comparison, the 68 local school systems are divided into *quintiles,* which are derived by ranking the districts from low to high according to their RTS, where each quintile contains approximately 20 perecent of the student membership. During fiscal year 2003–04, the fiscal capacity in the lowest quintile was $1,128 and the highest was $3,500. The total revenue varied from $7,330 to $8,739 and the total expenditures ranged from $7,420 in the lowest quintile to $8,378 in the highest. The average revenue provided by the state was 48.1 percent, local was 38.3 percent, and federal 13.6 percent. The property tax mill levy ranged from 34.0 mills in the lowest quintile to 31.34 in the highest.

School districts in Louisiana have considerable leeway to raise local revenues to supplement the state's contribution. The flexibility afforded school districts in raising local revenues from property tax and sales tax serves to increase interdistrict differences in local revenues. As in most states, there is considerable variation among school districts in Louisiana in fiscal capacity or "ability" to finance schools.[29]

Michigan

A reformation of sorts for school finance came about during 1993 and 1994 as the Michigan legislature and governor approved legislation that dramatically shifted the sources of funding for local school districts. Prior to fiscal 1995, local public schools received the majority of their funding from local property taxes. At the time, the statewide average mill rate on all property was just under 34 mills. However, dissatisfaction with inequities in funding caused by wide variations in the property tax base from district to district brought about an enactment of several laws that shifted the revenue sources for public education. The School Aid Act and related codes "marked the beginning of the foundation grant approach to State school aid payments. This was a departure from the district power equalizing approach that had been in effect for almost twenty years. The school finance reform plan also diminished the State's reliance on local school operating property taxes as a source of funding for K–12 public schools."[30]

The new law dramatically shifted the state and local tax burden (see Figure 7.4). In 1993, Michigan had a relatively low sales and use tax and had a considerably higher property tax burden compared to the national average. By 2003, the property tax more closely mirrored the national average, making the overall tax structure in the state more in line with national averages, resulting in greater revenue with a more equitable formula for taxpayers—based on a personal income "ability to pay" principal.[31] The foundation program provides a per-pupil amount for each school district. The formula is based on the previous year's allowance and increases by a specific amount each year through legislative action and establishes a per-student minimum figure. If a district does not reach the minimum with the specific amount awarded, an "equity payment" is appropriated to bring the state to the minimum. In fiscal year 2005–06, a $175 increase in the basic (minimum) foundation allowance provided $6,875 per pupil in all districts, bringing them all to at least the basic foundation level. The Michigan plan

FIGURE 7.4   Percent of K–12 General Funding for Michigan Schools

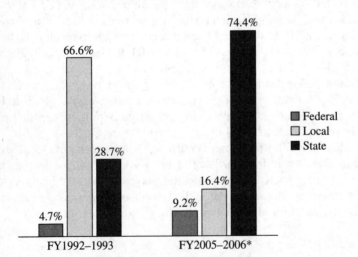

*All federal NCLB grants were transferred into the school aid budget—previously funded through the Michigan Department of Education.

Source: Office of Revenue and Tax Analysis, Michigan Department of Treasury.

is an equalizing foundation program providing districts with a set minimum dollar amount multiplied by the number of students in the membership. The legislature has been attempting to make equity payments part of the foundation allowance with a target of closing the gap between the lowest funded districts to 10 percent of the highest funded districts.[32]

The revenue for the basic (minimum) program comes from state and local funds. The state portion in fiscal year 2005–06 was provided by "the difference between the product of the district's foundation allowance per pupil and the district's pupil membership (excluding special education pupils) less the local revenue on 18 mills or the number of mills levied in 1993, whichever is less."[33] The local share is raised from limited local operating mills as designated by the legislature. In fiscal year 2005–06, the "local portion of the foundation allowance is the school operating property tax revenue from 18 mills (or the number of school operating mills levied in 1993, whichever is less) levied on nonhomestead property in the district."[34]

Utah

The Constitution of Utah indicates that "the legislature shall provide for the establishment and maintenance of a uniform system of public schools, which shall be open to all children of the State, and free from sectarian control."[35] In order to accomplish that mandate, the state operates a school finance foundation program that guarantees a certain basic level of expenditure for each student with a minimum uniform local property tax rate that each district must levy. In fiscal 2007, the required amount was 0.001593. The following example shows how this levy affects a local district in meeting its obligation toward the basic program.

District	WPUs	WPU Value	Basic Guarantee (millions)	Assessed Value (billions)	Rate	Local Share (millions)	State Share (millions)
A	18,000	$2,417	$43.51	$5.90	.001593	$9.40	$34.11
B	5,600	$2,417	$13.54	$1.77	.001593	$2.82	$10.72
C	3,200	$2,417	$ 7.73	$5.73	.001593	$9.13	($ 1.40)

The value of the WPU in fiscal 2007 was $2,417. In District A, the basic state guarantee was $43.51 million (18,000 × $2,417), with the local contribution raising $9.4 million ($5.90 billion × .001593). The state contribution was $34.11 million. District C has only 3,200 WPUs but has a healthy assessed valuation of $7.73 billion, generating $9.13 million toward the minimum program, or an overage of $1.40 million. This surplus is *recaptured* and becomes a part of the state Uniform School Fund. Of the 40 districts, 2 to 4 each year usually raise a greater amount locally than is required for their guaranteed minimum program.

The taxpayer with a $200,000 home assessed at 55 percent of market value would have an assessment of $175.23 ($200,000 × 0.55 × .001593) toward the state basic program. State revenues to guarantee the foundation program come from the Uniform

School Fund. The local property tax toward the basic program is only a portion of the overall local contribution needed for the operation of schools. Other mills with limits may be assessed for capital outlay, debt service, recreation, tort liability insurance, transportation, a voted leeway, and a board leeway. The average property tax for public schools in the state for all districts is about $950.00 on a $200,000 home.

The maintenance and operation budget responsibility for each student becomes a function of the total taxable wealth of the state and is not limited to the taxing ability of each local school district. Average daily membership (ADM) is used in the calculations. Pupils are weighted to reflect the cost associated with providing special services. For example, District A may have only 14,800 *regular* students but generate an additional 3,200 WPUs from other sources, including special education. Table 7.1 lists the basic programs at the state level funded on the WPU formula. Part II lists the areas that are funded a specific amount and are categorical in nature. Additional money is provided for *one-time appropriations* based on priority needs and surplus revenues.

State aid is provided by income tax, which, by constitutional fiat, is totally earmarked for the "schools established by the legislature."[36] Other sources of funds come from school land income, corporation franchise tax, mineral production, and other minor resources. If needed, revenue is transferred from the general fund in which the state sales tax is the largest revenue source.

Additional programs were awarded revenue by the legislature: social security and retirement, pupil transportation, one-time appropriations for library books and supplies, enrollment growth, charter schools, and classroom supplies. Table 7.1 is a good example of a basic uniform school program with additional block grant programs that receive a set amount rather than an amount based on the weighted pupil unit. Through the years these programs have fluctuated, often as a result of public pressure for a particular felt need. The funding source for the budget comes from the uniform school fund (basically state income taxes of $2,069,508,455) and local revenue (basically property taxes of $470,804,680).

State Ability to Support Education

Measurement of a state's ability to support education is difficult. Local districts confine their main tax effort to the property tax, but the states have no such limitations. Sales taxes, income taxes, and many others are available for state use, thereby complicating the problem of measuring and comparing total tax effort and ability.

The ability of the states to support education varies greatly, regardless of the criteria or devices used in its measurement. Here again, as with measurement of local ability, the question arises as to whether taxpaying ability should be measured in terms of potential revenues from all sources, many of which are not legally authorized, or in terms of the tax system that is authorized and operable. Does a state have the ability to produce any given amount of school revenue from a state sales tax if such a tax is not being used? Another unanswered question is related to the relative economic effects of varying forms and kinds of taxation. For example, what property tax rate is equivalent to a 6 percent sales and use tax?

TABLE 7.1   Utah Minimum School Program: Fiscal 2007

Program	WPUs	State Allocation
I. Basic with WPUs		
Kindergarten	23,680	$ 57,234,560
Grades 1–12	462,579	$1,118,053,443
Professional staff	43,909	$106,128,053
Administrative costs	1,629	$ 3,937,293
Necessarily small schools & consolidated schools	7,649	$18,487,633
Special education		
Preschool	8,158	$19,717,886
Regular	56,413	$136,350,221
Self-contained	13,301	$32,148,517
Extended year	367	$887,039
State institutions	1,443	$3,487,731
Applied technology	24,797	59,934,349
Technology agriculture	1,060	$ 2,562,020
Class size reduction	30,773	$74,378,341
II. Allocations—Not Based on WPU		
Social security and retirement		$310,891,038
Pupil transporation		$62,601,763
Local discretionary block grant		$21,820,748
Interventions for student success block grant		$16,792,888
Quality teaching block grant		$62,993,704
Highly impacted schools		$5,123,207
At-risk		$27,992,056
Adult education		$9,148,653
Accelerated learning		$12,010,853
Electronic high school		$1,300,000
School land trust		$15,000,000
State-supported voted leeway		$196,083,503
State-supported board leeway		$54,704,476
Charter schools		$21,552,450
K–3 reading improvement		$12,500,000
Board leeway for K–3 reading improvement		$15,000,000

Source: Office of the Legislative Fiscal Analyst, Utah State Government, May 27, 2006.

Some old ways of measuring state taxing ability have outworn their usefulness. An example is the use of per-capita wealth as measured by the assessed or the real value of taxable property within the state. The deemphasis or complete elimination of the state property tax and the introduction of sales and state income taxes have resulted in the demise of this method of comparing the abilities of states to finance education.

The most common method now used to compare the financial ability of states to support education seems to require the inclusion of income. The close relationship between some state income tax systems and the federal income tax program makes determination of total income relatively easy. Relating the total personal income to the total population does not consider the disparity among the states in the ratio of school-age children to total population. Using the average daily membership or average daily attendance of pupils in public schools does not consider the wide variation among the states in the numbers of pupils attending private or parochial schools. Some authorities in the field support the seemingly justifiable method of using total personal income minus total federal income taxes paid by the people of a state divided by the total number of children of school age as the best method of measuring state ability to pay for education. Still others advocate complex combinations of data and mathematical formulas, which are difficult to determine but which, once obtained, lend some validity to such methods of comparing the ability of states to finance education.

Since the ability of the 50 states to support education naturally varies, and since each spends a different amount per child being educated, it follows that their taxing efforts also vary. Study the ramifications of Table 7.2. As an example, the total state taxes in Hawaii is 9.87 percent of personal income, which ranks the state number 1. By comparison, in Colorado, only 4.36 percent of total state taxes come from personal income.

Those less wealthy states whose citizens choose to have good educational programs must necessarily make a greater effort than their more fortunate counterparts in more wealthy states. *Effort* is an elusive term, requiring complicated means of measurement. The important point is that real differences continue to exist among the states in their ability to finance education.

Summary

Early settlers apparently recognized the importance of education to the future of the United States, but they left the various states with the responsibility for its implementation and development. Education was not referred to specifically in the United States Constitution; interpretation of the Tenth Amendment delegated that responsibility to the individual states. Each state in the Union has interpreted its responsibility differently depending on language in their state constitutions and enabling legislation. Hence, there is no single public school system, but rather 50 distinct systems.

The states have developed their school finance systems largely by trial and error, with considerable difficulty and sacrifice. Public schools were originally financed largely by land grants, fees, tuition charges, and other nontax funds; as schools became more numerous, property taxes were introduced as a source of local revenue.

The Northwest Ordinances of 1785 and 1787 and later land grants did much to help the states develop public education. At first, local districts financed education with little or no state assistance, and there were vast differences in a district's ability to provide quality education programs. By the early part of the twentieth century, the states were making grants to local districts, for the most part based on the philosophy of Ellwood Cubberley. A quarter of a century later, the equalization principles of George D.

TABLE 7.2   State and Local Total Tax Burden per Person and Percent of Personal Income: Fiscal Year 2004

	CY2004 State Taxes (thousands)	CY2004 Population	CY2004 State Taxes per Person	Rank	CY2004 Personal Income (thousands)	CY 2004 Taxes as a % of Pers Inc	Rank
Alabama	$7,143,282	4,525,375	1,578.50	47	$125,166,703	5.71%	39
Alaska	$1,464,574	657,755	2,226.63	16	$22,340,402	6.56%	27
Arizona	$9,257,368	5,739,879	1,612.82	44	$164,323,943	5.63%	42
Arkansas	$5,991,086	2,750,000	2,178.58	17	$70,809,895	8.46%	5
California	$90,674,107	35,842,038	2,529.83	10	$1,262,454,026	7.18%	13
Colorado	$7,248,054	4,601,821	1,575.04	48	$166,152,653	4.36%	50
Connecticut	$10,540,921	3,498,966	3,012.58	4	$159,435,002	6.61%	24
Delaware	$2,519,769	830,069	3,035.61	3	$29,527,185	8.53%	4
Florida	$32,131,459	17,385,430	1848.18	34	$547,311,531	5.87%	36
Georgia	$15,526,633	8,918,129	1,710.74	41	$265,537,511	5.75%	38
Hawaii	$4,062,432	1,262,124	3,218.73	1	$41,175,569	9.87%	1
Idaho	$2,593,730	1,395,140	1,859.12	33	$37,393,570	6.94%	15
Illinois	$24,755,275	12,712,016	1,947.39	29	$441,485,267	5.61%	43
Indiana	$12,399,197	6,226,537	1,991.35	27	$187,565,068	6.61%	25
Iowa	$5,258,564	2,952,904	1,780.81	37	$91,499,771	5.75%	37
Kansas	$5,297,639	2,733,697	1,937.90	30	$84,809,871	6.25%	32
Kentucky	$8,209,368	4,141,835	1,982.06	28	$112,565,602	7.29%	11
Louisiana	$7,784,398	4,506,685	1,727.30	39	$122,913,214	6.33%	29
Maine	$2,961,329	1,314,985	2,251.99	15	$39,481,808	7.50%	9
Maryland	$13,029,228	5,561,332	2,342.83	11	$220,261,099	5.92%	35
Massachusetts	$17,184,561	6,407,382	2,681.99	7	$270,144,644	6.36%	28
Michigan	$21,566,909	10,104,206	2,134.45	19	$324,133,954	6.65%	22
Minnesota	$15,036,722	5,096,546	2,950.38	5	$184,514,849	8.15%	7
Mississippi	$5,210,608	2,900,768	1,796.29	36	$70,770,022	7.36%	10
Missouri	$9,272,137	5,759,532	1,609.88	46	$175,610,709	5.28%	46
Montana	$1,619,496	926,920	1,747.18	38	$25,642,844	6.32%	31
Nebraska	$3,768,985	1,747,704	2,156.54	18	$56,393,335	6.68%	21

(continued)

199

TABLE 7.2 Continued

	CY2004 State Taxes (thousands)	CY2004 Population	CY2004 State Taxes per Person	Rank	CY2004 Personal Income (thousands)	CY 2004 Taxes as a % of Pers Inc	Rank
Nevada	$4,460,997	2,332,898	$1,912.21	31	$78,875,571	5.66%	40
New Hampshire	$2,092,980	1,299,169	1,611.01	45	$47,660,890	4.39%	49
New Jersey	$22,218,403	8,685,166	2,558.20	8	$362,189,814	6.13%	34
New Mexico	$3,888,882	1,903,006	2,043.55	23	$49,777,827	7.81%	8
New York	$48,825,017	19,280,727	2,532.32	9	$737,038,528	6.62%	23
North Carolina	$17,343,133	8,540,468	2,030.70	25	$250,285,714	6.93%	16
North Dakota	$1,294,213	636,308	2,033.94	24	$18,553,456	6.98%	14
Ohio	$23,967,488	11,450,143	2,093.20	22	$356,773,618	6.72%	19
Oklahoma	$6,552,383	3,523,546	1,859.60	32	$98,019,976	6.68%	20
Oregon	$6,196,056	3,591,363	1,725.27	40	$109,935,032	5.64%	41
Pennsylvania	$26,121,502	12,394,471	2,107.51	20	$412,590,849	6.33%	30
Rhode Island	$2,511,693	1,079,916	2,325.82	13	$36,935,647	6.80%	18
South Carolina	$7,009,361	4,197,892	1,669.73	42	$113,988,229	6.15%	33
South Dakota	$1,094,319	770,621	1,420.05	49	$23,602,399	4.64%	47
Tennessee	$9,698,691	5,893,298	1,645.72	43	$175,884,974	5.51%	45
Texas	$31,178,124	22,471,549	1,387.45	50	$690,376,069	4.52%	48
Utah	$4,390,393	2,420,708	1,813.68	35	$64,375,986	6.82%	17
Vermont	$1,760,300	621,233	2,833.56	6	$19,721,154	8.93%	3
Virginia	$14,960,895	7,481,332	1,999.76	26	$269,861,839	5.54%	44
Washington	$14,359,257	6,207,046	2,313.38	14	$217,240,119	6.61%	26
West Virginia	$3,814,926	1,812,548	2,104.73	21	$46,619,385	8.18%	6
Wisconsin	$12,819,558	5,503,533	2,329.34	12	$176,635,877	7.26%	12
Wyoming	$1,561,180	505,887	3,086.03	2	$17,322,645	9.01%	2
United States	**$610,357,612**	**293,656,842**	**2,078.47**		**$9,702,525,000**	**6.29%**	

Note: State and local tax collections and population estimates are from the U.S. Census Bureau. Personal Income data is from the U.S. Department of Commerce, Bureau of Economic Analysis.

Source: Developed by Michigan House Fiscal Agency, March 2006.

Strayer and Robert M. Haig were being applied to school finance systems. Paul Mort and others did much to improve the equalization concept during the middle years of the twentieth century. In the latter part of the century and evolving into the past decade, various factors altered the focus on funding education. Continued emphasis on equity and adequacy are prevalent issues, and accountability involving student *outcomes* and teacher *quality* are receiving the attention of the courts, legislators, business leaders, and interested citizens.

Currently, there are a great variety of methods to allocate funds to local districts. Describing the finance systems of the 50 states is complex. Some commonalities include a basic or foundation program, a relationship between state and local contributions, and utilization of the categorical funding method. The trend has been toward greater state responsibility for financing public education, resulting in greater state control and an erosion of the power and authority of local school boards.

ASSIGNMENT PROJECTS

1. Provide a definition for each of the following terms: *flat grants, foundation program, minimum program, modified program, EPM, DPE, WPU, effort, level up, level down, categorical aid, basic program, recapture, rate bills.*
2. Trace the development of the school finance program in your state through the various stages, as outlined in the text. Indicate areas or aspects of the program that may still be in some of the earlier stages, such as state grants per pupil or other nonequalizing grants.
3. Develop arguments for and against full state funding of education.
4. Propose a program of district power equalization that you think would be desirable for your state.
5. Relate state financing of education with state control. Is it possible to have local control of education with complete state financing? Justify your answer.

Computer simulations and questions, research exercises, and website addresses relevant to this chapter can be found at

www.ablongman.com/edleadership

SELECTED READINGS

Alexander, Kern, and Richard Salmon. *Public School Finance.* Boston: Allyn and Bacon, 1995.

English, Fenwick W. *Theory in Educational Administration.* New York: HarperCollins, 1994.

Fowler, William J. Jr. *Developments in School Finance: 2001–02.* Washington, DC: National Center for Education Statistics, 2003.

Honeyman, D. S., D. C. Thompson, and R. C. Wood. *Financing Rural and Small Schools: Issues of Adequacy and Equity,* Gainesville: University of Florida Press, 1989.

King, Richard A., Austin D. Swanson, and Scott R. Sweetland. *School Finance Achieving High Standards with Equity and Efficiency.* Boston: Allyn and Bacon, 2003.

Medler, Alex. *State-Level K–12 Education Reform Activities.* Denver: Education Commission of the States, June 1994.

McDonnell, Lorraine, and Milbrey Wallin McLaughlin. *Education Policy and the Role of the States.* Santa Monica, CA: Rand Corp., 1981.

Mort, Paul R. *State Support for Public Education.* Washington, DC: American Council on Education, 1933.

Sarason, Seymour B. *How Schools Might Be Governed.* New York: Teachers College Press, 1997.

School Finance Trends in U.S. Education Spending. Washington, DC: U.S. Accounting Office, September 1995.

Theobald, Neil D., and Betty Malen, eds. *Balancing Local Control and State Responsibility for K–12 Education.* 2000 Yearbook of the American Education Association. Larchmont, NY: Eye on Education, 2000.

Thompson, David C., R. Craig Wood, and David S. Honeyman. *Fiscal Leadership for Schools, Concepts and Practices.* White Plains, NY: Addison-Wesley, 1994.

ENDNOTES

1. *State Aid to Local Government* (Washington, DC: Advisory Commission on Intergovernmental Relations, April 1969), p. 40.
2. Ellwood P. Cubberley, *School Funds and Their Apportionment* (New York: Teachers College, Columbia University, 1906), p. 17.
3. *State Aid to Local Government,* p. 40.
4. Paul R. Mort, as quoted by Erick L. Lindman in *Long-Range Planning in School Finance* (Washington, DC: National Education Association Committee on Educational Finance, 1963), pp. 38–39.
5. *State Aid to Local Government,* p. 40.
6. *Serrano* v. *Priest,* 96 Cal. Rptr. 601, 487 P.2d 1241 (Calif. 1971).
7. *San Antonio Independent School District* v. *Rodriguez,* 411 U.S. 1, 93 S. Ct. 1278 (1973), rehearing denied.
8. *School Finance 1996–97, EdSource Report,* October 1996, Palo Alto, CA, pp. 4–5.
9. Ibid., p. 5.
10. "School Finance Overview," EdSource Online, http://edsource.org/edu_fin_, March 2003.
11. Ibid.
12. Ibid.
13. Ibid.
14. "Categorical Programs," California Department of Education, www.cde.ca.gov/fiscal/categorical/, June 20, 2003. Updated May 2006.
15. Caryn Moore, California State Department of Education, updated May 2006.
16. Budget Brief, Connecticut State Board of Education, p. 1.
17. Ibid.
18. "Education Cost Sharing (ECS) Grant Program, Minimum Expenditure Requirement (MER), 2005–06," Connecticut State Department of Education Division of Finance and Internal Operations. "Governor Rell's Commission on Education Finance," prepared for the Commission by Robert Brewer and Brian Mahoney, presentation on January 1, 2006, and a PowerPoint presentation by Kathleen S. Guay, Section Director, State of Connecticut Office of Policy and Management, April 2006.
19. www.firn.educ/doe/bin00042/home0042.htm, 2002–03.
20. Ibid.
21. Ibid.
22. "Overview of Public School Funding," Office of Funding and Financial Reporting of the Bureau of School Business Services, Florida Department of Education, www.firn.edu/doe/fefp, 2006.
23. Ibid.
24. Ibid.
25. Reinventing Education Act of 2004 (REA—Act 51), Hawaii State Legislature, 2004. Update provided by Edwin Koyama, Hawaii Department of Education, Honolulu, May 2006.
26. Ibid.
27. Ibid.
28. Ibid.
29. Updated information provided by Paula Matherne, Louisana State Office of Education, 2006.
30. *School Finance in Michigan Before and After the Implementation of Proposal A: A Comparison of FY 1993 and FY 1994–95 Approaches to K–12 Funding in Michigan,* Senate Fiscal Agency, Lansing, December 1995, p. 3.
31. *The Michigan School Act Compiled and Appendices.* House Fiscal Agency, Lansing, August 2006.
32. Ibid.
33. Ibid.
34. Ibid.
35. Article X, Section 1, Utah Constitution.
36. Ibid.

8 Federal Interest in Education

> *There is disagreement among the people of the nation about the role of the federal government in financing education. A proper mixture of leadership at all levels of government is needed if public education is to continue to improve.*
>
> —Percy Burrup

The framers of the U.S. Constitution viewed with fear the possibility of a nationally controlled school system. Their distrust of a strong central power was a break from the philosophy of unitary governments in the European countries. They feared concentration of power, whether it was political or religious. The colonists' main purpose in coming to America—political and religious freedom—seemed to be antithetical to strong centralization of power in a national unit of government. In response to that apprehension, they established a government based on a federal system.

Federalism

Federalism is the vertical diffusion of power among the three levels (local, state, and federal) of government. The United States developed a system of federalism that historically has provided opportunity for a strong federal government, strong state governments, and strong local governments, all part of one creative whole. Alexander Hamilton, James Madison, and John Jay in the *Federalist Papers* wrote that the Constitution was the best document that the Constitutional Convention could develop, in part because the system that the Convention had created and described in the Constitution would create a strong federal government yet protect the rights of states and local governments.

Nearly all countries that are large in land mass, such as Brazil, Canada, Australia, and the United States, have federal systems. Many smaller countries, such as England, France, and Japan, are unitary. In a unitary system, powers are largely concentrated in a single central government. State governments in the United States are essentially unitary.

In a federal system, powers are divided between a central government and its component parts. In the United States, these powers are assigned to the central government or state governments, shared by both and/or denied to either of them. The Tenth Amendment to the U.S. Constitution has been interpreted as legal sanction for state responsibility for education, one of the important services of government. Also, since education is not mentioned in the U.S. Constitution, while in many state constitutions it is enumerated as a state responsibility, those state constitutional designations are viewed as verification that the Tenth Amendment reserves education to the states. Federal and state courts have judged education to be a state's obligation (see Chapter 9). Simply stated, education was to be a role for the *state* in America's federal governmental framework.

In keeping with that philosophy today, the role and percentage of funds expended at each level is as follows:

- State: 50 states   Responsible   48.7% of
                                for education   educational funds

- Local: 15,040 districts   Agency of   42.8% of
                                the state   educational funds

- Federal: 1 government   Responds to   8.5% of
                                national needs   educational funds

This allocation of power demanded policy and political actions to develop proper intergovernmental cooperation. Very early in the nation's history, the federal government began a policy of deference to the states in matters of education. Even the severe critics of education in the United States recognize that the federal-state-local partnership in education worked well for over a century. State constitutions and court decisions at all levels acknowledged and supported this relationship. The public schools, recognized as one of the truly great contributions of this country to the world, were developed under the aegis of this partnership system. Their vitality and accomplishments attested to the validity of this relationship.

Thus, for most of the duration of the republic, the constitutionally authorized advisory role of the federal government was accepted and followed, with only minor exceptions. The grass-roots level of school control that has been so vigorously defended seemed to be working well. The United States became a leader in many areas of science and culture; the schools played an important part in that achievement. Even the perennial problem of financing education was solved in most areas of the country with little or no involvement of the federal government.

To be sure, the federal government vacillated in its role. Periodic—even spasmodic—innovations and policy changes came and went without panic on the part of those who were dedicated to preventing change in the federal role. To a great degree, the occasional venture of the federal government into educational matters represented the philosophies of those in positions of power in the federal hierarchy rather than real changes in the educational philosophy of society in general.

Historical Role of the Federal Government

Historically, the federal role in education had been minor; its function was to conduct research, disseminate information, and provide advisory assistance to the other two levels of government—to exercise interest in education without direct responsibility or control. At various times, however, the federal government has provided financial support for education, usually eschewing extensive federal controls in the process. In its forays into providing financial assistance, the government has left decision making and administrative controls with the individual states.

Department of Education

For well over a century, the federal government's main thrust in the performance of its educational function came through the operations of the United States Office of Education. The agency was founded in 1867 and called the Department of Education, although not represented in the cabinet. The newly designated agency had three major functions: (1) to collect statistics and facts that would show the condition and progress of education in the several states and territories; (2) to diffuse information reflecting the organization and management of schools and school systems, and methods of teaching; and (3) to promote the cause of education throughout the country. The first Department of Education was quickly downgraded to the status of a department within the Bureau of Interior and remained there for 72 years, functioning as a small record-keeping office and collecting information on the modest federal education efforts.

In 1939, the Office of Education was transferred to the Federal Security Agency, which became the Department of Health, Education and Welfare (HEW) in 1953. During the 1960s, several studies of government organization recommended establishment of a separate department, as well as further reorganization that would bring all education programs under the administration of a single department.

In September 1979, Congress approved the creation of the Department of Education, with cabinet-level status. The legislation established a Department of Education, headed by a secretary to be appointed by the president and approved by the Senate. It formed within the department's six offices: elementary and secondary education, post-secondary education, vocational and adult education, special education and rehabilitation services, education research and improvement, and civil rights. Also established were an office of education for overseas dependents and an office of bilingual education and minority languages.

The legislation emphasized that the primary responsibility for education was reserved to the state and local school systems and specifically prohibited the department from increasing federal control over education or from exercising any control over the curriculum, administration, personnel, library resources, textbooks, or other instructional materials of any school, except to the extent authorized by law. "When Congress was writing the Department of Education Organization Act in 1979, lawmakers wanted to allay fears that the new Cabinet-level agency would bring Washington's political meddling into local classrooms. So language was written into the law that strictly forbids the department from wielding any control."[1]

A cursory look at the actions of former presidents puts in perspective the changing nature of federal interest in education finance. In the 1700s, both George Washington and Thomas Jefferson were committed to education. Washington called for a national university and Jefferson considered his role in helping establish the University of Virginia as one of his greatest accomplishments. However, it is important to note that neither president contemplated financial aid to the states' public schools.

A lone voice in the 1880s, President Rutherford B. Hayes called for Congress to appropriate money to supplement the educational budgets of the states to promote free popular education. Congress did not respond.[2] President Chester Arthur appealed for federal aid to education, suggesting that the government distribute money to the states on a ratio based on the amount of illiteracy in each state. His request was not legislated.[3]

It was not until the last half of the 1900s that presidents spoke often of education finance, when, in 1950, President Harry Truman called for federal aid to education while asserting his opposition to federal control of schools. Many believed that concept to be an oxymoron. They felt that federal aid and federal control were inseparable. President Dwight Eisenhower called for federal aid to school construction. He believed that in order to avoid federal control, the federal government's role should be in the capital outlay portion of school district and state budgets, for "bricks and mortar will not have a dilatory effect on instruction in the classroom."[4]

President John Kennedy favored general aid to states for school construction and teacher salaries but insisted that federal aid to education must be for both parochial and public schools.[5] President Lyndon Johnson's Great Society program "helped build more schools and more libraries than any single session of Congress in the history of the Republic."[6] And he instituted the original Elementary and Secondary Education Act of 1965. President Jimmy Carter established the Department of Education.

President Ronald Reagan called for the elimination of the Department of Education and the creation of a National Institute for Education, where the federal government can "put their money on a stump and then walk away," thereby assuaging any federal control.[7] (Many attribute the survival of the Department to the 1983 "A Nation at Risk" report developed under then Secretary of Education, Terrel H. Bell.) President Reagan's criticism of federal control was the department's attempt to instigate federal rules over the nation's teaching practices for children whose primary language was other than English. President George Bush held an education summit at which national performance goals were established. President William Clinton called for a commitment to education "worthy of this great nation."[8]

Constitutional Role

The Constitution of the United States provides indirectly for the federal government to exercise a lesser role in the three-way partnership of governmental responsibility for education. Government's role at all levels are specifically mentioned in, or derived from, the U.S. Constitution.

Enumerated powers for the federal government include the prerogative to coin money, raise an army, and declare war. *Implied* powers, at the national level, are those not specifically listed in the Constitution but are derived from the "necessary and proper clause." *Inherent* powers are those derived from the role of the nation as a sovereign in international affairs. *Prohibited* powers are certain actions forbidden to government. Finally, *reserved* powers are clearly stated in the Tenth Amendment, which "declares powers not delegated to the national government by the Constitution nor prohibited by it to the states, are reserved to the states respectively, or to the people."[9]

Nevertheless, this largely indirect legal relation of the federal government to education has been important. Federal courts have ruled on alleged violations of constitutional rights by the states and their local school districts. The impact of such federal court decisions on education, even though indirect, has been of great consequence and will continue to be so (see Chapters 9 and 10). When one considers the nationwide effect of the Supreme Court's desegregation ruling in *Brown* v. *Board of Education* (1954), it must be recognized that that indirect power has monumental implications.[10] The impacts of Title IX of the Education Amendments of 1972 (sex discrimination) and Section 504 of the Rehabilitation Act of 1973 (discrimination against the disabled) are excellent examples of how indirect controls may strongly influence schools and their organizational and administrative operations.

Evolution of Federal Interest

Most people believe that public education is still primarily a state responsibility with some degree of local control. When President Carter and the Congress separated the United States Department of Education from the Department of Health, Education and Welfare and created a Cabinet-level post, the enabling legislation was clear and precise. It declared: "The establishment of the Department of Education shall not increase the authority of the Federal Government over education or diminish the responsibility for education which is reserved to the States and the local school systems and other instrumentalities of the States."[11]

Generally, greater interest at the federal level comes when a perceived national need is identified and the federal establishment reacts to that need. Even before the adoption of the U.S. Constitution while the Continental Congress was meeting in Philadelphia, delegates under the auspices of the Articles of Confederation saw the need to colonize the Northwest Territory. Consequently, they legislated the Northwest Ordinances of 1785 and 1787, which contained a proviso to give section 16 of every township to provide for schools. These grants provided some incentive for the settlement of western lands and were the first acts of federal aid to education. As the territories became states, the newly formed federal government established a policy for land grants to be used as gifts to the newly formed states to finance state-sponsored public education systems.

As settlers moved west in the nineteenth century, the federal government passed the Morrill Acts, which provided land grants to establish universities in each state for the teaching of agriculture and applied sciences. The establishment of land-grant colleges was an answer to a national need to improve farm practices, since 97 percent of the national economy was agricultural.

The twentieth century was an era in which a federal interest in education, above and beyond land grants, started slowly, then was recognized and fostered to a degree. Needs surfaced that were not contained within state boundaries generating a national interest; the federal government then established programs to address those needs. When the United States entered World War I, for example, industrial skills were needed but were lacking in America. Several vocational education programs were established to develop industrial capacity. They were funded by the federal government and administered by the states. It was determined to be necessary to meet the challenges of the war effort.

When the nation was in the depths of a depression in the 1930s, federal interest was accelerated to meet the demands facing an impoverished nation. During this period, legislation established the Federal Surplus Commodities Corporation to distribute surplus food to schools. The National Youth Administration and the Civilian Conservation Corps were established to provide work and training for youths. The Public Works Administration made grants and extended loans for school construction.

The G.I. Bill followed World War II as the nation struggled to respond to postwar problems. That law authorized substantial educational benefits for veterans. At that time some proposed a general aid, "no strings attached," federal education bill—merely a certain amount given by student population—with the federal government not having any power on how the money would be spent. Issues such as no federal funds to segregated schools and school districts, church-state ramifications, and fear of federal control thwarted that effort for elementary and secondary schools.

The Soviet Union launched the satellite *Sputnik* in 1957 that led to fear of spying and Soviet power to control outer space. That created great interest at the federal level to rally support for education. The National Defense Education Act (NDEA) was passed, which provided revenue for math, science, foreign language, media, and counseling services.

Later, the Great Society concept established programs for ESEA Title I compensatory education, disability education, and Head Start. Also, during that period the Office of Economic Opportunity was formed that has some impact on education.

Common to all these perceived needs was the overriding element of finance—how much, what for, where the funds should go, what strings should be attached, and how much control and accountability would be required? With each program different procedures were adopted, often leading to confusion at the state and local levels.

In 1995, Congress passed the Unfunded Mandates Act, which disallowed the federal government from imposing requirements in the future on states and local governments, including school districts, for which no allocation of funds followed.

No Child Left Behind Law

At the turn of the twenty-first century, the federal government perceived a national need that students from certain socioeconomic and racial populations were suffering from a significant "achievement gap." Attendance in some schools was tantamount, it was thought, to being denied a good education. The reaction to that identified national need was to implement a dramatic alteration to and reauthorization of the Elementary and Secondary Education Act (ESEA). The timing was fortuitous, for the law was scheduled for renewal in 2001 and Congress reauthorized the act and changed its name to the No Child Left Behind Act of 2001 (NCLB).

Initiated by President George W. Bush, the NCLB requires every state to test students in grades 3 through 8 annually in reading and mathematics. The centerpiece of the legislation is to identify schools that are failing to meet student achievement goals and to label them as schools "in need of improvement." The linchpin of that identification and labeling process is accountability. The method used to determine if schools are in need of improvement is to test students and synthesize the aggregate results school by school and declare which schools are making adequate yearly progress (AYP).

Another aspect of the accountability activity is to evaluate the system with particular focus on having "highly qualified teachers" in every classroom. One aspect of being highly qualified is to be professionally certificated and/or licensed. Other factors include having a bachelor's degree, passing a test in each of the subjects one teaches, and having an academic major or equivalent in each subject taught. Determining if a teacher has a graduate degree or advanced certification results in being "highly qualified" demonstrably.

The requirements for testing and the oversight for highly qualified teachers were significant shifts from the historical role of the federal government in education. This raised the critical question: Since the federal government provides a minuscule fraction (historically 6 to 8.5 percent) of the amount spent on education in America, does that level of government have the right, in a federal system, to exercise such a vigorous oversight, including the power to withhold funds if a state does not comply with the federal mandates? State and local education leaders are concerned about the federal encroachment that they feel NCLB has wrought and that it is in absolute violation of the enabling legislation that was included in the creation of the Department of Education, which states:

> No provision of a program administered by the Secretary or any other officer of the department shall be construed to authorize the Secretary or any such officer to exercise any direction, supervision, or control over the curriculum, program of instruction, administration, or personnel of any educational institution, school, or school, or school system or any accrediting agency or association, or over the selection or content of library resources, textbooks, or other instructional materials by any educational institution or school system except to the extent authorized by law.[12]

It has been said that federal aid (money, property, and other capital) was given without federal control in the twentieth century. The requirements of NCLB, some maintain, have brought considerable federal control to education in the twenty-first century.

Federal Expenditures

The Department of Education administers a budget of about $88.9 billion a year—$57.6 billion in discretionary appropriations and $31.3 billion in mandatory appropriations—

and operates programs that touch on every level of education. That said, it is important to point out that education is primarily a state and local responsibility, and that the Education Department's budget is only a small part of both total national spending and the overall federal budget. Fiscal 2006 allocations for federal programs included:

- ESEA Title I Grants to Local Educational Agencies
- Reading First State Grants
- Even Start
- State Agency Program—Neglected and Delinquent
- Improving Teacher Quality State Grants
- Mathematics and Science Partnerships
- Education Technology State Grants
- 21st Century Community Learning Centers
- State Grants for Innovative Programs
- State Assessments
- Safe and Drug-Free Schools and Communities State Grants
- Language Acquisition State Grants
- Education for Homeless Children and Youth
- Impacted Aid
- Special Education
- Preschool Special Education State Grants for Incarcerated Youth Offenders
- Rural and Low Income School Programs

Department discretionary spending for FY 2006 included $1.6 billion in education assistance to areas affected by hurricanes Katrina and Rita. Discretionary appropriations—from 2001 until 2007—for the Department will have grown by almost $12.2 billion, or 29 percent (see Figure 8.1).

FIGURE 8.1 Department of Education Discretionary Appropriations (Billions of Dollars)

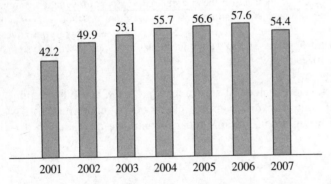

Note: 2007 reflects President Bush's request level.

Source: www.ed.gov/about/overview/budget/budget07/summary/edlite-section1.html.

Some critics of federal expenditures permit their children to participate in school lunch programs, attend agricultural colleges, pursue vocational education, and participate in many other federally subsidized programs. Even the most radical critic of federal assistance to education can find little to condemn in the tremendously important land grants or in the G.I. Bill, which provide federal funds for the education of war veterans. Both of these programs represent federal contributions to education. On the other hand, the most ardent advocate of federal aid can point to some programs that seem to have gone beyond generally acceptable limits in federal usurpation of control in education and/or the domination of the responsibility for education.

Notwithstanding different perceptions about federal expenditures, the contribution of the federal government provides from about 5 percent of the funds in New Jersey, New Hampshire, and Connecticut to nearly 18 percent in Alaska (see Figure 8.2). The percentage of education expenses funded by the federal government is 8.5 percent.

Fiscal Advantages and Disadvantages

The federal government's role in financing public education may be characterized as having begun as advisory and supplementary. The contribution of the federal government to the present state of development of public schools has been important, in spite of the disadvantages that this unit of government encounters as a partner in the system of education. It is the unit in the hierarchy of governance that is at the greatest distance from the ongoing process of education. By constitutional design, the federal government was to have only limited interest in educational matters. Education is the only function of the local school district and is an important function of state government, but it is only one of many important responsibilities at the national level. The federal government has a myriad of problems and programs that, of necessity, often upstage the federal interest in education—especially in periods of crisis or national emergency.

The federal government has certain advantages to assist in the operation of this important and expensive service of government. Chief among these is its ability as a tax collector. Using the graduated income tax, the federal government has become an effective tax-collecting agency. It uses the graduated income tax as its predominant source of revenue, followed by, historically, deficit financing. Total income, with proper deductions for dependents and other tax exclusions, provides a good comparison of the ability of people to pay their obligations to government. An income tax produces large amounts of revenue at a relatively low collection rate. It is collected for the most part by withholding taxes. It is paid by a high percentage of citizens, although it is too easy to evade, under certain conditions. Features of the tax can be regulated in such a way as to alter the economic pattern of the country. With all its limitations and unfairness in the treatment of some individuals or companies, the income tax remains the backbone of this country's federal tax structure. Inherent inequities in its application and its complexity are its greatest deficiencies; its power to produce large amounts of revenue while using the ability principle of taxation is its greatest virtue.

FIGURE 8.2   States Ranked by Percentage of Public Education Revenues Received from Federal Sources: School Year 2002–2003

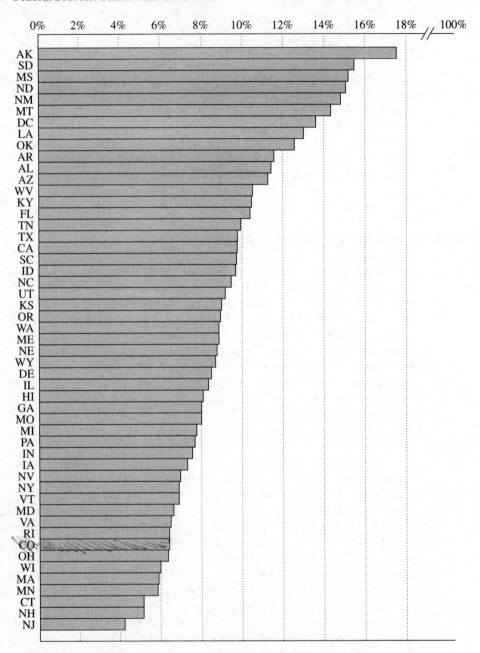

Source: U.S. Department of Education, National Center for Education Statistics, Common Core Data. "National Public Education Financial Survey," School Year 2002–2003. http://nces.ed.gov/edfin/graphs/topic.asp?INDEX=8.

A disadvantage to the federal government's role in financing education may be that educational personnel do not understand the budgetary process of the federal government. School personnel often remark that a certain program "has not been funded as it was supposed to have been." The procedure begins when the president presents a budget to Congress. The forwarded budget may or may not be accepted by the Congress. If not, when the amount that is finally made available is known, some could say that it was not what the president promised. In legislative actions there are two distinct levels—one is the authorizing effort and the other is the appropriations result. Concerning the financial part of the authorization effort one must consider the money authorized to be a ceiling above which the appropriations committee cannot exceed. Almost never in the appropriations phase of the process has the money appropriated equaled what was authorized—not only in education but also in every federal department or agency. Critics of a federal program may wail that the program is underfunded. If complaints adversely affect the perception of the role of the federal government, then it is, indeed, a disadvantage.

Neutral Position

The position of the federal government should be one of neutrality as far as providing educational advantages is concerned, for all the people are citizens of a nation, not just citizens of local communities and states. Potentially, federal tax money can be used in any state for education or in any school district, for every citizen can be viewed at the national level as being as important as every other one.

Although there has been considerable discussion over the years concerning the method or process of the distribution of federal funds, generally speaking, the modus operandi was using categorical funding (i.e., a certain category of need was determined to be in the federal interest and then that particular category was funded). Under this categorical aid approach, the federal government designates the exact purpose for which federal funds will be used. Examples of these categories are compensatory education (Title I, which was legislated in 1965 when it was determined that the poor needed some compensation in the school system because of their lack of opportunity), handicapped education, American Indian education, vocational education, school lunch programs, the NCLB, and early childhood education (Head Start and others). Bilingual education, migrant education, and programs of national significance, although not as extensive, are additional examples of categorical funding.

Some have criticized the imbalance that many of these federal activities have tended to create in the public schools and have suggested a block-grant approach. Educators see block grants as related to the categorical approach, involving broader categories and greater discretion within and among these categories. An example of block grants would be to combine bilingual education and migrant education. The term *block grant* has been used as if it were synonymous with general aid, but it is a middle-of-the-road approach between categorical aid and general aid.

General aid involves only a general expression of purpose or priority by the federal government, such as improving education at the elementary and secondary levels, and allows the states to solve their problems as they see fit. It also implies far less accountability, reporting, and evaluation. Some educators champion categorical aid, whereas others have accepted it only in lieu of general federal aid to education. General federal aid has not yet been authorized by congressional action. It would seem that the odds against obtaining general federal aid in any substantial amount are high. The chief argument raised against categorical aid is that it tends to give the federal government too much power and control in determining where the money is to be spent.

Future general federal aid programs, to be effective, must embody certain characteristics: (1) They must not be used to allow state and local support monies to be decreased. The main responsibility for financing education must remain at those levels; federal assistance must assure a supplemental, not a supplanting, function. (2) Funds should be based on the principle of equalization, but each state should expect to receive some funds, depending on its comparative wealth and need. (3) Funds should be provided for some specific programs that are in the national interest but that may be neglected because of their high costs, inconvenience, or emergency nature—education of the disadvantaged, the disabled, the exceptional, and similar groups.

Federal Aid in Lieu of Taxes

Federal aid to education does not represent a purely altruistic position of an affluent "uncle." Rather, some federal programs have been organized and implemented because of the financial obligations that the federal government has to the states. A prime example is the obligatory payments the federal government has to make in lieu of the taxes that would ordinarily be paid on the tremendous amount of land that it owns, particularly in the western states. The federal government owns about one-third of the land area of the country; this removes it from the reach of state, county, or school district property taxes.

A report in 2006 indicated that federal ownership of land in the 50 states had reached more than 700,000,000 acres. Most of the gains were due to expansions of national parks, national monuments, national wildlife refuges, and national forests. The Forest Service, National Park Service, Bureau of Land Management, and Fish and Wildlife Service manage 95 percent of the federally owned land. More than half of the land owned by the federal government is in five states. In Nevada, 84.5 percent of the state is owned by the federal government; in Alaska, 69.1 percent; in Utah, 57.4 percent; in Oregon, 53.1 percent; and in Idaho, 50.2 percent (see Figure 8.3).

Increased Governmental Services

It is impossible to understand the point of view that favors extended federal financial support for education unless one understands the change in philosophy about government services that has pervaded the country in the last several decades. Traditionally,

FIGURE 8.3   Percent of Federal Land Ownership in Each State

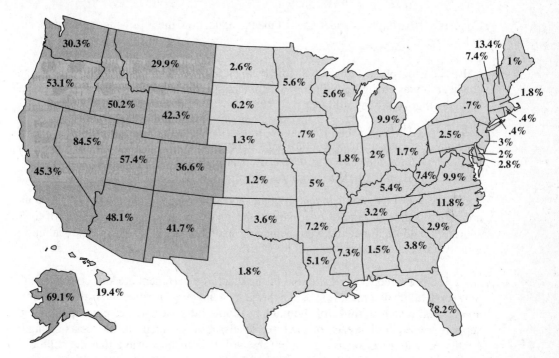

Source: U.S. General Services Administration. chriscannon.house.gov/wc/images/govt._own_land.pdf, 2006.

the federal role was accepted as one of maintaining law and order, providing for some degree of protection to individuals and their property, and in general maintaining a laissez-faire policy toward most other problems. Such a role was justifiable and worked for the maximum development of individual initiative and growth. Economists and political scientists supported this policy, and it served the country well for a long period of its early history.

The "let alone" policy of government is still an issue. The increasing complexity of social institutions, the economic order, and the political structure have resulted in increased services of government. The dangers of unlimited extension of such services are great, however. Thus, determining the services that should be provided by each level of government and those that should be left to individuals is now of paramount importance. The assumption here is that each unit of government is responsible for providing those services that will result in maximum benefits to the greatest possible number of citizens.

The Future of Federal Aid to Education

Concerning the future of federal assistance to education, the following facts now seem to be apparent:

1. The widespread and complex involvement of the federal government may change considerably as changing philosophies and changing leaders in the three branches of the federal government influence it.

2. If order is to be established in the administration of federal programs, it will be necessary to center primary responsibility in fewer educational agencies at the national level. The United States Department of Education is the logical agency to administer most, if not all, of the federal programs directly related to education.

3. Additional federal financial programs need not—indeed, should not—greatly increase the degree of control over education. Funds for education, regardless of their source, should be directed toward achieving national as well as state and local community goals of education.

The issues concerning the role of the federal government are still controversial. Some federal involvement is now supported by a majority of citizens. As the programs and official responsibilities of the public schools increase, greater participation and support are required at each of the three levels of government. As the costs of high-quality education continue their spiral upward, it is inconceivable that the solutions to the increasing problems of education should rest on only one or two of the party's concerned—the states and the local school districts. For the system to work as intended, each partner must assume some share of the additional responsibility for the educational programs that citizens will continue to demand in the years ahead.

Many federal funding elements from the twentieth century have endured, and are likely to continue in the future, primarily in the areas of American Indian education, vocational education, compensatory education, education for those with special needs, school foods, federal payments in lieu of taxes, and support through loans and grants to students in postsecondary and higher education institutions.

Summary

The role of the federal government in education has long been a controversial one that has had racial, religious, and political overtones. Historically, federal involvement with the public schools has been minor. However, at the turn of the twenty-first century, centered on a perceived need that certain populations were disadvantaged educationally, the No Child Left Behind Act of 2001 was legislated. The law changed the dynamics of the federal role in education.

The framers of the Constitution seemed to have feared the establishment of a nationally controlled school system. In effect, the adoption of the Tenth Amendment in

1791 relegated the federal government to an advisory role as far as education is concerned. Throughout the history of the United States, the comparative roles of the three levels of government have been in a state of change.

Federal education activities began in 1785 with the land grants in the Northwest Ordinances that were given for the purpose of establishing schools. Later, the Morrill Acts provided land for the establishment of land-grant colleges. These were followed by supplemental acts and by various vocational education grants. School lunch, relief and emergency programs, war on poverty, and payments in lieu of taxes are examples of federal involvement in financing education. Federal emphasis has been given to programs designed to help eliminate racial and sex discrimination, stress cultural awareness, provide funds for specialized categorical programs including, through NCLB, the educationally disadvantaged.

The federal government has the ability to collect taxes in an effective manner. One of its major concerns is how to determine the best method for distributing funds equitably. Federal funds are usually categorical in nature, with the result that the states and local school districts lose some of their control.

There is still wide disagreement among the people of the nation as to the degree to which the federal government should participate in financing public education. A proper mixture of leadership at all levels of government is needed if public education is to continue to improve and to provide the kind and amount of instruction that is so necessary for the youths of the nation.

ASSIGNMENT PROJECTS

1. Provide a definition for each of the following terms: *constitution, federalism, Tenth Amendment, categorical aid, block grants, general aid, in lieu of taxes, budgeted, authorized, appropriated, Northwest Ordinances.*

2. Trace the development of the Department of Education from its beginning to its present position. List the advantages and disadvantages of having a department of education at the national level.

3. Determine which of the long list of federal acts for financing education that have been in operation through the years have been generally accepted with little controversy and which have engendered great controversy.

4. Distinguish between general federal aid and categorical federal aid in terms of their advantages and disadvantages, their value to the states and to school districts, and the problem of getting each type enacted by Congress.

5. Trace the development of land grants by the federal government and indicate the current status of these lands in your state.

6. Examine the No Child Left Behind law and trace how its features, particularly in financial matters, are interpositional into states, school districts, and various schools. Determine what control the government has put on how the funds are spent, how the funds are administered, and how resources are used.

Computer simulations and questions, research exercises, and website
addresses relevant to this chapter can be found at

www.ablongman.com/edleadership

SELECTED READINGS

Centre for Educational Research and Innovation, Organization for Economic Cooperation and Development. *Education at a Glance, OECD Indicators of Education Systems and Organizations.* Paris: Author, 1995.

A Compilation of Federal Education Laws, Volume II-Elementary and Secondary Education. Individuals with Disabilities and Related Programs. Prepared for the use of the Committee on Education and Labor. Washington, DC: U.S. House of Representatives, July 1991.

The Condition of Education 2006. Washington, DC: U.S. Department of Education, 2006.

Education Funding Research Council. *Guide to Federal Funding for Education Volume I and II, 1996.* Arlington, VA: Author, 1996.

Moskowitz, Jay. *Targeting, Formula, and Resource Allocation Issues: Focusing Federal Funds Where the Needs Are Greatest.* Washington, DC: U.S. Department of Education, 1993.

National Center for Education Statistics. *Development in School Finances: 2001–02.* Washington, DC: U.S. Department of Education, Office of Education Research and Improvement, June 2003.

National Center for Educational Statistics. *Federal $upport for Education: Fiscal Years 1980–1998.* Washington DC: U.S. Department of Education, 1998.

Oates, Wallace, E. *Fiscal Federalism.* New York: Harcourt Brace Jovanovich, 1972.

ENDNOTES

1. *Education Week,* June 25, 1997, p. 2.
2. David C. Whitney, revised and updated by Robin Vaughn Whitney, *The American Presidents, Biographies of the Chief Executives from Washington through Clinton,* 8th ed. (New York: Doubleday Books and Music Clubs, 1993), pp. 162.
3. Ibid., p. 174.
4. Personal conversation, Dwight D. Eisenhower and Rulon R. Garfield, Washington, DC, June 13, 1957.
5. Whitney, *The American Presidents*, p. 306.
6. Ibid., pp. 321–322.
7. Personal conversation, President Ronald Reagan, Secretary of Education Terrel (Ted) H. Bell, and Rulon Garfield, Washington DC, January 1982.
8. Whitney, *The American Presidents*, p. 467.
9. Rulon R. Garfield, Gene J. Garfield, and J. D. Willardson, *Policy and Politics in American Education* (Atlanta: St. Barthelemy Press, Ltd., 2003), pp. 13, 14.
10. *Brown* v. *Board of Education* (1), 347 U.S. 483, 74 S. Ct. 686 [1954].
11. Public Law 96–88, October 17, 1979.
12. Ibid.

9 The Influence and Climate of the Courts

Many Americans are becoming concerned about the judiciary becoming super-legislatures. However, the courts tend to reflect the values and attitudes of a majority of the people toward the issues and questions on which they are ruling.

—Russell Carruth, 2007

Nowhere in the broad spectrum of activities in education is there a better example that financing education is in a climate of change than examining the actions of the courts as they scrutinize public school finance systems. Currently it is a rather stormy climate. One has only to read the history of U.S. education to be reminded of the many times the courts have altered its course because of a changing climate. As early as 1859, in *Springfield Township* v. *Quick et al.*[1]—a case concerning Section 16 of land that the Northwest Ordinances of 1785 and 1787 had set aside for the support of schools—the Supreme Court made the decision that a school finance law in Indiana "is a perfectly just one . . . those plaintiffs* have no right to call on this court to interfere with the power exercised by the state legislature in laying and collecting taxes and in appropriating them for educational purposes, at its discretion."[2] The *Kalamazoo* case of 1874[3] established a legal system of taxation for funding secondary education; the *Brown* case of 1954[4] pushed aside the indefensible doctrine of "separate but equal," facilitating opportunities for minorities; and the "one man–one vote" decision of 1962[5] changed the organization of state legislative bodies and ultimately obliterated the requirement that voters must pay property taxes in order to vote in certain school elections. In 1971, the *Serrano* decision of the California Supreme Court[6] put legal pressure on the California state legislature to revise the state finance formula to effect greater equity and equality for the students in all school districts within the state.

In *San Antonio Independent School District* v. *Rodriguez* (1973),[7] the United States Supreme Court upheld the Texas school financing system stating that education was not a federal fundamental right under the U.S. Constitution. This case had remark-

---

*In this chapter the word *plaintiff* is used to denote those who challenged a state's school finance system.

able impact on school finance cases and it ended appeals to the federal court system on such matters in the twentieth and thus far in the twenty-first century. It is expected to stop similar appeals in the future as well. Basically, the Court ruled, "Though education is one of the most important services performed by the State, it is not within the limited category of rights recognized by this Court as guaranteed by the Constitution."[8] Justice Powell delivered the opinion of the Court, which was decided by a 5–4 vote. Powell stated:

> Education, of course, is not among the rights afforded explicit protection under our Federal Constitution. Nor do we find any basis for saying it is implicitly protected
> . . . We have carefully considered each of the arguments supportive of the District Court's findings that education is a fundamental right or liberty and have found these arguments unpersuasive.[9]

Powell continued to discuss the issue of state and national roles in educational finance matters. His frame of reference was in relation to federalism. He maintained:

> It must be remembered also that every claim under the Equal Protection Clause has implications for the relationship between national and state power under our federal system. Questions of federalism are always inherent in the process of determining whether a State's laws are to be accorded the traditional presumption of constitutionality, or are to be subjected instead to rigorous judicial scrutiny. While the maintenance of the principles is a foremost consideration in interpreting any of the pertinent constitutional provisions under which the Court examines state action, it would be difficult to imagine a case having a greater potential impact on our federal system than the one now before us, in which we are urged to abrogate systems of financing public education presently in existence in virtually every State.[10]

Since *Rodriguez*, a plethora of cases in state courts has either sustained or required alteration of school finance systems. These cases, which have been pursued in state courts, recognize the principle of federalism—that education is a state responsibility and that state legislatures, and perhaps state courts, should be where school finance issues are decided. If state courts sustained their state's school finance system, they generally followed the rationale of Justice Powell in *Rodriguez* where he stated, "Ultimate solutions must come from the lawmakers and from the democratic pressures of those that elect them." In those states where an alteration of their school finance system was required, they have followed a *Serrano* approach as well as proceeded as Justice Thurgood Marshall suggested when writing for the minority in *Rodriguez*: "Of course, nothing in the Court's decision today should inhibit further reviews of state educational funding schemes under state constitutional provisions."[11]

Following Marshall's point of view, 40 states have had school finance disputes adjudicated at the state supreme court level. In 20 states, plaintiffs who were challenging the state finance systems have won; in 20 states, the plaintiffs lost (see Figure 9.3 on pages 235–236). In the remainder of the states, either no litigation took place or their state supreme courts did not or have not rendered a decision. Some scholars maintain that in the early twenty-first century, emulating *Serrano*/Marshall, plaintiffs are on a winning streak with recent wins in Arkansas, Idaho, Kansas, and North Carolina. Conversely, others declare that the early twenty-first century trend supports the *Rodriquez*/Powell view because of rulings in Massachusetts and Texas for the state, by supporting legislative actions.

Such bifurcation is not without precedence. Following *Serrano*, three state supreme courts ruled for the plaintiffs: Arizona, New Jersey, and Minnesota. After *Rodriguez*, plaintiffs lost in the supreme courts of Michigan and Pennsylvania. Later, plaintiffs had a list of victories in Connecticut, Washington, and West Virginia. The beginning of the 1980s resulted in wins for the states of Georgia, Colorado, New York, and Maryland. In the mid-80s, it was a draw with a win for the plaintiffs in Arkansas and a loss in Oklahoma. A banner year for plaintiffs was 1989, when they won in Kentucky, Montana, and Texas, which carried over into 1990 with another victory in New Jersey, *Abbott* v. *Burke I*—an extension of the *Robinson* case. In the late 90s and 2000, the states of South Carolina, Wisconsin, and Alabama were successful in defending their school finance systems. Plaintiffs were victorious in their challenge to Montana's finance formula and they acquired a partial victory in Ohio.

Diversity in State Court Rulings

Opinions of the various state supreme courts demonstrate distinct differences, which have led to questions about the efficacy of judicial fiat being the manner through which educational finance decisions are made. "One may think that relying on court-ordered [opinions] would be more rational and responsible than leaving spending decisions to politicians. The exact opposite is the case. For all its defects, legislators can be held responsible for wasting taxpayer dollars, and courts . . . generally cannot. This gives courts . . . license to use pseudoscience to drive education spending higher, where legislators might be more skeptical and frugal."[11] Pseudoscience has resulted in judicial activism "which has substituted judicial appropriations for democratic appropriations."[12]

There are four standards that courts have used to determine if the state is adequately financing the schools:

1. *Professional judgment.* Professionals design a school that they believe to be optimal.
2. *Expert state of the art.* Consultants acquire evidence and define what a quality school should be.
3. *Successful school.* Successful schools are identified and they need to be emulated.
4. *Cost function.* Analyze the relationship between cost and achievement.

Hanuchek maintains that these standards "have no relation to empirical reality." He renames the professional judgment standard as "Educator's Wish List," the expert state of the art method as "Consultant's Avis (we're number 2 and we want to be number 1 like Hertz)," the successful school system as the "superior student method," and the cost function analysis as the "expert accounting method."[13]

Debate about the Role of the Courts Has Intensified

There has been a continuing debate about the role of the courts in school finance matters but in the twenty-first century the debate has become more heated. "Courts in school finance matters have usurped legislative actions causing a constitutional crisis."14 "It is endemic to American politics that there are three separate and equal branches of government. These three branches have as a supernumerary the Constitution. However, the wording in state constitutions may not have a clear, precise meaning. Judges must choose which of the several meanings should be adopted."15 In school finance matters, language in state constitutions leaves much leeway for interpretation. Such words as fundamental, equity, adequate, thorough, efficient, reasonable, support free common schools, effective, appropriate, productive, and suitable are used by judges diversely. Also, in determining the intent of the constitutional writers, the courts may act much like a legislator. Many fear that conclusions reflect individual biases. James Landis has pointed out that "strong judges prefer to override the intent of the legislature in order to make law according to their own views."[16] Not all judges are convinced of the desirability of achieving objectivity, or of withdrawing from the field of policy making. Such judges are characterized as "judicial activists." The judicial "self-restrainers" take another view. They recognize a judge's difficulty in rising above his or her own biases, but insist that objectivity is the goal for which one should aim. Self-restrainers insist judges must be very careful to avoid injecting their own wishes into the judicial process, since it is not their responsibility to determine public policy, and that judges should be especially hesitant to check the full play of the democratic process. The people's political representatives, legislators,[17] and executives, have the right to work out the accommodation of interests that is the essence of legislation. United States Supreme Court Justice Stone stated it succinctly: "While unconstitutional exercise of power by the executive and legislative branches of government is subject to judicial restraint, the only check upon our own exercise of power is our own sense of self-restraint, for the removal of unwise laws from the statue books, appeal lies not to the courts, but to the ballot and to the processes of democratic government.[18]

Those who favor court action rather than legislative action view the courts as unbiased. In the half of the states that have adjudicated favoring the plaintiffs' position, supporters of judicial action maintain that the decisions are based on law and that the state should provide a basic education within the parameters decided by the courts. Language in various state constitutions may be similar to that of the Kansas Constitution. That constitution contains a clause that indicates that:

> The Kansas legislature shall be responsible for making "suitable" provision for the finance of the educational interests of the state (Article 6, Section 6). It is primarily the state legislature's responsibility to figure out exactly what "suitable" is supposed to mean and how to make "suitable" provisions of finance. However, Kansas like other states also has a judicial branch and one responsibility of that branch of government is to review challenges brought by individuals against laws adopted by the state legislature. As its broad framework for review, the state court relies primarily on the state constitution. That is, it is a responsibility of both the state courts and the state legislature to figure out what exactly "suitable" means and whether current policies are, in fact, "suitable."[19]

In determining what "thorough" and "efficient" mean, "*Abbott I* (a continuation of *Robinson* v. *Cahill*), *Abbott II, Abbott III, Abbott IV,* and *Abbott V* are significant. The New Jersey courts judged "thorough" and "efficient" differently than the state legislature did. This litany of cases followed a prolonged schedule of the courts demanding more "thorough" and "efficient" legislative actions, and then returning over and over again, saying what the legislature had done, was not satisfactory.

In Massachusetts (*Hancock* v. *Driscoll, the Commissioner of Education*) and Texas (*West-OrangeCoveISD* v. *the State of Texas*), the state supreme courts stunned plaintiffs by "upholding the adequacy of funding received by K–12 school districts" in both Texas and Massachusetts. Furthermore, in Massachusetts the plaintiffs alleged " 'that the Commonwealth was violating its constitutional obligation to educate children in poorer communities' . . . [In addition] the [Supreme] Court declined to adopt the conclusion of a Superior Court judge that the Commonwealth was not meeting its obligation under the Massachusetts Constitution." In the Ohio (*DeRolph*) case, even though Ohio's Supreme Court had declared the school finance system unconstitutional, the court ruled that "there would be no fiscal relief for the districts and that the court prohibited the state high court itself or any other court jurisdiction over the case."[20] In Wisconsin's *Vincent* v. *Voight*, four of seven judges ruled the school finance system unconstitutional or a fundamental right; nevertheless, Wisconsin's finance system was considered acceptable. Even in the *Abbott* cases the New Jersey Supreme Court for 2006–2007 granted a stay on state funding due to a $4 billion budget shortfall—a remarkable turn-around.

The debate is not over. Critics are declaring that the "responsibility for school funding and policy should lay with the legislature outside the jurisdiction of the court."[21] Others are organizing efforts to "rethink Rodriguez; Education as a fundamental right."[22] They are "examining possible strategies for creating a new paradigm so that education can acquire judicial affirmation of a fundamental right status; arguing in favor of court involvement in school funding litigations to help achieve that end."[23] It is expected that these disputations will continue.

Court Decision Guidelines

Certain general guidelines have emerged from the numerous state and federal court decisions about financing education. Some of the most important are the following:

1. Since education is neither an explicit nor implicit right under the United States Constitution, financing education is a state responsibility. Numerous court cases at the state level strengthen that principle. State courts measure the educational finance system within a state against the respective states' constitutions and educational statutes, and reach diverse conclusions.

2. The courts are generally inclined to construe statutes concerning taxation strictly. They usually favor the taxpayer over the school district. A Florida court, for example, pointed out that "in deciding questions relating to procedure employed by a governmental taxing agency one must bear in mind at the outset that laws providing for taxation must be construed most strongly against the government and liberally in favor of the taxpayer."[24]

3. School finance funds, including tax monies, are state funds, not local ones. Local school districts are agencies of the state and are in reality acting for the state. The courts are therefore inclined to the same care and efficiency in the administration of school funds that are required for other state agencies and institutions.

4. The courts have held consistently to the opinion that school taxes need not be imposed so that a direct relation exists between the benefits individual taxpayers receive and the amount of taxes they pay. In the words of one court, "The benefits are intangible and incapable of pecuniary ascertainment, but it is constitutionally sufficient if the taxes are uniform and are for public purposes in which the whole city has an interest."[25]

5. The legislature of each state has power to control public school funds and to determine how the public schools shall be financed, subject only to the restrictions imposed by the constitution and statutes of the state involved. Consequently, the legislature has wide discretion in determining how school funds shall be apportioned, so long as the basis for such apportionment is just and not arbitrary.

6. State public school finance systems do not rise to the level of strict judicial scrutiny in the federal courts. The United States Supreme Court in Rodriguez stated, "Public school finance is an inappropriate candidate for strict judicial scrutiny."[26] Standards used by the federal courts to review legislation include reasonable, intermediate, and strict scrutiny. Reasonable scrutiny requires a state to demonstrate a mere rational basis behind most laws concerning education and has minimal, if any, federal protection. Examples of statutes reviewed under the reasonable level of scrutiny would be compulsory education statutes and policies for extracurricular school activities. Intermediate scrutiny is applied to laws that address issues concerning gender and age. Strict scrutiny requires a state to demonstrate a compelling state interest to justify any law that has an impact on matters of race, color, creed, national origin, and First Amendment fundamental rights such as speech, religion, press, and association—not public school finance (see Figure 9.1). Concerning *Brown* v. *Board of Education*,[27] the U.S. Supreme Court ruled that equal education opportunity on the basis of race came under the strict scrutiny level of constitutional protection. Therefore, the students' rights reviewed in *Brown* v. *Board of Education* stated that education must be provided on equal terms. In sum, a student cannot be discriminated against in school but has no federal constitutional right to be treated financially equitably.

Generally, the courts tend to reflect the values and attitudes of a majority of the people toward the issues and questions on which they are ruling. Court decisions illustrate the attitude of the general public toward some of the legal principles involved in financing education. This attitude can be illustrated by the controversy over Supreme Court nominees. Stuart Taylor Jr., speaking of the nomination process to choose justices for the Supreme Court, declared, "A change in the ideological balance could swing the court to the right or left."[28] When the president of the United States nominates some-

FIGURE 9.1   Standards Used by the Federal Courts in Equal Protection Cases under the Fourteenth Amendment*

Strict Scrutiny Compelling State Interest	First Amendment rights (speech, religion, press, association, etc.), race, color, creed, national origin Federal Constitution
Intermediate Scrutiny Medium State Interest	Gender, handicap, age Federal Statutes
Reasonable Scrutiny Rational Basis	Compulsory education, lifestyle, extracurricular school activities, public school finance systems Minimal, if any, federal protection

*The standards courts use when applying strict scrutiny, intermediate scrutiny, and reasonable scrutiny may change over time. The scrutiny with which courts examine legislative actions changes when legal philosophy is altered or when justices with different legal persuasions are appointed.

one to the Court, often the nominee's political—not judicial—philosophy becomes the target of the inquiry. In the early twenty-first century, several federal presidential appointments were delayed for months by filibusters, or held up in committee because of political persuasion.

Power of the Courts before 1971

Until the early 1970s, most higher courts refused to interfere or to rule in school finance cases, with the rationale that the methods used to collect and distribute funds to local school districts were a legislative, not a judicial, problem. For example, in *Sawyer* v. *Gilmore* (1912),[29] the Supreme Court of Maine said, "The method of distribution of the proceeds of such a tax rests in the wise discretion and sound judgment of the Legislature. If this discretion is unwisely exercised, the remedy is with the people and not with the court." No one seriously questioned the philosophy of the Sawyer court at that time.

Perhaps the most publicized court case before 1971 that involved the provision of unequal revenues per pupil in different school districts in the same state was *McInnis* v. *Shapiro* in Illinois in 1969.[30] The complaint was that there was inequality in the provision of funds in various school districts in the state. A three-judge court dismissed the complaint, even though it recognized the wide range of expenditures among Illinois school districts. The court ruled that the Illinois plan for financing public education reflected a rational policy that was consistent with the mandate of the Illinois Constitution. It stated that the unequal expenditures per pupil did not amount to an invidious discrimination and that the laws that permit such unequal expenditures were neither arbitrary nor unreasonable. It further ruled that equal educational opportunity was not a constitutional requisite and that the court could not decide the issue.

The plaintiffs appealed the case (now *McInnis* v. *Ogilvie*) to the United States Supreme Court. The Court, without hearing the case, affirmed the decision of the lower court. The trial court had emphasized judicial lack of power or authority to change state school finance programs when it said, "The courts have neither the knowledge, nor the means, nor the power to tailor the public moneys to fit the varying needs of these students throughout the state. We can only see to it that the outlays on one group are not invidiously greater or less than that of another."[31] In this case, educational advocates of equal protection had hoped for a constitutional guarantee under the Fourteenth Amendment.

Serrano v. *Priest* (1971)

A landmark decision that altered the general view of state school financing formulas occurred on August 30, 1971, when the California Supreme Court ruled that John Serrano's complaint against the state's public school financial pattern was justifiable and that the pattern must be revised to make it constitutional.[32] At the time the *Serrano* suit was brought to court, educational expenditures per person in California ranged from $274 in one district to $1,710 in another—a ratio of 1 to 6.2. In the same year, two districts in the same county (Beverly Hills and Baldwin Park) expended $1,223 and $577 per pupil, respectively. This inequity was due to the difference in the assessed valuation of property per pupil to be educated ($50,885 in Beverly Hills and $3,706 in Baldwin Park—a ratio of nearly 14 to 1). The taxpayers in Baldwin Park paid a school tax of 54.8 mills ($5.48 per $100 of assessed valuation), whereas those in Beverly Hills paid school taxes of only 23.8 mills ($2.38 per $100 of assessed valuation). Thus, a tax effort in the poorer district twice as high as that in the wealthier one resulted in school expenditures of only 47 percent of that in the wealthier district.

The disparities in school funds available per pupil that led to the *Serrano* lawsuit could have been found in nearly all of the 50 states. It should be noted that the differences in ability to pay for education in Beverly Hills and Baldwin Park were not exceedingly great when compared with the extremes in the entire state or with those that could have been found in other states. Had the case been concerned with the extremes then existing in all of California, they would have been about 50 to 1, and 14 to 1 in New York. Thus, the issue in Serrano was concerned with differences in ability to pay—not necessarily in the size of those differences. In *Serrano*, the California court considered questions related to the comparative wealth of districts, the classification of education as a fundamental interest, and whether the financing system was necessary to the attainment of any compelling state interest. In a 6 to 1 opinion, the court declared the state's public school financing system to be unconstitutional. It declared that dependence on

local property taxes was the "root of the constitutional defect." It noted what school finance analysts have long known: Under such a system, with heavy reliance on property
taxation, school districts with a low value of taxable property per child cannot levy taxes
at high enough rates to compete with more affluent districts; in many instances, they cannot even provide funds for a minimum program of education. The following statement
summarizes the rationale of the court in the *Serrano* v. *Priest* decision:

> The California public school financing system, as presented to us by the plaintiff's com-
> plaint supplemented by matters judicially noticed, since it deals intimately with education,
> obviously touches upon a fundamental interest. For the reasons we have explained in detail,
> this system conditions the full entitlement to such interest on wealth, classifies its recipi-
> ents on the basis of their collective affluence and makes the quality of a child's education
> depend upon the resources of his school district and ultimately upon the pocketbook of his
> parents. We find that such a financing system as presently constituted is not necessary to the
> attainment of any compelling state interest. Since it does not withstand the requisite "strict
> scrutiny," it denies to the plaintiffs and others similarly situated the equal protection of the
> laws. . . . If the allegations of the complaint are sustained, the financial system must fall and
> the statutes comprising it must be found unconstitutional.[33]

The trial court held that the California system of financing public education
violated the equal protection provisions of the California Constitution and the Fourteenth Amendment to the U.S. Constitution because a disparity of tax money to support education existed among the districts of the state. According to the court, it made
no difference that the existing system might provide an adequate education for all the
children of the state. The disparity in the amount of money available for the education
of children among the districts was constitutionally significant because it permitted
some school districts to offer a higher quality of education than others. This differential
treatment of children was in the area of the fundamental interest of education and was
not justified by any compelling reason. Therefore, the court reasoned, the disparity
must be corrected within a reasonable period of time. It ordered the state to provide a
better equalization program by August 1980.

The trial court asserted that providing a school finance law was a responsibility
of the California legislature, but it took the liberty of suggesting four possible plans to
meet the requirements of equal protection:

1. Implement full state funding with statewide imposition and control of real property taxes.

2. Reorganize the 1,067 then existing school districts into about 500 districts with
boundary realignments to equalize assessed valuations of real property among all
school districts.

3. Retain the school district boundaries but remove commercial and industrial property from local taxation for school purposes.

4. School district power equalizing is based on the concept that school districts
could choose to spend at different levels. But for each level of expenditure chosen, the

tax effort would be the same for each school choosing such level, whether it is a high-wealth or a low-wealth school district.

Demurring in 1971, the California Supreme Court looked past all previous contrary decisions of other courts. Previous rulings in such states as Michigan, Virginia, Texas, and Illinois had implied that the equal protection clause of the Fourteenth Amendment did not apply to school financing patterns. Thus, *Serrano* became a landmark case—the first major decision by a higher court ruling against a state's school finance program on the basis of violation of equal protection for all the school pupils of a state.

Consequences of *Serrano*

The following statements are representative of the reactions of school finance scholars and writers to the *Serrano* decision:

> Despite the fact that the school-finance systems of every state but Hawaii were subjected to fundamental challenge, the decision was widely hailed on all sides. The press, legislative groups, educators at all levels in the administrative hierarchy, and taxpayer organizations were all enthused. Liberal civil rights adherents rejoiced at the apparent triumph of egalitarianism and conservative property owners rejoiced at the apparently impending demise of the local property tax.[34]

Wickert stated, "A new era was introduced with California's *Serrano* v. *Priest* court decision, which required school funding to be determined on some basis other than district property wealth."[35] However, many members of the educational community viewed the *Serrano* decision with a degree of skepticism. They feared that rather than being a great promise for the future in the field of educational finance, it might bring a leveling of the growth curve of revenues provided for education. A period of retrenchment was anticipated for taxpayers, who were beginning to rebel against the local property tax.

Educators, along with numerous lay citizens, were quite concerned with the spiraling costs of educational programs and services. The *Serrano* decision was followed with some inaccurate statements and faulty interpretations concerning what the California Supreme Court had actually said in condemning the finance law in that state. The following statement clarifies some of the misunderstandings that developed:

> Since the *Serrano* decision is a major factor in setting the criteria for education finance reform, it is important to be clear about what the court did and did not say. The court did not say that equal dollars had to be expended per child. It did not explicitly rule out plans providing more funds to higher cost pupils—such as disadvantaged, vocational, gifted, or handicapped students—as long as the distribution of these funds is not related to district wealth. Finally, the court did not exclude the property tax as a basis of education finance, but rather said that the level of educational expenditures could not be a function of district wealth.[36]

Serrano established judicial standards that courts from other states used.[37] Those standards were per-pupil expenditures and fiscal neutrality, holding that funding for schools should not be limited by local district wealth but reflect the wealth of the state as a whole.

The immediate consequences of the *Serrano* decision were significant in matters of school finance. Within five months after the announcement, three other state courts had made similar rulings. States that formerly seemed to be satisfied with maintaining their traditional financing programs began to study and restyle them. Such prompt state action was considered necessary in the face of an apparent legal threat of nationwide school tax and funding reform. The traditional local property tax, which had formed the chief framework for financing education, was diminished in importance. Although the *Serrano* decision did not condemn property taxes per se, it did condemn the unfairness that resulted from their use in California. State officials faced with apprehension the prospect of providing equitable school finance formulas if local property taxes were reduced or eliminated. They viewed with alarm the possibility of *Serrano*-type litigation in their states. Consequently, research studies were organized to correct formula inequities before court action was initiated.

Van Dusartz v. *Hatfield* (1971)

In October 1971, only six weeks after *Serrano*, Minnesota became the second state to have its system of financing education declared unconstitutional. A federal district court judge accepted the California arguments and findings as being equally applicable in Minnesota. According to him, "The level of spending for a child's education may not be a function of wealth other than the wealth of the state as a whole." The court recognized that pupils in publicly financed schools have a right under the equal protection guarantee of the Fourteenth Amendment to have money spent on them "unaffected by variations in the taxable wealth of their school districts or their parents." The court said:

> This is not the simple instance in which a poor man is injured by his lack of funds. Here the poverty is that of a governmental unit that the State itself has defined and commissioned. The heaviest burdens of this system surely fall defacto upon those poor families residing in poor districts who cannot escape to private schools, but this effect only magnifies the odiousness of the explicit discrimination by the law itself against all children living in relatively poor districts.[38]

Spano v. *Board of Education* (1972)

The first ruling after *Serrano* against the claims of the plaintiffs came in New York with the *Spano* case.[39] Andrew Spano and other residents and property holders in Lakeland Central School District No. 1 sued the Board of Education and various state officials because of the alleged unfairness of New York's legislative and constitutional provisions for levying and distributing school tax funds. Although the claims were much the same as in *Serrano,* the court based its decision on two previous cases (*McInnis* v. *Ogilvie* [Illinois, 1969] and *Burruss* v. *Wilkerson,* [Virginia 1969]).[40] Although acknowledging that there may be inadequacies and unfairness in state school financing systems, the New York Court of Appeals (New York's highest court; comparable to other states' supreme courts) indicated that, in its view, changes to correct such inequities should be the duty of the legislature rather than the court. It further stated that the "one scholar–one dollar" version of the "one man–one vote" mandate would have to be the prerogative of the U.S. Supreme Court.

San Antonio Independent School District v. Rodriguez (1973)

The United States Supreme Court spoke in 1973 while deciding the *Rodriguez* case. In 1970, three urban school districts in Texas brought suit against the Texas Board of Education and the State Commissioner of Education to determine whether the Texas system of allocating state funds for education was unfair. This case was based on the charge that underassessment of taxable property in many rural school districts resulted in their obtaining disproportionate amounts of state funds. In late 1971, a federal court ruled that the Texas financing system violated both the federal and the Texas Constitutions. The court went a step beyond the California and Minnesota decisions by giving Texas two years to reorganize its school financing system. The court threatened that if the legislature should fail to act, the court would take such further steps as may be necessary to implement both the purpose and spirit of this order.

The *Rodriguez* case was accepted for review by the United States Supreme Court and became the first and only equal protection case concerning school finance to be considered by the high court to date. The facts of the case were as follows:

1. The financing of elementary and secondary schools in Texas came from state and local funding.
2. Almost half of the revenues came from the state's Minimum Foundation Program, which was designed to provide a minimum educational offering in every school in the state.
3. To provide for this program, the school districts as a single unit provided 20 percent of the funding.
4. Each district contributed its share as determined by a formula designed to reflect its relative taxpaying ability. These funds were raised by property taxes.
5. All districts raised additional monies to support schools.

Rodriguez held that the revenue source varied with the value of taxable property in the districts, thus causing great disparities in per-pupil spending among districts. The lower courts concluded that the Texas system of public school finance violated the equal protection clause of the Fourteenth Amendment, finding that wealth is a "suspect" classification and that education is a "fundamental" interest. On March 21, 1973, the U.S. Supreme Court, by a vote of 5 to 4, reversed the lower court decision, which also nullified the *Van Dusartz* decision in Minnesota and negated all related pending federal court actions. In general, the Court ruled that reforms with respect to state taxation and education are matters reserved for the legislative processes of the various states. Education is not a constitutional federal interest and the Texas school finance system did not discriminate against any class of persons considered suspect, because it dealt with property-poor school districts, not individuals.

Rodriguez found that variations in local wealth were permissible under the state's constitution. The court also made it clear that education was not a fundamental right under the U.S. Constitution. *Rodriguez* was heard in the U.S. Supreme Court and the decision was based on the equal protection clause of the Fourteenth Amendment to the United States Constitution. This decision halted school finance challenges in federal courts, but it did not directly affect actions of a similar nature in state courts. Melvin stated, "The U.S. Supreme Court decision in *Rodriguez* effectively removed school finance reform litigation from the federal courts. Further court action was forced to rely on violation of state constitutional provisions if any relief was to be afforded."[41]

Justice Powell indicated that the Court did not support or agree with the disparities in per-pupil expenditures so evident in the *Rodriguez* case in the following statement:

> We hardly need add that this Court's action today is not to be viewed as placing its judicial imprimatur on the status quo. The need is apparent for reform in tax systems which may have relied too long and too heavily on the local property tax. And certainly innovative new thinking as to public education, its methods and its funding is necessary to assure both a higher level of quality and greater uniformity of opportunity. These matters merit the continued attention of the scholars who already have contributed much by their challenges. But the ultimate solutions must come from the lawmakers and from the democratic pressures of those who elect them.[42]

This action of the Supreme Court in effect stopped plaintiffs from using the federal court system to promote school finance reform and supported property taxation as a source of local school funding. It did not stop the momentum generated in the several states to use the states' court systems to effectuate school finance reform. State courts were faced with interpreting their state constitutions in light of *Serrano*/Marshall or *Rodriguez*/Powell.

State Court Cases

Because *Rodriguez* was tried in federal courts, and the United States Supreme Court stated that education is not a federal constitutional right, the ruling moved similar cases away from the federal court system to state courts. This shifting was made possible in part by the U.S. Supreme Court's decisions that state constitutional law can be separated from federal interpretation. In *Oregon* v. *Hass*,[43] the Court stated that a "state is free as a matter of its own law to impose greater restrictions . . . than those this Court holds to be necessary."

In fact, the Supreme Court refused to hear cases from Wyoming, Ohio, and California *(Serrano II)*,[43] verifying that school finance is a state matter. Melvin stated, "The Supreme Court of the United States has spoken and it is clear that the problem of reform must be handled by the states." The decision in *Rodriguez* pointed out that the high court considered the matter one for states to solve. This posture has been strengthened by the fact that the high court has refused to review decisions of state supreme courts in this area since *Rodriguez*.[45]

In their interpretations of state constitutions and school finance statutes, state courts have ruled in opposing ways, some in favor of the *Serrano*/Marshall doctrine, some in favor of the *Rodriguez*/Powell philosophy. Those that have used the *Serrano*/ Marshall decision as precedent have ruled on the basis that school finance formulas violated the equal protection or equal educational opportunity clauses of their state constitutions or that education is a fundamental interest protected by the state constitution, as well as that the funds expended are not adequate.[46] Those state courts that have followed the *Rodriguez*/Powell philosophy have been unable to find a rationale in state constitutions that require equalizing per-pupil expenditures[47] or find, as the Virginia Supreme Court ruled, that "the matter is for the legislature rather than judicial action."[48] The Michigan and New York high courts originally overturned their school finance systems based on the *Serrano* decision, but these courts later reversed those rulings, citing *Rodriguez*.[49]

Complexities of Judicial Review

Illustrative of dissimilar state court cases are two decisions—one finding for the plaintiffs, one for the state, but each with complicating factors. The Ohio Supreme Court ruled for the plaintiffs in *DeRolph* v. *State of Ohio*,[50] maintaining that the system failed to meet the Ohio "thorough and efficient" standard for financing schools laid out in the Ohio Constitution. The Ohio State Supreme Court, however, "declined to appoint a special master to oversee the state's further efforts to comply with" provisions of the state constitution. The state supreme court maintained continued jurisdiction for a while. The decision was an ambivalent one for the plaintiffs, as they did not get a master appointed nor did they get immediate relief. They did, however, gain a declaration that the school finance system in Ohio was unconstitutional.

In early 2001, the governor of Ohio presented an education program to the legislature designed to meet the demands of the state supreme court that had twice declared the school funding system unconstitutional in the *DeRolph* v. *State of Ohio* case. The Ohio Senate proposed an alternative plan. Both measures raised per-pupil expenditures, which relied on a formula that averaged expenditures in high-achieving schools. In 2003, *DeRolph* was revisited with Ohio's Supreme Court ruling, once again ruling that the state's school finance system was unconstitutional. The court provided no fiscal relief in the decision, indicating that the state legislature had that responsibility—not the courts. In a rather dramatic announcement, the *court* prohibited the *state high court itself*, or *any other court*, jurisdiction over the case. Further jurisdiction was sought, however, with the plaintiffs appealing to the United States Supreme Court later that year, arguing that the state court had violated equal protection rights for the students guaranteed in the Fourteenth Amendment of the United States Constitution. The Court declined without comment to review the case.[51] Once again, at this point, *Rodriguez* was reinforced; school finance matters have no federal jurisdiction.

The Wisconsin Supreme Court ruled in favor of the state with an even more complicated decision in *Vincent* v. *Voight*.[52] There are seven members on the Wisconsin Supreme Court, four of whom said that education was a fundamental right because the Wisconsin Constitution required a finance system that provided an equal education to the students of the state. Three of the four also stated that the plaintiffs had proved that the finance system in Wisconsin was in violation of that state's constitution. One of the four agreed that education was a fundamental right in Wisconsin's Constitution but opined that the plaintiffs had not proved that the finance system did not provide the required equal education. Three of the seven justices ruled that the Wisconsin Constitution does not require that the educational opportunities provided by school districts be equal, for the state constitution does not say that education is a fundamental right. The plaintiffs lost 4 to 3, since only three judges decided that the plaintiffs had proved their point that the finance system did not provide sufficient resources to the poorer districts to produce equal education. Not succeeding in the courts, plaintiffs turned to the legislature. Desideratum has proven evasive.

The issues in these two cases paralleled one another in that the public school finance formulas did not provide for equitable school financing to the poorer districts. The finance frameworks were measured against the two states' constitutions and state statutes. In Ohio, the court ruled that the most glaring weakness is the failure to specifically address the over reliance on local property taxes. In Wisconsin, however, the majority of the court ruled that so long as the legislature is providing sufficient resources so that the school districts offer students the equal opportunity for a sound basic education as required by the constitution, the state school system will pass constitutional muster. Therefore, even though a majority of the court felt disposed to declare the Wisconsin system unconstitutional, Wisconsin's finance system was considered acceptable to the provisions of its state constitution. These two cases, as well as *Hancock* v. *Driscoll, the Commissioner of Education* and *West-OrangeCoveISD* v. *The State of Texas*, portray the issue that courts can declare a state's school system unconstitutional but disallow any judicial action for reform. A giant in school finance reform, Charles Scott Benson, in testimony before a committee of Congress, added a somber note to the school finance issue. He noted that one must be careful when wishing for things because one may just get what one wished for. People worked hard for equity in California. They got it. Now they don't like it!

This decision-making process raises broader issues, such as the lawmaking authority of the various state legislatures and usurpation of that authority by judicial activists, the judicial power of the courts and the failure of governmental entities to comply. Who best understands education and who has the authority to finance it is controversial.

Court Cases: Equity and Adequacy

Financing education equitably is an important issue. In those states where the state supreme courts ruled that school finance formulas violated their state constitutions, language such as this was used: "While precisely equal funding may not be achieved or even necessary, district wealth alone should not determine educational opportunity."[53] In states that ruled their finance formulas were acceptable, statements such as these were used: "Plaintiffs failed to prove that the state is not fulfilling its responsibility and that the courts need to step in. . . . The state's method of funding [is] for the governor and the legislature to address."[54] It is relatively easy to make mechanical arithmetic adjustments to improve financial funding formulas. The problem has been negotiating the differing political points of view, which has prevented legislation that could perhaps correct the financial problems. The action in the courts is dramatic. When either side loses, other suits often follow. The denouement of the court cases has been perplexing.

Figure 9.2 shows state court activity, in a map form, as of January 2007. The status of school finance constitutional litigation, by state, title, and result, is shown in Figure 9.3.

FIGURE 9.2   Results of Education Finance Litigation Determined in the Various States' Highest Court

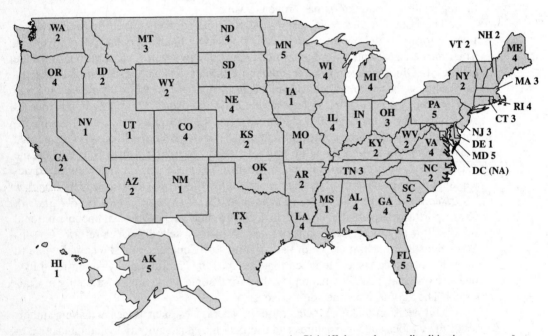

1 = No litigation or state supreme court decision

2 = Plaintiffs won

3 = Plaintiffs won with complications

4 = Plaintiffs lost and no pending litigation

5 = Plaintiffs lost but variances exist

FIGURE 9.3   Status of School Finance State Constitutional Litigation

1. No litigation filed or the state supreme court has not rendered a decision on the school finance system: **10 total**

   Delaware
   Hawaii
   Indiana
   Iowa
   Mississippi
   Missouri
   Nevada
   New Mexico (a case has been filed in federal court because it centered on American Indian inability to assess property taxes)
   South Dakota
   Utah

2. Plaintiffs won at the state supreme court or the state supreme court approved a trial court decision for plaintiffs: **13 total**

   Arizona *Roosevelt Elementary School District 66* v. *Bishop,* 1994; *Hull* v. *Albrecht,* 1998
   Arkansas *Dupree* v. *Alma School District,* 1985; *Tucker* v. *Lake View School District No. 25,* 1996, 1998; *Huckabee* 2002, 2005
   California *Serrano* v. *Priest,* 1971, 1976
   Idaho *Idaho Schools for Equal Educational Opportunity (ISEEO)* v. *Evans,* 1993 (now *State* v. *ISEEOV,* 2005)
   Kansas *Montoy* v. *State,* 2005, accepting Kentucky's strong opinion as to the power of the Courts; *Montoy II,* 2005
   Kentucky *Rose* v. *Council for Better Education,* 1989
   New Hampshire *Claremont School District* v. *Governor,* 1993, 1997, 1998
   New York *Campaign for Fiscal Equity* v. *State,* 1995; *CFE II* (herein numbered for the Court of Appeals), 2003
   North Carolina *Britt* v. *State Board of Education,* 1987; *Leandro* v. *State,* 1997
   Vermont *Brigham* v. *State,* 1997
   Washington *Northshore School District* v. *Kinnear,* 1974; *Seattle School District* v. *State,* 1978

   West Virginia *Pauly* v. *Kelly,* 1979; *Tomblin* v. *Gainer,* 1997
   Wyoming *Washakie County School District* v. *Herschler,* 1980; *Campbell County School District* v. *State,* 1995, 2001

3. Plaintiffs won but further complications exist: **7 total**

   Connecticut *Horton* v. *Meskill,* 1977, 1985; *Sheff* v. *O'Neill* (special consideration for Hartford), 1996
   Massachusetts *McDuffy* v. *Secretary of Education,* 1993 (in 2005 declined to adopt the conclusion of a Superior Court Judge that the Commonwealth was not meeting its obligation under the Massachusetts Constitution)
   Montana *State ex. rel. Woodahl* v. *Straub,* 1974; *Helena Elementary School District No. 1* v. *State,* 1989, 1990; *Columbia Falls Public Schools* v. *State,* 2005 (funding not adequate, state doesn't pay its share, no commitment to American Indian culture, expect suit in 2007 for progress report)
   New Jersey *Robinson* v. *Cahill,* 1973; *Abbott* v. *Burke,* 1985; *Abbott II,* 1990; *Abbott III,* 1994; *Abbott IV,* 1997; *Abbott V,* 1998 (for the 2006–07 school year a hold has been placed on funding, must live with 2005–06 amount)
   Ohio *DeRolph* v. *State,* 2000; *DeRolph* v. *State,* 2001; *DeRolph* v. *State,* 2003 (the court provided no fiscal relief in the decision, indicating the state legislature had that responsibility—not the courts; and the court prohibited the state high court itself, or any other court, jurisdiction over the case)
   Tennessee *Tennessee Small School System* v. *McWerter,* 1993 (then after legislature revised the system in *McWerter II,* 1995, the court ruled that the finance program was acceptable)
   Texas *Edgewood Independent School District* v. *Kirby,* 1989, 1990, 1991, 1992, 1995; *West Orange-Cove ISD* v. *Alanis,* 2005 (the court "stunned plaintiffs" by "upholding the

(continued)

FIGURE 9.3 Continued

adequacy of funding received by K–12 school districts")

4. Plaintiffs lost at the state supreme court level and no later case is pending: **14 total**

Alabama *Alabama Coalition for Equity (ACE)* v. *Siegelman,* 2002

Colorado *Lujan* v. *Colorado State Board of Education,* 1982

Georgia *McDaniel* v. *Thomas,* 1981

Illinois *Committee for Educational Rights* v. *Edgar,* 1996; revisited with *Lewis E.* v. *Spagnolo,* 1999 (defeated anew in which the court chastened the plaintiffs for "once again" asking the court to "enter the arena of Illinois public school policy")

Louisiana *Charlet* v. *State,* 1998 consolidated with *Minimum Foundation Commission v. State,* 1998

Maine *School Administrative District No. 1* v. *Commissioner,* 1994

Michigan *Milliken* v. *Green,* 1973; *East Jackson Public Schools* v. *State,* 1984

Nebraska *Gould* v. *Orr,* 1993; then another case filed, *Douglas County School District* v. *Johanns,* 2005; lost again

North Dakota *Bismarck Public School* v. *North Dakota,* 1993

Oklahoma *Fair School Finance Council of Oklahoma, Inc.* v. *State,* 1991

Oregon *Olsen* v. *State,* 1976; *Coalition for Equitable School Funding, Inc.* v. *State,* 1991; *Withers* v. *State,* 1995, 1999

Rhode Island *City of Pawtucket* v. *Sundlun,* 1995

Virginia *Scott* v. *Commonwealth,* 1994

Wisconsin *Kukor* v. *Grover,* 1989; *Vincent* v. *Voight,* 2000

5. Plaintiffs lost at the state supreme court level but variances exist: **6 total**

Alaska *Kasayulie* v. *State,* 1999 (partial summary judgment for facilities but state still uses dual funding method)

Florida *Coalition for Adequacy and Fairness in School Funding* v. *Chiles,* 1995 (constitutional amendment strengthening education clause passed, pending is *Honore* v. *Florida,* 2000, which claims amendment not being followed)

Maryland *Hornbeck* v. *Somerset Bd. of Ed.,* 1983; *Bradford* v. *Maryland State Board of Education,* consent decree, 1996

Minnesota *Skeen* v. *Minnesota,* 1993 (NAACP sued in 1995 was settled with a new accounting system for Minneapolis)

Pennsylvania *Danson* v. *Casey,* 1979; *Marrero* v. *Commonwealth,* 1998; *Penn Ass'n for Rural and Small Schools* v. *Ridge,* 1999

South Carolina *Abbeville County School District* v. *State of South Carolina,* 2005 (except in preschool education)

Campaign for Fiscal Equity v. The State of New York (2003) and CFE II (2006)

A 2003 decision in the *Campaign for Fiscal Equity* v. *The State of New York*[55] (reaffirmed in 2006) case has had impact in many parts of the country. It raised issues dealing with financing education equitably and adequately by requiring the legislature to provide revenue for a "sound basic education."

The court ordered the governor and the legislature "to reform the State's funding formula to ensure necessary resources, and to implement a fair accountability system to ensure that students actually receive that opportunity." It defined a "sound basic education" as one that includes a meaningful high school education with the skills and knowledge to "function productively as civic participants in 21st-century society, including being capable and knowledgeable voters and jurors, and able to sustain employment."[56]

Although the case technically involved New York City only, the ramifications have been noted statewide, and the governor and legislature were expected to study the system for funding schools throughout the state. With the victory, the executive director of the Campaign for Fiscal Equity (CFE) and co-counsel, Michael A. Rebel, called the decision "a ringing triumph for every child in New York City, New York State, and throughout the nation. The Court has declared in no uncertain terms that New York's children are more important than backroom politics. The Court joins the people of New York in agreeing that all children should have a true educational opportunity to succeed in the workplace and in life."[57]

Analyzing the implications of the case, Heubert stated:

> The bottom line in this decision is that it's the states' responsibility to make sure all children are getting an education of sufficiently high quality and have a real opportunity to meet standards. The decision has national significance because all of the states are adopting high standards and accepting the notion that all kids can reach these standards and yet virtually all of the states are much less forthcoming when it comes to putting up the money to get the job done.[58]

Others maintain that since the Education Article of the New York Constitution (Article XI–1) states, "The legislature shall provide for the maintenance and support of a system of free common schools, wherein all the children of this state may be educated," that it is an improper use of judicial power to order specific funding levels when the legislature has, in fact, developed common schools for all the children in the state of New York. They declare that the judicial funding order fosters a festering constitutional problem of enormous dimensions.

The *CFE* v. *The State of New York* case demonstrated a shift by plaintiffs to circumvent decisions based on *Serrano* and *Rodriguez*. Instead of concentrating on per-pupil expenditure or fiscal neutrality in a case, an emerging pattern is to approach the issue on providing *adequate* educational funding. It also broke with accepted practice when the court ordered the New York legislature to determine the cost of providing a "sound basic education" and fund those costs in each school. The cost-study was made but the legislature didn't respond to a July 30, 2004, deadline to "fund those costs" imposed by the trial court. Then the trial court appointed a panel of three masters to hold hearings. The masters urged the court to order the state to enact legislation within 90 days that would include an additional $5.63 billion for annual operation and $9.2 billion for facilities.

In March 2005, the trial court confirmed the special master's report to which the state appealed. One year later, in March 2006, the intermediate appeals court ordered the state to increase the annual operating funds of New York City's schools by at least $4.7 billion annually and at least $9.2 billion in facilities within five years. The court set an April 1, 2006, deadline. On that day, the legislature funded *facilities* that met the court's requirement but did not comply with the *operational* funding order.

Another action occurred when the plaintiffs asked the state's highest court to issue an *enforceable order* that would mandate the state legislature to comply fully and spend between $4.7 billion and $5.63 billion in annual operating funds. This *Campaign for Fiscal Equity* v. *State of New York, 111070/1993 New York State Supreme Court, Manhattan* case was the largest and longest-lasting education case in the country. Constitutional scholars watched carefully because the primary point the court has asked the counsel to address was the contention that the separation of powers doctrine was being abrogated if the court were to command the legislature to fund an incontrovertible amount of money.

Oral arguments were held October 10, 2006. On November 20 of that year, the New York State Supreme Court reaffirmed that funding a sound basic education was a constitutional right of the children of New York. The Justices, however, rejected the intermediate appeals court decree and the plaintiffs' request for the enforceable order. The state of New York argued that $1.93 billion was enough to provide for a sound basic education. The court concurred. By a 4 to 2 vote, the court ruled that the state needed to provide $1.93 billion more aid, less than half the amount that the plaintiffs had requested and the intermediate court had commanded.

Apparently the oral arguments concerning the separation of powers doctrine impacted the court as the decision included the statement that "when we review the acts of the Legislature and the Exclusive we do so to protects rights not to make policy." The judges left the decision whether to add to the $1.93 billion by indicating it was the prerogative of lawmakers, "empowered by the separation of powers, to make policy and enact budgets."[59]

Shift in Cases from Equity to Adequacy

Historically, plaintiffs in several states have gone to court to challenge the disparity among districts about the amount of money that one district had to spend compared to others. The twenty-first century brought a transformation in which plaintiffs brought suits maintaining that the amount of money the state was spending was not enough (adequate). The deviation developed in the aforementioned *CFE* v. *The State of New York* case in which the court required the legislature to spend a certain amount of money to provide an adequate education—those seemingly simple words added an emphasis and new focus on adequacy. The trial court defined a "sound basic education" as one that includes a meaningful high school education with the skills and knowledge to "function productively as civic participants" in twenty-first–century society, including being capable and knowledgeable voters and jurors and being able to sustain employment.

Some scholars have criticized the courts for assuming legislature powers in their decisions when they instructed the legislature that they had to expend a certain amount of money. This perception has not slowed the desire of plaintiffs to go to court to challenge the states about the amount of money needed for an adequate education. In 32 states plaintiffs have filed adequacy cases. In 17 states the cases have had a decision declared by the state supreme court of which 8 (Arkansas, Kansas, Montana, New

Hampshire, New Jersey, New York, North Carolina, and Washington) have ruled for the plaintiffs and 9 (Alabama, Arizona, Illinois, Louisiana, Massachusetts, Ohio, Pennsylvania, Rhode Island, and Texas) for the state. Similar to equity cases the courts have revealed considerable disparity of opinion. In Illinois the plaintiffs were chastened for once again asking the court to enter the arena of Illinois public school policy. On the other hand, in Arkansas the court declared it has a constitutional duty to ensure the state meets its goal of an adequate education and reserves the right to exercise power at any time. The impact of this case in future school finance litigation will be of interest to those who follow the progress of adequacy and equity in financing education, particularly as it relates to the constitutions of the various states. The question is: Can the courts assume responsibility for determining how much money must be spent rather than allowing school boards and legislatures to decide?

Principles Established by Court Decisions

The court decisions of *Serrano, Rodriguez,* and other related state cases have seemed to agree with the following general principles or conclusions:

1. It is reaffirmed that financing education is the responsibility of the state.
2. Since educational needs vary from district to district, the state does not have to require all of its school districts to spend the same amount of money per pupil or offer identical educational programs.
3. State legislatures are not required to eliminate property taxes in favor of taxes on other sources of revenue.
4. Schools may make additional expenditures for programs for exceptional children, compensatory programs for culturally disadvantaged children, and programs for other educational needs that are significant and worthy of special treatment.

Pressure for Reform

After the *Rodriguez* decision, many feared that the school finance reform process would be slowed if the court actions alone were used. Therefore, the school finance court decisions resulted in general pressure on most state legislative bodies to bring reform to school finance systems. Kirp wrote, "The Supreme Court's decision in *Rodriguez* demolished the hope that the courts would lead a school finance revolution of national scope. Although suits premised on equal protection and specific educational provisions in state constitutions have subsequently been filed, the judicial response has been at best mixed."[60]

Legislative bodies, whether or not they are faced with mandates from the courts, have had much activity in developing legislation regarding the equity and adequacy issues. Following Justice Powell's admonition in *Rodriguez* that these matters merit the continued attention of scholars, lawmakers, and the people, some different prerogatives were used. They included full state funding; elimination or reduction of local tax levies; use of a statewide property tax; increase in state income taxes, sales taxes, or lotteries;

assumption by the state of all capital-outlay costs; increases in school expenditures in poor districts, with or without a decrease in expenditures in more affluent ones; and provisions for additional local revenue to supplement a state-funded school program.

Finance Studies and Reform Efforts

Several studies have had an impact on state school finance programs. Perhaps the most influential report was the historic "A Nation at Risk: The Imperative for Educational Reform." The report maintained that a major cause of the once unchallenged preeminence of education in the United States affecting commerce, industry, technology, and innovation was mediocrity in the nation's public schools.

Verifying public sentiment, the report from the National Commission on Excellence in Education indicated that the U.S. schools inadequately met the challenges of global competition. The now famous document stated:

> Our nation is at risk. Our once unchallenged preeminence in commerce, industry, science, and competitors throughout the world are overtaking technological innovation. This report is concerned with only one of the many causes and dimensions of the problem, but it is the one that undergirds American prosperity, security, and civility. We report to the American people that while we can take justifiable pride in what our schools and colleges have historically accomplished and contributed to the United States and the well-being of its people, the educational foundations of our society are presently being eroded by a rising tide of mediocrity that threatens our very future as a nation and a people. What was unimaginable a generation ago has begun to occur—others are matching and surpassing our educational attainments. If an unfriendly foreign power had attempted to impose on America the mediocre educational performance that exists today, we might well have viewed it as an act of war.[61]

The Commission viewed the decline in standardized test scores, illiteracy rates, and poor achievement in mathematics and science as a disaster. They called for increased high school graduation requirements in English, mathematics, science, social studies, and computer science. More time for education by extending the school day or the school year was recommended. Teachers were to work longer, have career ladder opportunities, and act as mentors if experienced, or be mentored if novices.

Factors Limiting School Finance Reform

After "A Nation at Risk," governors from many states assumed leadership for education, pressuring state departments of education and legislative bodies to mandate reform measures. The movement saw the development of two distinct groups of citizens seeking reform, with divergent backgrounds and approaches to the problems they were trying to solve. In the first group were those with professional experience in education, many of whom had vested interests and some degree of expertise and practical understanding of the problems to be solved. These were school finance professors, public school administrators, and specialists in state departments of education—the "friends" of public education. These were the "authorities" in the field, working for improvement of their profession.

The second group of reformers included those who saw the problem from a different perspective—lawyers, economists, political scientists, representatives of the disadvantaged, members of state legislatures, representatives and members of minority groups, and others with only secondary interest in education per se. This group usually worked with community and state political leaders (and now the courts) to bring about reform sufficient to avoid *Serrano*-type court decisions, or to revise or defeat proposed laws that would repudiate their state school finance systems.

Unfortunately for the schools, these two groups did not always agree about goals or methods. Communication and collaboration were often neglected or minimized, and consequently the results were not always satisfactory.

Other problems plagued the advocates of school finance reform. The differences that have always existed among urban, suburban, and rural districts were not decreased in the struggle to improve the financing of education. For example, there was seldom any solution to the question of providing additional funds for city districts to compensate for municipal overburden. The problem of getting laws enacted to satisfy the rulings of courts was always difficult when such proposals were thrown into the political arena. Many legislative bodies found it politically impossible to enact legislation that would meet the "requirements" established by courts in the same state—largely due to the fact that any school finance program would inevitably favor one kind of school district over another.

California's Proposition 13

Students of physics frequently cite the law, "Action equals reaction." They observe the swing of the pendulum that moves an apparently equal distance in two opposite directions. Applying such observations to the real world outside the laboratory, one can observe this physical law operating with more dramatic and perhaps more consequential results in the realm of the social sciences. Everywhere are examples of the inevitability of movement to the liberal side, bringing reverse action to the conservative, and vice versa. A few steps one way, followed immediately by almost equivalent steps in the other direction, too often mark the progress of a society and its institutions in the direction of its ultimate goals.

This phenomenon has been observed many times in the field of public school finance. California's Proposition 13, said by its ardent sponsors to be a panacea for a taxpaying society, came more quickly and with more force and national influence than was generally anticipated. In one massive effort, the voters of California, by almost a 2 to 1 margin, voted to restrict property taxes to 1 percent of the 1976 assessed market value of such property, thus reducing property tax revenues by about 57 percent. The act also provided that a two-thirds favorable vote of the legislature would be necessary to increase future annual tax assessments to a maximum of 2 percent.

Although the quick and convincing passage of Proposition 13 caught many people by surprise, knowledgeable people in the field of school finance had long anticipated some voter reaction to inflationary costs of education and increasing taxes. Persistent resistance to taxes could be seen on every hand—defeated bond and school budget elections, increases in the number and size of circuit-breaker and other tax relief measures, and increases in high-cost services to the elderly and the disabled were strong and persuasive indicators of difficulties to come in providing adequate funds for public education and other government services.

California was an extremely fertile ground for tax retrenchment. In addition to high property values due to extreme inflation, the state had a highly progressive income tax, a high sales tax, and a record of high and steadily increasing property taxes. Its system of keeping assessments in line with the inflationary market value of property, although philosophically desirable, also worked to the benefit of the instigators of Proposition 13. Increases in market values were quickly transformed into higher personal taxes on real property, while in many other states increased assessments tended to lag far behind market value increases. Then, too, it appeared to be "popular" practice in California to keep the tax structure producing revenues greater than expenditures, with a consequent buildup of reserves that could be used in emergencies. Present, too, was the political notion that a surplus of state government revenues represented high efficiency in state administration rather than simply excessive taxation. The California legislature seemed to be reluctant to enact a satisfactory tax relief measure in spite of numerous attempts to do so.

The passage of Proposition 13 instantaneously affected other states. A survey of all 50 states conducted one year later revealed the following: 22 states reduced property taxes, 18 states reduced income taxes, 15 states curtailed in some fashion the collection of sales taxes, 8 states voted spending limits, and 12 states repealed or reduced various other taxes.[62]

Proposition 13 was not immune from judicial review. Over time, it resulted in dramatic disparities in the taxes paid by persons owning similar pieces of property. Long-term owners paid lower taxes, while newer owners paid higher taxes. One such new owner, Stephanie Nordlinger, claimed the "scheme violated the Equal Protection Clause of the Fourteenth Amendment" and brought suit in *Nordlinger* v. *Hahn*.[63] The County Superior Court dismissed the complaint and the state Court of Appeals affirmed. Nordlinger appealed to the U.S. Supreme Court and on June 18, 1992, the case was decided, with the Court ruling (8–1) that Proposition 13 and its attendant tax disparity did not violate the Equal Protection Clause. Speaking for the Court, Justice Blackman stated:

> The Equal Protection Clause of the Fourteenth Amendment commands that no state shall "deny to any person within its jurisdiction the equal protection of the laws." The Equal Protection Clause does not forbid classifications . . . and as a general rule "legislatures are presumed to have acted within their constitutional power despite the fact that, in practice, their laws result in some inequality . . . and judicial intervention is generally unwarranted" . . . and we must decline petitioner's request to upset the will of the people of California. The judgement of the Court of Appeal is affirmed.[64]

Finance Reform or Tax Reduction?

In each case where limits have been imposed, the state faces the paradox of substantially altering property taxes while preserving school programs. To the degree that tax reductions are made and/or school services reduced, it appears that the friends of education have failed to make a legitimate case for the high costs of school services. That there is conflict between the forces favoring school finance reform and those favoring tax reduction is shown in the following statement:

> There is an impending clash between two major public finance movements. One is stimulating a large increase in state/local public spending while the other is galvanizing a trend toward lower expenditures. The first is known as the "school finance reform movement." Its supporters . . . have developed a new focus on equity in recent years. A strong network of state policy makers who are pushing for tax or spending limitations leads the second movement.[65]

Thus, the "battle" between those who view equity in educational finance as a top priority and those who feel that tax reduction is necessary has continued. It was apparent that taxpayers were demanding some relief from the heavy burden of high taxes. Gradual decreases rather than abrupt and destructive decreases in taxes, placing reasonable limits on the expenditures of government, the establishment of tax levy limits, the liberalization of circuit-breaker laws for the tax relief of the poor and the disabled, and greater centralization and consolidation of schools in many areas of the country are better methods of obtaining taxpayer justice than indiscriminate cuts that slowly destroy social institutions.

Summary

The courts exert considerable pressure on the states to improve their school finance systems. The decisions have been divided and there is no clear trend in these decisions. Some guiding principles have emerged for school finance formulas.

Serrano v. *Priest* in California was an influential court case involving school finance. As a result of *Serrano,* many states made an effort to improve their method of financing education. *San Antonio Independent School District* v. *Rodriguez* ended appeals in the federal courts, when it was ruled that education was not a federal constitutional right. The school finance issues continued in state courts and were measured against state constitutional rights. States that followed the *Serrano* philosophy found education to be a fundamental right for the students in those several states, or found school financing patterns to be in violation of state education clauses (20 states have ruled thusly). States that followed the *Rodriguez* philosophy found no justification for equal per-pupil expenditures in their state constitutions, or ruled that the matter was for legislatures to decide (20 states have ruled that way). In 10 states, the state supreme courts have not rendered decisions or no case has been filed.

Questions are being raised by critics as to the function of the courts in solving school finance problems. Others are working hard to maintain judicial oversight, which includes efforts to undo *Rodriguez*. Some state courts have determined a certain amount to provide for an adequate sound basic education, such as the *CFE* v. *The State of New York* case. This is a deviation from past court action, with a new focus—of adequacy joined with the matter of equity.

A tax-reduction movement and/or legislatures deciding they did not have the funds to comply altered the impact of the courts. The tax-reduction movement was heightened by the passage of Proposition 13 in California. Several states followed California's lead in reducing taxes. The effect of court actions, school finance reform, and tax reduction will be an ongoing matter—the results of which are not yet known.

ASSIGNMENT PROJECTS

1. Provide a definition for each of the following terms: *strict scrutiny, intermediate scrutiny, rational basis, equal protection, Serrano philosophy, Rodriguez doctrine, equal protection clause, constitutional provision, Powell's answer, Marshall's answer, impact of CFE v. The State of New York.*
2. Trace the history of tax-restrictive legislation in one particular state. Indicate the major forces favoring such tax restrictions as well as those opposing it.
3. Produce the evidence to show that tax-restrictive legislation penalizes schools more than any other function of state and local government.
4. In class, organize into groups and debate the consequences of California's Proposition 13.
5. Interview a school finance professor, a public school administrator, and a school finance specialist in a state department of education about financing of education in the next 10 years. Then interview a state legislator, a tax lawyer, an economist, a political scientist, a spokesperson for the disadvantaged, and a spokesperson for a minority group about the same subject. Compare and contrast their opinions and viewpoints.

Computer simulations and questions, research exercises, and website addresses relevant to this chapter can be found at

www.ablongman.com/edleadership

SELECTED READINGS

Clune, W. H. "New Answers to Hard Questions Posed by Rodriguez: Ending the Separation of School Finance and Educational Policy by Bridging the Gap between Wrong and Remedy." *Connecticut Law Review,* Vol, 24, No. 3, 1992.

Garfield, Rulon R., Gene J. Garfield, and J. D. Willardson. *Policy and Politics in American Education.* Atlanta: St. Barthelemy Press, Ltd., 2003.

Hickrod, G. Alan. "Testimony to the Subcommittee on Education, Arts, and Humanities on the Committee on Labor and Human Resources, U.S. Senate." In W. B. Fowler, Jr., ed., *Developments in School Finance: Fiscal Proceedings from the Annual NCES Sate Data Conference,* Washington, DC: U.S.

Honeyman, D. S., D. C. Thompson, and R. C. Wood. *Financing Rural and Small Schools: Issues of Adequacy and Equity.* Gainesville: University of Florida Press, 1989.

King, Richard A., Austin D. Swanson, and Scott Sweetland. *School Finance Achieving High Standards with Equity and Efficiency.* Boston: Allyn and Bacon, 2003.

Lunonburg, Fred C., and Allan C. Ornstein. *Education Administration Concepts and Practices,* 3rd ed. Belmont, CA: Wadsworth/Thomson Learning, 2000.

Nowak, John E., Ronald D. Rotunda, and J. Nelson Young, *Constitutional Law.* St. Paul: West Publishing, 1986.

Minorini, P. A., and S. D. Sugarman. *Equity and Adequacy in Education Finance: Issues and Perspectives.* Washington, DC: National Academy Press, 1999.

Odden, A. R., & Picus, L. O. (2004). *School finance: A Policy Perspective,* 2nd ed. New York: McGraw-Hill.

Reutter, E. Edmond. *The Law and Public Education.* Westbury, NY: Foundation Press, 1999.

Sperry, David J., Dixie Huefner, T. K. Daniels, and E. Gordon Gee. *Education-Law-and-the-Public-Schools: A Compendium,* 2nd ed. Norwood, MA: Christopher-Gordon, 1998.

Strahan, Richard D., and L. Charles Turner. *The Courts and the Schools.* New York: Longman, 1987.

Thomas, Gloria Jean, David J. Sperry, and F. Del Wasden. *The Law and Teacher Employment.* New York: West Publishing, 1991.

Underwood, Julie K., and Deborah A. Verstegen, eds. *The Impact of Litigation and Legislation on Public School Finance: Adequacy, Equity and Excellence.* New York: Harper & Row, 1990.

ENDNOTES

1. *Springfield* v. *Quick et al.,* Supreme Court, December Term, 1859, pp. 56–60.
2. Ibid.
3. *Stuart* v. *School District No. 1 of the Village of Kalamazoo,* 30 MI 69 1874.
4. *Brown* v. *Board of Education* (1) 347 U.S. 483, 74 S. Ct. 686 (1954).
5. *Baker v. Carr,* 369 U.S. 186, 82 S. Ct. 691 (1962).
6. *Serrano* v. *Priest* (I), 96 Cal. Rptr. 601, 487 P.2nd 1241 (Calif.) 1971.
7. *San Antonio Independent School District v. Rodriguez,* 411 U.S. 1, 93 S. Ct 1278, 1973.
8. Ibid.
9. Ibid.
10. Ibid
11. Ibid.
12. Jay P. Greene, "Educating From the Bench," *The Wall Street Journal,* April 27, 2006, p. A19.
13. Eric Hanuchek, Notes from presentation by him at the American Education Finance Association, 2006, Denver CO.
14. Jay Chambers, Senior Research Fellow, American Institutes/Research, Presentation, American Education Finance Association Convention, 2006, Denver, CO.
15. Rulon R. Garfield, Gene J. Garfield, and J. D. Willardson, *Policy and Politics in American Education* (Atlanta: St. Barthelemy Press, 2003), pp. 222, 223.
16. James Landis, *Harvard Law Review,* April 1930, p. 886.
17. Garfield et al., *Policy and Politics,* pp. 224, 225.
18. *U.S.* v. *Butler,* 297 U.S. Code 2 (1936).

19. Bruce D. Baker, University of Kansas, "Response to Eric Hanushek's Assault on Educational Adequacy," bbaker@ku.edu.
20. *DeRolph* v. *The State of Ohio.*
21. *West-OrangeCoveISD* v. *State of Texas.*
22. "California Symposium Proposes Quality Education as a Fundamental Right," www.schoolfunding.info/news/policy/5-9-06rethingrodriguez.php3.
23. Ibid.
24. *Lewis* v. *Mosley,* 204 So. 2d 197 (Fla. 1967).
25. *Morton Salt Co.* v. *City of South Hutchinson,* 177 F. 2d 889 (10th Cir. 1949).
26. *San Antonio Independent School District* v. *Rodriguez.*
27. *Brown* v. *Board of Education.*
28. Stuart Taylor Jr. "The Supremes in the Dock," *Newsweek,* April 10, 2000.
29. *Sawyer* v. *Gilmore,* 109 Me.169, 83A 673 (Me. 1912).
30. *McInnis* v. *Ogilvie* (Shapiro), 349 U.S. 322, 89 S. Ct. 1197 (1969).
31. Ibid.
32. *Serrano* v. *Priest* (1) 5 Cal. 3d. 584, 96 Cal. Rpt. 601, 487 P.2d 1241 (Calif. 1971).
33. Ibid.
34. Paul D. Carrington, "Equal Justice Under Law and School Finance," *School Finance in Transition* (Gainesville, FL: National Conference on School Finance, 1973), p. 162.
35. Donald Wickert, "Some School Finance Issues Related to the Implementation of Serrano and Proposition 13," *Journal of Education Finance,* Spring 1985, p. 535.

36. Betsy Levin et al., *Praying for Public Schools* (Washington, DC: Urban Institute, 1972), p. 8.

37. John Dayton, "Three Decades of School Funding Litigation: Has It Been Worthwhile and When Will it End?" *School Business Affairs,* May 2002, pp. 7–9.

38. *Van Dusartz* v. *Hatfield,* 334 F. Supp. 8709 (D.C. Minn. 1971).

39. *Spano* v. *Board of Education* (329 N. Y. 1972).

40. *Burress* v. *Wilkerson,* 310 F. Supp. 572 (W. D. Va. 1969), cert. denied, 90 S. Ct. 812 (1969).

41. Leland D. Melvin, "The Law of Public School Finance," *Contemporary Education,* Spring 1984, p. 149.

42. *San Antonio Independent School District* v. *Rodriguez.*

43. *Oregon* v. *Hass,* 420 U.S. 714, 719 (1975).

44. *Washakie County School District No. 1* v. *Herschler,* 606 P.2d 310 (Wyo. 1980), cert. denied, 101 S. Ct. 86, 449 U.S. 824 (1980); *Board of Education of the City School District of Cincinnati* v. *Walter,* 390 N. E.2d 813 (Ohio, 1979); *Serrano* v. *Priest (II),* 557 P.2d 929 (Calif. 1977), cert. denied, 432 U.S. 907 (1977).

45. Melvin, "The Law of Public School Finance," p. 153.

46. *Horton* v. *Meskill,* 376 A.2d 359 (Conn. 1977); *Horton* v. *Meskill,* 486 A.2d 1099 (Conn. 1985); *Seattle School District No. 1 of King County* v. *State of Washington,* 585 P.2d 71 (Wash. 1978); *Washakie County School District No. 1* v. *Herschler,* 606 P.2d 310 (Wyo. 1980), cert. denied, 101 S. Ct, 86, 449 U.S. 824 (1980).

47. *Shofstall* v. *Hollins,* 515 F.2d 590 (Ariz. 1973); *Thompson* v. *Engelking,* 537 P.2d 635 (Idaho 1975); *Olsen* v. *State of Oregon,* 554 P.2d 139 (Ore. 1976); *State ex rel. Woodahl* v. *Straub,* 520 P.2d 776 (Mont. 1974); *Knowles* v. *State Board of Education,* 547 P.2d 699 (Kans. 1976); *Blase v. State of Illinois,* 302 N.E.2d 46 (Ill. 1973); *People of Illinois ex rel. Jones* v. *Adams,* 350 N.E.2d 767 (III. 1976); *Lujan* v. *Colorado State Board of Education,* 649 P.2d 1005 (Colo. 1982); *McDaniel* v. *Thomas,* 285 S.E.2d 156 (Ga. 1981); *Board of Education of the City School District of Cincinnati* v. *Walter,* 390 N.E.2d 813 (Ohio 1979); Virginia (Burruss, 310 F. Supp).

47. Oral arguments, October 10, 2006. www.courts .state.ny.us/ctapps/crtnews.htm.

48. *Scott* v. *Virginia,* 112 S. Ct. 3017 (Virginia, 1994).

49. *Milliken* v. *Green,* 203 N.W.2d 457 (Mich. 1972); *Milliken* v. *Green,* 212 N.W.2d 711 (Mich. 1973); *Board of Education of Levittown Union Free School District* v. *Nyquist,* 408 N.Y.S.2d 606 (Nassau Co. Supreme Court 1978), aff'd, 443 N.Y.S.2d 843 (1982), rev'd, 453 N.Y.S.2d 643, 439 N.E.2d 359 (N. Y. 1982).

50. *DeRolph* v. *State,* 789 N.E.2d 195 (Ohio), Docket 03-245-Writ of prohibition against further exercise of court jurisdiction. Case denied review October 20, 2003. www.supremecourtus.gov/orders.

51. *DeRolph* v. *State,* 789 N.E.2d 195 (Ohio), Docket 03–245-Writ of prohibition against further exercise of court jurisdiction. Case denied review October 20, 2003. www.supremecourtus.gov/orders.

52. Wisconsin Supreme Court, http://www.wisbar.org/ Wis3/97–3174.htm.

53. *Education Week,* February 12, 1997, p. 16.

54. Ibid. January 17, 1997, p. 20. See also December 4, 1996, p. 17.

55. *Campaign for Fiscal Equity* v. *The State of New York,* Decision 1, No. 74. www.4law.cornell.edu/ cgi-bin/htm, June 26, 2003. See also 86NY 2d 307–1995

56. "Highest Court Rules For CFE; Declares That All Children Are Entitled to a Meaningful High School Education," Campaign For Fiscal Equity, p. 267. www.cfequity.org/ns-nys1.htm.

57. Ibid.

58. "Highest Court Rules For CFE; Declares That All Children Are Entitled to a Meaningful High School Education," Campaign For Fiscal Equity, p. 267. www.cfequity.org/ns-nys1.htm.

59. The National Access Network at Teachers College, Columbia University, www.schoolfunding .info; Michael Quinn on the Economy: "Court Orders Aid Boost for New York City Schools, www.bloomberg.com/apps/news?pid=2061103& sid=afqJ.s0V9avI&refer=us, abb2116@columbia .edu. Actual arguments of the New York Court of Appeals' hearing may be viewed/heard at www .courts.state.ny.us/ctapps/CFEOG.asx.

60. David L. Kirp, "Law, Politics, and Equal Educational Opportunity: The Limits of Judicial Involvement," *Harvard Educational Review,* Vol. 47, No. 2, May 1988, pp. 122–123.

61. The National Commission on Excellence in Education, "A Nation at Risk: The Imperative for Education Reform," April 1983, p. 5.

62. *Phi Delta Kappan,* October 1979, p. 84.

63. *Nordlinger* v. *Hahn,* 1992 WL 132447 (U.S. 1992).

64. Ibid.

65. Michael J. Kirst, "The New Politics of State Education Finance," *Phi Delta Kappan,* February 1979, p. 427.

10 Public Funds and Nonpublic Schools

School choice and its requisite financing is an intense debate in American education today. It encompasses and addresses every other educational concern.

—John Updike, 2007

Using public funds for private schools has a major impact on the overall aspects of school finance. Although the public, in general, supports its local schools, forces continue to promote using taxpayer dollars to assist in providing revenues for nonpublic schools. Legislators, private entrepreneurs, and some citizens are questioning the ability of personnel in the public sector to operate the schools efficiently and to offer enough options to meet the needs of students. Privately sponsored schools have been encouraged for those groups and individuals who are willing to support them financially in addition to participating in financing the public school system. However, such groups have become more vocal and stress that because the states have a responsibility to provide a free education for the school-age population, they should provide for students in both private and public schools. The dilemma is complicated by the fact that the majority of private schools are parochial, making the First Amendment of the Constitution an issue.

A Controversial Issue

Historically, the illegality of direct government support for private and parochial schools was well established in the codes of the states and at the federal level. However, some state governments and the federal government are enacting legislation that provides some tax funds for use by nonpublic schools. The courts, particularly the U.S. Supreme Court, have usually disallowed direct state financial support to private and parochial schools. They have allowed Congress and state legislatures to provide support that promotes a secular principle, does not foster excessive government entanglement, and does not advance or inhibit religion.

Those who favor direct public aid to nonpublic schools base their arguments on the following points:

1. Parents should have freedom of choice in the education of their children. Proponents cite the case of *Pierce* v. *Society of Sisters* (1925) as a guarantee of such choice. Said the court, "The fundamental theory of liberty under which all governments in this union repose excludes any general power of the State to standardize its children by forcing them to accept instruction from public teachers only."[1]
2. There is no evidence to support the fear that divisiveness in education will be caused by the existence and operation of nonpublic schools.
3. The failure of nonpublic schools would create a tremendous impact on the financing of public education. From the economic point of view, it would be better to finance nonpublic schools to the extent necessary to keep them solvent.
4. The free exercise clause of the First Amendment allows such actions.

Opponents of direct aid to nonpublic schools argue:

1. Parochial aid represents a backward step, since this country once maintained such a system of education but has since altered the concept.
2. Private schools may tend to discriminate against students in terms of race and religious background.
3. Such a practice violates the establishment clause of the First Amendment.
4. Solution of the problem should be based on principle, not on economic considerations.
5. Public education is underfunded and if additional revenue becomes available, it should be expended in public schools.

One of the basic principles of U.S. education that has received general acceptance through the years is that public funds used by sectarian or other nonpublic schools must pass judicial muster. The principle is still debated, as indicated in the following opinion expressed by Justice Brenner:

> We have often grappled with the problem of state aid to non-public, religious schools. In all of these cases, our goal has been to give meaning to the sparse language and broad purposes of the cause while not unduly infringing on the ability of the states to provide for the welfare of their people in accordance with their own particular circumstances. . . . We have noted that the three-part test first articulated in *Lemon* v. *Kurtzman* guides the general nature of inquiry in this area (*Mueller* v. *Allen*, 1983). . . . First the statute must have a secular legislative purpose; second, its principal or primary effect must be one that neither advances nor inhibits religion; finally, the statute must not foster an excessive government entanglement with religion.[2]

The courts have relied on the so-called *Lemon* test since 1971 in all cases involving the sensitive relationship between government and religion in the education of children.[3] Although not directed to the finance issue, the *Lee* v. *Weisman* case, which was decided in 1992,[4] the *Jones* v. *Clear Creek Independent School District* case, which was decided in 1992,[5] and the *Goluba* v. *Ripon* case, which was decided in 1995,[6] were examples of the uncertainty of how the church-state relationship operates. These cases involved the constitutionality of ceremonial prayer at public school events such as graduation. In *Weisman,* the U.S. Supreme Court held that "religious exercises may not be conducted at a graduation where those who object to the prayer are induced to conform."[7] In *Jones,* the Fifth Circuit held that such prayers were constitutional, if they were student initiated. The Court stated, "The practical result of our decision . . . is that students can do what the state acting on its own cannot do to incorporate prayer in public high school graduation ceremonies.[8] The case was appealed to the U.S. Supreme Court. The Court remanded to the Circuit Court. In 1995, the Seventh Circuit ruled in *Goluba* that when a graduating student's initiated prayer occurred—even when school officials were aware that it would happen—such action was acceptable. The Justice Department, in their friend-of-the-court brief had urged the Supreme Court to scrap the *Lemon* test and allow "for greater 'civic acknowledgments of religion in public life.'"[9]

In 2000, in a case involving prayer at high school football games, the U.S. Supreme Court in *Sante Fe Independent School District* v. *Doe* (Case No. 99–62) struck down student-led prayer. One reason given was that the microphone used in prayer was purchased with taxpayers' money. Prayers in the South have continued without using a microphone. Court cases in that regard are expected to continue, as well as additional challenges to prayer at graduation, citing *Sante Fe* as a precedent.

Nonpublic School Enrollment

About 10 percent of U.S. students in kindergarten through grade 12 are enrolled in nonpublic schools. In the fall of 2003, there were 28,384 private schools in the United States, enrolling 5,122,772 students and employing 425,238 teachers. Of the private schools, 76 percent are parochial and 24 percent are privately sponsored. The percentage has remained relatively constant and is projected to continue to do so.[10] Table 10.1 shows the percentage of students in private schools in six states.

TABLE 10.1   Enrollment and Percentage of Students in Private Schools in Six States

	Number of Private schools	Number of Students	Percent of State K–12 Total Enrollment
California	3,377	623,105	8.80
Florida	1,803	323,766	11.12
Illinois	1,346	270,490	11.47
New York	1,959	458,079	13.81
Pennsylvania	2,009	316,337	14.95
Texas	1,282	220,206	4.85
U.S.	**28,384**	**5,122,772**	**9.59**

Source: U.S. Department of Education Digest of Education Statistics, Table 37, 2004, and Department of Education, National Center for Education Statistics, *Private School Universe Survey,* March 2006.

The problem of the state financing education of nonpublic schools is not merely a question of the number of students or the number of schools involved; there is also the question of where those schools and students are located. Nonpublic schools and students are concentrated particularly in large populated states. Major closings of nonpublic schools in these states would cause tremendous financial burden on the public schools. The effect may be even more dramatic for smaller states with a large percentage of private school students, such as Rhode Island (15 percent). Failure of nonpublic schools in such states as Oklahoma and Utah (where only 2.0 percent of school children attend nonpublic schools) may not cause a significant financial adjustment to state budgets.

The Law and Church-State Relations

Determining an acceptable relationship of church and state has been a concern in this country since its founding. The early New England colonies, except for Rhode Island, made the Congregational Church their official church, whereas the colonies south of Maryland were Anglican. New York had a "multiple establishment" pattern of church-state relationship. Only Rhode Island, Pennsylvania, and Delaware had no officially established church. Vestiges of church-state relations have continued to exist in one form or another.

Legal Provisions for Separation

The U.S. Constitution Article VI, Section 3, and especially the First Amendment that was included in 1791 in the Bill of Rights (10 amendments that delineated the rights of individuals), placed in U.S. law the principles of freedom of religion and separation of church and state. Article VI provides that "no religious test should ever be required as a qualification to any office or public trust under the United States." The First Amendment, in establishing church-state separation, declares, "Congress shall make no law respecting an establishment of religion, or prohibiting the free exercise thereof." How to provide the proper and complete application of these principles is highly controversial. The Fourteenth Amendment, often referred to as the "due process" amendment, was established in 1868. In the years since that time, it has been interpreted by the courts as applying the First Amendment and other federal guarantees to the individual states. It provides that "no state shall make or enforce any law which shall abridge the privileges or immunities of citizens of the United States; nor shall any State deprive any person of life, liberty, or property without due process of law, nor deny any person within its jurisdiction the equal protection of the laws."

The Courts and the Child-Benefit Theory

The Supreme Court of the United States has ruled a number of times on the legal relationship of church and state as intended by the amendments to the Constitution. For the various state legislative bodies and for the people generally, the Court's decisions have had varying degrees of palatability. The lack of complete support by the states for the federal position is partially vindicated by the general lack of unanimity among the

Court members themselves in many of these decisions, some of which were made by the narrowest possible vote of the Court.

In *Cochran* v. *Louisiana State Board of Education,*[11] the United States Supreme Court upheld the practice of Louisiana in providing free textbooks, paid for by tax funds, for pupils attending nonpublic schools. In the view of the Court, this was not a violation of the First or Fourteenth Amendment and was therefore legal. The basis for this reasoning was the "child-benefit" theory, according to which the children benefited directly, not the churches (which benefited indirectly).

In the verdict in *Everson* v. *Board of Education,*[12] the United States Supreme Court held that using New Jersey tax funds allocated to school districts to reimburse parents for the cost of bus fares to attend nonpublic schools was legal and did not violate the First or Fourteenth Amendment. Seeking the protective cloak of the child-benefit theory, the Court regarded the action as safe, legal, and expeditious public welfare legislation. The actions in *Cochran* and *Everson* are not binding on other states. Such actions are still an individual state decision.

A few of the states have reacted in support of the *Cochran* decision; about half of them have accepted the essence of the *Everson* verdict. State courts in Alaska, Wisconsin, Oklahoma, and Delaware "have struck down enactments authorizing free busing of children attending denomination schools."[13] Connecticut and Pennsylvania courts upheld some variations of the *Everson* decision.

The U.S. Supreme Court (*Meek* v. *Pittenger,* 421 U.S. 349, 95 S. Ct. 1753) allowed textbooks to be loaned to nonpublic school students but disallowed the use of public funds for services, equipment, and instructional materials. The Court (*Wolman* v. *Walter,* 433 U.S. 229, 97 S. Ct. 2593) ruled that the provision of books, testing and scoring, and diagnostic and therapeutic services was constitutional, based on the child-benefit theory. State support of field trips, instructional materials, and equipment was ruled unconstitutional, as they aided schools rather than children per se. One of the first setbacks for opponents of using state funds for parochial schools came in Pennsylvania. In 1968, that state passed an act authorizing the state superintendent of public instruction to contract for the purchase of secular education services for students from nonpublic schools located in the Commonwealth of Pennsylvania. It provided that certain revenues from state harness racing should go into a nonpublic elementary and secondary education fund for the financing for all of these expenditures. No public school funds were involved. The court ruled the law "neither creates nor supports the establishment of religion."

Because the Pennsylvania legislation was controversial and might potentially influence other states, litigation was expected. It soon materialized; suit was brought against the state superintendent of public instruction and the state auditor general. The plaintiffs, including many professional and religious groups, charged that the legislation violated the First and Fourteenth Amendments to the U.S. Constitution.

Intervention by the Courts

Acclaim for the action in Pennsylvania was short-lived. The U.S. Supreme Court overruled the district court and declared the Pennsylvania law to be in violation of the principle of separation of church and state. The decision was accompanied, however, by a contrary one regarding public support of nonpublic colleges and universities in Connecticut.

In these rulings, the U.S. Supreme Court acted simultaneously on three appeals of cases concerned with the use of public funds for nonpublic schools. These cases included *Tilton* v. *Richardson* (public funds for higher education in Connecticut), *Lemon* v. *Kurtzman* (public funds for providing educational services in nonpublic elementary and secondary schools in Pennsylvania), and *DiCenso* v. *Robinson* (public funds to provide supplements to the salaries of teachers in certain nonpublic elementary schools in Rhode Island).[14]

In considering the three cases, the Court looked at a number of issues: (1) Is aid to church-related colleges and universities constitutionally different from similar aid to church-related elementary and secondary schools? (2) May the state or the federal government or both provide direct aid to nonpublic schools, or must they confine themselves to indirect assistance like that already approved in the *Everson* and *Cochran* cases? (3) To what extent do these cases support or violate the establishment clause, which requires avoidance of excessive government involvement or entanglement with religion?[15]

In *Tilton,* the Court sustained the Connecticut issue for public aid to colleges and universities. In *Lemon,* it rejected the Pennsylvania law to aid nonpublic elementary and secondary schools, and it also rejected the Rhode Island plan for supplementing teacher salaries in nonpublic schools. These cases determined that there is less likelihood of state involvement or entanglement in the affairs of a church-related college than in a church-related elementary or secondary school.

Evidence of the controversial nature of many other state and federal plans for using or not using public funds for nonpublic schools is shown by the following representative examples of many laws and court rulings:

- The U.S. Supreme Court ruled against tax benefits for any private segregated school set up in Mississippi to avoid integration.
- The Maine Supreme Court ruled against church-state–related legislation. The court pointed out that financial conditions created by closing parochial schools were not the issue—the Constitution, not economics, was at stake.
- The California legislature made profit-making enterprises not connected to their tax-exempt purpose (religion) subject to the state's 7 percent tax on net income.
- The West Virginia Supreme Court ruled that county school systems must furnish bus transportation to parochial school students.
- A New York law that would have provided $33 million a year to church-related schools for teacher salaries, instructional materials, and other costs of instruction was declared unconstitutional by a three-judge federal panel.
- Ohio's law permitting aid to nonpublic schools was upheld by the Ohio Supreme Court, but the U.S. Supreme Court affirmed the decision of a federal district court that had ruled against the state's making direct grants to parents of children attending nonpublic schools.
- The National Defense Education Act, the Elementary and Secondary Education Act, the Education and Consolidation and Improvement Act of 1981, the Improv-

ing America's Act of 1994, and the No Child Left Behind Act of 2001 have all provided federal funds to public school districts that aid students in nonpublic schools through the "pass-through" provision.

■ The U.S. Supreme Court, in *Mueller* v. *Allen*,[16] approved a Minnesota law that permits taxpayers to deduct from their state income tax expenses for tuition, textbooks, and transportation. The deduction is neutrally available to every family with children of school age but is especially beneficial for parents who send their children to private schools.

■ In *Aguilar* v. *Felton*,[17] the U.S. Supreme Court held that the practice of nonpublic schools being used part time as public schools and receiving state aid was unconstitutional because nonpublic schools in that situation are "pervasively sectarian" (changed by *Agostini* in June 1997.)[18]

■ The U.S. Eighth Circuit Court of Appeals unanimously overturned a lower court decision in a Missouri case (*Pulido* v. *Cavazo*) which held that the U.S. Department of Education allocation of Chapter I funds that provided "off the top" money to provide leased mobile vans or portable classrooms for pupils in religious schools was unconstitutional. In a split vote, the panel also overturned the lower court's ruling that such vans and portable units could not be placed on the property of a church-affiliated school. The circuit court said that the units would be viewed as "religiously neutral" under proper circumstances.[19]

In *Sloan* v. *Lemon*,[19] the U.S. Supreme Court held that Pennsylvania's Parent Reimbursement Act for Nonpublic Education was unconstitutional. The act provided funds to reimburse parents for some of the tuition expenses they paid to send their children to nonpublic schools. The Court also held unconstitutional a New York statute that provided funds for nonpublic schools serving low-income families. The funds were to be spent for the maintenance and repair of buildings, for tuition grants, and for certain tax benefits for low-income parents of students attending nonpublic schools.

The major arguments presented against the Pennsylvania and New York laws were:

1. Providing state funds for nonpublic schools violates the Establishment Clause of the First Amendment to the Constitution.
2. Such allocation of funds could have a serious effect on the capability of the public schools to discharge their responsibility.
3. Such funding would divert money from public education to private education.
4. This funding would tend to renew the conflict over church-state relations.
5. Such funding would increase the number of students in nonpublic schools and change the mix of students in public schools.

In reviewing *Sloan* v. *Lemon* (Pennsylvania) and *Committee for Public Education and Religious Liberty* v. *Nyquist* (New York),[20] the Supreme Court, rejected both statutes, stating that the "maintenance and repair provisions violate the Establishment Clause because their effect, inevitably, is to subsidize and advance the religious mission of sectarian schools." It held that the tuition reimbursement parts of both statutes fail the "effect" test for the same reason as those governing the maintenance and repair grants. The court ruled that the tax benefit to parents of nonpublic school children did not fit the pattern of property tax exemptions sustained in *Walz* v. *Tax Commission.*[21] (In the view of the Court, tax exemptions for property used solely for religious purposes tended to reinforce the separation of church and state and to avoid excessive government entanglement with religion.) The controlling factor, in the view of the Court, was that although both statutes would aid all nonpublic schools, 90 percent of the students affected were attending schools controlled by religious organizations. Thus, the statutes had the practical effect of advancing religion.

In *Aguilar* v. *Felton*, the point at issue was that nonpublic schools were being used (and reimbursed by the state) as "part-time public schools." These religious schools identified themselves as public during the time they were teaching secular subjects. The Supreme Court held that the procedure was unconstitutional, stating:

> Schools in this case are thus "pervasively sectarian," [and] the challenged public school programs operating in the religious schools may impermissibly advance religion in three different ways. First, the teachers participating in the programs may unintentionally or inadvertently inculcate particular religious tenets or beliefs into the curriculum. Second, the programs may provide a crucial symbolic link between government and the school indicating a support of the religious denomination operating the school. Third, the programs may have the effect of directly promoting religion by impermissibly providing a subsidy to the primary religious mission of the institutions affected.[22]

To circumvent the ruling, many districts in the country, including New York City, leased or purchased mobile classrooms (vans or trailers) that traveled to parochial schools to provide the mandated services to qualifying Title I students. Congress appropriated some capital expense money for compliance with *Aguilar* v. *Felton* and the U.S. Department of Education required that if the allocated funds were insufficient, money would need to come "off the top" of their entire Title I allocation.[23]

The issue was readdressed in *Agostini* v. *Felton,*[24] which was presented to the U.S. Supreme Court.[24] The appeal was based on the premise that the previous ruling had cost taxpayers millions of dollars and that a new look at the entanglement question should be evaluated. A brief filed on behalf of the U.S. Department of Education noted, "*Aguilar* has led to considerable cost to education and the public but has yielded little constitutional benefit, in the sense of preventing any real entanglement between governmental and religious institutions."[25]

The court reviewed the case, and by a 5–4 vote, overturned the 1985 decision. *Agostini* altered the thinking of the *Lemon* test and changed the requirements in the *Aguilar* decision. Justice Sandra Day O'Connor, writing for the majority, stated:

> New York City's Title I program does not run afoul of any of three primary criteria we currently use to evaluate whether government aid has the effect of advancing religion. It does not result in government indoctrination, define its recipients by referent to religion, create an excessive entanglement between government and religion. We therefore hold that a federally

funded program providing supplemental, remedial instruction to disadvantaged children on a neutral basis is not invalid.[26]

The United States Supreme Court upheld the *Agostini* doctrine when it ruled in the Louisiana *Mitchell* v. *Helms* case.[27] Three issues were considered: (1) the on-site delivery of special education for children in religiously affiliated nonpublic schools, (2) the constitutionality of providing the use of equipment owned by the school district but used by nonpublic parochial schools, and (3) the legality of providing transportation to students who attended religiously affiliated private schools. The third issue was deemed constitutional by the District Court and the Fifth Circuit and was not part of the appeal in *Mitchell* v. *Helms*. Those courts' decisions and the omission in the appeal confirmed other rulings that have upheld the child benefit theory in issues dealing with transporting students to private/parochial schools. The Court upheld the *Agostini* tenets by concluding that the law "neither results in religious indoctrination by the government nor defines its recipients by reference to religion."[28]

Another significant case dealing with the church-state issue made its way to the U.S. Supreme Court. The *Joel Village School District et al.* v. *Louis Grumet and Albert W. Hawk* suit dealt with a school district that was established by the New York State Legislature in a special act. The Monroe-Woodbury Central School District and the Satmar religious community within the district were enmeshed in several disputes over ways to accommodate some of the religious traditions that were in conflict with district policies and procedures. The Second Circuit U.S. Court of Appeals determined that the New York City Board of Education's arrangement with the Satmar community to educate its children in a walled-off, segregated section of a public school in the Williamsburg section of New York City was an unconstitutional accommodation of religion.

The Monroe-Woodbury school district attempted to meet the requests of the Satmar community by assigning only male bus drivers to service public school bus routes assigned to transport male Satmar students to private schools in the Village of Kiryas Joel. The federal district court ruled that the school district had violated the Establishment Clause of the U.S. Constitution. After the legislative action, the New York State School Boards Association filed suit. Louis Grumet, executive director, indicated:

> We believe the state statute establishing a public school district in an exclusively Satmar community, the Village of Kiryas Joel, violates the First Amendment's Establishment Clause. What the statute provides is almost without precedent in the history of the United States: It confers on an exclusively religious community the extraordinary governmental benefits of a separate public school district system serving the village. Public tax dollars are being spent to support this clear violation of the Establishment Clause.[29]

The Supreme Court agreed with Grumet when they affirmed the Second Circuit's opinion that the arrangement with the Satmar community was an "unconstitutional accommodation of religion."[30] The New York Court of Appeals visited the issue again in *Grumet* v. *Cuomo*. Another ruling stated that the new legislation also violated the establishment clause of the U.S. Constitution.[31]

Educational Choice

An issue needing to be addressed for various reasons, including the great implications on finance, is school choice. The subject has been greatly debated at the national level and governors throughout the country have endorsed the concept as a way to restructure education. Choice is not a new issue. Since the founding of the United States, it has often been discussed whether the public or the private sector should be charged with the major responsibility of providing education. The negative claims against the public schools have included their alleged discrimination against the gifted and the disabled, their presumed failure to teach students fundamental skills, and their reputation for fostering inequality among the races and between the sexes. These and numerous other charges have resulted in various proposals for radical changes in the organization and administration of schools. Some of these proposals purport to be panaceas; others are proposed as partial solutions to the many problems that education critics claim are not solvable under the present public school systems of the 50 states. "School choice initiatives are based on the premise that allowing parents to choose what schools their children attend is not only the fair thing to do, but also an important strategy for im- proving public education. Instead of a one-size-fits-all mode, choice programs offer parents various alternatives from which to pick the educational settings they believe will work best for their children."[32]

The Education Commission of the States describes some of the choice options for parents and students:

Open enrollment. Allows parents to send their children to a public school within their school district. Interdistrict open enrollment allows parents to send their children to a public school of their choice in surrounding school districts.

Magnet school. Schools specializing in a certain curricular area. Typically such schools draw students from various attendance areas within and without the district.

Dual/concurrent enrollment. Allows secondary school students to enroll in post- secondary courses and apply course credit at the secondary or postsecondary institution or both.

Charter schools. Parents, community groups, or private organizations establish charter schools, which are essentially deregulated public schools. Charter schools are funded with public taxpayer money.

Vouchers. Payments made to a parent, or an institution on a parent's behalf, to be used to pay for a child's education expenses, usually at a private or parochial school. Some voucher programs are financed through private sources, others use public tax dollars to fund tuition at private institutions.

Tax credits and deductions. Some tax credits and deductions allow parents to redirect their tax dollars to offset some expenses incurred by sending their child to a private school. Other tax credits and deductions allow individuals and/or corporations to redirect tax dollars to scholarship granting organizations, which, in turn, redistribute these contributions to students in the form of private school scholarships.

Home school. Home schooling is an alternative form of education in which parents or guardians bypass the public school system and teach their children at home.[33]

In addition to this listing, public schools may offer alternative schools in and out of the district, high school graduation incentives, on-line courses for credit, and area learning centers that offer a broader curriculum than some high schools. The areas of choice that are most controversial and that have an impact on school finance center on vouchers, tax credits, and charter schools.

Education Vouchers

A frequently proposed solution to the choice issue is that of providing a voucher to be spent at the school selected by the parents and student. Numerous versions of this approach have been suggested through the years. Milton Friedman espoused its use in his *Capitalism and Freedom.* Reduced to its simplest form, his plan recommended: (1) the determination of a minimum level of education by each state, (2) the issuance of vouchers that parents could use in approved schools to purchase the education obtainable in that school, and (3) the payment by parents of the additional amount of money required by a particular school over and above the amount of the voucher.

It is claimed that such an arrangement would allow parents a choice among the educational programs available to their children by paying the amount required above the cost allowed by the voucher. The schools could be of any type—private, parochial, or public—provided they met the established state standards. McCarthy described the basic voucher system as "one where parents can use state-funded vouchers of a designated amount to pay for their children to attend a public or private school of their choice. Plans vary as to the amount of government regulation involved and whether participating private schools can charge more for tuition than the basic voucher amount."[34]

Advantages and Disadvantages.   It is relatively easy to see limitations and possible defects in this organizational system. It seems apparent that the affluent would be able to purchase education at the more expensive and prestigious schools, whereas the less affluent would be forced to purchase education for their children at less expensive institutions. Undoubtedly, this would accentuate undesirable economic segregation and social class distinction. Although such a program might offer a choice of schools and curricula for students in central cities or in other areas of dense population, the idea of competitive schools in rural areas is not feasible from the point of view of basic economics, considering the limited number of students available.

Some of the advocates of a voucher system argue that it would result in greater decentralization of schools. This, they say, is highly desirable, since it would bring the schools closer to the people whose children attend them. However, chaos could potentially develop if each school were allowed to set its own standards or values, to determine the subjects to be taught, and to establish its own costs of attendance.

Advocates say that such a plan would give parents a wider choice of education for their children and that the schools would be better as a result of the natural competition that would arise. They point to the fact that the public schools now maintain a natural monopoly and are very slow to react to public pressure and criticism, but that private schools that are dependent on favorable public opinion react quickly to the desires and needs of their students. The legal implications that make the issue the most controversial focus on the state-supported voucher programs that include parochial schools. The basic question is whether the participation of schools with religious ties violates the various constitutions of the states and the establishment clause of the First Amendment of the U.S. Constitution. This is a large issue, as nearly 80 percent of the private schools are religious in nature.

The Milwaukee Parental Choice Plan (MPCP), established in 1990, allowed 1,000 public school students the opportunity of attending nonsectarian private schools at state expense. The measure was specifically aimed at low-income students who were currently enrolled or who had dropped out of school. The plan was expanded to include parochial schools and increased the number of student participation to 15,000. A circuit court ruled that the inclusion of religious schools in the voucher program violated the state constitution, indicating that "millions of dollars would be directed to religious institutions." The ruling also struck down the expansion of the program. The Wisconsin Supreme Court reversed the decision and upheld the inclusion of parochial schools in the voucher program.[35] The U.S. Supreme Court declined to review the case. In January 2006, there were 121 private schools in the MPCP, enrolling over 14,000 students.[36]

The courts have been reviewing cases dealing with vouchers with various results. The Supreme Court of Wisconsin (*Jackson* v. *Benson*, 1998) upheld vouchers for students who attended religious schools. The Florida court did as well (*Holmes* v. *Bush*, 2000, 2001), then rejected the program on state constitution grounds.[37] In *Bagley* v. *Raymond School Department* (1999), Maine's appellate court approved the voucher program but prohibited schools with religious ties from qualifying for the funds. The action resulted in a case challenging that decision. (See *Eulitt* v. *State of Maine*, October 2004.)[38] The Maine First Circuit Court ruled, "[The] case calls to decide whether the protection clause requires Maine to extend tuition payments to private sectarian secondary schools on behalf of students who reside in a school district that makes such payments available on a limited basis to private nonsectarian secondary schools. We hold that the equal protection clause does not impose any such obligation." The Vermont Supreme Court (*Chittendon Town School District* v. *Vermont Department of Education*) struck down a school district's policy allowing tuition payments for children to attend sectarian high schools, noting that the practice violated the state constitution, which prohibits citizens to support religious worship in schools. The U.S. Supreme Court refused to hear the case.[39]

The Ohio General Assembly enacted a law that had as its intent to give greater educational choices to students and parents. The Ohio Pilot Project Scholarship Program (OPPSP) made it possible for students to attend alternative schools and, for some students, to receive tutor services. In addition, the OPPSP made a provision for the creation of community schools (charter) and magnet schools. Students and parents could select a *registered* private school, including one sponsored by a religious organization located in Cleveland, or one in an adjoining district. Out of the qualifying schools, 82 percent were parochial with 96 percent of the students in the religiously oriented schools. Funding was provided through tax dollars by issuing scholarships (vouchers) to qualifying students. Checks were sent directly to parents, who then had to turn the checks over to the participating school.[40]

The Supreme Court of Ohio upheld the OPPSP but determined that the program violated the state constitution's "one-subject" rule in *Simmons-Harris* v. *Goff*. The general assembly changed the statute that year to more directly meet court demands. A federal trial court in Ohio ruled that the voucher program violated the establishment clause, but the court allowed for the continuation of the program for a semester.[41]

The Sixth Circuit Court of Ohio ruled in *Simmons-Harris* v. *Zelman* that the OPPSP violated the establishment clause by having the impermissible effect of advancing religion. In June 2002, the *Zelman* case was heard in the U.S. Supreme Court, which relied heavily on the *Agostini* v. *Felton* decision. The Court indicated that in the Ohio program the "aid is allocated on the basis of neutral secular criteria that neither favors nor disfavors religion and secular beneficiaries on a nondiscrimination basis."[42] Reasoning in the case was based on the fact "that the program was one of true private choice, with no evidence that the State deliberately skewed incentives toward religious schools, [which] was sufficient for the program to survive scrutiny under the Establishment Clause."[43]

In summary, students in the Ohio pilot project may use vouchers to attend religious schools, and the legislature in 2006 increased the program from 20,000 eligible students to 50,000.[44]

The Florida Supreme Court (*Holmes* v. *Bush,* January 2006) ruled that a private school voucher plan (Opportunity School Program) violated the state constitution's requirement to provide "a uniform, efficient, safe, secure, and high quality system of free public schools." The court indicated that vouchers diverted public revenues to private schools, contrary to the requirement that the state fund only "public schools." In addition, "because voucher payments reduce funding for the public education system . . . by its very nature (the voucher) undermines the system of 'high quality' free public schools."[45]

Voters have defeated propositions in several states. In California, a measure was defeated by a 70.5 percent *no* vote to a 29.5 percent *yes* vote. Michigan defeated a measure by a similar margin: 69.1 against and 30.9 for the proposal. In Colorado, voters rejected two proposals that would provide vouchers to some students. This has not discouraged legislators in these states and others to pursue legislation that will circumvent voter resolutions to provide funds for students in nonpublic schools—including parochial schools. Interest is drawn to the District of Columbia, where the federal government provided funds for a voucher program with an attachment to an appropriations bill that was passed in 2004.[46] Arizona, Utah, and Wisconsin passed legislation in their 2006 sessions, with more states raising the issue in 2007. McCarthy notes, "No topic is generating more volatile debate in legislative, judicial and educational forum than voucher systems to fund schooling. Discussions elicit strong emotions, positions are entrenched, and few people are objective about or neutral toward this issue!"[47]

Public attitudes regarding the voucher issue have fluctuated over the past decade. In 1993, the Phi Delta Kappa/Gallup Poll reported that 24 percent of respondents were in favor of students and parents choosing a private school to attend at public expense. Since then, the highest number favoring the issue was in 2002, with 46 percent. In 2006, there was a decrease to 36 percent of respondents favoring providing public funds for students to attend private school; 60 percent opposed.[48] Note the following figures:

Do you favor or oppose allowing students and parents to choose a private school to attend at public expense?

	National Totals							
	'06 %	'05 %	'04 %	'03 %	'02 %	'01 %	'97 %	'93 %
Favor	36	38	42	38	46	34	44	24
Oppose	60	57	54	60	52	64	52	74
Don't Know	4	5	4	2	2	2	4	2

Source: Phi Delta Kappa/Gallup Poll, *Phi Delta Kappan,* 2006. Reprinted with permission.

Tax Credits

Some states have ventured into tax relief programs that indirectly divert some public funds to the support of activities related to nonpublic school education. Minnesota allows tax credit for purchase of educational services of various types. In Illinois, legislation was passed to award families state income-tax credits to help pay costs of private schools. The law allows for $500 per family toward private school costs, including tuition, books, fees, and other expenditures. A lawsuit filed by several families and supported by the Illinois Education Association challenged the law as unconstitutional. A U.S. District Judge ruled that the tax credits were constitutional if they are offered to parents of public school students as well.[49]

The legislature in Arizona enacted a law that provides tax credits for those making contributions to a "school tuition organization." The law allows funds to flow to private schools, including religious institutions. Taxpayers can generate up to $500 state income tax credit for voluntary contributions made to school tuition organizations that in turn provide scholarships for elementary and secondary students. Up to $200 tax credit is allowed against the taxes imposed for the amount of any fees paid by a taxpayer for the support of extracurricular activities of the public schools.[50] When a case was presented to the Arizona Supreme Court, it ruled that parochial schools were only "incidental beneficiaries" of the tax deduction allowance. The U.S. Supreme Court denied a hearing, allowing the program to continue.[51] The Arizona Individual Scholarship plan was enhanced in 2006 by legislation that provided matching dollar-for-dollar tax credits to corporations making donations to the fund.[52] Both Florida and Pennsylvania have similar tax credit programs, following Arizona's lead. The approach circumvents the First Amendment issue by making donations to private scholarship organizations. The fact that donations are being matched by revenue generated by *taxpayers* and that scholarships eventually benefit students in parochial schools in these cases may provide the incentive for other states to pass similar legislation.

Charter Schools

The *choice* movement, including voucher programs and tax credit proposals, historically made slow gains. Presently, the two concepts combined through the process of donating to private scholarship funds, have given it momentum, while charter schools have become established and accepted. Proponents for school choice have been excited about the expansion of options charter schools provide. The concept has been hailed by entrepreneurs as a real breakthrough for free enterprise, because it allows, in some states, private businesses to compete for billions of dollars that go into education budgets throughout the country. (See Local Control by Contract in Chapter 6.)

Defining *charter schools* is challenging because the state requirements for charter holders differ markedly. This dilemma holds true today, as descriptions make it difficult to narrow down categories for the various approaches. Thus, this early description by Harrington-Lueker has not changed much in the past decade:

> Laws vary so much from state to state that no single definition of a charter school applies. In general, though, charter schools are nonsectarian public schools that cannot discriminate on the basis of ethnicity, race, or disability. Charter schools generally set out specific results they will achieve—a certain attendance level, for example, or a certain percentage of improvement on standardized tests. If these outcomes aren't met, whoever granted the charter can revoke it.[53]

The Education Commission of the States offers this definition:

> Charter schools are semiautonomous public schools, founded by educators, parents, community groups or private organizations that operate under a written contract with a state, district or other entity. This contract, or charter, details how the school will be organized and managed, what students will be taught and expected to achieve, and how success will be measured. Many charter schools enjoy the freedom from rules and regulations affecting public schools, as long as they can meet the terms of their charters. Charter schools can be closed for failing to satisfy these terms.[54]

Federal Public Law 103-382 suggests the following features for charter schools:

- Charter schools are public schools that are exempted from significant state or local rules that inhibit the flexible operation and management of public schools.
- Charter schools are created by developers as public schools or adapted from existing public schools, and are operated under public supervision and direction.
- Charter schools operate in pursuit of a specific set of educational objectives determined by the schools' developers and agreed to by the authorized public chartering agency.
- Charter schools provide a program of elementary or secondary education or both.

- Charter schools are nonsectarian in their programs, admissions policy, employment practices, and all other operations and are not affiliated with a sectarian school or a religious institution.
- Charter schools do not charge tuition.
- Charter schools comply with federal civil rights legislation.
- Charter schools admit students based on a lottery if more students apply for admission than can be accommodated.
- Charter schools agree to comply with the same federal and state audit requirements as do other elementary and secondary schools in the state unless the requirements are specifically waived.
- Charter schools meet all the applicable federal, state, and local heath and safety requirements.
- Charter schools operate in accordance with state law.[55]

The Phi Delta Kappa/Gallup Poll in 2006 indicated that there was a lack of understanding of the charter school concept. Following are poll findings:

Public approval of charter schools has climbed from 42% in 2000 to 53% in 2006. This finding must be weighed against responses indicating that the concept is not clearly understood. Here are some comparisons:

- 39% of respondents say charter schools are public schools; 53% say they are not (fact: they are public schools).
- 50% say charters are free to teach religion; 34% say they are not (fact: they are not).
- 60% say charters can charge tuition; 29% say they cannot (fact: they cannot).
- 58% say charters can base student selection on ability; 29% say they cannot (fact: they cannot).[56]

The public response to the question related to favoring or opposing charter schools is noted in the following:

As you may know, charter schools operate under a charter or contract that frees them from many of the state regulations imposed on public schools and permits them to operate independently. Do you favor or oppose the idea of charter schools?

	National Totals				No Children in School				Public School Parents			
	'06 %	'05 %	'02 %	'00 %	'06 %	'05 %	'02 %	'00 %	'06 %	'05 %	'02 %	'00 %
Favor	53	49	44	42	50	49	44	42	49	48	44	40
Oppose	34	41	43	47	37	40	43	47	31	43	44	47
Don't know	13	10	13	11	13	11	13	11	10	9	12	13

The charter school movement has grown significantly since the first one was established in Minnesota in 1992–93. The Center for Education Reform reported in their directory in fiscal 2006 that 3,617 charter schools served 1,074,809 students in 41 states and the District of Columbia. An additional 90 charter schools began operations in fiscal 2007.[57]

Generally, at the state level, the charter recipients are awarded the same per-pupil revenue provided local school districts. Arizona has added state capital facilities aid for charter schools[58] and the school district in Anchorage, Alaska, approved a charter school for home-schoolers,[59] a concept that was struck down by the courts in Michigan. The home school issue takes the private school finance question to an extended dimension as the numbers continue to increase. Estimates are that nearly 900,000 students are taught at home.[60] The question arises: Should students who are home-schooled be eligible for the per-pupil state revenue provided to public schools? The arguments are strong for such support if the state has the responsibility to provide funding for the education of each student in the state, irrespective of the delivery system. The impact and strain on education dollars could be staggering.

Controversy Not Solved

The relation of church and state and now the broader issue of school choice have serious implications for school finance, some of which become more apparent each year. For example, the constantly increasing costs of education for nonpublic schools have caused the sponsoring agencies to take a serious look at the operation of such institutions. There is some merit to their argument that some governmental financial assistance may be required to keep their operation solvent so that they can continue to supplement and abet the educational programs of the public schools. Their contention is that nonpublic school bankruptcy would bring hundreds of thousands of abandoned students back into the public education system, at a very high cost.

Despite the obvious fact that nonpublic school failures will result in higher costs of public education, most citizens prefer to view the church-state issue on the basis of principle rather than economics. Either approach to the problem has its limitations, its defenders, and its critics. Consequently, litigation in this area of financing education is becoming more common and controversial than ever before in history.

Unfortunately, even though many courts have ruled on the problem, there is no clearly determined answer to whether statutes adopted in some of the states are contraventions of the First and Fourteenth Amendments. The controversy over the church-state conflict and the implications of sharing public revenue with private schools pose many questions for both private and public school administrators. The future is difficult to predict, but one thing is certain: The courts and legislators will be challenged with this issue again and again.

Summary

The principle of separation of church and state is lauded in this country, but it has caused a dilemma of some importance in the field of education. Direct government financial support for private and parochial schools has continually been repudiated by the courts. Proponents of financial aid to nonpublic schools argue that parents should have a choice in the type of school their children attend, that nonpublic schools cannot function properly without financial support, and that the elimination of such schools would cause economic stress on public schools.

Opponents argue that parochial aid represents a big step backwards in educational philosophy, that the practice would violate the Establishment Clause of the First Amendment to the U.S. Constitution, and that the problem should be solved on the basis of principle rather than its economic effect. The principle of separation has generally been observed, but interpretation of it has sometimes changed. The courts have sometimes supported a child-benefit theory and some forms of tax credit payments for elementary and secondary school students, if such action passed the *Lemon* test.

The topic of *choice* is receiving much exposure in the literature. A frequently proposed solution to the choice issue is that of providing a voucher to parents to be spent at the school they wish their child to attend. Interest was renewed in the concept with the Ohio case *(Zelman),* which allowed students with vouchers to attend schools with religious ties. Tax credits are another option that expands the possibilities for choice and at the same time proposes a way to divert federal and state public funds to nonpublic schools.

Private scholarship programs giving tax credits to contributors and some revenue matched by the state are providing an avenue for vouchers to be presented to students in both parochial and nonparochial private schools. In addition, charter schools have become more accepted as an option for choice, and continue to expand throughout the United States.

The church-state controversy has had and will continue to have an important effect on state school finance systems. Nonpublic schools, like public schools, are being adversely affected by continually rising costs, which sometimes force nonpublic schools to discontinue their services. This, of course, places a greater financial burden on the public schools.

The issue of financial support to nonpublic schools remains unresolved. The debate over its merits and drawbacks goes on unabated.

ASSIGNMENT PROJECTS

1. Provide a definition for each of the following terms: *Lemon test, Zelman, Weisman perception, Goluba perspective, child benefit theory, First Amendment, Tenth Amendment, Aguilar-Agostini logic, choice, tuition tax credits, vouchers, charter schools, establishment clause, free exercise clause.*
2. Trace the history of the church-state controversy in education in your own state since the adoption of the U.S. Constitution.
3. Review three important court decisions that have had an effect on public financing of church schools.
4. Summarize the arguments in favor and those opposed to the granting of public funds for the support of nonpublic schools.

5. Some states have made greater efforts than others to provide public funds for nonpublic schools. Trace the history of a particular state in its efforts to come to a satisfactory solution to this problem.

6. The "choice" issue has implications for diverting public funds to nonpublic schools. Prepare a paper that discusses the pros and cons of this point of view.

7. Prepare a paper indicating your position on the question of using public funds to help support nonpublic schools.

Computer simulations and questions, research exercises, and website addresses relevant to this chapter can be found at

www.ablongman.com/edleadership

SELECTED READINGS

Beales, J. R., and M. Wahl. *Private Vouchers*. Stanford, CA: Stanford University, Hoover Institution Press, 1995.

Bierlein, Louann A., and Mary F. Fulton. *Emerging Issues in Charter Schools Financing: Policy Brief*. Denver: Education Commission of the States, May 1996.

Chubb, J. E., and T. M. Moe. *Politics, Markets, and America's Schools*. Washington, DC: Brookings Institution, 1990.

Coleman, James, Thomas Hoffer, and Sally Kilgore. *Public and Private Schools*. Washington, DC: National Center for Educational Statistics, 1981.

Cookson, Peter W. Jr. *School Choice: The Struggle for the Soul of American Education*. New Haven, CT: Yale University Press, 1994.

Coons, John E., and Stephen D. Sugarman. *Education by Choice: The Case for Family Control*. Berkeley: University of California Press, 1978.

Everhart, Robert. *The Public School Monopoly: A Critical Analysis of Education and the State in American Society*. Cambridge, MA: Ballinger, 1982.

Finn, Chester. *We Must Take Charge: Our Schools and Our Future*. New York: The Free Press, 1991.

Fliegel, Seymour, and James MacGuire. *Miracle in East Harlem: The Fight for Choice in Public Education*. New York: Times Book, 1993.

Fuller, Bruce, and Richard F. Elmore with Gary Orfield, eds. *Who Chooses? Who Loses? Culture, Institutions, and the Unequal Effects of School Choice*. New York: Teachers College Press, 1996.

Gill, B. P., P. M. Timpane, K. E. Ross, and D. J. Brewer. *Rhetoric versus Reality: What We Know and What We Need to Know about Vouchers and Charter Schools*. Santa Monica CA: Rand, 2001.

Henig, Jeffrey R. *Rethinking School Choice: Limits of the Market Metaphor*. Princeton, NJ: Princeton University Press, 1994.

Howell, W. G., and P. E. Peterson. *The Education Gap: Vouchers and Urban Schools*. Washington DC: Brookings Institution, 2002.

Kirkpatrick, David W. *Choice in Schooling: A Case for Tuition Vouchers*. Chicago: Loyola University Press, 1990.

McCarthy, Martha M. *A Delicate Balance: Church, State and the Schools*. Bloomington, IN: Phi Delta Kappan Educational Foundation, 1983.

Nathan, Joe, ed. *Public Schools by Choice: Expanding Opportunities for Parents, Students, and Teachers*. St. Paul, MN: Institute for Learning and Teaching, 1989.

Peterson, P. E., and D. E. Campbell. *Charters Vouchers and Public Education*. Washington DC: Brookings Insitution, 2001.

Quade, Quenton L. *Financing Education: The Struggle between Governmental Monopoly and Parental Control*. New Brunswick, NJ: Transaction Publishers, 1996.

RPP International. *The State of Charter Schools: Fourth-Year Report*. Washington DC: Department of Education, U.S. Government Printing Office, 2000.

ENDNOTES

1. *Pierce* v. *Society of Sisters,* 268 U.S. 510, 45 S. Ct. 571 (1925).
2. *Aguilar* v. *Felton,* 105 S. Ct. 3232 (1985).
3. *Lemon* v. *Kurtzman,* 403 U.S. 602, 91 S. Ct. 2105 (1971), *rehearing denied.*
4. *Lee* v. *Weisman,* 505 U.S. 577 (1992).
5. *Jones* v. *Clear Creek Independent School District,* Federal Reporter, 2d Series, Vol. 977, pp. 963–972.
6. *Nikki M. Goluba, Plaintiff-Appellant* v. *The School District of Ripon, a municipal corporation; and Roland Alger, Defendants-Appellees.* 1995 WL 8235 (7th Cir. (Wis.)).
7. *Lee* v. *Weisman.*
8. *Jones* v. *Clear Creek Independent School District.*
9. Mark Walsh, "Court Opens Term with Several Major School Cases on Docket," *Education Week,* October 2, 1991, p. 25.
10. "Characteristics of Private Schools in the United States: Results from the 2003–2004 Private School Universe Survey," *National Center for Education Statistics,* nes.ed.gov/program, March 2006.
11. *Cochran* v. *Louisiana State Board of Education,* 281 U.S. 370, 50 S. Ct. 335 (1930).
12. *Everson* v. *Board of Education,* 330 U.S. 1, 67 S. Ct. 504 (1947), *rehearing denied.*
13. National Education Association, *Research Bulletin 45,* No. 2, May 1967, p. 44.
14. *Tilton* v. *Richardson,* 403 U.S. 672, 91 S. Ct. 2091 (1971); *Lemon* v. *Kurtzman,* and *DiCenso* v. *Robinson,* 403 U.S. 602, 91 S. Ct. 2105 (1971), *rehearing denied.*
15. The Supreme Court previously addressed this question in *Walz* v. *Tax Commission* (397 U.S. 664, 90 S. Ct. 1409) and upheld by an 8 to 1 vote a constitutional and statutory provision in New York exempting church property from taxation.
16. *Mueller* v. *Allen,* 463 U.S. 388, 103 S. Ct. 3062 (1983).
17. *Aguilar* v. *Felton.*
18. *Agostini* v. *Felton,* Case No. 96–552, and *Chancellor of the Board of Education of New York* v. *Felton,* Case No. 96–553.
19. *Pullido* v. *Cavazos,* 934 F.2d 912 (8th Cir. 1991).
20. *Committee for Public Education* v. *Nyquist,* 413 U.S. 756, 93 S. Ct. 2955 (1973).
21. *Walz* v. *Tax Commission,* 397 U.S. 664, 90 S. Ct. 1409 (1970).
22. *Aguilar* v. *Felton.*
23. Mark Walsh, "Case Limiting Title I Gets New Day in Court," *Education Week,* April 9, 1997, p. 30.
24. *Agostini* v. *Felton.*
25. Walsh, "Case Limiting Title I," p. 30.
26. *Agostini* v. *Felton.*
27. *Mitchell* v. *Helms* (98-1648) 151 F. 3d 347, reversed also, http://supct.law.cornell.educ/supct/html/98-1648.ZS.html.
28. Ibid.
29. Louis Grumet, "Breeching the Wall," *The American School Board Journal,* May 1994, p. 26.
30. *Grumet* v. *Board of Education of the Kiryas Joel Village School District,* 114 S. Ct. 544 (1993).
31. 90. N. Y. 2d p. 57.
32. "Choice and Vouchers," *Education Week,* March 2, 2000, www.edweek.org/context/topics/choice.
33. Education Commission of the States, *Helping State Leaders Shape Education Policy: Choice,* www.ecs.org/html/issue, 2006.
34. Martha M. McCarthy, "What Is the Verdict on School Vouchers?" *Phi Delta Kappan,* January 2000, p. 372.
35. Ibid.
36. "Milwaukee Parental Choice Program (MPCP)," MPCP Facts and Figures for 2005–2006, January 2006.
37. Charles J. Russo and Ralph D. Mawdsley, "The Supreme Court and Vouchers Revisited," *School Business Affairs,* January 2003, p. 41.
38. *Eulitt* v. *State of Maine,* No. 04-1496 (1st Circ. October 22, 2004).
39. Russo and Mawdsley, "The Supreme Court and Vouchers Revisisted."
40. Ibid.
41. Ibid.
42. *Zelman* v. *Simmons-Harris,* 00-1751, Supreme Court Files, First Amendment Center. www.freedom forum.org.
43. Ibid. Quote from Chief Justice Renquist.
44. "Ohio and Utah Pass Bills Expanding School Choice Programs," Alliance for School Choice Programs, www.allianceforschoolchoice.or/media, March 30, 2006.
45. *Holmes* v. *Bush,* No. 0402323 (Florida, January 5, 2006).
46. "D.C. School Voucher Plan Failing to Meet Goals," *Issues in Education, National Education Association,* www.nea.org/vouchers.
47. McCarthy, "What Is the Verdict?" p. 371.
48. *The Phi Delta Kappa/Gallup Poll of the Public's Attitude Toward the Public Schools,* September 2006.
49. Alan Richards, "Judge Upholds Illinois Tax Credits," *Education Week,* May 3, 2000, p. 28.

50. Title 43, Chapter 10, Article 5, Arizona Revised Statutes, section 43–1087, Laws, 1997.

51. McCarthy, "What Is the Verdict?" p. 374; see *Kotterman* v. *Killian,* 972 P. 2d 606, 616 (Ariz. 1999), *cert. denied.*

52. "Tuition Tax Credits: A Model for School Choice," *National Center for Policy Analysis,* www.ncpa.org/ pub, April 2006.

53. Donna Harrington-Lueker, "Charter Schools," *The American School Board Journal,* September 1994, p. 25.

54. "Charter Schools," Education Commission of the States, Denver, CO, 2003. www. ecs.org/html/issue .asp? Issue ID=20.

55. Public Law 103–383, reported in *A Study of Charter Schools,* p. 5.

56. *The Phi Delta Kappa/Gallup Poll of the Public's Attitude Toward the Public Schools.*

57. "Charter Schools," CEA Quick Facts, www .edreform.com/index, November 1, 2005.

58. Lynn Schnalberg, "State Charter Laws Get New Round of Attention," *Education Week,* June 25, 1997, p. 16.

59. Mark Walsh, "Alaska Charter for Home Schoolers Approved," *Education Week,* February 12, 1997.

60. "Homeschooling," *Education Policy Issue Site: Homeschooling.* Education Commission of the States, Denver, CO, April 2006.

11 Financing School Facilities

*In too many communities, a school building still reflects the wealth
of its neighborhood. Whether or not a school has a decent library,
computer lab, theater department or even proper ventilation depends
largely on the local tax base—a base which is systematically being
eroded. Ironically, the best-kept secret in economic development
is that the greatest bang for the buck on virtually every level is
the investment in a great public school in the neighborhood.*

—Lily Eskelsen, 2007

Capital outlay along with debt services, transportation, federal programs, school lunch, special education, and categorical programs are large budgets that school officials under the direction of the board of education administer. These funds are in addition to the maintenance and operation (M&O) budget, which receives the greatest attention from the majority of educators, since revenues are utilized for salaries (75 to 80 percent), textbooks, and supplies, and, to a large extent, control the teacher-pupil ratio (classroom size).

Capital funds are generally used for fixed assets, equipment, construction projects, and purchase of property. At one time, in many states, debt services were included as part of capital outlay. Presently, it is a separate budget category, including expenditures for principal and interest on bonds, leases, and long-term financial obligations.

For many years, revenues for capital projects were generated solely by local property taxes. The uncomplicated and formerly satisfactory system of financing public school capital outlays in this manner is obsolete and impractical for present-day use. Historically, most school districts were able to finance their own capital-outlay expenditures without assistance. Their school building problems had not yet reached the magnitude they have attained in recent years. There were many reasons for this:

1. A smaller percentage of the school-age population attended school.
2. Building costs were much lower for a number of reasons: buildings were much less pretentious, labor costs were much lower, and fewer special areas and less expensive equipment were required.

3. There was no accumulation of need for buildings.

4. Since extensive changes and innovations were minimal, relatively few facilities or buildings were discarded because of obsolescence.

As the need for state involvement increased in the early years of the twentieth century, a few states made a feeble start toward helping finance school district capital outlays. About half a dozen southern states provided emergency funds to the hardship districts least capable of providing school buildings with local tax funds alone.

Since the problems of financing public school facilities are much the same as those of financing current expenditures, it would seem that reforms and improvements in one would bring similar improvements in the other. Such had not been the case, however, as the movement toward equalizing capital outlay was slow. Walter G. Hack noted the similarities and differences in these two related problems of financing education in the post-*Serrano* reform period:

> Both types (financing current expenditures and financing facilities) have apparently felt the effects of the economic slowdown, . . . inflation, and the wrath of the taxpayers' revenge. There is one major difference, however, significantly more recent attention has been given to problems related to financing the current expense programs. This attention is certainly legitimate and logical, given the proportion of school dollars expended between the two programs. It appears now, however, that attention could and should be at least shared with needs to finance capital outlay expenditures.[1]

Early Capital-Outlay Programs

One of the strong traditions that began to develop early in school finance history was that capital-outlay costs were of local concern only, in spite of strong and almost universal acceptance of state responsibility for education. The soundness of such a position is open to serious debate, but the general acceptance of this local responsibility, and the almost complete indifference on the part of state governments, is a matter of open record. In spite of recommendations for state participation in capital outlays by such finance planners as Updegraff and Mort, the main concern of most authorities in the Strayer-Haig era of influence was with state support of current operational costs only. This may have been because current expenditures included about 85 percent of the total school budget, with only 15 percent being spent for capital outlay.

A big factor working against local responsibility for building school facilities has been the low assessed valuations in thousands of small school districts. Regardless of the statutes and the willingness of people to tax themselves, bonding small districts to build school buildings was often mathematically impossible. In some school districts, for example, the cost of a new building might well exceed the assessed valuation of the entire district, whereas in other districts in the same state, a small tax levy would be adequate to build needed buildings on a pay-as-you-go basis. Such inequity undermines the concept of providing equality of educational opportunity for all children within a state.

Another argument against complete local responsibility for construction of school buildings is that such costs would then be paid almost entirely by payers of property tax. Some people would then escape paying their share of these capital-outlay costs. The property tax may once have been a reasonably fair measure of taxpaying ability, but it is not so today. *Using property tax payments exclusively for capital outlays repudiates our long-held belief in taxing people in terms of their ability to pay for education.* Only state participation in such costs can provide parity for this inequity. Such relief should be provided on an equalization basis. This would bring some relief to payers of property taxes and would broaden the tax base to include revenues from many different kinds of taxes, an absolute necessity in any tax system.

Complete local support for financing capital outlays was an appropriate and practical method of collecting the money to build and equip new school buildings for many years. The rationale for such a method of collecting capital outlay and debt service funds has virtually disappeared in the face of fairer methods of financing education. Some of the changes in school finance philosophy include the following:

1. Since responsibility for education is legally a state function, responsibility for its financing rests firmly with each state.
2. There is difficulty in equitably incorporating the varied capital-outlay debt of the many districts within a state.
3. There is little justification for financing capital outlays on a different basis from current expenditures. If state financing of current operations is fair, so is state financing of capital outlays.
4. There is no defense for the traditional method of financing school facilities by relying on local property tax when more tax resources are available at the state level.
5. It is false economy to indebt school districts for long periods of time with excessive interest costs.
6. It is paradoxical to provide adequate funds for current expenditures for all districts and then deny some of them good educational programs because low assessed valuations and state-imposed limitations on debt service maximums limit their fiscal ability to provide satisfactory facilities.

State Support

States did little to help in financing local public school capital outlays until the second quarter of the twentieth century, as Thompson pointed out: "State involvement in assisting local communities with facilities funding provides a checkered history. At various times the effort has been enthusiastic, but at other times denial of responsibility has been evident. In general, there has been less than enthusiastic support among the states for the concept of state participation in school building costs."[2] Since an initial action of Delaware in 1927 that provided for significant state support for local district debt-service costs in the foundation program, most of the 50 states have made some progress in this aspect of school finance. Barr and Wilkerson note:

State participation in financing local facilities ranges from Delaware's major support to California's billion dollar loan plan, from the Pennsylvania State School Building Authority to Indiana's and Kentucky's "do it yourself" holding companies—originated in the 1920's from Florida's, Washington's, and New York's scientifically conceived state grant programs to South Dakota's purchase of local bonds and Oregon's support of construction of junior colleges only.[3]

Some states seek solutions by making grants from accumulated surpluses; others provide equalized matching plans; and still others experiment with including capital-outlay monies as a fundamental part of their foundation programs. Variety in the solutions to the problem and inadequacy of funds are the chief ingredients of such state-local partnership plans. In recent years, it has become evident that changes will have to be made in the method of financing capital outlays. Many financially weak districts have been unable to meet their own building needs.

The current situation on state financing of local district capital outlays is characterized by the following points:

1. Emergency state grants often precede regular appropriations or provision for capital-outlay funds in a state's foundation program. Relatively few districts share in the use of such emergency funds. The success of these plans is largely a function of the objectivity of the guidelines and standards required for participation. Over time, these emergency programs very often develop into more or less permanent patterns for such diversion of funds for school construction.

2. Only a few states include capital outlays as a part of a foundation program. Flat grants, incentive funds (such as matching funds or reorganization grants), emergency grants-in-aid, special grants to financially feeble districts, repayable loans, building authorities, and equalized foundation grants are the main ways used to allocate state funds to local districts for financing capital outlays.

3. There is little similarity among the methods used by the states for providing capital outlays and debt-service funds to school districts; state appropriations and state loans are probably the two most used methods. Although flat grants and incentive grants help all districts, they are not equalized and therefore tend to be limited in scope and in their effect on solving the capital-outlay problem. Some of these grants have been utilized to encourage school district reorganization and attendance area consolidation. Matching grants used by some states have given greater aid to wealthy than to poor districts; on that basis, they are not satisfactory.

4. Many states use more than one program or device in getting state school money converted into local buildings; some allow local districts to accumulate funds for future building needs.

5. The state usually supervises rather carefully the expenditure of state monies for local school building construction, as it does with other state funds. The state often provides such supervision even when no state funds are directly involved in local school construction. This often involves required state approval of plans for new construction, observance of state-established building standards, and the services of state school-building consultants in the planning of local schools.

6. Increased control and supervision of local districts seems to accompany the provision of state funds to help pay local school building costs. Some state courts have ruled that the state legislature must provide a certain amount of funds to provide proper public school facilities.

7. Some states have adopted a policy of making loans to districts for capital-outlay purposes. The conditions of repayment usually include a standard effort for each district. The districts unable to repay the loans with a preestablished degree of tax effort receive the unpaid part of the loan as a state grant. The plan works well but sometimes results in overburdening certain districts with tax effort in order to meet stated requirements for eligibility to use such loans. Such handling of loan grants provides a degree of equalization, for the more wealthy districts would have no chance to default in repaying their loans, but poorer districts would often find it impossible to do otherwise.

8. Building authority plans offer a temporary solution to the problem of obtaining adequate buildings in some school districts. However, many of the financially weaker districts are hard pressed to provide funds for the high cost of such building authority rentals. There seems to be no more reason for the state to subsidize weak district rental costs than to subsidize and liberalize the construction practices involved in building their own buildings in the first place.

The use of school-building authorities in a rental agreement is an oblique attack on the problem of providing adequate school buildings. Under one plan, a building company constructs a building and rents it to the school district. The chief virtue of the plan is that it provides facilities for use by financially weak districts that could not bond to build their own because of low assessed valuations and unduly restrictive debt limitations. Adequate planning, construction of school plants with modern educational specifications, and the difficulties involved in fitting changing programs to inflexible facilities are some of the problem that this kind of program generates.

In addition to the many direct methods that the states used to facilitate construction of needed school buildings—grants, loans, creation of building authorities, inclusion of such costs in foundation programs, and others—there were indirect provisions that allowed some local districts to solve their own problems. One of the most important of these indirect provisions was the liberalization of school district debt and tax-levy limitations. Debt limitations, usually expressed as some percentage of the assessed value of taxable property, were changed in one or more of several possible ways. Some states changed the total debt limitation of a school district from a percentage of assessed value to a similar percentage of true value; others increased the limit by a stated dollar amount; and still others provided for additional tax-rate levies.

The matter of relating a school district's debt limits to a specified percentage of the assessed valuation is open to serious question, as Barr and Garvue have indicated:

Debt limits should not be related to the amount of local assessed evaluation. A more appropriate overall limit for financing capital outlays would be a limit of 25 percent of school revenue allocated to reserve funds, debt service, lease rental, and current construction. Experience has shown that this, or even higher allocation of public school revenues for school building purposes is feasible [and] prudent, and does not adversely affect bond ratings.[4]

Honeyman stressed the need for both local and state agencies to be involved in solving the capital-outlay problem:

Deferred maintenance and school construction needs are a serious concern throughout the United States. The problems associated with financing of facilities by school districts place many school districts in potential distress. The problem is crucial to the long-term success of many rural and poor school districts that lack an adequate tax base to support the levels of debt needed to resolve the problem. Regardless of the mechanisms that can be used to resolve deferred maintenance and facility needs, local districts and state education agencies must plan to address this growing problem.[5]

Current Capital-Outlay Rulings

The focus on capital projects increased as court cases provided an impetus for states to analyze their system of providing revenue for capital projects. Often the issue is based on adequacy in providing moneys to districts throughout the state in relation to the state constitution. In West Virginia, a case was introduced in 1975 with a decision rendered in 1984. The *Pauley* v. *Bailey* (1984)[6] case established that adequate facilities are a necessary part of a thorough and efficient education system that is required in the state constitution. West Virginia legislators and education leaders were given the challenge of developing a system of equitable financing for the schools, including capital outlays. Since facilities ranged from deplorable to exemplary and there was a wide variation of resources among the counties, the state assumed a greater role in funding school facilities. The estimate for bringing buildings up to a basic standard was over $800 million. The state proposed a bond election in 1986 for $200 million for building needs, in an attempt to meet the requirements of the court order. However, the voters of West Virginia rejected the bond issue on three occasions. Still determined to meet the court order, lawmakers created the independent School Building Authority (SBA).

In 2006, the executive director of the SBA reported that since August 1989 five new bond issues were passed, $1.1 billion of state funds was provided to capital projects, $948 million was generated through local bond and other initiatives, and a statewide school construction program exceeding $2 billion was completed. The report noted that 117 new school buildings were constructed and renovations and additions at 87 existing buildings were completed. Through the SBA, West Virginia is currently on a *pay-as-you-go* funding plan with revenue coming from state sales tax and video lottery profits.[7]

The *Robinson* v. *Cahill* (1973)[8] case in New Jersey followed closely after *Serrano* and *Rodriguez*. The New Jersey Supreme Court declared that the education school funding statute was unconstitutional, violating the "thorough and efficient education" clause in the state constitution. That opened the door for the *Abbott* v. *Burke* (1990)[9] case, which more directly affected school facilities and capital outlay. The court brought pressure on the legislature to equalize expenditures in capital outlay. In July 2003, the state attempted to meet the court demands by establishing a $12 billion school construction project, with $6 billion designated for *Abbott* districts (30 poorest districts in the state). The issue was hindered by a revenue shortfall because of economic factors. The state attorney general on behalf of the Department of Education filed suit, which resulted in a relaxed deadline for providing revenue for the *Abbott* districts. A freeze was granted to hold level the funding in 2006–07.[10]

The *DeRolph* v. *State of Ohio* (2001) case included implications for equalizing expenditures for facilities. The court "held that an efficient system of common schools is one in which school districts throughout the state have 'sound buildings that are in compliance with state building and fire codes.'"[11] The state legislature responded to the decision and designed plans to provide revenue to meet the demands of the court. The final decision was based on the progress made.

> But in deciding whether the school-funding system created in the legislation under review is constitutional, we must determine only whether, when fully implemented, the legislation enacted in response to *DeRolph* will likely have the effect of bringing these facilities into compliance within a reasonable time. When determining what is reasonable time, we must realize that construction and renovation are necessarily lengthy and complex processes and are not amenable to a one-year or even a five-year deadline.
>
> There is a well-documented need for many of Ohio's school buildings to be renovated, repaired, or replaced, or for completely new facilities to be constructed, in order to meet the standards established by *DeRolph*. Construction of this magnitude will necessarily be complex and time consuming.[12]

In analyzing the progress made and noting the plaintiff's concerns, the court stated, "We decline to find that the guidelines as promulgated by the Ohio School Facilities Commission result in inadequate buildings."[13] In May 2003, the Ohio Supreme Court ruled that the court itself, or "any other court," no longer has any jurisdiction over the case. On other grounds, the plaintiffs referred the case to the U.S. Supreme Court, which refused to hear the case.

In Arizona, a law passed in 1998 required improvements in schools and shifted the costs of upgrading from the local district to the state. The "existing deficiencies" were considerably higher than original estimates. A ballot initiative (Proposition 301) was passed in 2002 by a significant margin, which raised the sales tax from 5 percent to 5.6 percent with proceeds going to upgrade the schools.[14]

In response to three lawsuits and a state judge's decision that the formula for distributing capital-outlay funds was unconstitutional, the legislature in New Mexico passed a law in 2000 providing $60 million per year over a 10-year period for bonds for districts in need of school facilities.[15] A listing of needs for the capital projects was created based on the state definition of *adequacy* and the taxing capacity of each district. In 2002, a Special Master was appointed by the state to evaluate the progress being made in abiding by the requirements of the legislation. In 2006, the legislature provided an additional $90 million for "high-growth" districts. Plaintiffs in a new lawsuit indicated that the original $60 million was underfunded and questioned the constitutionality of the new allocation for high-growth districts.[16]

The state supreme court in Idaho *(ISEEO* v. *State,* 1998) ruled that the state legislature has the responsibility to "provide means for school districts to fund facilities that offer a safe environment conducive to learning."[17] After a few minimal attempts to meet the court ruling, the legislature passed House Bill 403 in 2003 to answer the demands of the court and prevent further proceedings. The Fourth District Court ruled on that legislation indicating, "HB 403 is an unconstitutional attempt by the Idaho legislature to evade its responsibilities under the Constitution by establishing pointless procedures which serve no useful or permissible purpose. . . . The special procedures established by HB 403 also violates the doctrine of separation of powers." The court further stated, "The Idaho Constitution imposes a clear duty on the legislature to establish and maintain a general, thorough and adequate system of public schools. The current system fails to provide a minimally adequate means for struggling school districts in economically depressed areas to replace dangerous buildings. The system's sole reliance on property taxes for school construction leaves out the poorest districts who often have the oldest and most dangerous structures"[18] Further proceedings are pending.

Colorado increased spending on school repairs and construction after a lawsuit, and voters passed Amendment 23 in 2000 that requires the legislature to increase spending for public schools for a 10-year period based on the rate of inflation plus 1 percent.[19] Alaska continues to grapple with constitutional demands in funding facilities based on "racially discriminatory" issues and isolated community needs.[20] A Wyoming court *(State of Wyoming* v. *Campbell)* stated, "This court reluctantly concludes that, while great effort has been made by many and some improvement has been achieved, the constitutional mandate for a fair, complete, and equal education 'appropriate for the times' in Wyoming has not been fully met."[21] The court required the legislature to provide a plan to meet the capital aspects of the case by July 2002, with an outline to remedy the deficiencies by 2008.[22] In March 2006, the New York Supreme Court, Appellate Division, ruled that New York City was not receiving an appropriate amount of revenue for its schools and that it was a responsibility of the governor and the legislature to determine the exact amount of aid necessary. For capital projects, the court ordered funding of at least $9.2 billion over a five-year period and to undertake periodic studies to provide facilities sufficient to provide all of its students with the opportunity for a sound basic education. In April 2006, the legislature provided the appropriate revenue to satisfy the court[23] (see Chapter 9).

In the 2006 general election, California voters passed Proposition 1D with a 56.6 percent *yes* vote. The approval provides $10.4 billion in general obligation bonds to relieve public school overcrowding, repair older schools, and improve earthquake safety. The revenue for K–12 is $7.3 billion and for higher education $3.1 billion. A fiscal note on the impact of the bond measure demonstrates the actual projected costs to be $20.3 billion ($9.9 billion interest) with payments of about $680 million per year.[24]

Equity in Financing Educational Facilities

The debate between the courts and legislatures continue. The legal actions have had a significant influence on states, causing them to analyze their own needs, prioritize projects, and determine methods to fund them adequately. The focus on equity and adequacy in capital outlay draws attention to these issues:

1. It is unfair, discriminatory, and certainly unjustified for the state not to provide proper facilities in which to house educational programs.
2. There is a high degree of unfairness in those districts that are required to build and equip several buildings each year, as compared to those that do not face such requirements. Increases in district school population, such as required to house students after Hurricane Katrina and by the mobility of people are a problem of the state, not simply of the districts affected by increases in student enrollment.
3. Programs for vocational education, education of the disabled, and education of minority and compensatory students are often found in property-poor school districts.
4. Bonded debt revenue from property tax levies increases criticism and the inequity of the property tax within a given district.
5. The long-term bonding debts incurred by taxpayers in less wealthy districts are often considerably higher than in wealthier districts because of the more favorable interest rates obtainable on bond issues in the latter.

In reality, school buildings belong to the state, rather than to the community in which they are located. That being true, the state is obligated to assume major responsibility for their construction. There is no point in state equalization of current expenditure funds if some local districts cannot provide the funds to build adequate facilities for school programs. There is not complete equity in financing education if a wealthy school district can provide luxurious buildings and facilities with very little tax effort at the same time that property-poor districts cannot provide minimum or acceptable facilities even with tremendous effort.

One proposal to solve the problem of providing school facilities through equal effort in poor districts as in rich ones, while relieving property taxpayers of some of the burden of that responsibility, is as follows:

1. Levy a small statewide property tax to be collected by the state for school building purposes.
2. Match the amount received (in some multiple or ratio as determined by state law) from that tax with revenue from other sources—income taxes, sales taxes, or others utilized in that particular state.
3. Combine the two amounts into a state school-building fund to be used for that purpose only.
4. Determine the need for and priority of school buildings to be built for a fixed period of time. (This, of course, may be changed as conditions and the needs of school districts change.)

5. Finance the buildings approved on a pay-as-you-go basis, thereby eliminating the interest costs being paid by most local districts that are required to borrow money over a long period of time.

Those who favor local financing of school construction—usually people in property-rich districts—point to one possible weakness of such a plan: Not all districts would be able to get their needed buildings each year because of the extremely high cost. They also say that the political influence of larger districts would give them higher priority and that state control would be complete—an undesirable result. It is difficult to deny the assertion that state control of school buildings is fairer and much more desirable than state control of the financing and administration of the school program: Once the buildings are built, the state cannot control their use and certainly has no reason to do so.

The Federal Government and Capital Outlays

There has been ambivalence at the federal level to assist states and local districts with financial aid for capital-outlay expenditures. The federal government's involvement is relatively insignificant. The prevailing opinion that school-plant construction was exclusively a local problem was not challenged by federal relief until the emergency programs of the Depression years were undertaken. At that time, the Public Works Administration and the Works Progress Administration constructed many school buildings in the 1930s and then released them to local school boards. This gave some evidence that funds for capital outlay might be provided to local districts without concern for federal control.

During its existence, the United States Office of Education did much to stimulate the states to provide plans for helping local districts to finance capital outlays. In 1951, it proposed that each state should include capital-outlay financing in its foundation program for current and long-range building programs. State departments of education were to establish specific programs and help administer them. Current funds were to be used and reserves were to be established when practicable. By 1965, about 80 percent of the states had used some method of assisting local districts in financing capital outlays and debt service. Legislative grants and appropriations—including, for example, a part of the foundation program, state loans, state guarantees of local indebtedness, and state purchases of local district bonds—are the most important devices used by the states to help local districts finance capital outlays.

In 1950, Public Law 815 was passed. It provided federal capital-outlay funds for school districts in areas affected by federal installations and defense projects (now Title VIII of the 2002 No Child Left Behind law). It also demonstrated that the federal government was cognizant of the need to provide some funds for local governments that were entitled to revenues *in lieu* of tax dollars.

As part of the reauthorization of the Elementary and Secondary Education Act, the fiscal 1995 federal budget included $100 million for the Education Infrastructure Act (Title XII). The act was designed "to help urban and rural school districts ensure the health and safety of students through the repair, renovation, alteration, and construction of public elementary and secondary school facilities." Although the amount was minuscule, no appropriation was awarded for the program.

In March 2006, the Hurricane Education Recovery Act provided a total of $1.1 billion for hurricane relief efforts. Part of the funds were distributed to 49 states and the District of Columbia as emergency aid to help cover costs of displaced students. Although capital outlay costs were not specifically earmarked in the legislation, Louisiana, Mississippi, and Texas received aid "to help local school districts and nonpublic schools defray expenses related to the reopening of, restart of operations in, and the re-enrollment of students in elementary and secondary schools that serve the areas affected by hurricanes Katrina and Rita."[25] The initial revenue was distributed under the Immediate Aid to Restart School Operations Program.

Basically, the position of the U.S. Department of Education toward school construction, renovation, and other capital outlay expenditures is that they should remain the responsibility of states and local districts. [26]

Capital-Outlay Finance Plans

During the many years of almost exclusive local support for financing capital outlays, several different plans and procedures have evolved in the states. Chief among these have been pay-as-you-go, use of tax reserve funds, and bonding.

Pay-as-You-Go Financing

Pay-as-you-go financing, which has been feasible in some large and relatively wealthy school districts, is an ideal way to finance capital outlays. It is the quickest and perhaps the easiest way of getting the necessary resources from the private sector to the public sector of the economy. It eliminates the expenditure of large sums of money for interest, costs of bond attorney fees, and election costs. It is convenient and tends to reduce the time required to obtain school facilities. This is particularly important in periods of high interest rates and inflation. As the costs of education have risen year after year, fewer districts have been able to take advantage of this method without creating a hardship for some payers of property tax.

Pay-as-you-go plans usually do not produce adequate revenue to finance school-plant construction because of two factors: (1) relatively low assessed valuations in small and average-sized districts compared with the high cost of building and (2) low tax levies due to restrictive legal limitations and high tax rates on property for obtaining the revenue for current expenditures. Many school districts that used this plan successfully in the years of relatively low-cost construction have found it impractical in recent years.

Building Reserve Plan

The accumulation of tax funds to be held in reserve for future building needs has been practiced in a few states; in some others, it is illegal. This plan provides for spreading construction costs over a period of time *before* the buildings are erected—as contrasted with bonding, which spreads the cost over time *after* the schools are constructed. At first consideration, this reserve plan would appear to be a good method of solving this financial problem. However, there are a number of legitimate (and also some controversial) objections to this process:

1. The accumulated funds paid by taxpayers before the money was needed will have cost them the use of such funds with interest that might have been earned, and in many instances they may be funds that were borrowed by taxpayers at rates considerably higher than those available to the school district if these accumulated funds had been invested until they were needed.
2. Changes in the membership of the board of education, changes in the apparent needs of the school district, or both may sometimes result in diversion of these reserve funds to purposes other than those for which they were collected.
3. Some taxpayers who pay into the reserve fund may never receive the attendant benefits because they move from the school district or, over time, their children complete school.
4. Inflation tends to erode the value of the reserve and reduce its purchasing power, rather than increase it as a result of interest accumulation.
5. Some argue, rather feebly, that all those who use the buildings should pay their fair share of the cost of such facilities. This is possible only when the costs are paid over a long period of time—not feasible when pay-as-you-go or pay-in-advance procedures are used.

The validity of this "intergeneration equity" philosophy is open to question. If one espouses the point of view that each generation should pay for the benefits it receives from use of school facilities, one is rejecting the ability-to-pay principle of financing education and reverting to the benefit principle—an untenable position that has long since been rejected in school finance theory. At this point, too, it seems reasonable to assume that each generation will be called on to make sizable payments for school facilities without concern for which generation is getting more or less than its share of benefits.

Although it is usually illegal to combine funds from the current-expenditure budget and the capital-outlay budget, except under certain legally established conditions, the effect of high tax rates in one area is that taxpayer resistance often forces lower tax rates in the other. Thus, the high rates necessary for pay-as-you-go or pay-in-advance payments for capital outlay may force lower rates for current expenditures, resulting in district curtailment of educational programs and services or other presumed economies such as reduced salary increases or increased pupil-teacher ratios.

Some districts that use the building reserve plan make a practice of earmarking certain voted revenues that are accumulated in a sinking fund to finance capital outlays. In practice, the plan is much like the pay-as-you-go process.

Under certain conditions, surpluses may be transferred from current expenditures at the end of a fiscal period to building reserve funds. The use of building reserves is usually subject to prior approval by the eligible voters of a district. In some states, its potential utilization is limited to new construction; in others, it may be used for any construction, including renovation and remodeling.

Bonding

The most common of all local programs for financing capital-outlay and debt-service expenditures is bonding. The process involves obtaining taxpayer favor for the district to issue long-term bonds to obtain funds to construct buildings and provide other facilities. Bond retirement involves levying property taxes to obtain funds to repay the principal and accrued interest. Bonding practices are required in districts with low assessed valuations of property, where tax revenues are not large enough to finance building costs on a current basis, and where the accumulation of reserve funds is either impracticable or illegal.

The principal advantages of the bonding system of raising school construction monies are the following:

1. Relative stability may be maintained in the tax levies necessary for construction. The tax burden is usually small enough each year so that it does not disturb the taxing plan for current-expenditure revenue.
2. Most districts can bond for large enough amounts to meet their building needs, whereas pay-as-you-go financing does not usually provide this opportunity.
3. School buildings and facilities necessary to operate a new program can be obtained when they are needed. Waiting for new construction until the required funds are in the school treasury would result in the denial of many educational benefits to the unfortunate students who were going through the school program when the facilities were needed but not provided.
4. The generations of people who get the greatest use of the facilities would be the ones to pay for them.
5. In an inflationary period, building costs may exceed interest costs.

There are also some disadvantages to the use of a bonding process for school building construction. These drawbacks include:

1. Total cost of the facilities is greater due to the necessity of paying large amounts of interest. However, the position of most school finance authorities is that the interest cost is small when compared with the benefits obtained by the almost immediate procurement of school facilities when they are needed.
2. Deferred payments often result in the construction of larger and more elaborate facilities than are needed; cash payments tend to reduce the desires of those who supply the funds at the time of purchase.
3. Bonding puts the entire cost of school construction on payers of property tax.

School Bonding Practices

Local school districts or states that are in need of large capital-outlay funds find it necessary, like individuals, to borrow money from some source, to be repaid with interest over a relatively long period of time. Typically, the individual borrowing money signs a short-term note and receives the amount of the loan in cash or credit, to be repaid at an agreed-upon rate of interest over a predetermined period. The process is much the same for a school board needing capital-outlay funds. The board, after receiving formal approval from the school patrons (required in nearly all states), issues and sells bonds to one or more competing companies on the basis of the lowest bid for interest rates. Typically the principal and interest on these bonds are to be paid according to an agreed-upon plan, usually over a 10-, 20-, or 30-year period.

There are several ways to classify bonds: according to the agency (municipality or state) issuing them, the degree of security protecting bondholders, or the procedure to be used in paying them. The most common way of classifying them is by the method used to pay or retire the bond principal. Under this classification, there are two main types: serial bonds and straight-term bonds.

Serial Bonds

The advantages offered by the serial type of bonding are such that its use is required in most of the states. This kind of bond provides for payment of accrued interest each year and also for retirement of part of the principal each year on an amortized basis. This reduces the total interest cost, since interest is charged only on the unpaid balance of the principal. It also affords an extension of further bonding capacity as the amounts on the principal are paid. It is not necessary under this type of bonding to amass large surpluses or sums of money in a sinking fund in anticipation of bond maturity at a later date. Taxes can be held to the total amount required to pay the predetermined costs of debt retirement each year. Such a plan is inflexible and may cause problems in periods of unanticipated decline or reduction in yearly tax receipts for such purposes.

Straight-Term Bonds

Straight-term bonds are those that mature at the end of the bonding period; they have very little real value to a school district. Although they are said to have been important and useful in financing capital outlays in years past, their history has been one of mismanagement and poor planning. Hence, they are not used extensively today. There is little to be gained by a district's delaying retirement of a debt until the end of the bonding period. The arguments were forcefully stated by *The Bond Buyer:* "The debt retirement plan should provide for: (1) the retirement of principal at least as rapidly as the capital assets acquired while the proceeds depreciate; (2) declining debt service on existing debt, otherwise the almost inevitable sale of emergency or unanticipated issues will result in debt service having a decidedly upward bias; (3) a maturity schedule that does not add undue rigidity to the budget."[27]

A variation of the straight-term bond saw the development of legal requirements for establishing and maintaining "sinking funds" for the payment of bonded indebtedness. These requirements called for the proceeds of debt retirement tax levies to be placed in a specific fund for payment of the bond principal at maturity. The usually anticipated problems of administering reserve funds—proper and safe investment, protection against mismanagement, and avoidance of making loans or transfers to other accounts—have continued in the administration of this kind of bond.

Callable Bonds

Bond amortization plans are usually rigid and prevent adjustment over the period of their retirement. Bonds that are sold during a period of high interest rates may thereby become a heavy burden if interest rates drop appreciably during the life of the bond issue. For that reason, "callable" or "refundable" options are available to the school district at the time of the original issue of the bonds. These provide for premature payment of the debt, with reissue of the bonds at a more favorable rate of interest. Since this feature protects only the school district from falling interest rates (with no protection to the bonding company for increasing rates), the cost of such an option makes callable bonds a little more expensive than ordinary serial or straight-term bonds.

Registered Bonds

Registered bonds, as the name implies, require that all payments be made solely to the registered owners on record. Historically, school districts used bearer or coupon bonds rather than registered bonds because of the lack of need to keep meticulous records, negotiability, and easy transferability of ownership. That option no longer exists.

Now, bonds sold must be registered, a result of the Tax Equity and Fiscal Responsibilities Act (TEFRA). Sponsors of the law believed that owners of bearer bonds were not paying their fair share of taxes. With bearer bonds, no list of owners is kept. Interest is paid to the owner by taking the bond coupon from a booklet and presenting it for payment. To transfer ownership, a person merely gives the bond to another. Because no one can positively identify the bearer, one could avoid paying taxes. A person could use bearer bonds as gifts and not have to report the transfer. The IRS believed that in excess of $100 million of unreported income was the result. The act has not gone unnoticed in the courts. South Carolina filed suit, and the National Governor's Association joined, but the Supreme Court upheld TEFRA.

Institutions that issue bonds in registered form must keep records of the owners' names, addresses, and social security numbers. Interest paid and ownership transfers must be recorded, which means increased costs for maintaining records.

Bonding Rates

It is important for school districts to establish and maintain a good bond rating, which results in lower interest when bonds are sold. Bonds range from a high rating of AAA, to a low rating of a junk bond. Some of the other categories are Aaa, B, b, C, and c. These ratings reflect the fiscal condition of the district and are determined by the amount of debt, record of debt payment, and the correlation between assessed value within the district and the amount of debt. Local districts must not only rely on their own pecuniary management procedures, but ratings are influenced by the financial condition of the city or county in which they are located.

Some states are now allowing local districts to utilize the state's rating and guaranteeing that obligations will be met. A state with a strong financial profile may have a AAA rating, whereas the district may have an underlying A1 position. This provides a stronger base for districts, making bonds easier to market and resulting in lower interest payments.

The ratings are established and compiled by a variety of agencies. Personnel in a district should support actions that maintain high bond ratings.

Bond Sales

Bonds are sold through competitive bidding. Interest rates are determined by the economic conditions at the time the bonds are sold, the extent and degree of competition in the market, the bond rating, and the length of the term for which they are issued. School bonds are attractive investments because of their exemption from federal and state income taxes.

Bonding Power

Bonding is not an implied power that school districts may use at their discretion and convenience; it must be expressed in the body of state law. The legislature has full power to determine the conditions required for bonding and the limits of bond issues available to each district. Likewise, it has plenary power to determine the qualifications of voters, how the bonds are to be sold, and any other pertinent conditions surrounding the transaction. However, the statutory conditions concerning bonding are often directory rather than mandatory, and courts usually support bond business where substantial compliance with the law has existed. Strict compliance is expected, but the intent of the statutes is to determine the will of the voters. Consequently, the legality of bond elections and sales is usually determined by whether the procedures have achieved what the people actually wanted.

Bond Attorney

The increasing complexity of state requirements for bonding and the increasing legal and financial problems facing the school administrator make it almost mandatory for school districts to employ a bond attorney when a bond issue is contemplated. The attorney's experience and training provide the school board and superintendent with advice and legal information necessary to complete this important aspect of financing the construction of school facilities. Services include securing legally accepted affirmation of bonding by the voters and arranging proper and advantageous sale of bonds to the best interest of the school district.

Bonds Are Debentures

School district bonds are debentures acknowledging a debt that the school district owes to the bondholder; they do not have collateral backing or ordinary mortgage rights, however. They are not mortgages in the typical sense of the word, for they do not permit bondholders to foreclose and take over the physical assets of a district in the event of default in payment. The various lawmaking bodies and the courts, while recognizing that taking possession of school property by an unpaid bondholder would be against the interest of the people in general, protect the bondholders by requiring that certain tax funds be earmarked and set aside in special funds or accounts for bond redemption.

Amortization Schedules

The selection of the best schedule for a district to retire a bond issue depends on whether additional bonds will be involved before the issue in question is repaid. It requires no particular skill to amortize one issue over a period of years, keeping total interest and principal payments (and consequently tax levies) at a nearly constant figure. The problem is rather complicated, however, in districts that require frequent bond issues of varying amounts and with varying interest rates.

Long-range planning in school districts involves anticipation of school construction and bonding for several years ahead. Although there is no mathematical or exact rule for amortizing bond issues, a few practical guidelines may help the school administrator plan when frequent issues are expected:

1. The bond principal should be retired in an orderly fashion as soon as possible, in order to reduce bond interest cost and to increase future debt capacity.
2. Bond levies should ordinarily be kept somewhat constant, with the highest levy being set at the time of voter approval and with legal reserves being kept reasonably high. (Taxpayers often resent frequent increases in tax rates, particularly when they come as a result of poor planning or lack of foresight by the school board.)
3. Promises made by school personnel concerning bond-redemption tax levies should be made only on the basis of careful long-range planning. Such promises should be kept.
4. Surplus sums of money held in anticipation of bond payments should be invested within the restrictions of state law.
5. Bonds should be refunded whenever it is to the financial interest of the district to do so.
6. School boards should utilize consultant help from finance authorities in planning long-range bonding programs.
7. Bond and debt service levies should not be so high that taxpayer resistance forces a reduction of the levy for current expenditures.
8. The people should be kept informed concerning the long-range construction and bonding plans of the school district.

9. Indices of amortization can often be used to advantage in preparing complex amortization schedules.

10. So far as possible, bond payment schedules should anticipate future school facts and figures that affect fiscal matters. Changes in projected school population, expected fluctuations in property assessment values, economic trends, and changes foreseen in the policies of the community and state toward indebtedness and future educational needs are a few of the most important matters to consider.

Refunding Bonds

Lower interest rates and the need for additional capital outlays have motivated some districts to refund outstanding bonds. The concept is similar to an individual borrowing money to consolidate debts, paying off existing obligations, extending the months (or years) of payments, and making only one payment to a single lending source. The advantages of refunding or refinancing are (1) interest rates are generally lower; (2) obligations are consolidated, and there is only one expiration date; and (3) a lower payment frees capital for other needed projects. Disadvantages include (1) the public does not have the opportunity to vote on the measure, except in board meeting hearings; (2) the obligation is spread over a longer period of time; and (3) total interest throughout the full transaction may be greater.

Table 11.1 shows a cash flow analysis for a school district after refunding bonds of $5,920,000. The goal was to lower debt-service payments and collect revenue toward future capital costs. Outlined in the table are the principal and interest due yearly, a comparison with the prior issues, and the savings accrued from refinancing over the 10-year period. Needless to say, when school administrators and boards of education refund bonds, much analysis of the fiscal position of the district is needed. As with the issuance of other bonds, the costs are a factor. For example, in this particular district, the charges for the services not shown in the table amount to $72,615. These expenses include attorney fees, bank fees, and sales costs, which result in actual savings of $384,362.50. Following is a summary of the costs and savings resulting in the refunding bond issue for district XYZ.

Old debt obligation	$8,002,012.50
New bond issue	$5,920,000.00
Interest payment	$1,615,212.50
Total new issue	$7,535,212.50
New issue savings	$ 466,800.00
Expenses (not shown)	$ 72,615.00
Actual reissue savings	$ 384,362.50

Salmon and Wilkerson emphasized another caution dealing with refunding:

Advance refunding of municipal bonds by school districts is legally permissible in many states and would be a desirable policy option for all states. The Internal Revenue Service

TABLE 11.1   Refunding Bond Issue

The Board of Education of XYZ School District

$5,920,000 General Obligation Refunding Bonds

Series 2006

Gross Debt Service Comparison

Date	Principal	Coupon	Interest	New D/S	OLD D/S	Savings	Fiscal Total
12/15/2006	—	—	—	—	—	—	—
06/15/2007	—	—	128,925.00	128,925.00	177,515.00	48,590.00	48,590.00
12/15/2007	—	—	128,925.00	128,925.00	177,515.00	48,590.00	—
06/15/2008	50,000.00	4.000%	128,925.00	178,925.00	177,515.00	(1,410.00)	47,180.00
12/15/2008	—	—	127,925.00	127,925.00	177,515.00	49,590.00	—
06/15/2009	630,000.00	4.000%	127,925.00	757,925.00	757,515.00	(410.00)	49,180.00
12/15/2009	—	—	115,325.00	115,325.00	160,115.00	44,790.00	—
06/15/2010	660,000.00	4.250%	115,325.00	775,325.00	775,115.00	(210.00)	44,580.00
12/15/2010	—	—	101,300.00	101,300.00	141,511.25	40,211.25	—
06/15/2011	685,000.00	4.250%	101,300.00	786,300.00	791,511.25	5,211.25	45,422.50
12/15/2011	—	—	86,743.75	86,743.75	121,686.25	34,942.50	—
06/15/2012	715,000.00	4.250%	86,743.75	801,743.75	811,686.25	9,942.50	44,885.00
12/15/2012	—	—	71,550.00	71,550.00	100,468.75	28,918.75	—
06/15/2013	740,000.00	4.500%	71,550.00	811,550.00	830,468.75	18,918.75	47,837.50
12/15/2013	—	—	54,900.00	54,900.00	77,656.25	22,756.25	—
06/15/2014	780,000.00	4.500%	54,900.00	834,900.00	857,656.25	22,756.25	45,512.50
12/15/2014	—	—	37,350.00	37,350.00	53,281.25	15,931.25	—
06/15/2015	810,000.00	4.500%	37,350.00	847,350.00	878,281.25	30,931.25	46,862.50
12/15/2015	—	—	19,125.00	19,125.00	27,500.00	8,375.00	—
06/15/2016	850,000.00	4.500%	19,125.00	869,125.00	907,500.00	38,375.00	46,750.00
Total	**$5,920,000.00**	—	**$1,615,212.50**	**$7,535,212.50**	**$8,002,012.50**	**$466,800.00**	—

Source: Zions Bank, Public Finance, Salt Lake City, UT. Reprinted by permission.

(IRS) has promulgated a series of regulations that provide the framework for such refunding (Code of Federal Regulations). The primary intent of the IRS regulations is to deny unreasonable profits to the underwriters and to prohibit issuance of tax-exempt securities by governmental units that invest the proceeds in materially higher yield, taxable securities. If the IRS regulations are not followed properly, such municipal bonds might be classified as "arbitrage bonds" and the school district could lose its tax-exempt status (United States Code Service 1983).[28]

Bonding Authorities

The tightening of budgets and tax-limiting legislation has made it necessary for states and local districts to seek creative ways to finance new facilities and to make better utilization of existing buildings. Some states are broadening the concept of bonding authorities and bond banks to provide some flexible alternatives in solving capital-outlay problems. Camp and Salmon described the concept in this way:

> The bonding authority concept, first developed at the turn of the century to circumvent constitutional debt limitations, and the bond bank concept, introduced in the early 1960s to consolidate the issues of subordinate political entities under the auspices of a state corporation issue, have evolved in many cases as effective and efficient methods of assisting local education agencies in financing school facility construction and other capital improvement programs. A series of these public corporations has developed in varying forms in over one-third of the states by entering into lease-purchase agreements with or purchasing bonds of local education agencies, thus supplying badly needed funds for the construction and improvement of local school buildings.[29]

Camp and Salmon list the following as characteristics of a public bonding corporation:

1. It acts as an alternative financing vehicle that provides credit assistance to local governments and acts as an intermediary between the investment market and the local government. It is an autonomous governmental corporation that issues its own bonds for the purpose of constructing public elementary and secondary school buildings. It does not enter into the assessment of need or initial evaluations surrounding the determination of physical characteristics of the buildings, and it does not participate in the actual operation of the facilities following construction. It acts primarily in a financing capacity.

2. It operates as a "quasi-business" organization with strong exclusion-principal and/or private-good characteristics. In general, it operates without yearly state appropriations, even though it can use certain state accounts as a reserve to secure better bond ratings. In addition to its other services as a financial intermediary, it is empowered to accept certain state grants, helping to defer a portion of the costs to local districts.

3. It has the power to incur debt and to issue bonds that are not considered a debt of the state, but it cannot tax except in special emergency conditions. The proceeds of the issue are used to purchase bonds and other evidences of indebtedness, including leases for the purpose of school construction. Receipts from rents, fees, or bonds are used to secure and service bonded indebtedness.

4. It purchases revenue or general obligation bonds from or enters into leases with the local school governing units, and issues revenue bonds and/or general or moral obligation bonds.

5. It assists local units with marketing debt issues and often creates a market of size for the debt of small local education agencies.[30]

A typical building authority project is established by a state statute that allows municipal bonds to be sold for planning and building schools. "The building authority leases the school facilities to the school system at a cost that covers the principal and interest on the bonds and the cost of the building authority operation. Provision is usually made for the facilities to become the property of the school system upon the retirement of the bonds, and attendant costs."[31] The debt is considered a short-term obligation and provides some additional risks for those who purchase the bonds, which often results in a higher interest rate. The district benefits by being able to provide facilities to meet present needs and by not requiring a bond election.

States providing local districts the opportunity to use certain state accounts as a reserve to secure better bond ratings is gaining more support. The concept allows local districts to issue bonds with the state ensuring that the bonds will be paid in full and within the time limit specified. With such support, bonding agencies are able to increase ratings and usually provide much better interest rates to local districts. The state, through its capacity to control financial resources to districts, provides a service that is virtually cost free.

Impact Fees

Local governments have utilized impact fees and special assessments to cover the costs of certain infrastructure projects for a number of years. Recently, some school districts have moved to require that purchasers of homes in newly developed areas be assessed such a fee to cover costs of a new school in the impacted area. The rationale for assessing an impact fee is that it would reduce the financial burden of current residents who may otherwise share the cost of additional facilities through higher taxes.

Politically, this approach becomes popular with current residents. On the other hand, those who are assessed the impact fee argue that such a fee is unfair because it requires them to make double payments—one for the initial fee and one through property taxes used to retire public debt for existing schools.

In some instances, land developers may donate or be requested to provide enough acreage in a subdivision to accommodate a new school. Although having a school within a neighborhood is a plus in selling homes, the cost for donated property may, in actuality, be a hidden cost for home buyers that could be equivalent to an impact fee.

The legality of impact fees, per se, has been challenged in the courts on the basis of violating due process and equal protection, and is held to constitute taking of private property without just compensation. In education finance, the question may be asked: Is it equitable to charge a local impact fee when it is a state responsibility to equalize capital outlay as well as maintenance and operation? This and other legal issues may be raised as more and more financially strapped local school districts look at impact fees as a way to assist in providing much needed facilities.

Other Alternatives

An option certain districts are using and some states are encouraging is the fuller utilization of buildings through the adoption of a year-round schedule. Students attend the prescribed number of days of school, but they are spread throughout the year in various combinations (e.g., 45 days in school, 15 days out). Theoretically, on a four-track system, one-third more students can attend the school, saving the costs of a new building for every four schools on the plan. Proponents of the year-round schedule point out that other savings accrue in the maintenance and operation area.

Earthman discussed other options for meeting facility needs and freeing capital outlays. He suggested (1) selling or exchanging existing school facilities or property, (2) entering into lease agreements, (3) leasing air rights over a school site, and (4) cooperating with other agencies in sharing facilities. He summarized:

> None of these alternatives are complete solutions to the crunch that school systems feel for housing students and none of the alternatives are even new ideas to most educational administrators, but the identified alternatives might be means that can be used in combination to help meet a need. Because of unstable demographic conditions and subsequent change in program demand, the schools may need to more fully explore the use of these alternatives than previously.[32]

Summary

Historically, providing funds for school construction has developed slowly at the state level. Although most states presently offer assistance to local districts, in the main, the major revenue has come from local property taxes. This has brought actions in the courts in several states, including New Jersey, Texas, West Virginia, Idaho, Alaska, Ohio, and a major case in New York. The suits are based on both adequacy and equity, and have influenced most states in the nation to consider their funding for capital projects in relation to their state constitutions. The emphasis has caused them to focus on analyzing the needs in the state, prioritizing projects, and determining methods to fund them. Federal involvement has been minimal in providing funds for building projects and capital needs, with the position that it is a state and local district responsibility. Funds were provided to some states as relief from the devastation of Hurricanes Katrina and Rita. None was specifically earmarked for capital improvement projects.

One of the major factors that has restrained many districts from needed construction has been the low assessment value of their taxable property. Largely because of such low assessment values, most school construction has been financed by some form of bonding. Pay-as-you-go financing, a building reserve plan (where legal), and bonding have advantages as well as disadvantages as methods of financing capital outlays. Less used but feasible approaches for acquiring needed revenues include bonding authorities, refunding bonds, switching to year-round operations, and impact fees.

The bonding process is fairly complicated and results in a major expenditure. School districts that handle construction in this way should use the services of a bonding attorney. Bonding rates are an important factor to consider for those districts that need to sell bonds for capital-outlay needs. Ratings reflect the fiscal condition of the district and influence the interest that would be required on the bonds. Some states are allowing local districts to utilize their better rates, which make bonds more marketable and result in lower interest payments.

Providing school facilities is a responsibility of the state. Property taxes should not bear the entire cost of financing school facilities. Increasing the amount the state pays for financing such facilities, of course, puts the burden of taxes on forms of wealth other than real property. As with the maintenance and operations equalization formulas, equity for taxpayers statewide needs to be a consideration.

ASSIGNMENT PROJECTS

1. Provide a definition for each of the following terms: *capital-outlay, expenditures, pay-as-you-go financing, building reserve fund, bonding, serial bonds, straight-term bonds, callable bonds, registered bonds, debentures, amortization, refunding bonds, bonding authorities, impact fees.*

2. Some districts in the United States are faced with the problem of eliminating buildings at the same time that others are in dire need of building additional ones. Determine the type of school-building problem in the city or county in which you live and what methods are being used by the school boards to solve their building problems.

3. Summarize the arguments for and against local school districts being required to finance their own school construction, regardless of their taxable wealth.

4. Outline a plan for greater state financial support for the construction of local school district buildings.

5. A few states now provide most of the funds for new school construction. Find out what kinds of problems accompany such an arrangement and the methods used to overcome these problems.

6. Determine what criteria a state should use to equalize capital-outlay expenditures in districts. How should it be decided where new buildings are to be built? When buildings are needed? What kinds of capital equipment should be provided? When capital equipment should be replaced? When school districts are "equal" in terms of capital expenditures?

7. Year-round schools, extended days, and double shifts are methods of utilizing school buildings more fully. Discuss the pros and cons of each plan.

8. Several buildings in your district were built over 50 years ago and are now outdated and crowded. Citizens in your district say that when they were students, these buildings were adequate, so why should they have to pay for new buildings? What approaches would you take to convince the voters that new buildings are needed?

Computer simulations and questions, research exercises, and website
addresses relevant to this chapter can be found at

www.ablongman.com/edleadership

SELECTED READINGS

Campbell, Roald F., Luvern L. Cunningham, Raphael O. Nystrand, and Michael D. Usdan. *The Organization and Control of American Schools,* 6th ed. Columbus, OH: Merrill, 1990.

Codification of Governmental Accounting and Financial Reporting Standards. Stanford, CT: Governmental Accounting Standards Board and Government Accounting Research Foundation of the Government Finance Officers Association, 2003.

Earthman, Glen I. *Planning Educational Facilities for the Next Century.* Reston, VA: ASBO, 1992.

Graves, Ben. *School Ways: The Planning and Design of America's Schools.* New York: McGraw-Hill, 1993.

Guide for Planning Educational Facilities. Columbus, OH: Council of Educational Facility Planners, International, 1985.

Kozol, Jonathan. *Savage Inequalities.* New York: Harper Perennial, 1991.

Odden, Allen R., and Lawrence O. Picus. *School Finance: A Policy Perspective,* 2nd ed. New York: McGraw-Hill, 2000.

Ray, John R., Walter G. Hack, and I. Carl Candoli. *School Business Administration: A Planning Approach,* 7th ed. Boston: Allyn and Bacon, 2001.

Sergiovanni, Thomas J., et al. *Educational Governance and Administration,* 4th ed. Boston: Allyn and Bacon, 1999.

Sarason, Seymour B. *Political Leadership and Educational Failure.* San Francisco: Jossey-Bass, 1998.

Theobald, Neil D., and Betty Malen, eds. *Balancing Local Control and State Responsibility for K–12 Education.* Larchmont, NY: Eye on Education, 2000.

Thompson, David, C., and R. C. Wood. *Money and Schools,* 2nd ed. Larchmont, NY: Eye on Education, 2001.

ENDNOTES

1. Walter G. Hack, "School District Bond Issues: Implications for Reform in Financing Capital Outlay," *Journal Education Finance,* Fall 1976, p. 156.

2. David C. Thompson, William E. Camp, Jerry C. Horn, and G. Kent Steward, *State Involvement in Capital Outlay Financing: Policy Implications for the Future* (Manhattan, KA: Center of Extended Services and Studies, Kansas State University, 1991), p. 4.

3. W. Monfort Barr and W. R. Wilkerson, "State Participation in Financing Local School Facilities," in *Trends in Financing Public Education* (Washington, DC: National Education Association, 1965), p. 225.

4. W. Monfort Barr and R. J. Garvue, "Financing Public School Capital Outlays," in *The Theory and Practice School Finance* (Chicago: Rand McNally, 1967), pp. 276–277.

5. David S. Honeyman, "School Facilities and State Mechanisms That Support School Construction: A Report from the Fifty States," *Journal of Education Finance,* Fall 1990, p. 248.

6. *Pauley* v. *Bailey,* 324 S.E. 2d 128 (W. Va. 1984).

7. Personal Conversation and e-mail from Dr. Clacy E. Williams, Executive Director, School Building Authority of West Virginia, June 2006.

8. *Robinson* v. *Cahill,* 303 A. 2d 273 (N.J. 1990).

9. *Abbott* v. *Burke (Abbott),* 575 A. 2d 359 (N.J. 2002).

10. Fred G. Burke, Commissioner of Education. Case brought to the New Jersey Supreme Court by the State Attorney General. Ruled July 23, 2003.

11. *DeRolph* v. *State* (2001), 93 Ohio St. 3d 309, May 2003.
12. Ibid.
13. Ibid.
14. Darcia Harris Bowman, "Arizona Leaders Urge Tax Hike for Education," *Education Week,* April 5, 2000, pp. 19, 22.
15. Catherine Gervertz, "New Mexico Retools Facilities Plan Overturned by Judge," *Education Week,* April 19, 2000, p. 33.
16. Nelly Ward, "New Mexico Plaintiffs Claim State Is Backtracking on Capital Funding," *Access,* May 11, 2006, pp. 1–2.
17. *ISEEO* v. *State,* 976 p. 2d 913 (Idaho, 1998).
18. District Court of the Fourth Judicial District of the State of Idaho, in and for the County of ADA, case no. 94008, October 27, 2003.
19. Molly A. Hunter, "Colorado," *Access,* Teachers College, Columbia University, April 10, 2006.
20. Molly A. Hunter, "Alaska," *Access,* Teachers College, Columbia University, September 16, 2005.
21. *State of Wyoming* v. *Campbell County Schools,* Legisweb.state.wy.us, February 23, 2001, reviewed June 2006.
22. Ibid.
23. *Campaign for Fiscal Equity, Inc., et al, Plaintiffs-Respondents* v. *The State of New York, et al.,* 2006 NY Slip Op 02284, decided March 23, 2006.
24. www.smartvoter.org/11/07/ca/state/prop.
25. "Secretary Spellings, Gulf Coast Rebuilding Coordinator Powell Announce $1.1 Billion for Hurricane-Affecteed Students and Schools," U.S. Department of Education, www.ed.gov/news/pressreleases/2006/03/03022006.
26. Jim Mould, Information Resource Specialist, U.S. Department of Education, by e-mail, July 24, 2003. (See also www.ed.gov/inits/hope/taxact.html.)
27. "Preparing a Bond Offering," *The Bond Buyer,* 1962, p. 9.
28. Richard Salmon and William Wilkerson, "Financing Public School Facilities," in *Managing Limit Resources: New Demands on Public School Management. Fifth Annual Yearbook of the American Education Finance Association,* ed. L. Dean Webb and Van D. Mueller (Cambridge, MA: Ballinger, 1984), p. 123.
29. William E. Camp and Richard G. Salmon, "Public School Bonding Corporations Financing Public Elementary and Secondary School Facilities," *Journal of Education Finance,* Spring 1985, p. 495.
30. Ibid., pp. 496–497.
31. Walter G. Hack, I. Carl Candoli, and John R. Ray, *School Business Administration: A Planning Approach,* 7th ed. (Boston: Allyn and Bacon, 2001), p. 279.
32. Glen I. Earthman, "Problems and Alternatives in Housing Students: What a School Business Administrator Should Know," *Journal of Education Finance,* Fall 1984, p. 171.

12 Administering the School Budget

Because they are responsible for the use and the preservation of financial and human resources, it should be an imperative of every successful educational executive to strategically plan and utilize well the budgeting process.

—Brent Pulsipher, 2007

The innovations that are currently receiving emphasis in curricular and administrative aspects of education have their counterparts in school finance theories and practices, including budgeting and accounting. Present budgetary practices are the result of a long evolutionary development, which has recently been accelerating rather than stabilizing or decelerating. The traditional principles and practices of budgeting, which seemed to be well established and proven, are now being supplanted or supplemented by more sophisticated systems of interpreting the educational program of the school.

Evolution of Budgetary Practices

Historians report that budgetary practices originated in and received their greatest early development in England. The British government was using budgeting procedures two centuries before their use by the U.S. government and was practicing full-fledged budgeting by 1822. As developed in England, budgeting involved budget preparation by the executive branch of government, approval of the budget by the legislative branch (with amendments when deemed necessary or appropriate), authorization of tax levies by the legislative branch to meet the expected expenditures, and administration by the executive branch. Johns and Morphet noted the importance of these developments in budgetary theory: "This may seem like a very simple and natural arrangement. But it took hundreds of years for the people to wrest from ruling monarchs the authority to levy taxes and to determine governmental expenditures. . . . The budget is not just a document containing a list of receipts and expenditures but it is a process by which the people in a democracy exercise their constitutional right to govern themselves."[1]

Budgeting Developed Slowly in America

In the early history of this country, the presence of seemingly boundless wealth thwarted the development of sound budgetary practices in government. Petty jealousies between members of Congress and the executive branch also contributed in large measure to the slow metamorphosis of budgeting practices. The first law providing for a national budget was passed in 1921; it set the pattern for the present budgetary procedures of the federal government.[2]

Budgetary practices became common in business and industry before local boards of education accepted them generally. Until the end of the first quarter of the twentieth century, public school budgetary practices were unrefined and not standardized to any appreciable degree. As in the case of many other innovative practices, urban school systems developed budgetary patterns and routines before rural schools did. Gradually, the various states enacted laws that established guidelines and specifics required of all districts in the receiving and disbursing of school funds. The extent of these requirements and the degree of detail of accounting have increased until such practices have become relatively standardized for similar kinds of districts within each state.

The Budget

Because everyone uses the word *budget* in government, business, industry, education, and even the home, it is presumed to be commonly understood. Technically, however, *budget* may mean different things to different people. Certainly, the purposes for which budgets are prepared and the degree of adherence to budgetary detail and administration vary considerably among the people and agencies that use them. In a desire for more uniformity in the education community, the National Center for Education Statistics (NCES) developed a handbook, *Financial Accounting for State and Local School Systems*. Its initial publication was in 1980 with a modest update in 1990. The handbook represents a national set of standards and guidance for school systems with the most recent update published in 2003.[3]

Definition

A *budget* is a financial plan that involves at least four elements: (1) planning, (2) receiving funds, (3) spending funds, and (4) evaluating results—all performed within the limits of a predetermined time. Thus, budgeting is defining priorities and needs, and receiving and spending funds over a particular period, usually a year for school districts. The evaluative aspects cover examining previous budgets in order to build better budgets for succeeding periods.

Roe defined the educational budget "as the translation of educational needs into a financial plan which is interpreted to the public in such a way that when formally adopted it expresses the kind of educational program the community is willing to support, financially and morally, for a one-year period."[4] Translating those needs into a budget can follow the pattern of (1) identifying needs, (2) establishing goals, (3) organizing

FIGURE 12.1 Steps for Developing a Financial Plan

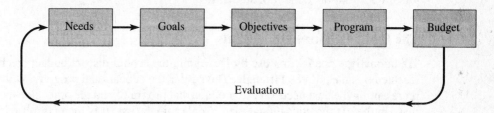

objectives, (4) building a program in meeting those objectives, and (5) providing a budget to fund those programs (see Figure 12.1).

Few people question the importance of budgeting in the public schools, the branches of government, business, industry, or any activity that involves receiving and expending large sums of money. Its importance in school districts increases as its function develops from purely mechanical and mathematical accounting to appraisal and translation of the educational program into meaningful terms. In the words of Ray and associates, some of the benefits of budgeting are:

1. It requires a plan of action for the future.
2. It requires an appraisal of past activities in relation to planned activities.
3. It necessitates the formulation of work plans.
4. It necessitates expenditures and estimating revenues.
5. It mandates orderly planning and coordination throughout the organization.
6. It establishes a system of management controls.
7. It serves as a public information system.[5]

Purposes of Budgetary Practices

The school district budget serves a number of important functions:

1. It projects the proposed school program and educational plan of the district for the next fiscal period.
2. It shows the sources of funds, anticipated expenditures, and allocation of authority for administering budgetary items.
3. It serves to inform the public about the educational program of the school.
4. It provides a guide for evaluating a year's program and a means of comparing school services with those that have been offered in other years.
5. It provides the motivation for careful planning, for establishing systems of control, and for wise and effective expenditure of funds.
6. It points out the relationship of the state, federal, and local units of government in supporting education.

Budgetary administration varies with state laws and with administrative interpretation. To some, it may be the master to be followed with strictness and complete propriety. To others, it is a guide that need not be followed blindly; its structure must not take precedence over the effects on the educational program that school administrators propose for the benefit of students.

The Budget's Three Dimensions

Traditionally, since its first use by De Young, the school district budget has been represented by an equilateral triangle: The base is the educational program, with one side representing the cost necessary to produce that program, and the other side the revenue plan. In theory, the educational plan is determined first. It is then converted into cost terms, and finally the determination of the sources of required revenues is made. The rationale for such a sequence is that educational programs are to be planned for the peculiar needs of the pupils, without letting the available funds be the master or limiting factor in determining the bounds of the educational program.

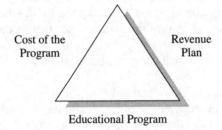

Cost of the Program   Revenue Plan

Educational Program

In the past, affluent school districts were able to follow sound principles and accepted procedures in preparing the budget. Where revenue limitations were not too severe, the process worked well. In districts with restricted revenue, budget building was often reversed in sequence of preparation; the revenue was determined and then school officials decided what kinds of programs and services could be purchased for the amount of the expected revenue. This procedure often resulted in selection of programs and services that were inexpensive rather than those that responded to the real needs of the pupils. Such planners resemble the prospective consumer who, in the restaurant or the variety store, reads the menu or price list from right to left. He or she may purchase goods or services that do not meet his or her dietary or other needs simply because they are less expensive than those that would be appropriate.

Determining the Educational Program

The educational program is directly related to the purposes and objectives of the school. Unfortunately, the aims and objectives of educational institutions are not always clear or well defined. This makes determination of programs and services very difficult. The superintendent is faced with a myriad of questions. What services of the school should be increased next year? Should the school provide more guidance services, or should it put more emphasis on equipping teachers with better facilities and instructional media? Should more emphasis be placed on expensive programs such as driver education, or should the social science offerings be increased? Are funds available to meet required testing and other state and federal requirements? Has the district included revenue for pension funds, benefits, and requirements of the Governmental Accounting Standards Board? Should the school provide for kindergartens and early school admission programs? To what extent should pupils participate in paying the costs of education with incidental fees and charges? These and countless other questions must be answered in preparing the proposed educational program to be sponsored by each school district.

The superintendent, regardless of the complexity of school problems, must work with the staff, the school board, and the parents in the community to determine the proposed educational objectives and programs for the subsequent fiscal year and for several years ahead. Superintendents who suggest to their boards of education that, since there is a potential increase of 5 percent in school revenue, each area of the budget will automatically be increased by that amount are making at least three errors. (1) They are presuming that the previous budget was perfect and that since costs have increased, each part of the budget must therefore be increased by the same amount. (2) They are ignoring the need for evaluating the past year's budget and examining and resolving such imbalances as it may have had. (3) They are denying those with an interest in the school—teachers, staff members, school board members, pupils, and the general public—their right and responsibility of continuous evaluation of the public school program.

Superintendents working with boards of education are responsible for involving people in determining educational policies and objectives. They should use all their public relations know-how to get committees or representatives of the PTA, the press, radio, television, and other parent groups to participate in such policy making. Final decisions regarding proposed program changes and innovations must rest with the board of education, acting on the advice and recommendations of the superintendent and his or her staff.

Preparing the Budget Document

For budgetary purposes, the educational plan is valueless until converted into dollar costs. Under the direction of the superintendent, those who will be responsible for specific parts of the educational plan determine the needs of these programs. Sound budgeting theory dictates that teachers and other school personnel should be given forms and figures indicating budget allotments and expenditures for one or more past years, with blanks for estimates of next year's needs. As years pass, the budget histories that are established become useful in providing fiscal information for succeeding years.

With increasing frequency, districts are using another aspect of budget building by school personnel. In addition to having teachers and others suggest what they *need* for the following year, many progressive districts ask teachers also to submit requests for those supplies and facilities required for an optimum or superior program, or even for an alternative program. The administration is, in effect, asking school personnel to indicate their *wants* or *desires* that, if granted, would provide the best possible program that each individual can envision at that moment. Teachers who in past years may not have received the supplies and equipment they requested may not be too anxious to make the extra effort to determine what they could use effectively, if such were to be available. However, regardless of the final disposition of the individual's requests according to needs or desires, it is a worthwhile experience in itself for each school employee to suggest how much money should be allocated and for what it should be spent to provide the best possible educational program. Such a problem as determining the kind and frequency of use of instructional media under an ideal budget arrangement will cause the teacher to evaluate carefully the many alternatives available in the teaching process. Besides, there is always the possibility that the requested optimum program may be accepted and implemented in the final budget document.

Unfortunately, the extent of involvement of teachers and other staff members in determining the educational program and allocating resources to attain the school's objectives is minimal in practice. For various reasons, many school administrators use the previous year's budget as the sole basis for the budget for the next year. In this way, inequities and imbalances tend to become perpetuated. Some administrators find that district office determination of budget needs is easier, less frustrating, and more acceptable to many teachers and staff members who treat the business of budgeting with apathy or indifference.

> This concept views the development of the budget as strictly a responsibility of management. No staff help is asked for or desired. The central office gives the impression that budgeting is a very complex process, and that only the "chosen few" are sufficiently sophisticated to participate. The prevailing philosophy seems to be that if fewer people know about the budget, there will be less static and fewer questions. Often, value judgments are made without proper evaluation and with no options offered to those affected. This tight-ship approach is symptomatic of authoritarian systems and has hastened the coming of our present era of negotiations, citizen involvement, and student awareness.[6]

In the districts that follow the staff participation method of budgetary preparation, the principal of each of the various attendance areas combines the budget requests of all staff members working under his or her direction, checks them for omissions, duplications, and errors, and then submits them (usually in combined form) to the school district office, where they are summarized and combined into totals for the district. From these reports and from similar requests from district employees, a tentative budget document is prepared.

The tentative budget is presented to the board of education for its study and recommendations for changes. The board is free to make whatever changes it desires within the limits of the statutes governing such practices in the state. The tentative budget is then accepted, summaries are prepared, and the board of education and the superintendent prepare for a budget hearing.

The budget does not stand by itself. It is related to many other records involved in the school district's business affairs, such as salary schedules, insurance policies, and inventories, and is influenced by them. Many of these schedules should accompany the budget document as it is presented to the board for study and adoption. They aid greatly in interpreting the message that the budget conveys. Ovsiew and Castetter made an excellent and inclusive list of materials that should be included in the budget document:

- Letter of transmittal
- Statement of introduction, especially relating to the school philosophy
- Justifications
    Curriculum review, by unit, divisions, and departments
    Audited statements of funds
    Bonding schedule
- Recapitulations of sections of the budget
- Salary schedules
- Statistical summary of salary program, showing experience, training, and classifications
- Enrollment, showing trends and projections
    Numerical adequacy of staff
    Average daily attendance
    Pupil-teacher ratio in instruction
    Per pupil costs by budget categories
    Enrollment by curriculum in the high school
    State-aid provisions, indicating changes
    Insurance in force
    Transportation schedules
    Property tax experience, including relationship to assessments, market values, percent of collection, and millage limits
    Nonproperty tax experience, by type levied and by potential
    Cost experience, by trends in prices of selected items
    Retirement and social security schedules
- Expenditure and revenue items for two to three previous years
    Policy statements mandating expenditures
    Unmet needs report
    Items mandated by new laws or official directives
    Inventory report
    Budget transfers during previous year
    Summary of germane committee reports
    Comparative costs data with selected school district[7]

The Budget Hearing

Superintendents have long since discovered that there is little interest in budget hearings if no effort is made to summarize and interpret the massive lists of figures and minute details of the budget document. In preparing for a hearing, the superintendent must exercise ingenuity in devising an interesting and informative way of presenting the pertinent facts about the budget so that they can be easily understood by lay citizens. The use of audiovisual materials—PowerPoint presentations, videotapes, charts, slides, films, computer models, transparencies, and the like—helps greatly in elucidating the points that are of most interest and concern to school patrons.

Not all states have laws that require a formal hearing before adoption of the annual school district budget. In those that do, the board and the administrative staff present and explain the tentative budget, listen to the suggestions and criticisms of school patrons, and make any necessary justifications of questioned items or policies. Final approval of the budget usually rests with the school board in fiscally independent districts. In fiscally dependent districts, a city or county board usually must pass on the total budget levy authorized by the school board, relating it to the tentative budgets of other agencies of government under its general jurisdiction. In such districts, the city or county board usually has the power to require a reduction of the budget levy if necessary, but detailed alterations are left to the board of education, within the accepted total levy approved.

General Provisions of the Budget

Budgets should provide for classification of receipts and expenditures in line with the accounting system that the federal, state, and local school district require. The budget should provide for separation of general expenditure funds from bond and debt-service funds. The current-expenditures budget should provide for emergencies by means of a contingency fund. Provision should be made, where possible, for a cash surplus at the beginning of the fiscal period to minimize the need for borrowing money until local tax money or state allocations are received.

School administrators often find it advantageous to provide a comparison of new budget items with similar considerations of the past year or two. There is much to be said in favor of a written explanation and justification of some budget items. Unexplained arithmetical figures in the budget may mean little to the uninformed person, who sees them without perspective or rationale. This is particularly true when unusual changes are being made for specific items. Critics of unexplained items or changes often become supporters of them when they understand the reasons behind them.

Some administrators and students of budgetary practice urge the establishment of priorities in the spending plan of the school district. Such priorities can only be established after much study of the relative value of alternative parts of the school program. The practical advantages of this procedure become obvious when revenues are less than expected or when costs exceed expectations.

Administration of the Budget

Once the budget is formally adopted, it becomes effective on the first day of the new fiscal period. The superintendent (by law in some states and by assignment in others) is the executive officer charged with carrying out the programs that the budget authorizes. Unfortunately, some school districts try to differentiate between the strictly educational responsibilities of the superintendent and the fiscal policies, which are supervised by a clerk or business administrator who is responsible directly to the board of education.

The dilemma that such an arrangement creates is antithetical to the purposes of the school. A dual head to a school system, with one administrator in charge of the instructional program and the other guarding the treasury, can work satisfactorily only under ideal conditions, and these seldom exist. The board of education should recognize that the superintendent as its executive officer must be in charge of the entire school operation. The official in charge of the business functions of the school, regardless of title, must be directly responsible to the superintendent. Only with such an arrangement can the board hold the superintendent accountable for the educational program of the school district.

Expending Money

Once the budget is formally adopted, the various line items and amounts are formally entered into the district's accounting system. The new budget then becomes a daily guide for the expenditure of school funds. Work plans and expenditure policies must be established so that the money can be dispensed for the purposes for which it was intended without undue red tape or unnecessary inconvenience. A district administrator or building principal who deems it prudent to *save* money from a fiscal year budget to build up a surplus balance for subsequent years is not being fiscally responsible to students currently enrolled, staff members, taxpayers, or the budgetary process. The purpose of the budget is not to save money; it is to help spend it wisely and expeditiously when needed. All school employees need to know the policies and specific procedures to be followed in carrying out the budgetary plan. It should not be hoped or planned that complicated or time-wasting procedures will discourage proper expenditure of the necessary funds to operate any aspects of the school program that have been approved.

Evaluation of the Budget

No person, least of all the school administrator, expects a perfect budget. He or she knows that careful planning and evaluation may reduce but never completely eliminate the need for making changes in the current budget. The board of education can do this when necessary, operating within the legal requirements of such adjustments. Of course, if the budget is changed at will with impunity, it becomes a meaningless document, of questionable value to the school district.

Superintendents are responsible for seeing that the budget is more than just an accounting system built and administered around a legal requirement to make guesses or estimates about receipts and expenditures. They have the obligation to demonstrate that the budget is a well-conceived monetary summary of the educational plan of the school district for a specific time. They must be able to demonstrate that it is constructed around the specific purposes or objectives of the schools and the plans, services, personnel, and systems to be used in achieving those objectives.

Each succeeding budget should be an improvement over the previous one in terms of utility and effectiveness. It should indicate steady progress toward achieving its main processes and purposes, such as more significant involvement of school personnel and citizens in its preparation, more concerted effort to avoid program imbalance, more conferring and more effective rationale to justify budgetary items, greater effort toward continuous planning, and greater emphasis on program budgeting, with the provision for alternative programs to meet specific objectives.

One of the important lessons school administrators learn is that the budget is the business of all the people in the district, not just the official concern of the superintendent and the school board. This concept has been a long time in receiving wide acceptance. School patrons cannot be expected to support financial claims against them without some degree of understanding of purpose. In reality, budget critics often become budget defenders when they understand the objectives the school is attempting to achieve and the financial limitations under which it operates.

The superintendent is responsible for keeping the board of education and the public informed about the operation and the effectiveness of the budget. He or she usually issues financial reports to the board on a regular basis, showing total expenditures to date, balances in the chief accounts, and anticipated problems in keeping within main budget item limitations. The superintendent determines the extent to which the budget has been effective, what improvements should be made in the next budget, what imbalances have been created between programs that are overfinanced compared with those that are underfinanced, and other necessary subjective and objective evaluations of budget performance. He or she takes special note and reports from time to time to the board concerning the everpresent problems of protecting the school's funds against dishonest, unethical, or careless handling by school personnel. Experience has shown that any precautions or guidelines used to protect public funds, as well as to protect the reputation of the people using them, will be effort well spent.

The Budget Calendar

School administrators realize that maximally effective budget building must be a continuous process. They recognize a need to follow a fairly specific budget preparation calendar. The details to be followed and the actual time to be assigned to budget preparation depend on the size of the school district, the number of employees involved in budget preparation, and the degree of difficulty encountered in obtaining three-sided balance in the budget triangle. Regardless of these factors, however, budget building should start as soon as the current budget is put into operation.

The fiscal year in most school districts starts on July 1. On the day the current year's budget begins, the superintendent starts planning for the next year. The details involved in the preparation of a new budget will not be the same in all districts, since the legal requirements and the number of staff members responsible for budget planning will not always be the same.

The budget calendar should be organized to include certain minimum requirements. Fixed dates, or at least suggested dates, should be predetermined for the completion of certain actions, such as when new program requests should be recommended, when required supplies and instructional materials should be reported, when the initial and tentative budget document will be presented to the board of education, and when and where budget planning and budget hearings will be held. Although the school district must follow whatever budget preparation requirements are written in the state code, other performance dates and deadlines are usually advisory and need not be followed to the letter if it seems in the best interest of the school district to deviate from them. Superintendents make serious mistakes if they procrastinate on budgetary preparation to the point where approaching deadlines interfere with conscientious budget-building practices.

Ray and colleagues outlined a budget calendar, with elements to be considered on a monthly basis throughout the fiscal year:

Month 1	Budget year begins
Month 3	Quarterly revision—to incorporate accurate revenue and enrollment figures (present budget)
Month 4	Population (enrollment) projections Staff needs projections Program changes and additional projections Facilities needs projection
Month 5	Staff requisitions—supplies Capital outlay preliminary requests
Month 6	Budget revisions (present budget) Central staff sessions on needs Maintenance and operations requests
Month 7	Rough draft of needs budget
Month 8	Meet with staffs and principals to establish priorities Citizen committees' reports and reviews Central staff and board of education budget sessions
Month 9	Budget revision (present budget)
Month 10	Working budget draft Meet with staff and community groups to revise working budget
Month 11	Final draft of working budget
Month 12	Budget hearings and adoption of working budget[8]

Although the new budget may begin on a specific date, in most districts, the previous year's budget is not concluded for the business office at that time. Accrued encumbrances as well as final reviews and reporting may extend involvement for several months into the new fiscal year. In essence, the budget process overlaps and includes operation of the current budget, finalizing the previous year's budget, and planning for the following year.

Budgeting at the School Level

At the building level, there is a need to follow sound budgetary and expenditure practices. With the large amount of revenue generated at the school level from athletic receipts, various fees, textbook rentals, bookstore operations, school food funds, field trips, weekly and scholastic readers, apportioned district funds, individual school fund-raisers, and other kinds of funds that flow through individual schools, principals must understand financial information. After all, it is they who are the chief financial officers of schools, with primary responsibility for thousands or, in some cases, millions of dollars. Appropriate handling of such funds must be in compliance with generally accepted accounting principles and federal-, state-, and district-mandated policies and procedures.

In basic terms, the principal must administer the budget by dividing the revenues from the expenditures.

> First, principals need to identify the sources of the funds received at their school. This may sound simpler than it really is. But this identification is important because the source of the funds determines how the funds are to be used and who is able to use them. For example, funds donated by supportive parents may have restrictions attached. Parents may indicate that the donated funds are to be used only for the school band where their child is a participant.
>
> Other restricted funds may include student fees paid by students for specific school programs or activities. These funds should only be used for the purpose for which the fees were collected. Revenues collected for student activities such as dances and athletic events need to be accounted separately so not to be co-mingled with funds from another school program.[9]

It is essential that all funds be recorded and deposited into one school account. Also, all funds should be processed through the principal's office, for it is the principal who carries the responsibility for school funds. Good practice suggests that individually signed prenumbered receipts be given to each person (or activity) who turns over funds to the school account. Thus, there is a record of the transaction at its base source. Deposits should be made daily, if possible, with a small cash drawer to handle change kept. Overnight security is difficult within a school building; it is seldom comparable to that of a banking institution. Copies of deposit slips should be retained by both the depositor and the school bookkeeper for the principal.

A specific notation must be made in the accounting records for every financial transaction that takes place. Most computerized and many manual accounting systems are double entry accounting systems. In such a system, an increase in assets of a fund is noted with a debit entry and a decrease in fund assets is recorded with a credit entry. The difference between increases and decreases in the fund assets affects the fund balance.

The simplest manual school accounting form used to record a financial transaction reflects a single entry system where each activity to be monitored is listed on a separate form. The form contains a single vertical line which divides debits (indicating increases in fund assets) on the left from credits (indicating decreases in fund assets) on the right side of the vertical line. Figure 12.2 illustrates a simple single entry accounting form.

Flexibility is essential on the expenditure side of the ledger. Perhaps the senior class decides to sell a product to acquire money to purchase a gift to the school and they can save considerable cash if they pay as they order. A loan could be made to the class from the resources available, and the loan would be canceled when the sales receipts

FIGURE 12.2   Sample School Activity Balance Sheet: Band Fund

	Receipts (Debits)			Expenditures (Credits)		
Date	*Source*	*Amount*	*Date*	*Payee*	*Amount*	*Balance*
1/3/08	Previous Balance	$700.00				$700.00
			1/5/08	Photo Shop	$67.97	$632.03
			1/9/08	Post Office	$64.00	$568.03
			1/18/08	Post-its	$8.50	$559.53
1/19/08	Contributions for Trip	$75.00				$634.53
			1/20/08	Tour Company	$50.00	$584.53
1/21/08	Ticket Sales	$225.00				$809.53
1/31/08	Candy Sales	$340.00	1/23/08	Booster Buttons	$85.00	$1064.53
			1/24/08	Candy	$300.00	$764.53
						$764.53

are received. Further, idle funds may be invested in safe short-term endeavors such as certificates of deposits or money market accounts.

One inflexible rule for school principals is that student fees and other receipts from current students must be used for the students who have paid them. It is imperative that student fees be expended in the school year in which they are collected. It is simply not fair to charge someone for something and then use the funds for the benefit of someone else. If student fee balances are carried over to the next year, then the fee charged was too much.

In a survey of the 50 states, researchers identified 21 states that used fees for additional revenue, noting in many cases that the fees were used mainly for noncurricular or required programs. Charging fees is regressive in nature, discriminating against low-income families.[10]

Monthly reports should be rendered, showing the opening balance on the first of the month, and receipts and expenditures and the closing balance on the last day of the month (see Figure 12.3 as an example).

The National Center for Education Statistics handbook, using the Governmental Accounting Standards Board's 2003 activity fund guidelines, notes that "activity funds are unique to school districts. Two classifications are commonly recognized as Student activity funds, which belong to the students and are used to support student organizations and clubs and District activity funds, which belong to the school district used to support district programs."[11] Examples of student activity funds are various clubs, such as Art, Auto, Cheerleaders, Chorus, Debate, Drama, Foreign Language, Journalism, Pep, and Photography as well as class (Sophomore, Junior, Senior) funds, the Marching Band, the National Honor Society, and the Student Council. Examples of district activity funds are Athletics, Book Fair, Lyceums, Concerts, and Plays.[12]

FIGURE 12.3   Hypothetical High School Monthly Report

Activity	Beginning Balance	Receipts	Monthly Total	Expenditures	Balance
Band Fund	$344.70	—	$344.70	$19.50	$325.20
Cheerleaders	140.75	$10.00	150.75	50.74	100.01
Drama Club	234.50	65.55	300.05	100.02	200.03
Junior Class	1,239.85	320.00	1,559.85	59.85	1,500.00
Just Say No Club	8.32	112.50	120.82	12.16	108.66
Senior Class	2,583.99	55.40	2,639.39	339.15	2,300.24
Sophomore Class	678.90	10.00	688.90	244.45	444.45
Store	234.56	453.00	687.56	99.83	587.73
Varsity Club	100.00	—	100.00	12.00	88.00
Yearbook	2,567.00	—	2,567.00	1,914.08	652.92
					6,307.24

To make certain that the financial affairs of a school are in order, an independent, timely, annual audit should be conducted at the close of the school year or whenever there seems to be some inconsistencies in the fiscal operations of a school. The independent auditor should examine source documents and transactions in order to certify that all activities were conducted with generally accepted accounting principles and in accordance with authorized actions and legal requirements. An audit that is not conducted in a timely fashion is worthless.

In summary, funds that are provided to the individual school must be handled properly. Such funds must be protected and verified by prudent use of purchase orders, reports, imprest fund utilization, and account flexibility. The money should be used for those who paid the fees, and timely annual audits should be conducted.

School/District Coordination

With the appointment to the position of principal comes the stewardship of a large institution. The extent to which financial information is understood by school principals is vital for decision making. As the chief financial officer of the school, the principal has the responsibility for thousands or even millions of dollars. Most principals have limited formal training in the principles of accounting for overseeing such a la
rge financial operation. Outlining some of the budgetary responsibilities in the school setting, Willardson stated:

> The variety in the kinds of funds that are used in schools adds to the complexity of determining where they stand financially. Funds that schools handle include those appropriated by federal and state programs that flow through the district to the schools; funds contributed from supportive donors; revenues received from such miscellaneous sources as vending machines, sale of supplies and materials, fines for parking, ticket sales for athletic and student

activities; and monies collected from students for school lunches, textbooks and yearbooks. The appropriate handling of funds from these sources is important to insure compliance with generally accepted accounting procedures and with federal, state and board mandated policies and practices.

Principals are not expected to be expert accountants. However, familiarity with some of the more common expected day-to-day responsibilities of school finance can help reduce a number of mistakes and can increase the principals' confidence in handling and resolving school finance problems.[13]

The business office of the district usually assigns a budget to the principal (school) on an annual basis. Funds are divided into various budget categories. Most districts have thorough procedures for tracking expenditures. At the school level, the purchasing process begins with a requisition from a staff member or the principal (see Figure 12.4). Note the billing instructions (budget categories) at the top of the form. At the school level, the principal is responsible for determining the budget category for the expenditure. It is important for the local school administrator to carefully monitor budgets and make certain that items purchased are allowable in specific programs. For example,

FIGURE 12.4 Sample Requisition Form

XYZ SCHOOL DISTRICT

REQUISITION

Requisition No. ____________

Purchase Order # ____________

School ____________ Requested by ____________

Administrator's Approval ____________ Date ____________

BILLING INSTRUCTIONS Check one of the following:

☐ A.V. Materials	☐ Food Service	☐ Periodical	☐ Special Program Title:
☐ Custodial Supply	☐ Furniture	☐ Teaching Supply	
☐ Equipment	☐ Library Book	☐ Textbook	Special Program Acct. #:
☐ Equipment Replacement	☐ Library Supply	☐ Other	

DATE DELIVERED		BATCH NUMBER
		RECORD NUMBER
INITIAL	INITIAL	VENDOR NUMBER

STOCK #	QTY. ORD.	QTY. SHIPPED	✓	DESCRIPTION	ORDER FORM—NAME AND ADDRESS	UNIT COST	TOTAL COST

Merchandise Received by

Total Amount of the Requisition $

White — Purchasing Dept.
Green — Purchasing Dept.
Yellow — Principal

APPROVED BY

FOR PURCHASING DEPARTMENT USE ONLY

CHARGE						CREDIT					
FUND	LOC.	FY	PROGRAM	FUNCTION	OBJ.	FUND	LOC.	FY	PROGRAM	FUNCTION	OBJ.

certain equipment may not be approved in particular federal programs, or an audit may reveal that expenditures were not in line with board policy.

In some districts, principals may be authorized to send purchase orders directly to the vendor, with certain restrictions. Careful follow-up is necessary to see that the requested material has been received. The final stage of the purchasing transaction requires an invoice from the vendor, approved by the receiver and paid for with a check from the district or school, depending on whose budget the purchase is to be charged.

Computer programs have eliminated *hard copy* forms in many districts. A principal's budget, requisitions, purchase orders, delivery confirmation, and authorization for payment are all part of the school's network with the district business office.

In summary, these seven steps should be followed in the expenditure procedure in a district: (1) A requisition form should be utilized to begin the process. (2) When a request is made on a requisition form, the principal should designate the fund category. (3) A purchase order is generated and signed by the appropriate authority. (4) The purchase order is mailed to the vendor (see Figure 12.5). (5) When the article is received, it is accompanied by an invoice to be signed by the person receiving the material. (6) Payment is made by check when the vendor submits the invoice to the school or district. (7) A copy of the purchase order, the invoice, and a copy of the check are filed together. With the canceled check, a good audit trail has been established, completing the transaction.

Since the handling and processing costs of a single purchase order may approach $50, it is not cost efficient to issue purchase orders for anything less than that sum. To facilitate small expenditures, a revolving imprest fund (approved by the board of education) of up to $500 should be maintained in the school for nominal purchases. The authorized person dispenses the funds upon request from the person who has or will soon pay cash for incidental expenditures. The purchaser provides a proof-of-payment slip, which may be self-generated, but preferably provides a sales slip from the vendor. These numerous small transactions are then charged to the proper account. Funds revolve through the imprest fund to and from the appropriate account and should be carefully monitored.

Principals may have authority to write a district check for an amount not to exceed a prescribed figure (in the range of $300 to $500) that is charged to the school account. This approach may save money while still maintaining the integrity of the process. This *limited purchase draft* (see Figure 12.6) should require two signatures for the protection of the issuer. Though it is a commonsense issue with most administrators, it still is a caution that needs to be stated: *Never mingle school funds with personal accounts.*

In the spring of the year, the principal may be asked to submit an *annual* order so that the district may pool all school requests to secure the lowest bid on materials, supplies, and equipment. Larger districts with warehouse facilities are in a position to estimate needs and make purchases in large quantities and at times of the year that are most advantageous for purchasing.

Often, two yearly budgets may *overlap*. Some purchase orders may be issued late in the fiscal year and the materials or supplies may not be received and/or billed by the vendor and payment authorization given until several months after the new fiscal year has begun. These *encumbrances* can be confusing unless good records are maintained.

FIGURE 12.5   Sample Purchase Order Form

XYZ SCHOOL DISTRICT
PURCHASE ORDER

ADDRESS

TELEPHONE
FAX

No.
PLEASE SHOW THIS NUMBER ON ALL INVOICES, PACKING SLIPS, PACKAGES, AND CORRESPONDENCE.

DATE:

VENDOR: Ship to:

SUBMITTED BY:			LOCATION:			
ACCOUNT NUMBER			ENCUMBER AMOUNT	PAY AMOUNT	REQUISITION NO.	
						VENDOR NO.
INVOICE NUMBER		PARTIAL	FULL	APPROVED FOR PAYMENT		DATE

THIS IS A TAX EXEMPT PURCHASE.
DO NOT INCLUDE FEDERAL EXCISE TAXES.

ITEM	QUANTITY	UNIT	DESCRIPTION	UNIT PRICE	TOTAL PRICE	WHSE. NO.

_____
PURCHASING COORDINATOR

Systems of Budget Administration

To the casual observer, it would seem that budgeting is a simple process of calculating the costs of operating a projected educational program and then applying the legal provisions of state, local, and federal government laws and restrictions to determine the sources of revenue and the amounts obtainable to meet the anticipated expenditures. Such hit-and-miss procedures were common in the budgeting practices of school districts years ago. They involved little or no direct relationship between the objectives of the school program and the expenditures. Seldom were alternatives considered or

FIGURE 12.6 Sample Limited Purchase Draft Form

LIMITED PURCHASE DRAFT

THIS IS A TAX EXEMPT PURCHASE. DO NOT INCLUDE FEDERAL OR STATE TAX.

DEPARTMENT _____   VENDOR NO. _____

INVOICE NO.	DESCRIPTION	COST

ACCOUNT CODE(S)	AMOUNT

FUND	SUB FUND	DIRECTOR	PROGRAM	LOCATION	OBJECT	FUNCTION

THIS LIMITED PURCHASE DRAFT VERIFIES OUR TAX EXEMPT STATUS

XYZ SCHOOL DISTRICT

Check No.

ADDRESS
TELEPHONE NUMBER

MO	DAY	YR

THIS WARRANT IS ISSUED ACCORDING TO LAW AND IS WITHIN THE LAWFUL DEBT LIMIT OF THE BOARD OF EDUCATION OF THE XYZ SCHOOL DISTRICT

CASH IMMEDIATELY – VOID IF NOT CASHED WITHIN SIX MONTHS OF DATE OF ISSUE.

BANK
ADDRESS

LIMITED PURCHASE DRAFT
NOT VALID FOR MORE THAN
(BOARD-APPROVED AMOUNT)

PAY AMOUNT _____   PAY $ [   ]

PAY TO THE ORDER OF:

BANK AND ACCOUNT INFORMATION   2 SIGNATURES REQUIRED

found necessary. There was little consideration given to systematic analysis of the budget, and long-range budgeting practices were yet to be developed.

The development of theory in educational administration, with an emphasis on the study of administrative behavior, was accompanied by the beginning of what has become known as *systems analysis* (or the *systems approach*), a way of looking at the functions involved in administration. According to the AASA Commission on Administrative Technology, the beginnings of the systems approach can be traced to the first efforts to introduce science into the management of organizations; some crude efforts occurred at the beginning of the twentieth century.[14]

During the early 1950s, many of the leaders in educational administration became vitally interested in developing basic theories involved in the practice of their profession. New kinds of textbooks were written, and theory classes in school administration began to appear in the curricula of the graduate programs at many of the progressive colleges and universities. The rationale for this departure from the past was that research and practice in educational administration were too heavily involved with empiricism. The front-line thinkers in the field noted, rather apologetically and almost unbelievingly, that the discipline up to that point had almost completely ignored theory in the study and practice of school administration. In the 1960s, with the advancement of technology and the thrust for accountability, education administrators joined the movement to develop a systems analysis approach to planning the school program and link it to developing the budget.

Systems analysis is a practical philosophy on how to assist a decision maker with complex problems of choice under conditions of uncertainty. It is a systematic approach to help a decision maker choose a course of action by investigating the entire problem, searching out alternatives, and comparing these alternatives in the light of their consequences, using an analytic framework to bring expert judgment and intuition to bear on the problem. It includes these elements:

Formulation:	Defining the issues of concern clarifying the objectives, and limiting the problems.
Search:	Determining the relevant data and seeking alternative programs of action to resolve the issues.
Explanation:	Building a model and using it to explore the consequences of the alternative programs, usually by obtaining estimates of their cost and performance.
Interpretation:	Deriving the conclusions and indicating a preferred alternative course of action. This may be a combination of features from previously considered alternatives or their modification to reflect factors not taken into account earlier.
Verification:	Testing the conclusion by experimentation. Rarely is it possible to carry out this step until a program is implemented. A program plan should call for evaluations that can provide after-the-fact verification.
Structuring of the problem, design of the analysis, and the conceptual framework:	The correct questions must be asked and the problem must be properly structured. The objectives of the policies and programs must be clearly stated in policy terms, the relevant population must be defined, and the alternatives for evaluation must be selected. The two principal approaches are the *fixed output approach* where, for a specified level of output, the analyst attempts to attain the output at the lowest possible economic cost, and the *fixed budget approach,* where the analyst attempts to determine which alternatives (or combinations thereof) are likely to produce the highest output within the given budget level.

Planning/Programming/Budgeting Systems

The United States Department of Defense introduced and applied some aspects of systems analysis to certain difficult problems, with the purpose of facilitating a much more precise evaluation of the outcome of programs. The success of the process prompted other government departments to institute similar planning techniques. The concept was the *planning/programming/budgeting system* (commonly referred to as *PPBS*).

A planning/programming/budgeting system is an integrated system devised to provide administrators and other school staff members with better and more objective information for planning educational programs and making choices among the alternative ways for spending funds to achieve the school's educational objectives. Some advocates of the system who felt that *evaluation* was not stressed sufficiently added an *E* to the acronym, making it PPBES. The Association of School Business Officials was not yet satisfied with the designation and substituted ERMD (educational resource management division), which it felt was more descriptive of this approach to budgetary planning.

The PPBS is a way of extending the planning period and duration of a program budget, often for five or more years. Its chief thrust is in the direction of replacing broad, traditional objectives with specific, measurable ones. It involves a cycle in planning that includes (1) establishing objective goals, (2) determining the financial cost of alternative plans for reaching the objectives, (3) evaluating the results, (4) improving the objectives, and (5) adding to and improving the alternative plans to reach the revised objectives.

Zero-Base Budgeting

Just as many serious reform efforts were made in the 1970s to improve school finance formulas to meet the standards of *Serrano* and other court rulings, so were efforts made to improve budgeting practices in school districts. In addition to PPBS, a budgetary plan known as *zero-base budgeting (ZBB)* was developed. Although the idea of planning a budget from zero has existed for more than a century, it was little used until the 1970s, when Peter A. Phyrr began writing about it. The idea soon gained a degree of popularity, particularly in Texas, Georgia, and New Mexico. The concept received widespread attention when Jimmy Carter, running for the U.S. presidency, proclaimed that he would use ZBB techniques in developing the federal budget. The one cardinal principle for ZBB is that nothing is sacred. Every program, if it is to receive continued funding, must be justified during each budget development.[15] There is no standard or universally accepted definition of ZBB. The following two definitions represent the general and the specific approaches:

> Perhaps the essence of zero-base budgeting is simply that an agency provides a defense of its budget request that makes no reference to the level of previous appropriations.[16]

> Zero-base planning and budgeting involves decision making from the lowest levels of management to the top. Managers are required to analyze each budget item—whether already existing or newly proposed—so that the starting point for the development of the budget is zero.[17]

Zero-base budgeting is a rational budgeting approach. It is more of a decision-making process than a complete resource allocation system. It works bottom-up from

basic organizational activities, rather than top-down from organizational goals and objectives. Developed for industry and adapted for use in the public sector, ZBB emphasizes identifying, ranking, and choosing alternatives.[18] There are several advantages
of this type of budgeting, including involvement of staff members, the requirement
of annual evaluation of all programs, accurate determination of programs, and the
development of priorities with alternatives. The critics of the zero-base system point to
the great amount of paperwork involved, the need for more administrative time in the
preparation of the budget, and the feeling that the system is too complicated and thus
too impractical for small school districts.

Site-Based Budgeting

Site-based budgeting (SBB) is a concept of developing a district budget through the involvement of teachers, community, and administrators at the school level. The process
provides an opportunity for the school staff to assist in building a budget that will have
an impact on the final decisions made by the board of education. It is a decentralized
system of providing revenues for instructional supplies, materials, equipment, texts,
and library books and, in some districts, is extended to salaries for teachers, aides, and
custodians. Some schools using SBB techniques analyze student needs in relation to
teaching resources and may have the latitude to purchase the services of two teacher
aides in place of one certificated teacher. Such a degree of decision-making power is
not always possible because of union or association influences, but it does demonstrate
the flexibility possible in a site-based budget process.

To be effective, SBB requires that principals and staff be able to match student
needs with available resources. It is not simply a matter of providing a principal with an
amount of money based on the number of pupils in the building, to be spent in three or
four categories at the school level rather than at the district level. The employees in the
building must be a part of the planning and must recognize cultural, ethnic, and socioeconomic factors that may influence student needs and then establish priorities and budget to meet those needs. Site-based budgeting is an essential element in charter schools.

District office administration assumes a different role in the preparation of site-
based budgets; central administrators become facilitators to the staff and community at
the school level. Budgeting for administration, capital outlays, and maintenance costs
usually remain a district responsibility, because of the need for large expenditures on
particular projects. A new roof on an older building, for example, may take a large
share of the district's total maintenance budget in one year. Lausberg summarized the
responsibility by indicating that the

> purpose of site-based management is to give the principal and instruction staff more control
> over budget, personnel, and organization at the school level. The concept's objectives are:
> greater involvement in decision making, less imposition of state or district level rules which
> restrict creativity or school level choices, and the development of innovative instructional
> methods which will ultimately improve educational results and public acceptance of school
> performance.
>
> Site-based management often gives authority to principals to move funds within a
> total school allocation among line items in the budget.

The role of the central office, whether it be in instruction, personnel, or business, shifts to one of balancing district-wide standards with local decision making, and providing training and support to school-based decision makers. It means sharing responsibility for many services formerly centrally controlled by the business office or other central office departments.[19]

Essentially, proponents of site-based management contend that schools will be improved because it:

- Enables site participants to exert substantial influence on school policy decisions,
- Enhances employee morale and motivation,
- Strengthens the quality of schoolwide planning processes,
- Fosters the development of characteristics associated with effective schools, and
- Improves the academic achievement of students.[20]

Strategic Planning

Patterned after a technique used in business and industry, educators have utilized a process of planning that has an influence on the school budget. Strategic planning is an approach to setting district goals for a three- to five-year period. Involvement includes a broad segment of the community that is brought together for intensive training and decision making that may cover two to five days. A mission statement is designed, belief statements may be outlined, and goals or vision statements are defined for the district. Action teams may be organized to refine the goals and prescribe strategies for achieving them. Finally, the board of education is required to adopt the plan to complete the process.

Planning is an integral part of the budget sequence. As with other approaches, the goals and outlined action recommendations usually exceed potential revenues, and priorities need to be determined. Too often, the budget covers the basic program and many action plans are put on hold.

Total Quality Management

Total quality management (TQM) has been suggested as a basis for achieving excellence in schools. It is an opportunity to conceptualize a systematic change for school districts. School board members, administrators, teachers, support staff, parents, and students meet on a peer level to reach consensus about a shared vision of excellence. In most organizations, the practice is to wait for decisions from the top. The TQM process requires the total organization to take the authority and the responsibility. Through brainstorming and discussion, the group develops a statement of the problem that is clearly understood by all its members (see Figure 12.7).[21]

The group task force collects specific data necessary to analyze a problem. Findings are then reduced to a format that allows the task force to recommend solutions. In a nonevaluative fashion, a list of many possible solutions is produced. Selecting

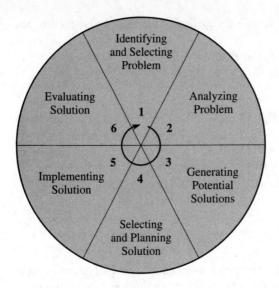

FIGURE 12.7   A Problem-Solving Wheel

Source: Lois Mastro and Frank Kerwin, "Implementing TQM in Maintenance and Operations," 1993.

and planning the optimum solution is done to plan the implementation. Implementing the solutions involves coordinating, assigning, monitoring, measuring, and developing action commitments. Control systems are established to monitor progress, collect data, and help contingency plans evolve. Then solutions are evaluated to determine any discrepancy between the actual and the desired results. The step involves reporting on what has been accomplished, tracking and monitoring the solution to verify its successes and setbacks, and determining if the solution met the original requirements. If the decision is judged to be successful, it becomes fixed in the process.

Challenge of Leadership

Each alternative—PPBS, ZBB, SBB, Strategic Planning, TQM, or other procedures—use common elements of analysis. These components are:

- *Objective(s).* Systems analysis is undertaken for the purpose of suggesting or helping to choose a course of action, which, in turn, must have an objective or an aim. Policies or strategies are then examined and compared, based on how efficiently and effectively they can accomplish the objective.
- *Alternatives.* These are the different programs or means by which the objective or objectives can be attained.
- *Costs.* Each alternative requires the use of specific quantities of resources which, once committed, cannot be used for other purposes.
- *Model(s).* These are representations of the situation under study designed to predict the resource inputs into a system, the effectiveness outputs, and, ideally, their

relationships to each alternative. It is an abstraction of the relevant characteristics of the situation.

■ *Criterion (Criteria)*. These rules or tests for the selection of one alternative over another provide a method for ordering the alternatives, using their costs, and measuring their effectiveness.

No single budget format dominates and no one fiscal innovation lies ahead. Many superintendents wisely incorporate the best elements of recent budget concepts: budgeting that is more responsive to local needs and does not highlight a particular acronym or fad. The leadership challenge is to develop the best possible budget process and document that will convey to the board and community the goals and expectations of the district.

Summary

Historians report that budgetary practices originated and underwent early development in England. In the United States, budgeting became common in business and industry before its use in the public schools. The first law providing for a national budget was passed in 1921; the practice has improved steadily since that time.

The term *budget* has many definitions. The process of budgeting involves planning, receiving, and spending funds, and evaluating results in a specified time frame—usually one year. Its purpose is to define the district's educational plan, determine the source of funds, and specify how revenues are to be expended. The budget document provides a guide for evaluating the school program and serves as a way of keeping the public informed about the activities of the school.

The superintendent of schools should administer the budget, and the school board has legal authority for its formal adoption. The budgeting process should be continuous and provide for citizen review and appraisal. In preparing the budget, the superintendent should work with the entire school staff in order to provide an instrument that reflects the goals and objectives of the district.

The principal, as the chief financial officer at the individual school level, should establish a basic two-sided budget and ledger sheet with receipts and expenditures. Generally accepted accounting practices should be used. An imprest fund is an excellent procedure at the school level. Flexibility should be used, monthly reports prepared, and annual independent audits conducted.

The systems approach to budgeting has gained some recognition in the field of education. Systems analysis is a practical philosophy on how to assist decision makers in choosing a course of action by investigating their entire problem.

The National Center for Educational Statistics (NCES) Handbook has been refined to conform to the national set of standards established by the Governmental Accounting Standards Board (GASB). School districts are beginning to use these NCES/GASB national standards.

ASSIGNMENT PROJECTS

1. Provide a definition for each of the following terms: *budget, revenue, expenditures, receipts, NCES, GASB, PPBS, zero-based budgeting, site-based budgeting, strategic planning, TQM, system analysis.*

2. Interview the business manager of a school district and report on the budgetary changes that have taken place in the last few years. Is an accounting system required by the state? What effect has the use of computers had on school district accounting and budgeting practices?

3. Determine the state requirements for local school district budgeting in your state.

4. Compare the budgetary responsibilities of a school superintendent in a small school district with those of a superintendent in a large school district.

5. Write a paper suggesting ways for school superintendents and boards of education to inform school patrons about budgetary practices.

6. Interview teachers and other school personnel about their involvement in the budgetary process. What information do they give regarding needs and desires for next year? Do they want to be more involved? Less involved? Do they understand how priorities are set and budget decisions made?

7. Prepare a presentation for a new superintendent and newly elected school board about budgetary practices. Outline their responsibilities. How should other school personnel and patrons be involved?

8. Prepare a paper describing the pros and cons in determining a school district budget when the district is committed to a site-based management approach.

Computer simulations and questions, research exercises, and website addresses relevant to this chapter can be found at

www.ablongman.com/edleadership

SELECTED READINGS

Campbell, Roald F., Luvern L. Cunningham, Raphael O. Nystrand, and Michael D. Usdan. *The Organization and Control of American Schools,* 6th ed. Columbus, OH: Merrill, 1990.

Candoli, I. Carl. *School District Administration: Strategic Planning for Site Based Management.* Lancaster, PA: Technomics Publishing, 1990.

Deming, W. Edwards. *The New Economics for Industry, Government, Education.* Cambridge, MA: Massachusetts Institute of Technology, 1993.

Guthrie, James W. *Understanding School Budgets.* Washington, DC: U.S. Department of Education, 1988.

Murphy, Joseph, and Karen S. Louis. *School Based Management as School Reform.* Thousand Oaks, CA: Corwin Press, 1995.

Ray, John R., I. Carl Candoli, and Walter G. Hack. *School Business Administration: A Planning Approach,* 8th ed. Boston: Allyn and Bacon, 2005.

Stevenson, Kenneth R., and John H. Lane, eds. *School Business Management in the 21st Century.* Reston, VA: Association of School Business Officials International, 1990.

ENDNOTES

1. Roe L. Johns and Edgar L. Morphet, *The Economics and Financing of Education* (Englewood Cliffs, NJ: Prentice-Hall, 1969), p. 441.
2. Ibid., p. 442.
3. *Financial Accounting for Local and State School Systems, 2003 Edition* (Washington, DC: National Center for Education Statistics).
4. William H. Roe, *School Business Management* (New York: McGraw-Hill, 1961), p. 81.
5. John R. Ray, I. Carl Candoli, and Walter G. Hack, *School Business Administration: A Planning Approach,* 8th ed. (Boston: Allyn and Bacon, 2005), p. 12.
6. Ibid., p. 12.
7. Leon Ovsiew and William B. Castetter, *Budgeting for Better Schools* (Englewood Cliffs, NJ: Prentice-Hall, 1960), p. 52.
8. Ray et al., *School Business Administration,* pp. 145–146.
9. J. D. Willardson, unpublished monograph, 2007, p. 3.
10. J. D. Willardson, "School Fees," unpublished monograph, October 2007.
11. *Financial Accounting for Local and State School Systems,* p. 10.
12. Ibid., p. 9.
13. J. D. Willardson, "Preparing Principals for Their Financial Stewardship," unpublished monograph, September 2007.
14. *Administrative Technology and the School Executive* (Washington, DC: AASA Commission on Administrative Technology, 1969), pp. 17–18.
15. David E. Weischadle, "Why You'll Be Hearing More about 'Zero-Base Budgeting' and What You Should Know About It," *American School Board Journal,* September 1977, pp. 33–34.
16. Leonard Merewitz, *The Budget's New Clothes: A Critique of Planning, Programming, Budgeting and Benefit-Cost Analysis* (Chicago: Markham, 1971), p. 61.
17. Paul J. Stonich, *Zero-Base Planning and Budgeting* (Homewood, IL: Dow Jones-Irwin, 1977), p. 37.
18. Peter A. Phyrr, "Zero-Base Budgeting: Peter Phyrr Defends His Brainchild," *MBA Magazine,* April 1977, p. 25.
19. Clement H. Lausberg, "Site-Based Management: Crisis or Opportunity," *School Business Affairs,* April 1990, p. 11.
20. Betty Malen, Rodney T. Ogawa, and Jennifer Kranz, "Evidence Says Site-Based Management Hindered by Many Factors," *The School Administrator,* February 1990, p. 32.
21. Lois, Mastro and Frank Kerwin, "Implementing TQM in Maintenance and Operations," *School Business Affairs,* November 1993, p. 32. Figure used by permission.

13 Accounting and Auditing

Incumbent upon every educator is the duty to assure that public funds are properly and efficiently used. Proper control and financial reporting must be based on a solid accounting system with school administrators understanding and fulfilling their fiduciary duties to the taxpayer.

—Janet J. Tanner, 2007

Schools are maintained for the purpose of providing a high-quality educational program. This means that they are operated to spend money—but it must be spent for the right purposes. Getting maximum benefits for the money expended, rather than saving money, is the function of the business administration of a school district. Certain key concepts are associated with this responsibility, such as economy, judicious spending, honesty, protection of property, and protection of individuals.

Revenue for public schools is provided primarily through governmental sources. With this funding comes the public expectation that the money expended for education will be wisely and efficiently spent in meeting educational goals. Administrators of educational units are accountable for the progress of their students as well as the financial resources entrusted to their care. The responsibility rests not only with district financial officers but also with principals and administrators at the school level. Teachers and other district personnel are responsible for understanding the ramifications of various reporting activities in meeting accounting and auditing requirements. The implication that this entails is magnified when a student of school finance realizes that in many districts in the United States resources to meet requirements noted in this chapter are limited because of the relative size of the district.

Everyone accepts in principle that the business of education should use the best possible system of collecting, expending, and accounting for the large sums of public money required to operate the public schools of this country. Yet the history of accounting for such funds, especially at the site-level unit of organization, has not been a particularly outstanding one. The practices and principles have evolved and today bear little relationship to the unstandardized system used by school districts of an earlier era. More stringent reporting requirements at both the state and federal levels have modified that position greatly.

The School Accounting System

The state offices of education and the local school districts have a fiduciary responsibility to make expenditures and keep financial records in accordance with legally approved budgets and prevailing accounting principles. School administrators must protect school funds and property as well as the reputation of those involved in disbursing school dollars. Shoddy or inadequate records can serve to impugn the actions of those in charge, even where there has been no dishonest intent.

Efficiency and effectiveness in school financial practice require a sound system of accounting for income and expenditures. Permanent records of these transactions are an integral part of a system of reporting the reception and disposition of public funds. Financial reports can be only as good as the data on which they are based. Effective accounting principles provide for collection of financial data in a timely, reliable, and consistent manner and have internal control systems to minimize the risk of misusing funds.

In a business setting, the accounting system provides important data for internal and external users. Management utilizes the data to determine the company's fiscal condition. Decisions are based on income, potential income, expenditures, and the "bottom line"—profit and loss. Reporting to regulatory agencies and to stockholders and potential investors is part of the external distribution of information. In the educational setting, accounting and financial reporting has a similar yet different focus than that of business. Education leaders also must report to regulatory agencies and must give an accounting of the progress made by their clientele—the students. In addition, an accounting must be made to the revenue providers—the taxpayers.

Whereas business must be concerned with having a profitable bottom line, governmental and education entities generally expect to be in a break-even position at the end of their fiscal year. Indeed, excess amounts of revenues over expenditures for an educational unit may indicate to taxpayers that tax levies have been too high—a potentially politically unpopular situation. In most states there is a legal preclusion from spending an amount greater than appropriations. In the public trust, getting the maximum benefit for the money provided and expended should be the concern of all district personnel. The business administrator and the principal at the school level have major roles in this function, with the ultimate responsibility resting with the superintendent and board of education.

Understanding the budgeting process as outlined in the previous chapter is important. At the end of a fiscal year, some funds may be encumbered and carried over for several months into the next fiscal year. In addition, a district, by fiat, may carry a small percentage of the total budget as a reserve. The reserves and encumbered balances may appear as a surplus, and negotiating teams may incorrectly attempt to put this perceived revenue on the bargaining table.

Principles

The business of school administration is to receive, spend, and account for taxpayers' dollars for education in the most effective and efficient way, in order to produce maximum educational benefits at minimum cost. Clearly, financial management of the schools is a means to an end, but that does not minimize its importance. Schools cannot achieve their instructional goals without the wise expenditure of public funds. Prudent disposition of funds requires that responsible school personnel adhere to generally accepted accounting principles (GAAP).

In brief, a school district employs an efficient accounting system in order to:

1. Protect public funds from the possibility of loss due to carelessness, expenditure for the wrong purpose, theft, embezzlement, or the malfeasant actions of school officers.
2. Provide a systematic way to relate expenditures to the attainment of educational objectives through the operation of a budget and related reports and processes.
3. Provide an objective method of appraising the performance of school personnel in attaining the school's objectives.
4. Meet the legal requirements of the state and other governmental units for reporting basic information for comparisons, reports, and reviews.
5. Provide local school patrons with important information concerning the fiscal and academic activities and needs of the district.

The Governmental Accounting Standards Board (GASB) emphasized:

> Accountability is the paramount objective of governmental financial reporting—the objective from which all other financial reporting objectives flow. Governments' duty to be accountable includes providing financial information that is useful for economic, social, and political decisions. Financial reports that contribute to these decisions include information useful for (a) comparing actual financial results with the legally adopted budget, (b) assessing financial condition and results of operations, (c) assisting in determining compliance with finance-related laws, rules, and regulations, and (d) assisting in evaluating efficiency and effectiveness.[1]

In spite of recommended principles and attempts to standardize practices, variations appear in every school accounting system. Administrators use those accounting procedures that will help most in implementing and accounting for the school's program. There are, however, certain general principles that may be applied to form the basis for an adequate and effective accounting system in every school.

1. *Accuracy.* There is little value in an accounting system that is not accurate. Audits are useful in discovering and reporting errors, but they are a very poor substitute for original accuracy. Errors not only make financial reports ineffective or useless but may jeopardize the reputation of the administration or ruin the positive image that the school business administrator may otherwise have created.

2. *Completeness and timeliness.* Incomplete records of transactions and accounting records that are out of date provide little help to the superintendent when following a budget, explaining a fiscal transaction, or defending future budgetary allocations or expenditures. Any information that the administrator or the school board needs should always be readily available. The actual fiscal condition of the school district should be known at all times. Reports of income, expenditures, encumbrances, unencumbered balances, and other useful kinds of information should be made periodically.

3. *Simplicity.* School accounting practices and procedures are intended to provide information to administrators, school boards, the state, and local citizens. They are valuable if understood and worthless if not. Simplicity is therefore a necessity in school accounting practices. Their purpose is to explain to a relatively unsophisticated clientele what the school has done, how much it cost, where the money came from, and what the fiscal condition of the district is at any particular time. There is no intent to deceive or confuse anyone by extremely complicated accounting systems or professional jargon in explaining the district's expenditures or other transactions.

4. *Uniformity.* Comparisons of costs between school districts are misleading unless the items being compared are uniform and to some degree standardized. Account classifications and funding practices must be the same in all types of districts if comparisons are to be valid and useful. State reports sent to the U.S. Department of Education must be made with sufficient uniformity to make them useful for such purposes.

The Changing Accounting Environment

The United States Office of Education exerted a leading role in establishing recommended practices in school accounting. The *Financial Accounting for Local and State Systems* handbook has been a financial reporting guide with various editions spanning over 60 years. The 1957 edition was one of the most significant issues outlining standard account codes and terminology that assisted school districts in establishing well-defined categories for operating a school budget and reporting system. With involvement from "a national panel of experts," the National Center for Education Statistics (NCES) published a new volume released in 2003 that made revisions to the 1990 handbook. The introduction to the new guide states:

> This handbook represents a national set of standards and guidance for school system accounting. Its purpose is to help ensure that education fiscal data are reported comprehensively and uniformly. To be accountable for public funds and to assist educational decision makers, school financial reports need to contain the same types of financial statements for the same categories and types of funds and account groups. This revised and restructured guidance focuses on
>
> - defining account classifications that provide meaningful financial management information for its users;
> - complying with generally accepted accounting principles (GAAP), established by the Governmental Accounting Standards Board (GASB);

- operationalizing the most recent position papers of GASB for accounting and reporting by governmental entities;
- recognizing the changes that have taken place in technology, safety, and security and recognizing other emerging issues; and
- supporting federal reporting requirements.[2]

Many governmental agencies, including state departments of education and local districts, have relied on the Governmental Accounting Standards Board's *Codification of Governmental Accounting and Financial Reporting Standards* as a guide to accounting practices. Unlike *Financial Accounting for Local and State School Systems,* account codes and budget categories are not specified. Most states require local education agencies to use uniform budgeting and accounting procedures and expect conformity with generally accepted accounting principles. The account code structure is designed to serve as an efficient coding facility and basic management tool and to establish a common language for reporting the financial activities of a school district.

Some states post their accounting manuals on-line. These manuals may direct governmental entities within the state, including school districts, as to what codes they must use in their accounting systems. This facilitates a more efficient combining of financial records when the state prepares its governmentwide financial reports at fiscal year end. Common accounting codes may also serve as a control feature during the budgeting process.

Various policy *statements* from the Governmental Accounting Standards Board have been issued to government entities, including school districts, since 1987. The GASB indicated that through extensive due process they have identified "what we believe are the most important objectives of financial reporting by governments."[3] The Preface of *Statement No. 34* (1999) noted, "This Statement establishes new financial reporting requirements for state and local governments throughout the United States. When implemented, it will create new information that governments have not presented in the past."[4] The requirements for activating the statement plan were based on the annual revenues of the individual government body. The effective date for compliance for all agencies was June 2003. For purposes of school finance, *Statement 34* includes state offices of education, local school districts, public higher education, and any other public education organization that receives federal funds.

The GASB model "can best be described as evolutionary. It builds on fund-based information that has been provided in the past with a fresh look, and it adds more information from an overview vantage point through requirements for management's discussion and analysis (MD&A) and governmentwide financial statements."[5] The standards required in the model make comparisons of the common core of data provided by the National Center for Education Statistics more accurate and meaningful.

Since its inception in 1984, the GASB has issued 3 Concept Statements, 47 Statements on technical accounting issues, 6 Interpretations, and numerous Exposure Drafts. Many of these publications have had substantial impact on the way that school districts structure their accounting systems, reporting requirements, and even run their day-to-day operations.

Recently there has been much concern among school districts as to the effects of GASB pronouncements regarding accounting for postemployment and retirement benefits. Statements No. 45 and 47 require governmental entities to record these benefits, which will be paid in future accounting periods, as they are earned, thus creating huge balance sheet liabilities. Previous to the GASB statements on this matter, governmental entities generally accounted for employment-related benefits on a pay-as-you-go basis.

The impact of these GASB pronouncements has reached from school hallways to state capital buildings. Many state legislatures have been reluctant to raise taxes to fund these benefits before they are actually paid out. There is a logical line of reasoning that maintains that the state has the authority, unlike businesses, to raise funds whenever they are needed. Taxes can be levied to meet the state's cash-flow needs.

Some states have recommended that a number of employee-related benefits be dropped, rather than face GASB compliance. Some school districts have ceased to offer retirement-related benefits. This has, in some school districts, caused a wave of early retirements. Employees are exiting their school systems so that their retirement packages are "locked in."

GASB has issued several pronouncements that are currently affecting accounting and business practices in school districts. It is imperative that school district administrators seek competent legal and accounting counsel in charting their course of actions regarding these pronouncements and their effects on the school district. A brief description of three of the most recent Statements follows:

- GASB Statement No. 47, *Accounting for Termination of Benefits,* issued in June of 2005, establishes accounting standards for termination benefits, both voluntary and involuntary. It prescribes treatment of expenses and recognized liabilities associated with these future benefits.
- GASB Statement No. 46, *Net Assets Restricted by Enabling Legislation—An Amendment of GASB Statement No. 34,* was issued in December of 2004. This statement clarifies the meaning of "legally enforceable" legislation.
- GASB Statement No. 45, *Accounting and Financial Reporting by Employees for Postemployment Benefits Other than Pensions,* issued June 2004, addresses the accounting treatment for other postemployment benefits (OPEB). OPEB includes postemployment health care, as well as other forms of postemployment benefits, such as life insurance, when provided separately from a pension plan. This Statement established standards for the measurement, recognition, and display of OPEB expense/expenditures and related liabilities, assets, note disclosures, and required supplementary information.[6]

Comprehensive Annual Financial Report (CAFR)

Many school districts are specifically required to file a Comprehensive Annual Financial Report (CAFR). This report must be prepared in accordance with generally accepted accounting principles set by GASB. The report should conform to all current, relevant pronouncements applicable to governmental entities throughout the United States. It generally contains both financial and nonfinancial information to meet the needs of a broad spectrum of readers. Portions of the CAFR may be audited by an external, independent auditor.

A CAFR must present at least three sections: introductory, financial, and statistical. A fourth section, compliance and controls, is finding more widespread usage as school districts and their auditors seek to combine all required financial reporting into one comprehensive document.

1. *Introductory section.* This section introduces the reader to the report and generally includes a transmittal letter signed by the chief financial officer and/or school superintendent, earned certificates of excellence in reporting, an overview of financial and economic conditions faced by the school district, key financial developments, an organizational chart of the district, a list of elected and appointed officials, and a map of the precincts of the board of education.

2. *Financial section.* This section comprises the main body of the CAFR. It includes the independent auditor's report, management's discussion and analysis, the basic financial statements, notes to the financial statements, and required supplementary information.

3. *Statistical section.* This section is generally not audited. It may contain substantial financial information, but may also present tables that differ from financial statements in that they may present nonaccounting data and cover several fiscal years. Statistical information may be presented in the following categories:
   a. Financial Trends Information
   b. Revenue Capacity Information
   c. Debt Capacity Information
   d. Demographic and Economic Information
   e. Operating Information

4. *Compliance and controls.* This section may include the annual single audit report by the independent auditor on the district's compliance with the provisions of the Single Audit Act of 1996 and the U.S Office of Management and Budget Circular A-133, *Audits of States, Local Governments and Non-Profit Organizations.* This section may also include the auditor's report on the internal control structure and compliance with applicable laws and regulations.

Governmentwide Statements

Two governmentwide financial statements are presented in a CAFR. They are both prepared on a full accrual basis. On the "statement of net assets," assets are listed net of their corresponding liabilities. In a school district, this residual amount is simply titled "net assets."

The second governmentwide statement, a statement of activities, shows the net cost of each of the school district's main functions and programs. Revenues and expenses are presented. This difference is shown as a "change in net assets." Revenues that cannot be directly associated with specific functions or programs are summarized in a separate section.

Individual Fund Statements

The Comprehensive Annual Financial Report contains financial statements for three types of funds. The specific statements are as follows:

1. Governmental funds
   a. Balance sheet
   b. Statement of revenues, expenditures, and changes in fund balance
2. Proprietary funds
   a. Balance sheet
   b. Statement of revenues, expenses, and changes in net assets
   c. Statement of cash flows
3. Fiduciary funds
   a. Statement of fiduciary net assets
   b. Statement of changes in fiduciary net assets

Notes to the Financial Statements

Notes are required and offer narrative explanations to supplement the numeric presentation of financial statement items. The notes may also include supplemental schedules such as changes in capital assets, changes in long-term liabilities, actual to budget comparisons, and pertinent supporting schedules.[7]

State Reports

School districts may be required by their governments to file other reports, fiscal as well as statistical. The value of such reports can hardly be overemphasized. They form the basis for legislative action and for information that various state agencies and groups use to debate the cause of education. The states submit a summary of these reports and other information to the U.S. Department of Education, which combines them and thereby provides comparative financial information that is available to all school districts in the nation.

Other Reports

Other reports are made as deemed important and relevant by the superintendent or the school board or possibly by other entities that may have funded some portion of the district's operations. Reports that include charts, graphs, pictures, and other visual devices have proven to be popular and effective in telling the financial story of the district. Many superintendents consider such reports to be excellent public relations devices.

Characteristics of Governmental (Fund) Accounting

Schools generally utilize fund accounting systems. A fund is a separate (and often legally determined) accounting and fiscal entity. The operations of each fund are accounted for with a separate set of self-balancing accounts comprised of assets, liabilities, fund equity, revenues, and expenditures or expenses, as appropriate. This facilitates the preparation of separate financial statements for each fund. A double-entry accounting system, with debits and credits, similar to a business accounting system, is utilized.

Depending on the characteristics of a specific fund, fund balances may be designated as "restricted," indicating that they can be legally used only for certain purposes, or as "unrestricted," meaning that they may be carried forward for reallocation in a future fiscal year.

Types of Funds

For reporting purposes, school funds are generally grouped into three classifications: governmental funds, proprietary funds, or fiduciary funds. Examples of typical funds and their classifications are as follows:

1. *Governmental funds.* These funds are generally financed through taxes and intergovernmental revenues. They may use a modified accrual basis of accounting.
   a. *General fund.* This fund is the general operating fund for a school district. It is used to account for all resources and for the cost of operations traditionally associated with school districts that are not specifically required to be accounted for in other funds.
   b. *Special revenue funds.* Revenues that are restricted and that require separate accounting are handled through special revenue funds.
   c. *Debt service funds.* The accumulation of resources to service (pay) for principle and interest associated with general obligation long-term debt (often in the form of bonds), as well as the actual recording of the payments, are recorded in this fund.
   d. *Capital projects funds.* This fund accounts for resources held for the acquisition or construction of major capital facilities.
2. *Proprietary funds.* These funds account for school district activities. Included are operations where the intent of the governing body is to charge fees to cover the cost (expenses including depreciation) of providing goods and services to schools and/or other locations on a continuing basis. User charges may be supplemented by federal subsidies. Examples of such operations include food services, insurance and risk management, and graphic arts production centers.

a. *Enterprise funds.* Business-type activities that may provide and charge for goods or services to customers or entities outside of the school district are accounted for in enterprise funds.

b. *Internal service funds.* Business-type activities that provide and charge for goods or services only to units within the school district are accounted for in internal service funds.

3. *Fiduciary funds.* These funds are used to report assets held in trustee or agency capacity for others and therefore cannot be used to support the school district's programs.

a. *Trust funds.* Funds from any number of sources other than regular governmental allocations may be contractually or legally restricted for specific purposes. The school district, as trustee of these funds, is in a position of fiduciary responsibility to use and account for the funds only in accordance with the granting entity's purposes.

b. *Agency funds.* A school district may hold, as an agent, funds related to school activities that are not owned or directly controlled by the school district itself. For example, a district may hold assets related to student activities of various schools in a single fiduciary fund entitled Student Activity Agency Fund.[8]

Encumbrance Accounting

Encumbrance accounting is important to any governmental-type budgetary system. An encumbrance represents a commitment related to unperformed contracts for goods and services. The issuance of a purchase order or the signing of a contract would create an encumbrance. The encumbrance account does not represent an expenditure for the period, only a commitment to expend resources.[9] As soon as some action involving future payments of money is made, the proper account should be encumbered by that amount. Without such an up-to-date record, the administrator may not always remember when the cash balance of a particular account has already been committed to another purpose. Encumbrance accounting serves the purpose of keeping the administrator informed concerning expenditure commitments. It is a necessary part of the accounting system of every school and school district. Proper use of this accounting device will not only help to keep the accounts in balance, but may save the administrator from the embarrassment that accompanies a second expenditure of money from an account that has already been depleted by a previous obligation.

The GASB provides the following summary for accounting and reporting encumbrances:

a. Encumbrance accounting should be used to the extent necessary to assure effective budgetary control and accountability and to facilitate effective cash planning and control.

b. Encumbrances outstanding at year-end represent the estimated amount of the expenditures ultimately to result if unperformed contracts in process at year-end are completed. Encumbrances outstanding at year-end do not constitute expenditures or liabilities.

    c. If performance on an executory contract is complete, or virtually complete, an expenditure and liability should be recognized rather than an encumbrance.

    d. Where appropriations lapse at year-end, even if encumbered, the governmental unit may intend either to honor the contracts in progress at year-end or cancel them. If the governmental unit intends to honor them, (1) encumbrances outstanding at year-end should be disclosed in the notes to the financial statements or by reservation of fund balance, and (2) the subsequent year's appropriations should provide authority to complete these transactions.

    e. Where appropriations do not lapse at year-end, or only unencumbered appropriations lapse, encumbrances outstanding at year-end should be reported as reservations of fund balance for subsequent year expenditures based on the encumbered appropriation authority carried over.[10]

Encumbrance accounting is so important that some states require it of all school districts, although some allow year-end reports either with or without encumbrances included.

Cost Accounting

Cost accounting has been an important element in business institutions for a long time. Although it is used to some degree in most larger school districts, the practice has never reached great popularity in smaller ones. The argument that it is not needed in schools because the profit motive is lacking holds little weight, for all schools are faced with the necessity of obtaining the greatest possible benefit out of the least possible expenditure.

Cost accounting provides the necessary information to answer a number of pertinent questions concerning various aspects of the school program. What are the relative costs of various programs—for example, the athletic program as compared with the physical education program? What is the cost (loss in state allocations of money) due to nonattendance of pupils? How do the costs of elementary education compare with those of secondary education? Speculation concerning the comparative costs of programs is of little value, but judgments based on actual expenditures may produce the evidence necessary to evaluate them more objectively.

The business of education requires sound judgment in decision making. Fortunate indeed are school administrators whose accounting system provides the information necessary to allow them and the school board to make decisions on the basis of adequate, reliable, and relevant facts and figures from a cost accounting system. No other basis can be considered as valid.

Cost accounting has two primary values: (1) It provides information for in-school choices and decisions in the expenditure of funds. (2) Costs for the same services can be compared with those of other schools. Too often, school personnel have seen the importance of this factor but have failed to recognize that the potential in-school values of cost accounting exceed those that might come from comparisons with other school systems.

In recent years, many school districts have been challenged to show the relationship between dollars spent for education and student output or achievement. Taxpayers and education specialists want to know that increased education budgets will result in a better "product" for students. A common method of comparing costs with outputs is known *as production function analysis.* Assessment is elusive in education because many uncontrolled factors enter into the input-output equation. Cost accounting, which tracks costs for specific programs, is crucial to this type of analysis.

Accrual Accounting

Accrual accounting is the superior method of accounting for the economic resources of the proprietary and fiduciary funds in a local education agency. "It results in accounting measurement based on the substance of transactions and events, rather than merely when cash is received or disbursed and thus enhances their relevance, neutrality, timeliness, completeness, and comparability."[11] The essential elements include (1) accrual of expenditures when incurred and amortization, (2) deferral of revenues until they are earned, and (3) capitalization of long-term expenditures and the subsequent depreciation of these costs.[12]

Some of the advantages of accrual basis accounting include:

- Providing a comprehensive measurement of financial position and results of operations;
- Providing accountability for individual assets within the accounting system at the earliest appropriate date;
- Providing comparability from period to period; and
- Reducing management's ability to control cash flows in such a way as to produce financial statements that will seem to present financial position and results of operations in either a more optimistic or more pessimistic context depending upon management's particular preference at the end of any given fiscal year.[13]

Receiving and Depositing Funds

The school accounting function begins with the receipt of funds from the taxing agency that allocates funds to local districts, as well as from local collections (e.g., fees, tuitions, and interest). There must be agreement between the instruments showing receipt of funds and the amount of such monies received.

The typical school district under the direction of the local school board has control of its own budget and has custody of its funds. Local property taxes are usually collected by a county tax collector who transfers the rightful share to the school district in the county. The district administration offices deposit tax warrants, state allocations, and all other school district funds in the bank (or banks) that the school board has designated as its depository.

The school district uses the same criteria for the selection of a depository for its funds as an individual would use when establishing a personal account. Many boards find it advantageous to accept bids from various banks when a selection for services is being made. Quality of service, financial standing, convenience, interest rates, and the integrity of bank officials are some of the most important factors to be considered when selecting a bank.

Expending School Funds

General authorization for the expenditure of funds comes from the budget and the minutes of the board of education meetings. Under the direction of the superintendent, charges and obligations are made against the district accounts as provided by these two documents. Some boards of education authorize charges against the district by sole action of the superintendent but with full accountability to the board; others require either preapproval or ratification at a board meeting of all expenditures or encumbrances above a predetermined amount.

As part of the internal control system, invoices received by the district office are checked for accuracy, approved by the responsible official, and then directed to the business office for payment. Other documents that legalize the payment of money from the school treasury include such items as contracts, time cards, and legal claims by government (social security payments, for example). All original documents must show evidence of proper authorization and satisfactory acceptance of services rendered or goods received before they can be authorized for payment.

Original documents that serve as supporting evidence of money received or expended must be filed as official records of fiscal transactions. They become the supporting records from which audits can be made. Usually the requisition, purchase order, and invoice or voucher for a particular transaction are clipped together and filed, forming a complete record of the events that authorized that particular expenditure. The original documents—receipts, contracts, invoices, checks and warrants, deposit slips, requisitions, purchase orders, payroll records, and similar documents—provide the information necessary for entries in the records maintained in the accounting system.

Auditing

When protection of property and money is being considered (as well as protection of the reputation of the employees involved), the administrator and the board of education turn to the audit for support. Auditing is usually the culminating act in the business of protecting the assets of the school district; it is used in some form and to some extent by all school districts.

An *audit* is a systematic process or procedure for verifying the financial operations of a school district to determine whether property and funds have been or are being used in a legal and efficient way. It provides a service that no business—least of all an institution receiving and expending public funds—can afford not to use on a regular basis. Timeliness is essential. Audits of worth are those that provide information that is *current.* Delayed audits are virtually worthless and fail to achieve the goal of protecting the accounting system.

Purposes

The purposes of auditing are the same now as they always have been, but the emphasis has changed dramatically. Discovery of fraud and detection of errors were once the main functions of auditing, but it has other, more important functions today, as indicated in the following statement by Welsch and Anthony:

> Its purpose is to lend credibility to the financial reports; that is, to assure that they are dependable. Primarily this function involves an examination of the financial reports prepared by the management in order to assure that they are in conformance with generally accepted accounting concepts and standards. In carrying out this function the independent CPA examines the underlying transactions, including the collection, classification, and assembly of the financial data incorporated in the financial reports. In performing these tasks, established professional standards must be maintained and the information reported must conform to "generally accepted accounting principles" appropriate for the entity involved. Additionally, the CPA is responsible for verifying that the financial reports "fairly present" the resource inflows and outflows and the financial position of the entity.[14]

In spite of the foregoing, it seems likely that the average citizen, perhaps even the average school administrator, views the audit as simply a means of discovering financial shortages or misuses of public funds. That, however, is becoming less and less its main value to the school district. Only a very small percentage of school audits disclose any acts of dishonesty in handling school money. On the other hand, every audit does result in some protection to the honest school officials who are responsible for the fiscal management of the district. In addition, the audit shows the degree or extent of observance of state and district laws and policies, expresses a professional opinion as to whether or not the financial statements present fairly the financial condition of the district, examines the adequacy or inadequacy of accounting procedures, provides suggestions to improve the system, and gives an official review of the operations of the school system for the period of the audit. These are the values that make the audit worth its cost.

Kinds of Audits

Audits or appraisals of school finance practices and records are of several kinds, but their purposes are the same—to satisfy state and local district requirements, to protect school funds, and to help establish public confidence in the operation of the schools. Audits rarely trace every financial transaction. Instead, specialized tests are made to ensure the integrity of the internal control and accounting systems.

The kinds of audits that school districts use are sometimes differentiated according to when they are made. For example, preaudits occur before the transactions actually occur, continuous audits occur during the length of the complete fiscal period, and postaudits occur after the fiscal period has elapsed. All types of audits form a basis for more efficient management of school funds and at the same time protect the school and its employees from what might otherwise be legitimate criticism of the school's handling of public funds.

The most common kinds of school audits in general use are internal, state, and external. These may be subdivided in turn according to when the audit is conducted and the degree of completeness.

Internal Audits.   Internal (continuous) audits are conducted by technically qualified personnel already employed by the school district. They may be preaudits, current audits, or even postaudits. Internal audits function as an integral part of a control system that districts use to assure school patrons of proper and careful management of school finances. By themselves, internal audits cannot guarantee such management, and they are in no sense a justifiable alternative to professional external audits that are required at regular intervals by the various states.

State Audits.   It has been pointed out that states are paying a high percentage of the cost of public education. School funds in reality are state funds. It follows, then, that the states have a direct interest in the management of local school district funds and therefore have a right, as well as a responsibility, to know how school finances are managed. Accordingly, the states require periodic audits of local district funds to ensure that the law is being observed in their utilization. The nature and extent of the audit vary considerably from one state to another. Those states that have many districts with limited resources and those that have many other institutions requiring state audits usually restrict the extent of state-required audits. Some states concern themselves only with local district observances of state laws governing the expenditure of school funds. A few states require such an audit only every three or four years. Many states solve this problem by requiring that independent auditors perform this function on a yearly or other regular basis.

External Audits.   External audits are conducted by qualified agencies or individuals (usually certified public accountants). They are usually of the postaudit variety and may or may not be comprehensive audits. Some districts may not require a comprehensive external audit every year because of the cost factor, but this varies with the district's policy and the state's requirement.

External auditing practices follow state laws established for such purposes, as well as certain generally accepted auditing standards (GAAS). Comprehensive year-end audits usually include the following activities:

1. A study of the minutes of the meetings of the board of education. These records are the official authorization for all transactions that occur in the operation of the schools. The financial records of the school must be reviewed in terms of their agreement with the school board minutes and the legal requirements and regulations provided in state laws.

2. Verification of all receipts from all sources—revenue, nonrevenue, and transfer funds. This action includes a check on the allocation of receipts to the current-expenditure fund, to capital outlay, and to debt service accounts.

3. Verification of expenditures—requisitions, purchase orders, vouchers, and checks issued.

4. Review of the entries in the journals, ledgers, payrolls, and similar books of entry and disbursement.

5. Reconciliation of bank statements, accounts, money transfers, and investments.

6. Review of all subsidiary records, deeds, supporting documents, inventories, insurance policies, trusts, sinking funds, and numerous other records related to the operation of the school.

7. Inclusion of student activity and other fiduciary accounts in every external postaudit. No school official should accept internal audits as meeting the audit requirements for such accounts (reasoning that they are not under the direct control of the board of education). There has been a tendency in the past to minimize or disregard the importance of spending taxpayers' money for such audits. In the typical school district, these accounts are more likely to be in need of review and audit than the regular district-level accounts.

Thus, it is evident that a comprehensive audit means exactly what the name suggests. In the words of Knezevich and Fowlkes, it is a "detailed study of the system of internal control of all books and accounts, including subsidiary records and supporting documents, to determine the legality, mathematical accuracy, complete accountability, and application of accounting principles."[15]

There are other kinds of audits in addition to the comprehensive audit. For example, special audits (considering some particular phase or part of the school operation) are used when suspicion of error or fraud may be involved. Such an audit may be for other than a full fiscal year and may sometimes cover parts of more than one fiscal period.

The preaudit is an informal system to prevent unauthorized, illegal, or questionable use of school funds. It is an administrative procedure to protect the school from spending money for the wrong purpose or from the wrong account. In practice, it becomes a system of administrative control to assure school officials that embarrassing, unwise, or even illegal transactions are prevented. A certain amount of preauditing takes place in every school's operation, where care is taken to prevent unwise expenditures of money. The officials of the school may not think of their informal preventive or protective measures as being preaudits, but they are, nonetheless.

The continuous audit is much like the preaudit, but carried through the entire fiscal period. Large districts may have a more formal organization, with a controller or other official to perform this function. It is important that this function be conducted for the good of the educational program. It should not become a position with the negative connotation of "watchdog of the treasury."

The audit requirements for state and local governments, including school districts, that administer assistance programs above a specified threshold are specified in the Single Audit Act of 1984, as amended in 1996. Audits may be performed in conjunction with the audit of the school district's CAFR. However, federal governmental standards must be followed for that portion of the audit that falls under the Single Audit. The external auditor's report must specify if the Single Audit is part of the comprehensive audit.

Selecting an Auditor

Boards of education may sometimes wish to employ the auditor who bids lowest. Other factors are usually much more important in the selection—such as the accountant's competence, reputation, experience with similar assignments, availability, and ability to get the job done in a reasonable time. Competitive bidding for the assignment should never be used. Such a process is analogous to competitive bidding for the position of teacher or school superintendent.

Occasionally, problems arise between the auditing agency and the school district. In no sense is the auditor being placed in a position of evaluating the judgment of the board of education in the use of school funds. It should be made clear to auditors before they accept the assignment that their function is to verify what has happened in the school operation and report the findings to the board—not to the individual who has been in charge of fiscal operations. As technical experts, auditors provide fact-finding and advisory services only. They should have a free hand in performing their services, and the records of the school district and the informational services of the school employees should be at their disposal. These matters seldom are cause for difficulty if they are understood before the beginning of the audit.

It is very important that the board of education and the auditor agree on the extent of the audit to be made and establish some reasonable relation between this assignment and the estimated cost. A comprehensive audit on a per diem cost basis might go well beyond the need of the school district or its ability to pay. A formal contract specifying the expectations and responsibilities of the audit team, as well as the school districts, should be negotiated and signed prior to the audit engagement. The contract, generally drawn up by the school district's legal counsel, should include dates, reports to be generated, and price. A binding contract reduces the chances of miscommunication or poor audit performance.

Administrators and Audits

No wise administrator advises the board of education to avoid or postpone periodic audits of all school district fiscal operations. The cost is little when compared with the input it may provide for improving and evaluating school business operations. Professional educators should not leave a position or accept a new one where they are responsible for the management of school funds until some kind of formal audit, preferably by a certified public accountant, has been performed. The reputation of a school administrator, and to a lesser degree a teacher, is inextricably related to how the public views the management of public funds. An audit protects the prudent and detects the imprudent. It is therefore a necessity, not a luxury. A comprehensive audit by a qualified agency is the public's best possible assurance of the honest and efficient operation of school fiscal affairs.

Protecting School Funds

A school does not ordinarily impose on itself the rigid legal and system-oriented rules for receiving and expending money that banks and many other businesses usually use. Unfortunately, some administrators and teachers have had little or no training in business and have not placed the necessary emphasis on this aspect of the educational program. Education administrators must handle public funds with strict compliance to fundamental and sound business practices—regardless of the amount of funds under their jurisdiction. Strict observance of basic accounting principles and the bonding of all school employees who manage school funds are absolute necessities in all schools.

Surety Bonds

The chief purpose of bonding school officials is sometimes misunderstood. Bonding is not done, as some suppose, because of questions about the integrity of the officials concerned. Rather, bonds are placed on officials because of the nature of the office itself. Bonding protects the school district against fraud or loss, but it also provides motivation to the official to be businesslike in handling the funds under his or her jurisdiction. Surety bonds are of three main types: fidelity, public official, and contract. There are many varieties and special forms of each of these.

Used as a legal term, *surety* is defined as one who has the responsibility for the debt, default, or failure of another. A surety bond guarantees the performance of a contract or obligation. For a fee, an agent assures the purchaser of the bond—the board of education—that those involved with the finances of the district will fulfill their duties within the law. If there is loss of money through a fraudulent act on the part of a bonded district official, the bonding agency reimburses the district for the loss and pursues action against the individual(s) to recover its loss. Surety bonds may be purchased for activities other than financial. A board may want to have protection against a malfeasance suit, for example.

Management of Cash Receipts

The receiving and disbursing of school district funds offer few problems with regard to the money that goes through the normal fiscal cycle. Receipts for income, board authorization for the payment of verified invoices and other obligations, two signatures on checks for all expenditures, regular internal and external audits, and periodic reports to the board of education are evidence of the careful and legal management of school district funds.

There is less agreement, however, on some methods of handling cash receipts, such as lunch money, fees, store sales receipts, student activity funds, and many others. School officials should establish guidelines, policies, and procedures to protect these incidental funds as well as the reputations of those who handle them. Personal integrity is important, but so are records. The accounting system for such funds should follow acceptable guidelines, such as a centralized account for all student activity funds, receipts issued for all money received, timely deposit of cash receipts (with only minimal amounts of cash left in the school safe at any time), an unlocked-safe policy when protecting small amounts of money of less value than the safe door, all payments made by two-signature checks issued only after proper authorization, accurate and complete records of all transactions, supervision of all accounting systems by a faculty member or administrator, continuous internal auditing by qualified personnel, and regular external audits.

Summary

Since schools perform their functions by receiving and expending public money, it is a major responsibility of school personnel to ensure that the money is spent wisely and that accurate and complete financial records are kept. School accounting records and principles have improved greatly since their early introduction into the schools.

There are benefits to be gained by school districts that follow the standardized accounting practices recommended by the U.S. Department of Education. These practices are refined and changed periodically.

Governmental agencies, including state departments of education and local districts, are now required to follow the Governmental Accounting Standards Board's Statement 34, *Basic Financial Statements*.

Auditing of accounts by an outside agency is a necessary function for all school districts. Audits serve many purposes—one is to determine whether the financial operations were proper, legal, and in agreement with the district's accepted accounting practices. Audits also assist the district in determining the presence of fraud. It is unreasonable for a district to eliminate audits because of their cost. Every school administrator should insist on a preaudit of the district books when assuming office and a postaudit when leaving.

ASSIGNMENT PROJECTS

1. Provide a definition for each of the following terms: *accounting, auditing, fund, CAFR, GAAS, encumbrance, cost accounting, accrual accounting, internal audits, external audits, surety bonds.*
2. Determine the requirements for accounting and auditing of school district financial accounts in your state.
3. Prepare arguments to justify annual auditing of school district accounts by a professional agency.

4. Interview a school district business manager to determine what improvements have been made in accounting and auditing practices in the last few years.

5. Report on incidents of misuse of funds that might have been avoided if proper accounting and auditing practices had been followed.

6. Determine how computers can assist in the auditing function. How are school districts protecting themselves against computer fraud? What type of computerized audit trails are available for use in school district business offices?

Computer simulations and questions, research exercises, and website addresses relevant to this chapter can be found at

www.ablongman.com/edleadership

SELECTED READINGS

Bailey, Larry P. *2003 Miller Governmental GAAP Guide.* Aspen, CO: Aspen Publishing, 2003, updated 2006 by Michael Crawford.

Bauer, Richard I. "Get the Most from Your Cash Flow," *School Business Affairs, 61,* 10, October 1995.

Budget Accounting and Auditing Handbook 1979, Updated 1991. Salt Lake City, UT: State Board of Education, 1991.

Bureau of the Census. *Statistical Abstract of the United States 2003* (published annually). Washington, DC: U.S. Government Printing Office, 2004.

Campbell, Roald F., Luvern L. Cunningham, Raphael O. Nystrand, and Michael D. Usdan. *The Organization and Control of American Schools,* 6th ed. Columbus, OH: Merrill, 1990.

Chorafas, Dimitris N. *The Handbook of Data Communications and Computer Networks.* Princeton, NJ: Petrocelli Books, 1985.

Codification of Governmental Accounting and Financial Reporting Standards. Norwalk, CT: Governmental Accounting Standards Board, June 30, 2003.

Cuzzetto, Charles. *Internal Auditing for School Districts.* Reston, VA: Association of School Business Officials International, 1993.

Everett, Ronald E., and Donald Johnson. *Managerial and Financial Accounting for School Administrators.* Reston, VA: Association of School Business Officials International, 1996.

Financial Accounting for Local and State School Systems. Washington DC: NCES, 2003.

Granof, M. H. (2004). *Government and Not-for-Profit Accounting: Concepts and Practices,* 3rd ed. New York: John Wiley & Sons.

Pritchett, L., and D. Filmer. "What Education Production Functions Really Show: A Positive Theory of Education Expenditures." *Economics of Education Review, 18* (2), 223–239.

Proposed Statement of Governmental Accounting Standards Board on Accounting and Financial Reporting for Derivatives, Exposure Draft. Project 26-4P. Norwalk, CT: Governmental Accounting Standards Board, 2006, www.gasb.org/exp/derivatives_plain-language.pdf.

Proposed Statement of Governmental Accounting Standards Board on Concepts Related to Elements of Financial Statements, Exposure Draft. Project No. 3-11. Norwalk, CT: Governmental Accounting Standards Board, 2006, www.gasb.org/exp/ed_elements_financial_statements.pdf.

Ray, John R., Walter, G. Hack, and I. Carl Candoli. *School Business Administration: A Planning Approach,* 8th ed. Boston: Allyn and Bacon, 2005.

Roberts, Charles T., and Allan R. Lichtenberger. *Financial Accounting: Classification and Standard Terminology for Local and State School Systems.* Washington, DC: Office of Education, U.S. Department of Health, Education, and Welfare, 1973.

Sarason, Seymour B. *How Schools Might Be Governed.* New York: Teachers College Press, 1997.

Wood, R. Craig, David Thompson, Lawrence O. Picus, and Don I. Tharpe. *Principles of School Business Administration,* 2nd ed. Reston, VA: Association of School Business Officials International, 1995.

ENDNOTES

1. *Basic Financial Statements—And Management's Discussion and Analysis—for State and Local Governments* (Norwalk, CT: Governmental Accounting Standards Board, June 1999), p. 1.

2. http://nces.ed.gov/forum/pdf/nces-financial-handbook-pdf.

3. *Basic Financial Statements—And Management's Discussion and Analysis—for State and Local Governments,* Statement No. 34 of the Governmental Accounting Standards Board (Norwalk, CT: Governmental Accounting Standards Board, June 1999), preface.

4. Ibid.

5. David Bean and Paul Glick, "GASB's New Financial Reporting Model: Implementation Project for School Districts," *School Business Affairs,* October 1999, p. 8.

6. www. gasb.org/, retrieved July 2006.

7. www.nyscpa.org/cpajournal/2004/104/perspectives/?v 2.htm, retrieved August 2006.

8. *Codification of Government Accounting and Financial Reporting Standards* (Norwalk, CT: Governmental Accounting Standards Board, June 30, 1994), p. 81.

9. Larry P. Bailey, *2003 Miller Governmental GAAP Guide* (Aspen, CO: Aspen Publishing). Updated yearly, 2006 edition by Michael Crawford.

10. *Codification of Government Accounting and Financial Reporting Standards.*

11. Ibid.

12. Ibid.

13. *Financial Accounting for Local and State School Systems,* National Center for Education Statistics, 2003 Edition, p. 3. http://nces.ed.gov/pubs2004/h2r2.

14. Glen A. Welsch and Robert W. Anthony, *Fundamentals of Financial Accounting,* rev. ed. (Homewood, IL: Richard D. Irwin, 1977), pp. 14, 741.

15. Stephen J. Knezevich and John Guy Fowlkes, *Business Management of Local School Systems* (New York: Harper & Row, 1960), p. 144.

14 Business Aspects of the School Community

*Educational leaders must make sound business decisions to provide
a safe, secure and ambient school environment, safety first including
transporting students securely, having timely and sufficient supplies
and equipment, and providing a quality food service program.*

—J. D. Willardson, 2007

Within a decade major events had a great influence on the operation of schools. Twelve students and one teacher were killed in a high school (Columbine) in Colorado when two students lobbed homemade bombs throughout the school and, with guns, fired on students, and then committed suicide. Other similar incidents were attempted in schools; some were successful, others were thwarted. Students and teachers were killed by students with weapons, and most schools throughout the country took measures to tighten or initiate security systems. The terrorist attacks of September 11, 2001, anthrax mailings, sniper shootings, and significant incidents of extreme violence challenged educational leaders to provide a safe and secure learning environment for students. Responsible governments and school administrators were warned to "feature schools prominently in any terrorism-preparedness efforts, as more than one-fifth of the nation's population can be found in its 119,000 schools on any given weekday during the academic year."[1]

Natural catastrophic disasters also played a role in the complexities of school operations. Hurricanes Katrina and Rita were a devastating force that caused millions of dollars of damage and displaced thousands of families. Many students who lost their homes were assimilated into school districts in various states, taxing original legislative budgets for schools. Floods in the northeastern United States, fires and floods in California, and other events throughout the nation played a role to a greater or lesser degree on the schools and had an impact on district finances. Educators are aware of the wealth of research that indicates that a requisite for an effective school is to provide "a safe and secure environment for learning."[2] Court decisions require it.

World events have had an influence on the management of schools. Record-breaking oil prices forced many districts that were unprepared to meet the rapidly

340

rising fuel costs to modify budgets. Also, the influx of illegal immigrants into the country caused great debate. Through the years, students from these families have been assimilated into the schools, and court decisions indicated that the students had a right to be educated at state expense. New legislation may alter this position and school enrollments in some states; especially Arizona, California, and Texas could be affected. These multifaceted events were challenges to school districts throughout the United States and demonstrate the *climate of change* that requires effective school leaders to be flexible and innovative in meeting the challenges such changes bring.

In a complex school community, regardless of its size, the superintendent's chief responsibility has been to provide educational leadership. In today's unremitting atmosphere, the chief school officer in the district, and the school board itself, must bring to the top of the school agenda the oft-quoted slogan, "Safety first." They must become anxiously engaged in developing prevention strategies and emergency measures to "plan, prepare, and practice for the worst possible incidents of violence."[3] Their actions must be handled deftly, for if the actions conceived are so apparent and stifling, the classroom may become not safe and secure but a place of anxiety and concern for everyone, but especially the students who should be able to work in a warm and comfortable situation. No executive can possibly perform all of the generally accepted functions of the superintendency alone; some of the duties of the office must be delegated to others. However, whether delegated or not, providing for safe and secure schools is a primary function of the business side of a superintendent's position.

Increased Safety Hazards

The purpose of the school is to provide its pupils with high-quality education of the variety and quantity that will improve their behavior and competence as law-abiding and self-supporting citizens. But that purpose is not all-inclusive; the school's first responsibility involves maintaining the safety and protecting the health and well-being of all who attend. Education has relatively little value to the seriously injured pupil or to the one whose physical or mental health has been jeopardized through negligence on the part of anyone in the school community.

Too often in the past, school employees have given only limited attention to protecting the safety and maintaining the health of their pupils. These activities, they reasoned, were the responsibility of other government agencies and of the home. They often found their own academic or administrative responsibilities too time consuming to permit significant involvement in the primary safety and health concerns of students.

The potential and the real hazards to the health and safety of pupils in the school complex are greater than is commonly believed. As schools have become larger, many of the dangers to its members have increased. From automobile/motorcycle/bicycle hazards outside the school itself, to the playground heavily stocked with potentially dangerous equipment, to the overcrowded classrooms, gymnasiums, and laboratories, the dangers to life and limb manifest themselves on every hand. As a result, the importance of eliminating safety hazards, protecting the health of pupils, providing adequate insurance, and using risk management principles is much greater today than ever before in the history of education. The usual method of guaranteeing protection for the educational community is to transfer risk to an insurance carrier. There is an emphasis now on reducing the probability of loss by eliminating safety hazards.

Most schools are not negligent in providing pupils with a safe and hazard-free environment, but a few are. Every school, regardless of its safety record in the past, should constantly be reviewing and improving its policies and procedures to protect the safety and well-being of all members of the school community.

Principals need to protect themselves from lawsuits through a systematic approach of determining how safe the school facilities are for students and staff. A survey of the buildings and grounds on a frequent basis is essential. Establishment of a safety committee—including a teacher, parent, school nurse, representative from the fire department, and school administrator—has proved a successful approach in taking inventory of safety needs in some districts. Use of a self-evaluation safety checklist has also proved helpful in identifying hazardous problems in the school setting. Often, such surveys reveal areas of concern that may be costly to modify or repair. However, the risk management approach of prevention may prove to be the least costly in the long run. In addition to the desire to protect school children, school staff members should remind themselves that courts will look very critically on an institution whose members, required to be present by edict of the state, have not been given the greatest possible personal protection while in attendance.

Lessons learned from high-profile school violence occurrences make security measures to protect student, staff, and facilities extremely important. There is no room for complacency. Unfortunately, schools provide "soft targets" for terrorists and other nefarious vandals. To combat this threat, educational leaders should:

- Create comprehensive plans, provide staff training, coordinate plans with other governmental agencies, screen vendors, schedule drills, and perform on-site evaluations.
- Provide for better control of access to school facilities, be careful with mail, and establish specific response protocols.
- Limit cell phone use (in an emergency, all the frequencies should be available to security workers).
- Develop systems to ascertain that persons coming into the school have a legitimate reason for doing so, scrutinize the campus for suspicious items, and evaluate food and beverage stock, storage, and protection procedures.
- Assess school health and medical preparedness.
- Identify higher-risk facilities and organizations as well as potential terrorist targets in the community nearby schools.[4]

Since the business aspects of the school are clearly secondary to the educational aspects, the superintendent should delegate some of the business duties to capable employees but retain direct leadership responsibility for the academic program. In delegating responsibilities to members of the staff, superintendents must remember that their major responsibility is that of educational leaders, not office clerks or purchasing agents, although the responsibility for supervising the work of all departments of the school operation remains with the superintendent.

Having selected managers to assist in performing the business affairs of the school district, superintendents are then free to devote their time and ability to improving the educational program. They cannot, however, escape responsibility for the conduct of the business affairs of the district. They must know what is being done, and they must remain qualified to advise and to confer with those who perform the functions of the business office. There is no school district large enough, wealthy enough, or with a large enough district office to justify the superintendent's ignoring fiscal and material resources management.

The Business Office

The school business office is often spoken about as if such an "office" always existed in a school system. Very often indeed there is no such place as an entity by itself; the office referred to is usually only a part of the all-inclusive function of the superintendent of schools. The superintendent in most small school systems is, in effect, the business manager, the purchasing agent, and perhaps even the accountant for the district. In some cases, the role may also include being the high school principal and even a part-time teacher. The purposes to be served by a business office and the problems encountered in school business management are much the same in all districts, however.

The superintendent of schools is directly responsible to the school board for the educational program in all its aspects. In small districts, duties include most of the functions of the business manager, sometimes with little clerical assistance. In medium-sized districts, an assistant superintendent or an official clerk may be classified as the business manager. In the larger districts, the office has a staff of assistants, clerks, and office workers who perform the business functions of the school, often under the direction of an assistant superintendent.

The functions of the business office increase as the size and demands of the school district increase. Some writers have designated the so-called business management assignment of this office "fiscal and material resources management" in an effort to describe its function more comprehensively and accurately.

Regardless of the size of the school district, there are certain services that must be provided as part of the business administration functions. Following are areas that may be considered part of business office operations:

Accounting and Budgeting
    Audits
Teacher Compensation
    Benefits
    Payroll
Building and Grounds
    Maintenance
Human Resource Responsibilities

Food Services
Purchasing
Risk Management
   Insurance
   Safety
Transportation
Warehousing

Although there is much responsibility in conducting the affairs of a business office, it is important for the administrator not to lose sight of the fact that the office exists to support the teaching/learning process. Hill wrote:

> School business administration is not an end in itself. It exists for the sole purpose of facilitating the educational program of a school and school district. It should operate to support the teacher in the classroom, the principal in the school, the school board and central administration as each strives to fulfill its responsibilities toward the accomplishment of the educational mission. . . . The best school business official is one who understands the primary goals of education and who works closely with others in promoting the best education the community can afford.[5]

Students of education finance will readily note that these ancillary aspects of operating a school system add significantly to the overall costs of education.

Supplies and Equipment

Instructional and administrative personnel would be severely handicapped and their contributions to the educational program greatly minimized in the absence or short supply of appropriate materials and equipment. This is particularly true in today's schools, with emphasis on instructional media and educational technology. The days of providing teachers with only limited supplies of absolute necessities were not difficult ones for the school purchaser—who often was also a teacher. Purchasing, storing, and distributing the vast array of machines and materials needed by the school staff today is another matter, however. Instructional devices, aids, office supplies and equipment, custodial materials and machines, transportation parts and fuel, food service preparation, and instructional materials centers have revolutionized education and brought management challenges to school district business offices. The costs of such devices have increased in relation to the change from such essentials as chalk, paper, pencils, textbooks, and a few maps and charts to the list today, which includes radios, recorders, television sets, projectors, computers and a vast amount of educational software, DVDs, PowerPoint packages, VCRs, interactive videos, globes, mockups, models, calculators, cameras, duplicating machines, and numerous other items.

    Increasing pressures on school administrators for economical use of the school tax dollar and mounting demands for additional quality and quantity in educational programs make it essential that school administrators take a critical look at their entire fiscal operation. The objective of producing high-quality education at minimum cost has never been emphasized more than at present. The movement for accountability, the main thrust of systems analysis, and the negative reaction of taxpayers all point to the need to operate schools more efficiently without reducing their quality.

Financial accounting systems treat supplies differently from equipment. Procurement of supplies represents a charge against the current operating expenditures of the district, but equipment (except replacement equipment) is a capital-outlay expenditure. It is therefore important to distinguish between the two terms.

A *supply item* is any article or material that meets any one or more of the following conditions:

1. It is consumed in use.
2. It loses its original shape or appearance with use.
3. It is expendable; that is, if the article is damaged or some of its parts are lost or worn out, it is usually more feasible to replace it with an entirely new unit than to repair it.
4. It is an inexpensive item; even if it has characteristics of equipment, its small cost makes it inadvisable to capitalize the item.
5. It loses its identity through incorporation into a different or more complex unit or substance.

An *equipment item* is a movable or fixed unit of furniture or furnishing, an instrument, a machine, an apparatus, or a set of articles that meets all the following conditions:

1. It retains its original shape and appearance with use.
2. It is nonexpendable; that is, if the article is damaged or some of its parts are lost or worn out, it is usually more feasible to repair it than to replace it with an entirely new unit.
3. It represents an investment of money that makes it feasible and advisable to capitalize the item.
4. It does not lose its identity through incorporation into a different or more complex unit or substance.[6]

The differentiation between supplies and equipment is sometimes very difficult to make. In the interest of consistency, schools and many other institutions sometimes use a fixed standard of cost as the arbitrary determinant of the classification of the materials used in the operation. Thus, a material costing $250 per single unit might be classified as a *supply,* whereas one costing more than that would be called *equipment.* Standardization and consistency in whatever distinction is made is important if cost comparisons are to be made from year to year or from one district to another.

Purchasing

Accountability in education might well start with the procurement of school materials. It is among the first of the school's business operations to be studied and improved when the pressure of public opinion is directed toward economizing school business operations. The increased size of schools and the recent influx of devices, machines, and gadgets necessary to implement innovative programs have combined to multiply the problems involved in purchasing supplies and equipment for a modern school program.

Purchasing supplies and equipment is not just a simple process of ordering something from a vendor, although some people may view it as such. Involved in the complicated process of purchasing are such problems as determining what is needed and in what quantity and quality, synchronizing the time of need and the time of delivery, providing the quality of the product needed without overspending the amount budgeted, storing what is required without keeping too much money invested in inventories, keeping unsuccessful bidders happy, and satisfying school personnel when recommended brands of items are not purchased, deliveries are late, or some other reason prevents delivery of essential materials or equipment.

Great as the purchaser's problems are, planning and efficiency of operation will solve most of them. Written policies concerning the use of requisitions, purchase orders, and statements of standards or specifications are mandatory for efficient procurement and use of materials.

The problems involved and the procedures used in purchasing materials for schools differ somewhat from those usually encountered in business and industry. Businesses tend to specialize to some degree in certain kinds of products; schools require a great variety of items spread over many areas. In private business, and to some degree in industry, procurement of necessary supplies and equipment is usually restricted within limited fields of a highly specialized nature. The materials required are usually selected, designed, or developed by technical staffs and passed on to the procurement officers. In general, school purchasing agents do not have the benefit of such specialized aids; they must devise their own methods of evaluating the characteristics of the many items that appear on their requisition lists. In so doing, they must satisfy the needs of teachers at all levels of education and in many special departments.

In all purchasing, economy, speed, and accuracy are important. The measure of efficient purchasing in any organization is having a particular item in the right place at the right time, at a fair price. If this ideal is to be realized, a procurement program must be established to provide adequate supplies and equipment that meet the immediate and long-range needs of the local school program.

Much has been written in textbooks and periodicals to help school administrators in establishing workable and efficient purchasing departments and improving those already in existence. Regardless of differences in the size of school districts or the character of materials procured or the sources from which they are obtained, some sound principles of purchasing procedures are commonly recognized. Purchasing practices in a school district should:

1. Accomplish a definite objective in the shortest possible time and in the easiest manner consistent with accuracy and efficiency.
2. Provide simplicity to speed operations and reduce possibilities of error.
3. Establish procedures that are definite and understandable to obviate friction, duplication, and confusion.
4. Fix responsibility for each step of performance.
5. Establish procedures that are sufficiently elastic to allow for expansion as the district grows.
6. Provide a system of procurement that is inexpensive and consistent with the job to be done.
7. Ensure that the system is adequate to perform the task for which it was created.

Policies Governing Purchasing

Effective school purchasing requires a systematic purchasing organization, operated by established procedure. The first step in establishing such an organization is for the board of education to adopt written policies concerning purchasing. Such policies are extremely valuable, not only to the board, school staff, and pupils, but also to the patrons of the school. They bring clarity and understanding to school operations. Carefully considered and well-written policies are the basis for all board functions. They legalize actions and relieve employees of the responsibility for making policy decisions under the pressure of time or expediency. Policies also help interpret institutional purposes and facilitate speed and accuracy in translating policy into action. They clarify the relationships among school board, superintendent, and staff in the matter of providing materials for the school program. Purchasing policies relate to (1) the staffing of the department, (2) objectivity in vendor relationships, and (3) user input and feedback.[7]

To supplement the policies that the school board has adopted, the superintendent of schools or the assistant superintendent in charge of the business office should establish procurement regulations that will serve as detailed guides for staff members. If the purchasing policies of a school district are to achieve the desired level of effectiveness, they must be known and understood by everyone affected by them. The most effective means of communication possible must be used to make the information available to staff personnel and to vendors and interested patrons in the community.

Those in charge of purchasing at the district level must be aware of codes and purchasing regulations that may be established at the state level and apply to all state government entities, including school districts. Some state purchasing requirements may supersede local policies, and districts may be held responsible to abide by the state-adopted procurement code.

A caution to public employees who have a responsibility of overseeing budgets or have authority to make purchases for the district, school, or department: It is imperative that no "perks" or gifts are received as an incentive to purchase materials, supplies, or equipment from a particular vendor. If any advantage is given in a purchase arrangement, it must be for the benefit of the district or school rather than any individual.

Standardization

Many of the supplies that a school district uses can be of a standard size and quality without loss in effectiveness. Where such standardization is possible, the use of standard lists has certain advantages. Unit costs can be reduced through buying larger quantities and through competitive bidding by vendors. Even when the personnel concerned help determine the standards and specifications of materials to be used, sometimes there will be justifiable reasons for buying special supplies or supplies with nonstandard specifications. Important as standards are in procuring supplies and equipment, no worthwhile school program should suffer unduly because of inability to use standardized materials.

Among other benefits, standardization:

1. Allows lower costs from bids on large quantities of one item
2. Reduces and facilitates repairs and replacements
3. Reduces inventories, thereby reducing storage costs, and at the same time increases the amount of school funds available for other purposes
4. Speeds delivery of materials or equipment
5. Reduces the number of materials and equipment for which specifications must be written
6. Reduces the work of the purchasing department, including that of business office recordkeeping

One of the problems involved in determining standards of quality (and therefore of price) is determining what quality in a product is required to achieve a particular function for a particular period. This is the same problem that the purchaser meets when buying an automobile for personal use. He or she must decide whether a second-hand car of a certain quality will provide the proper amount and quality of service for the duration of known needs, or whether additional investment in a new car will prove to be more economical in the long run. The school district purchasing agent facing the same problem may often be tempted to procure the least expensive item, in order to allow for purchases of other items. All too often, this results in employee dissatisfaction, poor performance, high repair costs, early replacement, and an unwise and uneconomical expenditure of school funds.

In determining the standard of quality, the purchaser should consider:

1. Length of term for which the product is to be used
2. The comparative service that each potential choice is known to have given
3. Prestige factors involved, if any

4. The extent of safety hazards involved, if any
5. The availability of the products under consideration
6. Initial cost and upkeep costs
7. Disposal problems and costs

Specifications for materials to be purchased often require much time and effort in preparation. Districts take advantage of the standard specifications already prepared by private companies or by the Federal Bureau of Standards. The use of brand-name products will save the time of the business office in soliciting quotations and in ordering the product. It also provides some foreknowledge of the quality of the product being purchased. It has one important disadvantage: The user is often required to use one brand-name product when experience and personal bias would strongly suggest the purchase of a different one, often at little or no additional increase in cost.

Quantity Purchasing

School districts usually try to buy in large quantities to save on original costs and to reduce office work and delivery problems. This kind of purchasing policy requires a knowledge of needs and assures the business office of budgetary control in all supply and equipment accounts. At the same time, the practice could result in tying up the funds of the district in unnecessary inventories and requiring large areas of district facilities for storage. It may also occasion early purchase of certain materials that later become undesirable because of changes in teacher preferences or because better materials are invented or discovered. This may result in having to use supplies or items of equipment that are outmoded, obsolete, or not as effective as newer items. There is no standard rule for the purchaser to follow in deciding between quantity orders and more frequent orders. Experience with the products, as well as with the desires and working policies of school staff members, is necessary to determine the best policy for each district in quantity purchasing.

Bidding

Most states and local districts have rules and regulations concerning the need for competitive bids for the purchase of school supplies and equipment. Ordinarily, purchases or contracts for services for more than a stipulated amount or cost must be by bid. Here again, determining the maximum amount that does not require a bid is difficult. If the amount is low, little saving is possible—advertising for and receiving bids is expensive to the district and also to the vendor. Low maximums also tie the hands of the purchasing agent, who may otherwise have the opportunity of making frequent small purchases at a saving. On the other hand, placing the maximum too high encourages the district to purchase required materials without the formality and the savings of competitive bidding.

Bidding requires advertising, establishing specifications, obtaining sealed bids to supply the materials at a certain price, and determination of the successful bidder by the board of education. Bids are let to the bidder under a general policy of "lowest-best bid." This is not always the lowest bid in terms of unit cost. Other factors to be considered are quality of product and quality of service; ability of the vendor to provide the product, service, or both (usually covered by a performance bond); time when delivery can be made; and reputation and fiscal responsibility of the vendor.

Often, states have bid contracts for particular equipment that school districts may find beneficial. With the state's ability to buy in large quantities, savings can be generated for smaller districts especially. Small rural districts may find it advantageous to form a consortium for obtaining bids on certain high-priced items.

Supply Management

Once the supplies have been ordered and received, the neophyte purchasing agent may think the problem is solved. But the problems of receiving, storing, and distributing supplies loom large in the average school district. Supplies or inventory have little value unless they are available when needed. The main functions involved in receiving supplies are checking purchase orders against the goods received, noting the differences, if any, calling any errors to the attention of the vendors, certifying delivery, and authorizing payment. This work requires a careful and well-trained person. Irresponsibility in the receiving of supplies may cost the district money through errors in shipment or difficulties with vending companies. One of the advantages to be gained by receiving all purchases at the district or a central receiving warehouse is that it eliminates the careless checking that often occurs when many individuals perform this service.

Supply Storage

In large school districts, the problem of supply storage is often a serious one. The district must decide between a central storage facility and several site-level facilities. The advantages of these two methods tend to balance out. Central storage provides for better district control and accountability and reduces the number of employees involved in storing and distributing supplies. The decentralized system assures more school unit control and guarantees the availability of materials whenever needed, but less experienced employees are involved in their handling.

Storage of school lunch supplies and commodities requires special consideration. Supervisors are not always aware of what types of foods might become available from the federal government to supplement the school lunch program. The costs of operating the program are increased with the need for refrigeration/freezer storage facilities. School lunch supervisors are faced with these questions when receiving various types of government commodities with little notice: Is a central cooler/freezer available? Can the acquired supplies be stored in existing school facilities? Is temporary storage available from a commercial company? Can a neighboring district provide space for a period of time? Without careful planning, consequences could be costly.

As pointed out before, the primary concern is for the fiscal implications of the school's operation. The details of storage, distribution, and use of school supplies are therefore beyond the purview of this brief treatment. However, it is within the purpose of this work to suggest certain policies and procedures that do affect the costs of education. The following list of six requirements for an effective storage system seems pertinent:

1. All supplies must be stored in spaces that are free of destructive factors such as excessive heat or cold, moisture, vermin and insects, and fire hazards.
2. All storage areas must be accessible for both incoming and outgoing supplies.
3. All supplies must be so stored as to be readily available when needed.
4. All storage materials must be administered under the rule that old stock is used first.
5. A current inventory should be kept for each storage area.
6. Responsibility for proper operation of storage areas must be specifically assigned and clearly understood by all involved.

Distribution of Supplies and Equipment

Each school district has its own special system for the distribution of supplies and equipment. The essential characteristics of any system involve use of requisitions, records of distribution, and stock or inventory records.

The policy involved in the distribution of school supplies in today's school is much different from the traditional policy of an earlier era. No longer are supplies stored in the darkest corner of the basement under lock and key, available only on certain days or at certain hours and distributed on the basis of a permanent short-supply philosophy. The modern approach encourages a policy of putting supplies where they can be seen and obtained with the least possible inconvenience by the teacher or other staff members. Modern administrative policy recognizes the value of materials in helping the staff achieve the purposes of the school. It is economically foolish to employ a teacher at a good salary and then deny that person a chance to succeed by limiting the supplies, devices, and other aids so essential to the educational program. The old fear that open shelves of readily accessible supplies would encourage waste has proved to be groundless. Today's teachers use more supplies and greater varieties of them, but there is little evidence of their misuse.

Risk Management

The concept of risk management has changed drastically in the past few years as litigation has put the onus on boards of education, administrators, and teachers as responsible parties for accidents that occur in the classroom and on the playground. As a result, many districts are taking positive steps to alleviate problems before they occur by assigning *risk management* responsibilities to a staff member. "The term 'risk management' did not come into use until the 1960s. However, the practice of risk management dates back to 4000 B.C. with the practice of Bottomry. Bottomry was the method used for spreading risk in maritime adventures through loans that were repayable at exorbitant interest rates for successful ventures."[8] In education, past history has been simply that of alerting schools of possible danger areas and providing some workshops related to health and accident hazards.

Business and industry have led the way in demonstrating the value of taking an aggressive approach in preventing accidents in the workplace and have found it financially beneficial to hire a person specifically assigned to risk management responsibilities. The public sector, including school districts, has become much more involved and more and more services are being handled through a risk management office. Constantino provided evidence that school districts might have an even greater need than other public entities:

> A school board needs to evaluate the relationship between risk management and the high cost of risk. Even if a town employs a risk manager, school district risk management differs from municipalities in its liability exposure. A municipality is primarily dealing with adults—school districts deal with young, immature adults. School districts face a tidal wave of new and expanding exposures to loss, not the least of which is the liability of public officials and public bodies such as school boards.[9]

Letzring stressed, "Instead of eliminating all risks, you manage them to the point that they have the least effect on your bottom line."[10] More importantly, "look at the situation in terms of a safe and healthy environment for the students."[11] He noted that this effort falls into four categories:

1. *Risk avoidance.* Eliminate high-risk activities such as gymnastics, scuba diving, use of trampolines, and other potentially hazardous activities.
2. *Risk control.* Give thorough instructions to staff and students concerning risks in science labs, wood, metal and auto shops, gym classes, playground equipment, and potential hazards in and around the building.
3. *Risk transfer.* Involve a third party, through contract, to cover costs for losses that fall under certain insurance terms. Transfer may be through waivers signed by parents. Courts may have to decide if such waivers are legal, but some recent cases have upheld such agreements.
4. *Risk retention.* When risks cannot be eliminated, controlled or transferred, evaluate whether insurance costs are too great or unavailable; expected losses are so small that costs can be considered a part of operating costs; or the risk is so remote that it does not justify insurance.[12]

One approach to transferring risk is with public entity risk pools. Governmental Accounting Standards Board 10 defines this as "a cooperative group of governmental entities joining together to finance an exposure, liability, or risk. Risk may include property and liability, workers' compensation, employee health care. A pool may be a stand alone entity or be included as part of a larger governmental entity that acts as the pool's sponsor."[13]

The public entity pools vary, but can be classified as follows:

- *Risk-sharing pool.* Governmental entities join together to share in the cost of losses.
- *Insurance-purchase pool (risk-purchasing group).* Governmental entities join together to acquire commercial insurance coverage.
- *Banking pool.* Governmental entities are allowed to borrow funds from a pool to pay losses.
- *Claims-servicing or account-pool.* Governmental entities join together to administer the separate account of each entity in the payment of losses.[14]

In Utah, the Office of Risk Management is charged by statute with the responsibility of establishing a risk control program for state agencies and participating school districts. The office identifies the following as its purpose:

> Risk control is the art of anticipation and action and is an inherent management responsibility. It is embedded in the risk management process and has to do with identifying risk of loss and then eliminating, reducing or avoiding risk in the most appropriate way in each circumstance. It encompasses safety programs, inspections and training, but goes beyond traditional concepts of "safety" to include management issues such as policies and procedures, programming and contracts. It should be as broad and pervasive as risk of loss is. Among the main objectives of our risk control program are these: (1) to save lives, (2) to eliminate human suffering, (3) to avoid disruption of the services you provide, and (4) to reduce the cost of losses and thereby meet the public trust you have for the resources you control.[15]

Although there is an apparent great need for school districts to have a risk manager, as with so many other aspects in education, finances dictate priorities. "Yet, despite its importance for cost-control, asset protection and employee safety, many school districts lack the resources to hire a full-time risk manager."[16] In the main, districts throughout the country have assigned a staff member this responsibility as an add-on to other duties and have provided limited training. Whether the position is full time or part time, it is necessary to be supported at the top administrative level. Bieber stated:

> Top management support is important for a full-time risk management program to be effective, and it's even more important for a part-time risk management program because much of the day-to-day activities are going to have to be done on a departmental basis. Top management must demonstrate to department heads and line supervisors the importance of their cooperation, explain the need for a part-time risk management function and introduce the manager responsible for it.[17]

Because of the many potential risks, a litigious society, and increasing costs necessary to cover liabilities, it is likely that the role of the risk manager will continue to become increasingly more important in school business affairs.

Insurance

Insurance is a method of providing for cooperative sharing of the risk of financial or other loss in the event of some unfortunate incident. School districts are concerned primarily with insurance protection against loss of life; acts of criminals; the alteration of, destruction of, or damage to school property; the liability of school personnel for tort action; and the personal welfare of school employees.

Insurance has been called a necessary expenditure to provide for benefits in case of an incident or emergency that the purchaser hopes will never occur. The risk taker (school or individual) purchases insurance from a professional risk bearer (the insurance company or risk pool) as financial security in the event that some undesirable event occurs. No person looks forward to the burning of a home or a school so that insurance will be collected. The insured is merely trying to soften the financial blow of a catastrophe in the hope that the loss will not be permanently damaging.

School Board Responsibility

The school board's responsibility for operating schools carries with it stated and implied powers for the protection of public funds and property. It is taken for granted that schools and their pupils must be given reasonable protection from interruption and loss from emergencies, disasters, or other less serious events. The legal responsibility for such protection rests solely with the board of education in each school district, except in states where such protection is provided at the state level. This is an important obligation that the board can ill afford to ignore or minimize. At stake are several needs: protection of the state's and local district's large investment in school buildings and property; financial protection for individuals in the event of injury, tort action, or death; and public protection against interruptions in the normal school process in the event of emergencies.

Just as prudent individuals protect themselves against financial loss from fire in homes or places of business, so a responsible board of education will protect a community from the same risks with its school buildings. This is best accomplished by buying insurance in amounts commensurate with the size of the investment the district has in such properties.

Unfortunately, it is often no longer possible to buy such insurance at a reasonable cost. Many school districts view the provision of adequate insurance as a necessity. Insurance premium rates have skyrocketed, juries award claimants large amounts of money, and some school districts and municipalities are simply unable to pay extraordinarily high insurance premiums.

Basic Principles

Since it would usually be unwise economically for a school district to provide insurance to protect it from all the possible risks such an enterprise might face, school boards are often faced with the problem of selecting those items or assets for which they are most obligated to provide insurance protection. There are a number of basic safety measures that school boards can use to help cover many of the areas of low risk, to supplement the insurance program considered necessary for high-risk facilities and operations. These would include loss prevention through good building design, safety programs, regular inspections of buildings, the provision of adequate fire-fighting equipment, and the accumulation of reserves to pay for any losses sustained.

As thousands of school boards have dealt with their insurance problems over a long period, certain basic rules or principles have evolved:

1. A well-organized and conscientiously administered safety and loss-prevention program is effective in reducing injuries and property losses through accidents. Such a program is needed for management, as well as humanitarian reasons, and it is also the best and least costly kind of insurance.

2. The board of education has a moral and legal responsibility to provide protection for its employees, its students, and its patrons against ordinary accidents that often occur within the jurisdiction of the school. Once a discretionary power of the board, the provision for a well-conceived insurance plan is now a mandatory duty of every board of education, acting within the legal framework and guidelines provided in each state.

3. The board of education has a moral (and sometimes a legal) obligation to formulate in writing its policies and regulations concerning the safety and protection of all those in the school community.

4. The insurance program of a school should be the result of careful study of risks involved, past experiences in the district, and the recommendations of consultants. The field of insurance is so broad and complex that school administrators cannot hope to advise their boards concerning such needs solely on the basis of their own knowledge and experience.

5. The insurance program should not be static and unchangeable but should reflect changing needs and risks. To continue an insurance program year after year without evaluation and change or adjustment is a practice that only the inexperienced, the careless, or the uninformed pursue.

Main Types of Insurance

Insurance on almost any risk can be purchased if cost is of no concern to the purchaser. Thus, insurance may be available for almost anything and everything the school board may want to insure. The establishment of insurance priorities is therefore highly important to the board. The following is a list of some of the most common kinds of insurance that a typical school board would want to consider. No priority is intended, for that would vary from one school to another.

1. *Fire.* Insurance on the building and its contents against loss from damage by fire; common to all school districts; may use coinsurance, blanket insurance, specific or specific-schedule insurance, or self-insurance.

2. *Extended coverage.* Insurance that is added to fire insurance policies to cover miscellaneous risks, usually windstorm or tornado, smoke, loss by vehicular or aircraft damage to buildings, hailstorm, or riot damage; often difficult to obtain and expensive in riot-prone areas.

3. *Glass.* Insurance against loss of windows or door glass; usually too expensive for buildings with extensive window areas. Some schools are experimenting with plastic windows that are unbreakable in order to reduce high insurance costs.

4. *Boiler.* Insurance for protection against property damage, injury, and death due to boiler or pressure-tank explosions; a *must* for high-pressure boilers but not as necessary for the low-pressure ones now being used in many schools.

5. *Floater.* Insurance to protect all valuables and equipment used by the school; originally was inland marine insurance, which protected property in transit from one location to another.

6. *Crime.* Protection against loss by burglary, robbery, or theft.

7. *Automobile and bus.* Protection against damage or destruction and liability for damage and injury to others caused by district-owned automobiles or buses.

8. *Liability.* Protection against bodily injury or damage caused by accidents due to the negligence of employees or those sustained on school-owned property; also protection to the school board in states that have waived the immunity rule for school boards.

9. *Worker's compensation.* State protection from loss to the employee because of injury or death resulting from employment.

10. *Surety bonds.* Protection for the school district against loss or damage through dishonesty of employees.

11. *Accident.* Protection for pupils for injury sustained in the activities of the school.

Fire Insurance

Fire insurance rates are determined in terms of the risks involved. The type of construction of the building, adequacy of the fire department and its water supply, kind and age of equipment, distance from the fire department to the school, and fire alarm systems are all determinants of the rates school districts must pay for insurance. Buildings that are not fire resistant require higher rates than those that are fire resistant. Rates are lower for buildings that are near adequate and modern fire departments. Rates are also lower for insurance issued for longer periods; the typical term of an insurance policy for school buildings is either three or five years.

Financial protection of the large investment that every school district has in buildings, equipment, and other property is an absolute necessity. The serious predicament of the small school with inadequate insurance that loses its only building to fire is not pleasant to contemplate. If such an event should occur, no amount of explanation based on the board's opinion that insurance costs were beyond its budgetary provisions would satisfy the local citizenry, replace the school building, or in any way provide for the future school program. Thus, fire insurance is a necessity in order to protect the capital assets of a school district.

Increasing Rates

Increases in vandalism have had an effect on the willingness of insurance companies to insure schools. At one time, schools were wooed by insurance companies eager to insure them. Now, schools are either refused the coverage or asked to pay a much higher premium or accept an increased deductible.

The fact that some insurance companies may have overreacted does not alter the possibility that social problems of the day may have a deleterious effect on schools' efforts to protect the assets required for their operation. The penalties—difficulty in getting adequate property insurance and being forced to pay high rates for coverage— fall on districts with a record of few claims just as they do on districts with a record of many high claims.

The current problem of securing insurance coverage is greatest in urban areas. Some city school systems have been forced to close their doors for a short time after policies were cancelled or their renewal refused. Some of the larger cities use self-insurance; smaller city school districts are almost forced to count on greater state or federal financial assistance to help solve this problem.

Determining Insurance Needs

Neither overinsurance nor underinsurance represents an economical expenditure of funds for a school district. Overinsurance is a financial waste, for the district can never collect more than the actual loss of a building. On the other hand, insurance companies never pay more than the value of the insurance policy, regardless of a greater amount of loss.

Determining the insurable values of buildings involves original cost (excluding the cost of the site, architectural fees, foundations, and other noninsurables), depreciation, and replacement costs. The insurable value is the replacement cost (minus noninsurables) minus the value of depreciation for the number of years the building has been in existence.

It is essential that school boards know the insurable value of their buildings at the time they are insured. The savings that a board may presume to make by determining its own values for original purchase of insurance may be lost when insurance adjusters determine the value of claims. The value of using qualified appraisers and professional services in determining insurance needs is obvious.

Coinsurance

School districts have generally favored a system of coinsurance for protection against fire losses. Coinsurance involves a sharing of the risk between the school district and the insuring company. Coinsurance policies are usually written with either 80 percent or 90 percent coverage. This means two things. (1) If the school district maintains its required coverage (the 80 or 90 percent of insurable value it chose), the rate will be less than if it allows its coverage to be less than the agreed-on percentage. (2) If full coverage of the 80 or 90 percent is maintained, the insurance company will sustain the total amount of fire loss up to the value of the insurance; but if full coverage is not maintained, the district will share proportionately in every fire loss regardless of how large or how small it may be.

Coinsurance uses lower rates as an incentive for districts to carry the maximum amount of insurance that it has agreed to carry. Since any amount less than that agreed on makes the district liable for some fraction of any fire loss, districts are motivated to keep their coverage at the maximum. Since most school building fires do not result in complete loss of the building, less than maximum insurance coverage would never fully protect the district for any of its fire losses.

A district must keep accurate and up-to-date records of property values and insurance coverage. Regular appraisal of property by qualified professionals is an absolute necessity. Appraisal services are often available through state agencies or insurance companies, usually at low cost to the school. Certain organizations, such as the National Board of Fire Underwriters, perform useful services that are now available to schools in the improvement of the fire insurance policies and standards necessary to protect public property.

Extended Coverage

All the real and imagined risks to buildings are not covered by ordinary fire insurance policies. For example, the risks of damage from riot, explosion, windstorm, tornado, hail, smoke, or aircraft are not ordinarily covered in such policies. Extended coverage policies, however, provide such insurance, at some additional cost. Just what kinds of insurance the district should carry and in what amounts are judgments each school board must decide for itself. Ideally, such decisions are made only after careful study of the experience, over time, of comparable districts in comparable locations and with the recommendations of the administrative staff (made only after consulting professionals in school building insurance).

No school board, regardless of its revenue-producing ability, can afford to protect the school district from all possible hazards or risks. The cost would be prohibitive and would represent a degree of misuse of public funds. The insurance carried by a district should be determined on a "degree of risk" basis. For example, a school building near an airport represents a different degree of risk than one located in open country. Again, fire-resistant (sometimes erroneously referred to as fireproof) buildings in open country represent a much different risk from frame construction buildings in the same location. The responsibility of the school board is to protect itself and its clientele as best it can, keeping in mind the cost as compared with the risk involved in each unit insured. Good rules of thumb for the board would be to provide adequate insurance on all high risks, establish priorities and exercise sound judgment on all average risks, and eliminate or minimize insurance on low-risk insurables.

Self-Insurance

Insurance costs are determined by many factors, including the probability of loss as determined by experience with large numbers of similar risks under similar circumstances. Thus, the danger of loss of several buildings in a school district may be slight, particularly if they are scattered at random within the district. Under such conditions, a very large school district with a large number of buildings and with adequate financial resources may decide to provide "self-insurance" for its buildings and other insurance needs. The board may reason that the risk of loss of one or more buildings is offset by the large sum necessary to pay the insurance premiums over time. It may then proceed in one of three ways: (1) with no insurance—losses to be paid out of tax revenues or from special bond issues; (2) with the provision of insurance only on property with the greatest risk of loss and no insurance on the rest; or (3) with the provision for reserve funds (instead of premium payments), from which future losses will be paid.

The use of self-insurance in protecting schools in the event of insurance loss is obviously controversial. The argument at one extreme is that such a procedure offers no protection whatever; the argument at the other extreme is that some districts could and should insure themselves. Consequently, state law and the judgment of the board of education must provide the answer regarding whether to self-insure.

Liability Insurance

With the demise of archaic immunity laws regarding school board liability for tort action in several states, providing liability insurance becomes a relevant consideration. May school funds be legally expended for liability insurance to protect school boards for the torts of its employees in common-law states? The question still produces more than a little controversy, but there is no such paradox in the states that have abrogated that rule. The law and a sense of fairness to pupils require that all those who have a responsibility for pupils' safety, welfare, and education be insured. In the common-law states that adhere to the immunity principle, this means liability insurance on school employees at district expense. To the gradually increasing number of states that have cast aside the immunity rule, by court edict or state statute or both, this means liability insurance on school employees *and* school boards should be provided at public expense.

Regardless of whether the law mandates or simply approves school district liability insurance on itself or its employees, school boards have moved to provide whatever liability insurance coverage is necessary to protect all those with legal liability. This is a necessary part of the cost of education—one that experienced boards of education will not refuse to approve.

Regulation of Insurance

It is necessary that the broad field of insurance be regulated by some agency of government to protect all parties concerned. Without regulation, the cost of insurance could be placed at almost any point at the same time that some companies could default in their insurance payments to the parties who had suffered losses.

Most states control insurance companies through the office of a state commissioner. Through that office, insurance companies are approved to sell insurance if they meet the state rules and regulations that apply. The possibility of deception or fraud is decreased under this form of state regulation. School boards need to become familiar with the general pattern in their state for control of this important service. Among many other benefits to be obtained by the school board from such regulatory procedures, there is the value that comes from obtaining a reliable rating of all insurance companies licensed to operate within the state.

Transportation

State laws require compulsory education and prescribe that each school-age student is entitled to a free public education. If students are unable to get to and from schools because of time, distance, hazards, or their age or physical limitations, they are effectively denied a free education. Consequently, as a regular and necessary part of operating schools, districts must provide some means of getting students to and from schools where, otherwise, their very attendance would be jeopardized. Transportation of students is usually left to local districts, though they must operate within guidelines and restrictions established by state and federal legislation and regulated on a statewide basis.

The transporting of students is part of the education process in many districts and it can have a big impact on district budgets. The ramifications of operating school buses may seem trivial on the surface for the noninformed. Few people are aware that the transporting of students in the United States is the largest ground transportation system in the country. *School Transportation News* reports the following statistics that emphasize the enormity of the transportation of K–12 students (about 55 percent of the school population) throughout the United States:

24.0 million daily *one-way* rides
2.0 million daily extracurricular rides
52.8 million total student rides *daily*
9.54 billion total student rides in 180 day school year
1 billion total rides for summer school, Head Start, child care
10.54 billion annual student rides[18]

"There are more than 450,000 yellow school buses on U.S. roads. . . . The industry spends more than $15.6 billion annually, most in the form of reimbursement to school districts for state-supported transportation costs."[19] In some cases where students are in an inaccessible area, or only a few students are in an isolated location, a school board may opt to pay parents a sum to cover transportation costs rather than provide them bus service.

It is expensive to purchase, operate, and maintain a fleet of school buses. A large school system with transportation needs must employ drivers, mechanics, and a supervisor to determine routes, schedule trips, and provide other functions to operate an efficient fleet. Buses get low miles per gallon, making fuel costs a huge concern. In the year 2006, oil prices increased dramatically and caused some districts to curtail services.

Small rural districts usually have a greater percentage of the overall budget assigned to transportation because of the number of students that need to be transported greater distances. In general, such districts must operate without the resources available in larger districts.

In most states, transportation revenues are provided in addition to other budgets. However, if expenditures are greater than money available, the operation budget may be tapped and may infringe on the main focus of educating students. In some states, hazardous routes are left to the discretion of local boards of education and may be costly, but necessary, in transporting students over railway crossings, water hazards, busy intersections, or other such hazards. A local board may have an option of assessing a mill levy to offset such costs.

The Individuals with Disabilities Education Act (IDEA) requires that special education students be transported in specially equipped buses. No federal dollars have been appropriated to assist states and districts in meeting these additional costs. The Department of Transportation standards have added to costs as more stringent safety standards have been required. Other increases have been added to transportation budgets as discipline and vandalism have become a greater problem. Video cameras have been installed in many buses and aides are required to control students.

To enhance the education program and extend the classroom, field trips are an integral part of the curriculum in most districts. Athletics are also a factor in the transportation budget. These areas are funded in various ways by individual districts.

There are many ramifications in operating a school district transportation program. The intent in this book is to draw attention to the financial impact on education, not to detail the functions necessary to operate an efficient program.

School Food Services

The National School Lunch Program (NSLP) is federally assisted and operates in more than 99,800 public and nonprofit private schools. It was established under the National School Lunch Act in 1946. Financial support and administration is through the Food and Nutrition Service within the Department of Agriculture. In most cases, the program is administered by the state education agencies with agreements with local school districts.[20]

Since its inception, the school lunch program has broadened to include school breakfasts, special milk programs, summer food services, and after-school snacks. Almost 99 percent of all public schools are involved and 58 percent of the school children to whom the lunch program is available participate. It is apparent that this program is big business and a financial issue for states, districts, and local schools.[21]

The local school district business office is involved in operating the school lunch program and is responsible under the direction of the superintendent and board for the fiscal soundness of the program. There are restrictions and regulations that must be adhered to, but in the final analysis, the program should be self-sufficient and efficiently managed so that it does not become a financial drain on the district's regular budget.

At the local school level, the responsibility, however, still remains with the principal or other administrative head.

Revenues are received from the U.S. Department of Agriculture, which provides a cash reimbursement for each meal served, and from funds collected from program participants. In addition, schools may receive commodities, called *entitlement* foods, at a value of 17.25 cents for each meal served. Schools can also get "bonus" commodities as they become available from surplus agricultural stocks, including fresh, canned, and frozen fruits and vegetables; meats; fruit juices; flour and other grains; and other surplus products.[22] As of June 30, 2006, the cash reimbursement rates were:

> Free lunches: $2.32
> Reduced-price lunches: $1.92
> Paid lunches: $0.22
> Free snacks: $0.63
> Reduced-price snacks: $0.31
> Paid snacks: $0.05

Higher reimbursement rates are provided to Alaska and Hawaii and some schools with a high percentage of low-income children. [23]

The eligibility requirements for reduced or free meals are contained in the *Federal Register* for the Department of Agriculture, Food and Nutrition Service, which indicates:

> The Department requires schools and institutions which charge for meals separately from other fees to serve *free meals* to all children from any household with income at or below 130 percent of the poverty guidelines. The Department also requires such schools and institutions to serve *reduced priced meals* to all children from any household with income higher than 130 percent of the poverty guidelines, but below 185 percent of the poverty guidelines.[24]

The poverty level and eligibility figures are listed in Table 14.1.

Students eligible for a reduced-price meal can be charged no more than 40 cents.[25] Children from families with incomes over 185 percent of poverty pay full price, though their meals are still subsidized to some extent. Local school boards set their own prices for full-price meals.[26]

Table 14.2 shows the total participation in the program for a three-year period. In 2005, more than 29.6 million children were served 4.97 billion meals at a cost to the government of $7.0 billion. Estimates for the total program for the year was $11.5 billion. Of the total lunches served, 59.4 percent were free or reduced in price.

There are critics of the child nutrition programs. Because of the vastness of the participation and the costs involved, critics—and even some educators—ask the question: Why are we in the food business? The basic answer is that "we can't expect our children to learn when they're hungry."[27] Studies have shown that children have improved academic performance when they have eaten school breakfasts, and studies have linked hunger in children to other problems, including absenteeism, tardiness, hyperactivity, and antisocial behavior.[28]

TABLE 14.1   Income Eligibility Guidelines: June 2007

Federal Poverty Guidelines		Reduced Price Meals—185%			Free Meals—130%		
Size of Family Unit	*48 Contiguous States* and D.C.*	*Annual*	*Month*	*Week*	*Annual*	*Month*	*Week*
1	$ 9,800	18,130	1,511	349	12,740	1,062	245
2	13,200	24,420	2,035	470	17,160	1,430	330
3	16,600	30,710	2,560	591	21,580	1,799	415
4	20,000	37,000	3,084	712	26,000	2,167	500
5	23,400	43,290	3,608	833	30,420	2,535	585
6	26,800	49,580	4,132	954	34,840	2,904	670
7	30,200	55,870	4,656	1,075	39,260	3,272	755
8	33,600	62,160	5,180	1,196	43,680	3,640	840
Each additional family member, add	3,400	6,290	525	121	4,420	369	85

*Alaska and Hawaii eligibility requirements are higher.

Source: Federal Register, Vol. 71, No. 50, March 15, 2006.

TABLE 14.2   National School Lunch Program Annual Summary

Fiscal Year	Total Participation	Total Lunches Served	% Free of Total Lunches	% RP of Total Lunches	Snacks Served	Cash Payments	Total Commodity Costs
FY 2005	29,630,164	4,973,190,487	49.8%	9.6%	163,223,902	7,050,086,881	975,465,771
FY 2004	28,963,922	4,841,849,706	49.5%	9.5%	150,929,234	6,662,060,954	963,014,962
FY 2003	28,387,983	4,763,106,915	49.0%	9.5%	139,191,714	6,340,627,019	848,652,070

Source: www.fns.usda.gov/pd/slmonthly.htm, data as of May 2006.

Summary

In today's unrelenting atmosphere, the chief school officer in the district, and the school board itself, must bring to the top of the school agenda the oft-quoted slogan, "Safety first." Prevention strategies and emergency measures to plan, prepare, and practice for the worst possible incidents of violence must be created. Their actions must be handled deftly so that students do not begin to feel anxiety in the school setting.

Good management skills are required to operate the business aspects of the school community. Every school district is faced with the problem of procuring, storing, and distributing supplies and equipment in the most efficient and economical manner possible. If school budgets are reduced, the need for effective management of fiscal and material resources increases. Regardless of the size of the school district, the chief school administrator is responsible for assuring that maximum benefits are provided by the expenditure of each dollar in every aspect of the school program. The person or persons who supervise and administer the supplies and equipment program of any school district should be capable and well trained. Even though this operation is secondary to the instructional program, it demands care and wisdom on the part of all those who are responsible for its administration.

Some school districts find it advantageous to assign a staff member to a risk management position. This concept is gaining greater acceptance in the public sector. As a preventive measure, boards of education and principals of local schools should survey the facilities on a systematic basis to be assured that hazardous areas for students and staff do not exist.

As the risks of operating schools increase, the need for evaluating and improving the insurance program increases. It is easy to overinsure or underinsure the property and potential loss and liability from a myriad of causes. In procuring insurance, the school board should be certain that its program is providing coverage at reasonable cost for risks that often exist and that it does not provide high-cost insurance for risks that seldom exist. Regardless of the insurance provided, the program should be under constant evaluation by knowledgeable insurance advisers in order to provide the necessary coverage at minimum cost, using sound risk management principles.

Because of higher premiums and districts being rejected for coverage, some districts have become self-insured. States are making it possible for agencies under their jurisdiction, including schools, to become a member of an agency pool. In an inflationary period, school boards may find that a district that was properly insured is now underinsured. Neglecting to carry adequate insurance is a common oversight of many school districts. In very large districts, but not in small ones, self-insurance can sometimes be substituted for a formal insurance program.

Transportation and food services are usually assigned to the business office to administer. Both have wide participation and are an important part of the overall education program. Effective management is necessary to work with these relatively large budgets and to comply with federal and state restrictions and requirements. Though the day-to-day operations may be the responsibility of the principal and business office, the superintendent and the board of education are ultimately held accountable for the soundness of the programs.

ASSIGNMENT PROJECTS

1. Provide a definition for each of the following terms: *business principles, risk management, supply, equipment, standardization, bid, insurance, food services, transportation, liability, coinsurance, extended coverage, self-insurance, tort.*
2. Determine the major changes that have taken place in school district insurance needs, particularly in the area of liability for lack of supervision of students, failure of students to learn, tort actions, and so on.
3. Develop a rationale for and against self-insurance for a school district.

4. List the arguments for and against state insurance of all school buildings within a state.
5. Determine what approach a local district and the state are using for risk management procedures. Is there evidence that employing a risk manager is fiscally sound?
6. Suggest a plan for the orderly procurement, storage, and distribution of school supplies and equipment as well as a plan for transportation and school food services for a medium-sized school district.
7. Determine what your school/district "plan, prepare, practice" safety policy is.

Computer simulations and questions, research exercises, and website addresses relevant to this chapter can be found at

www.ablongman.com/edleadership

SELECTED READINGS

Campbell, Roald F., Luvern L. Cunningham, Raphael O. Nystrand, and Michael D. Usdan. *The Organization and Control of American Schools,* 6th ed. Columbus, OH: Merrill, 1990.

Louberge, Henri (ed.). *Risk Information and Insurance.* Boston: Kluwer Academic, 1990.

Randall, David, and George Gills. *Risk Financing Survey.* Arlington, VA: Public Risk Management Associates, 1993.

Ray, John R., Walter G. Hack, and I. Carl Candoli. *School Business Administration,* 8th ed. Boston: Allyn and Bacon, 2005.

Rejda, George E. *Principles of Insurance,* 3rd ed. Glenview, IL: Scott, Foresman, 1986.

Ross, Bernard H. *Public Risk Management: An Annotated Bibliography.* Arlington, VA: Public Risk Management Associates, 1992.

Schael, L. D., and C. W. Haley. *Introduction to Financial Management,* 2nd ed. New York: McGraw-Hill, 1980.

School Business Affairs. June 1992 and June 1993 "Issues on Risk Management." Reston, VA: ASBO.

Short, James F., Jr., and Lee Clark. *Organizations, Uncertainties and Risk.* Boulder, CO: Westview Press, 1992.

Thomas, Hywell, and Jane Martin. *Managing Resources for School Improvement: Creating a Cost-Effective School.* London: Routledge, 1996.

Ubben, Gerald C., and Larry W. Hughes. *The Principal: Creative Leadership for Effective Schools,* 3rd ed. Boston: Allyn and Bacon, 1997.

Williams, C. Arthur, Jr., and Richard M. Heins. *Risk Management and Insurance,* 7th ed. New York: McGraw-Hill, 1995.

ENDNOTES

1. National Advisory Committee on Children and Terrorism, www.bt.cdc.gov/children.
2. Barabara O. Taylor, "The Effective Schools Process: Alive and Well," *Phi Delta Kappan,* January 2002, pp. 375–378.
3. Kenneth S. Trump and Curtis Lavarello, "No Safe Havens," *American School Board Journal,* March 2003, pp. 19–21.
4. Ibid.
5. Frederick Hill, as quoted by H. Ronald Smith, "From Your President: Business Administrators Play on Education Team, Too," *School Business Affairs,* June 1986, p. 6.
6. Charles T. Roberts and Allan R. Lichtenberger, *Financial Accounting* (Washington, DC: U.S. Department of Health, Education, and Welfare, 1973), pp. 93, 108.
7. Joyce E. Ferguson, "The Purchasing Administrator," *School Business Affairs,* August 1985, pp. 20–22.
8. Rita T. Constantino, "School Boards Need to Know This . . . ," *Public Risk,* July/August 1990, p. 7.

9. Ibid.

10. Timothy D. Letzring, "Risk Management and Prevention," *School Business Affairs,* June 1999, p. 26.

11. Ibid., p. 28.

12. Ibid., pp. 26–28. Referenced court cases included *Terry* v. *Indiana University,* 666 N.E. 2d 87 (Ind. Ct. Appl. 1996), *Toth* v. *Toledo Speedway,* 583 N.E. 2d 357 (Ohio Ct. App. 1989), *Boucher* v. *Riner,* 514 A. 2d 485 (Ct. App. Md. 1986), and *Loder* v. *State,* 607 N.Y.S. 2d 151 (App. Div. 1994).

13. Larry P. Bailey, *Miller Governmental GAAP Guide* (New York: Harcourt Brace, 1999), section 20.06. (The 2006 edition is by Michael A. Crawford and D. Scot Loyd, published by CCH Incorporated, Chicago, Illinois.)

14. Ibid.

15. "Risk Management for School Principals," Utah School Boards Association, Utah State Office of Risk Management, 1991, unpublished, Section 4, p. 1. Note: To further understand the depth to which risk management has become a part of the operation of schools, analyze the *State of Utah Risk Management Self Inspection Survey Reports. May 2006,* available on-line.

16. Robert M. Bieber, "Full-Time Risk, Part-Time Job Effective Part-Time Risk Management," *School Business Affairs,* January 1995, p. 45.

17. Ibid.

18. www.stnonline.com/stn/index.htm, April 2006.

19. Ibid.

20. "Nutrition Program Facts Food and Nutrition Program," USDA, www.fns.usda.gov, May 2006.

21. Ibid.

22. Ibid.

23. Ibid.

24. *Federal Register,* Vol. 71, No. 50, March 2006.

25. "Nutrition Program Facts Food and Nutrition Program."

26. Ibid.

27. George H. Ryan, Governor of Illinois, in a press release, September 1999, www.state.il.us/99/Sep/reelu.htm. p. 1.

28. Ibid.

15 Human Resources and School Finance

When all is said and done, it is teaching and learning that are the reasons for having schools. All our efforts to gather resources, to organize policy, to collect and expend revenue, to recruit, train and retain staff, are wasted if the result is not high quality teaching and learning for each child.

—Larry Shumway, 2007

The title of *human resource administrator* enlarges the role that once encompassed the areas of *personnel administrator.* The concentration on recruitment, salaries, benefits, certification, and retirement are now only a few of the responsibilities assigned to the area of human resources. The director of human resources is more a "people expert," with a broader consciousness on motivating employees and assisting in fulfilling their needs. Notwithstanding the importance of personnel duties, the role is broadened to include improving the ambiance of the profession.

Refined skills are needed by the professional human resource administrator because a certain sense of diminution has occurred among educators across the land in regard to how well they are perceived in their communities and their own feelings of worth as they pursue the professional goal of teaching the students with whom they work. A great deal of attention has been given to the profession with the passage of the No Child Left Behind law, resulting in vigorous discussions centered on "failing schools," "accountability through testing," and the need for "highly qualified teachers." These factors, by inference, question the quality of the pedagogy of the teaching profession. The human resource administrator serves a very important function when the realization is faced that a school's success and effectiveness are dependent on the well-being of personnel working in the teaching/learning environment. A quality education program depends greatly on three basic elements:

1. The quality of the human resources within the system
2. The extent to which productive human relationships are realized
3. The development and utilization of existing human qualities

The superintendent in a school district must be the leader in providing an atmosphere that promotes human resource development. Regardless of title or size of the educational enterprise, the superintendent is responsible for all activities within his or her stewardship. The assignment may be delegated, but the responsibility remains with that office. In a school, the principal must lead in that development. If the superintendent and the principal are effective leaders, satisfaction will resonate among the employees. Cultivating a warm and positive feeling for the art of teaching, keeping morale high, and promoting a warm school climate are important aspects of human resource activities.

The Expanded Role of Human Resource Administration

As the school complex has expanded, the need for improving school human resource services has increased. Similarly, as the number of teachers in a school community has increased, their educational level advanced, and their collective bargaining intensified, the profession has had a stronger voice in negotiating contracts. School boards and administrators continue to face concerns related to recruitment, orientation, assignments, and payment of instructional and auxiliary personnel. In addition to being involved in professional negotiations that may have some adversarial ramifications, human resource personnel are involved in professional development, teacher placement in periods of declining and shifting enrollment, and building morale in a climate that has changed dramatically because of violence in the school setting.

The role of human resources covers a broad spectrum (see Figure 15.1) and has expanded as a result of many factors—increasing program needs, escalating government encroachment, changing accounting practices, changing rosters, vacillating demographics, increased immigration issues, special education teaching requirements, and greater mobility of educators. Human resource managers must be directly involved in the strategic planning of the school district, since well-prepared and well-serviced professionals are essential in meeting the goals and mission of the board of education. Expertise of the highest order is required in areas such as analyzing economic, political, and social changes; assuring productivity and accountability; meeting the needs of a demographically diversified clientele; and performing all of these tasks equitably. For the human resource administrator, hiring teachers is only part of the responsibility. In many districts more than half of the personnel may be support staff, such as secretarial assistance, bus drivers, school lunch workers, maintenance staff, and others who are necessary for providing services to students.

Broad categories of human resources necessary to accomplish organizational goals include in-service programs that increase the skill level of employees and that provide adequate and equitable remuneration for employee performance based on effective evaluation. Recruitment and selection on the contemporary scene may include various screening procedures of applicants, such as drug testing, fingerprinting, and determining if there is a history of criminal or moral impropriety. Separation, which must be handled adroitly, may be adversarial (discharge and reduction in force [RIF], for example) or nonadversarial (such as retirement and/or promotion). The human resources function has expanded and is a dynamic force in enhancing a school district's effectiveness and efficiency. The role of the teacher in the district's professional de-

FIGURE 15.1   The Expanded Role of Human Resource Administration

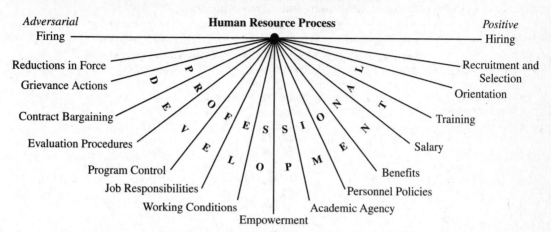

velopment strategies may change in an expanded understanding of human resources. Teachers can contribute in creating a comprehensive accountability model and could also be involved in budget matters and personnel hiring.

Teacher Compensation

Education administrators should allocate funds and provide facilities, personnel, and information in such a way that the improvement in educational achievement between entering and leaving students is maximized. To that end, the general purpose of the compensation process is to allocate resources for salaries, wages, benefits, and rewards in a manner that will attract and retain a school staff that can teach and prepare pupils well.[1] The chief costs of the labor-intensive industry of public education are salaries and benefits for instructional and supporting personnel. Such remunerations are deserving, for the function of the school is to provide high-quality academic instruction. The labyrinth of school finance is closely related to school employment.

Providing increases in teacher salaries and satisfactory benefits is not a new problem to the field of school administration. Teachers at entry level (educators graduating from college) receive less salary than graduates in other fields of employment (see Table 15.1). Note that offers to college graduates in other fields are substantially higher than average beginning teacher salaries. In 2004, the average job offer to college graduates who were noneducation majors was $40,472, whereas a teacher's average beginning salary was $31,704—a difference of $8,768. Teachers have done better, however, when compared to the average annual earnings of private-sector workers (see Figure 15.2). When compared with other professions, teachers are markedly disadvantaged (see Table 15.2). One possible explanation for the lackluster performance of teacher salaries contrasted to similar professions is that funds have been diverted to keep pace with the burgeoning cost of benefits since public-sector employees generally enjoy better health and retirements than workers in the private sector.[2] The average salary

TABLE 15.1   Trends in Beginning Teacher Salaries Compared to Job Offers to College Graduates with Majors Other Than Education: 1994–2004

Year	Beginning Teacher Salary (2004 Dollars)	Offers to Non-education Majors (2004 Dollars)	Offers to Education Majors as a Percentage of Other Offers
2004	$31,704	$40,472	78%
2003	32,186	41,109	78%
2002	30,095	43,723	69%
2001	31,738	45,914	69%
2000	30,463	44,089	69%
1999	30,450	42,064	72%
1998	29,793	41,502	72%
1997	29,438	39,031	75%
1996	29,238	37,953	77%
1995	29,744	37,214	80%
1994	29,611	37,278	79%

Source: Muir, E., Nelson, F. H., & Baldaro, A. (2005). *Survey and analysis of teacher salary trends, 2004.* Washington, DC: American Federation of Teachers. Reprinted with permission.

FIGURE 15.2   Real Wages for Teachers and All Workers

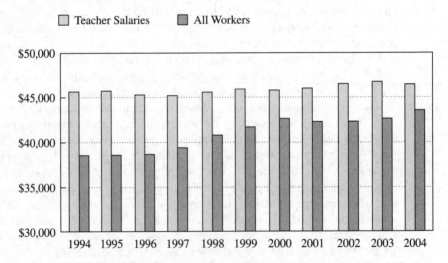

Source: Muir, E., Nelson, F. H., & Baldaro, A. (2005). *Survey and analysis of teacher salary trends, 2004.* Washington, DC: American Federation of Teachers. Reprinted with permission.

TABLE 15.2   Comparison of Teacher Pay to Other Professions: 2004

Profession	2004 Salary
Buyer	$64,813
Accountant	$56,102
Attorney	$89,989
Engineer	$78,023
Computer Systems Analyst	$73,269
Teacher	$46,597

Source: Muir, E., Nelson, F. H., & Baldaro, A. (2005). *Survey and analysis of teacher salary trends, 2004.* Washington, DC: American Federation of Teachers. Reprinted with permission.

TABLE 15.3   Average Salaries ($) of Public School Teachers: 2004–05

Rank	State	2004–05	Rank	State	2004–05
1	District of Columbia	58,456*	26	North Carolina	43,348
2	California	57,876*	27	Arizona	42,905*
3	Connecticut	57,737	28	Virginia	42,768
4	Michigan	56,973*	29	South Carolina	42,189
5	New Jersey	56,682*	30	Idaho	42,122*
6	New York	56,200	31	Tennessee	42,076
7	Illinois	55,421	32	Florida	41,590
8	Massachusetts	54,679	33	Texas	41,011
9	Rhode Island	53,473*	34	Kentucky	40,522
10	Pennsylvania	53,258*	35	Wyoming	40,497
11	Alaska	52,424	36	Arkansas	40,495*
12	Maryland	52,331	37	Maine	39,610
13	Delaware	50,595	38	Nebraska	39,456
14	Ohio	48,692*	39	Utah	39,456
15	Oregon	48,330	40	New Mexico	39,391
	United States	47,674*	41	Kansas	39,345
16	Minnesota	46,906	42	Iowa	39,284
17	Indiana	46,583	43	Missouri	39,067
18	Georgia	46,526	44	Louisiana	39,022
19	Hawaii	46,149	45	Montana	38,485
20	Washington	45,718	46	West Virginia	38,360
21	Vermont	44,535	47	Alabama	38,186
22	Wisconsin	44,299	48	Oklahoma	37,879
23	Colorado	43,949	49	North Dakota	36,695
24	New Hampshire	43,941	50	Mississippi	36,590*
25	Nevada	43,394	51	South Dakota	34,040

Source: NEA Research, Estimates Database (2006). From Rankings and Estimates 2005–2006, Rankings, Table C-11. Reprinted with permission of the National Education Association © 2006. Retrieved from www.nea.org/edstats/RankFull06b.htm. All rights reserved.

FIGURE 15.3   Teacher Salaries: 1964–2004

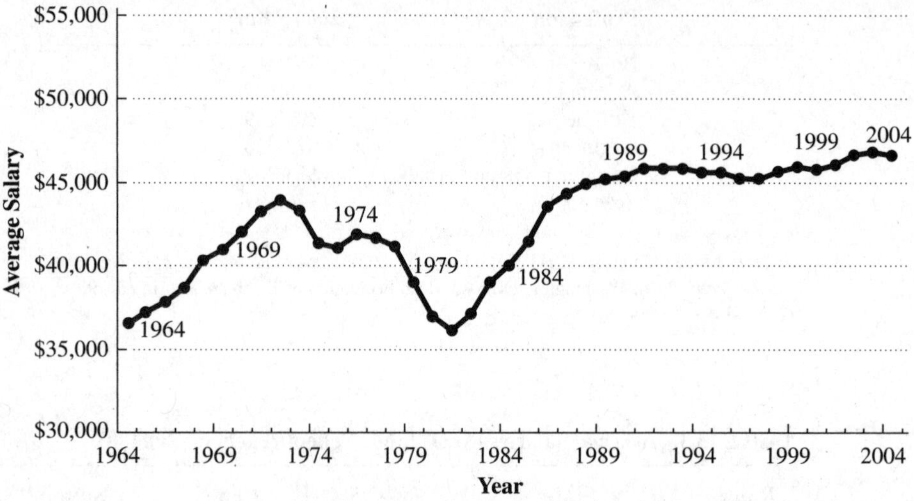

Source: Muir, E., Nelson, F. H., & Baldaro, A. (2005). *Survey and analysis of teacher salary trends, 2004.* Washington, DC: American Federation of Teachers. Reprinted with permission.

for teachers in 2004–05 was $47,674; the range was from $34,040 in South Dakota to $58,456 in the District of Columbia (see Table 15.3).

The salaries of public school teachers, which lost purchasing power to inflation during the 1970s, rose faster than the inflation rate in the 1980s and 1990s (see Figure 15.3). The rising salaries reflected an interest by state and local education agencies in boosting teacher salary schedules then. Since 1993–94 the trend has been for teachers to lose some of their salary advantage when compared to private workers—a positive pay ratio of 1.23 in 2003–04 ($46,597 to $37,765), whereas in 1993–94, it was a positive pay ratio of 1.36 ($45,584 to $33,592) (see Table 15.4).

Comparing salaries between public school teachers and earnings in the private sector is controversial. Podgursky maintains that teachers' salaries are very competitive: "When salaries are computed on an hourly basis, teachers generally earn more than registered nurses, accountants, engineers and other middle-class workers." Podgursky adds, "Some teachers enjoy fringe benefits that are superior to those in the private sector."[3] Sandra Feldman, president of the American Federation of Teachers (AFT), countered that "teaching is complex, demanding work that extends beyond the hours a teacher spends in the classroom."[4] The teacher is a public employee and as such suffers from the fact that salaries paid out of public funds are usually not competitive with professionals paid in the private sector. Individual operators and/or the board of directors of a business are free to pay whatever is required in the competitive complex in which one operates. Also, the latter can usually measure quite objectively the amount of production of the worker. On the other hand, the controlling board of education has

TABLE 15.4   Average Salary of Teachers in 2003–04 Compared to Annual Earnings in the Private Sector, 2003

State	2003–04 Average Teacher Salary	2003 Private Sector Annual Earnings	Pay Ratio Teachers to Private Sector		2003–04 Average Teacher Salary	2003 Private Sector Annual Earnings	Pay Ratio Teachers to Private Sector
Rhode Island	$54,809	$34,865	1.57	Wisconsin	41,687	32,998	1.26
Montana	37,184	25,659	1.45	Nevada	43,211	34,320	1.26
Pennsylvania	52,640	36,483	1.44	Kentucky	39,831	31,658	1.26
Hawaii	45,456	31,974	1.42	Delaware	51,122	40,884	1.25
Idaho	40,111	28,272	1.42	Georgia	45,848	36,863	1.24
Oregon	47,829	33,819	1.41	South Dakota	33,236	26,751	1.24
Alaska	51,136	36,504	1.40	Florida	40,598	32,915	1.23
Ohio	47,791	34,607	1.38	Arizona	42,324	34,602	1.22
Michigan	54,474	39,484	1.38	Kansas	38,622	31,794	1.21
Arkansas	39,226	28,494	1.38	Alabama	38,282	31,567	1.21
Indiana	45,791	33,395	1.37	Louisiana	37,123	30,615	1.21
Vermont	43,009	31,572	1.36	Tennessee	40,318	33,495	1.20
South Carolina	41,162	30,241	1.36	Oklahoma	35,061	29,264	1.20
West Virginia	38,496	28,359	1.36	Washington	45,437	38,673	1.17
Wyoming	39,537	29,148	1.36	New Jersey	53,663	45,981	1.17
California	56,444	41,864	1.35	Minnesota	45,010	38,693	1.16
Mississippi	36,217	27,138	1.33	Connecticut	56,516	48,935	1.15
New Mexico	38,469	28,941	1.33	New York	55,181	47,902	1.15
Illinois	53,820	40,574	1.33	Virginia	43,936	38,142	1.15
Nebraska	39,635	29,924	1.32	Massachusetts	53,274	46,569	1.14
Maine	39,864	30,229	1.32	New Hampshire	42,689	37,685	1.13
North Dakota	35,411	27,197	1.30	Missouri	38,247	33,944	1.13
North Carolina	43,211	33,313	1.30	Colorado	43,318	38,891	1.11
Maryland	50,303	39,155	1.28	Texas	40,476	37,442	1.08
Utah	38,976	30,522	1.28	**U.S. Average**	**$46,597**	**$37,765**	**1.23**
Iowa	38,381	30,220	1.27				

Source: Muir, E., Nelson, F. H., & Baldaro, A. (2005). *Survey and analysis of teacher salary trends, 2004.* Washington, DC: American Federation of Teachers. Reprinted with permission.

real difficulty in measuring the increased production of services resulting from the work of teachers on all levels of the salary schedule.

Teacher Salary Issues

Many difficult problems face the administrator and the board of education in the area of human resources. The best possible salary policy in terms of teacher and other staff requirements, in relation to the funds that are available, must be determined. Over time, the most common way to pay teachers is with a single-salary schedule. In this procedure, the amount of the beginning salary is determined; a number of classifications are established, such as bachelor's degree, bachelor's degree plus a certain number of hours, master's degree, master's degree plus a certain number of hours, and perhaps a doctorate's degree classification and then yearly increments for continued successful performance; and a maximum salary is determined.

In some school district programs that have been introduced, teachers are placed in categories patterned after college faculties, with five different levels of rank: apprentice, novice, career, advanced, and accomplished.[5] In other districts a performance-based compensation model has been adopted, which pays teachers for their abilities in improving student achievement and other agreed-on criteria.[6] Frequently used measures include parent satisfaction and involvement, teacher development, and teacher evaluations. Concerns with that approach are the subjective measurements where some biases and favoritism may be factors. Individual differences of children, alternate cultural standards, and the student achievement ratios become factors.

In still more districts knowledge and skill-based pay is being promoted to tie salaries to accountability. The system provides a mechanism to link pay to the knowledge and skills of teachers and, by extension, improved performance and increased student achievement.[7] Such skill dimensions may include National Board Certification, instruction abilities, assessment, self-reflection, family and community involvement, professional development, meeting individual differences, and course diversity. Opponents to the approach maintain that there is no legitimate rationale to correlate knowledge and skill dimensions to performance and student learning.

A new development in teacher salary issues occurred in Texas with the passing of a state minimum salary schedule. The mandate from the state to the local districts is: "In no instance may a school district pay classroom teachers, full-time librarians, full-time counselors, or full-time nurses less than the state base salary listed for that individual's years of experience."[8] The state base salary schedule emphasizes that there is no state minimum salary for any other position and that an educator employed under a 10-month contract must provide a minimum of 187 days of service. The 2006–07 school year minimum salary schedule is shown in Table 15.5.

Historically, instructional salaries have consumed between 65 and 80 percent of the operation and maintenance budget. In any study of financing education, human resource administration is of prime importance because of the major impact to provide the necessary labor. No school can attain its goals unless it has a corps of competent teachers and other staff members. At the same time, no school can attract and keep the qualified human resources so necessary for its purposes unless sufficient funds are available to provide adequate salaries and benefits. [9]

Salary Schedules

As salary schedules developed, they gradually became the single-salary variety (equal pay for personnel with the same qualifications and experience, without regard to gen-

TABLE 15.5   State Minimum Salary Schedule for Classroom Teachers, Full-Time Librarians, Full-Time Counselors, and Full-Time Nurses (Section 21.402(c), Texas Education Code): 2006–07

Years of Experience Credited	Monthly Salary	Annual Salary (10-month contract)
0	2,732	27,320
1	2,791	27,910
2	2,849	28,490
3	2,908	29,080
4	3,032	30,320
5	3,156	31,560
6	3,280	32,800
7	3,395	33,950
8	3,504	35,040
9	3,607	36,070
10	3,704	37,040
11	3,796	37,960
12	3,884	38,840
13	3,965	39,650
14	4,043	40,430
15	4,116	41,160
16	4,186	41,860
17	4,251	42,510
18	4,313	43,130
19	4,372	43,720
20 & Over	4,427	44,270

Note: Prepared by the Texas Education Agency for the 2006–07 school year. Monthly salary based on the standard 10-month contract.

Source: Texas Education Agency (TEA) Division of State Funding, June 2006.

der, grade level taught, number of dependents, or other previously used factors). An extension of single-salary schedules developed that included additional pay for yearly steps and additional schooling. They are still utilized by most districts. Another salary schedule is an indexed salary schedule with graduating step and lane changes based on a negotiated index. Teachers receive a higher salary based on experience and additional education. An expanded salary schedule continues to increase salaries for an extended number of years. Factors such as training, additional assignments, and education provide for supplementary remuneration.

An example of the single-salary schedule is included in Table 15.6. Negotiated salaries for teachers in the Clark County (Nevada) School District for 2006–07 are shown and it is a typical salary schedule used by most districts in the United States. Also, Table 15.7 from Clark County shows the salary schedule for teachers when ben-

TABLE 15.6   Clark County, Nevada, School District 2006–07 Annual Teacher Salary Schedule

Step	Class A B.A.	Class B B.A. + 16	Class C B.A. + 32	Class D M.A.	Class E M.A. + 16	Class F M.A. + 32	Class G PH.D.
1	$30,299	$32,084	$33,855	$35,641	$37,417	$39,192	$39,692
2	31,687	33,462	35,243	37,021	38,800	40,811	41,311
*3	33,073	34,845	36,624	38,403	40,184	42,438	42,938
4	34,453	36,227	38,010	39,786	41,573	44,059	44,559
5	35,835	37,618	39,391	41,173	42,953	45,681	46,181
6	37,222	38,999	40,775	42,555	44,330	47,297	47,797
7	38,600	40,380	42,159	43,939	45,716	48,921	49,421
8		41,768	43,554	45,321	47,100	50,541	51,041
9			44,926	46,706	48,485	52,162	52,662
10			46,310	48,088	49,866	53,783	54,283
11			47,694	49,476	51,250	55,402	55,902
12						57,125	57,625
13						58,641	59,141
14						60,596	61,096
15						61,808	62,308
16						63,044	63,544

Definition of Classes

Class A: Bachelor's degree and valid Nevada certification for the level or subject taught.

Class B: Bachelor's degree plus 16 increment growth units and valid Nevada certification for the level or subject taught. Units must be taken after receipt of Bachelor's degree.

Class C: Bachelor's degree plus 32 increment growth units and valid Nevada certification for the level or subject taught.

Class D: Master's degree from an accredited institution in a field pertinent to position and valid Nevada certification for level or subject taught.

Class E: Master's degree plus 16 increment growth units and valid Nevada certification for level or subject taught. Units must be taken after receipt of Master's degree.

Class F: Master's degree plus 32 increment growth units and valid Nevada certification for level or subject taught.

Class G: Doctorate degree from an accredited institution in a field pertinent to position and valid Nevada certification for level or subject taught.

Source: www.ccsd.net/jobs.LLPsalary.htm.

efits are included. That schedule demonstrates the additional compensation a licensed employee receives, which is considerably more than when salary alone is exhibited.

At issue in the remuneration of school employees are the benefits provided. Of importance in the salary schedule, dramatically demonstrated in comparing the two Clark County salary schedules, benefits have become numerous and expensive, covering items such as retirement, social security, sick leave, personal leaves, bereavement,

TABLE 15.7   Clark County, Nevada, School District: Licensed Employee Salary Schedule (Including Benefits) for the 2006–07 School Year

CLASS	STEP	Base Salary	Pers 19.75%	Annual Insurance Premium	Medicare 1.45%	Worker's Comp 0.83%	Total Value of Offer
CLASS A	1	$30,299	$5,984	$5,205	$439	$176	$42,103
BA/BS	2	31,687	6,258	5,205	459	184	43,793
	3	33,073	6,532	5,205	480	192	45,482
	4	34,453	6,804	5,205	500	200	47,162
	5	35,835	7,077	5,205	520	208	48,845
	6	37,222	7,351	5,205	540	216	50,534
	7	38,600	7,624	5,205	560	224	52,213
CLASS B	1	$32,084	$6,337	$5,205	$465	$186	$44,277
BA/BS +16	2	33,462	6,609	5,205	485	194	45,955
	3	34,845	6,882	5,205	505	202	47,639
	4	36,227	7,155	5,205	525	210	49,322
	5	37,618	7,430	5,205	545	218	51,016
	6	38,999	7,702	5,205	565	226	52,697
	7	40,380	7,975	5,205	586	234	54,380
	8	41,768	8,249	5,205	606	242	56,070
CLASS C	1	$33,855	$6,686	$5,205	$491	$196	$46,433
BA/BS	2	35,243	6,960	5,205	511	204	48,123
+32	3	36,624	7,233	5,205	531	212	49,805
	4	38,010	7,507	5,205	551	220	51,493
	5	39,391	7,780	5,205	571	228	53,175
	6	40,775	8,053	5,205	591	236	54,860
	7	42,159	8,326	5,205	611	245	56,546
	8	43,554	8,602	5,205	632	253	58,246
	9	44,926	8,873	5,205	651	261	59,916
	10	46,310	9,146	5,205	671	269	61,601
	11	47,694	9,420	5,205	692	277	63,288
CLASS D	1	$35,641	$7,039	$5,205	$517	$207	$48,609
MA/MS	2	37,021	7,312	5,205	537	215	50,290
	3	38,403	7,585	5,205	557	223	51,973
	4	39,786	7,858	5,205	577	231	53,657
	5	41,173	8,132	5,205	597	239	55,346
	6	42,555	8,405	5,205	617	247	57,029
	7	43,939	8,678	5,205	637	255	58,714
	8	45,321	8,951	5,205	657	263	60,397
	9	46,706	9,224	5,205	677	271	62,083
	10	48,088	9,497	5,205	697	279	63,766
	11	49,476	9,772	5,205	717	287	65,457
CLASS E	1	$37,417	$7,390	$5,205	$543	$217	$50,772
MA/MS	2	38,800	7,663	5,205	563	225	52,456
+16	3	40,184	7,936	5,205	583	233	54,141
	4	41,573	8,211	5,205	603	241	55,833

TABLE 15.7   Continued

CLASS	STEP	Base Salary	Pers 19.75%	Annual Insurance Premium	Medicare 1.45%	Worker's Comp 0.83%	Total Value of Offer
CLASS E	5	42,953	8,483	5,205	623	249	57,513
MA/MS	6	44,330	8,755	5,205	643	257	59,190
+16	7	45,716	9,029	5,205	663	265	60,878
(continued)	8	47,100	9,302	5,205	683	273	62,563
	9	48,485	9,576	5,205	703	281	64,250
	10	49,866	9,849	5,205	723	289	65,932
	11	51,250	10,122	5,205	743	297	67,617
CLASS F	1	$39,192	$7,740	$5,205	$568	$227	$52,932
MA/MS	2	40,811	8,060	5,205	592	237	54,905
+32	3	42,438	8,382	5,205	615	246	56,886
	4	44,059	8,702	5,205	639	256	58,861
	5	45,681	9,022	5,205	662	265	60,835
	6	47,297	9,341	5,205	686	274	62,803
	7	48,921	9,662	5,205	709	284	64,781
	8	50,541	9,982	5,205	733	293	66,754
	9	52,162	10,302	5,205	756	303	68,728
	10	53,783	10,622	5,205	780	312	70,702
	11	55,402	10,942	5,205	803	321	72,673
	12	57,125	11,282	5,205	828	331	74,771
	13	58,641	11,582	5,205	850	340	76,618
	14	60,596	11,968	5,205	879	351	78,999
	15	61,808	12,207	5,205	896	358	80,474
	16	63,044	12,451	5,205	914	366	81,980

Note: Add $500 for Ed.D or Ph.D.

Factors Regarding Placement on the Salary Schedule

1) All teachers must have a minimum of a bachelor's degree, awarded by an accredited institution recognized by the Commission on Professional Standards in Education.

2) Original college/university transcripts with degree conferred (foreign transcripts must be officially verified).

Source: www.ccsd.net/jobs/LLPsalary.htm.

insurance, worker's compensation, and professional improvement activities (see Table 15.8). Benefits have affected salary increases.

Benefits

School districts were generally slow in providing benefits to teachers and other school employees. Business and industry led the way in inaugurating such benefits as retirement plans, tenure, sick-leave privileges, and insurance coverage. For the most part, these are benefits that entered the educational scene in the last half of the twentieth century. Because wages were frozen during World War II, benefits were used to

TABLE 15.8   A Summary of Benefits

Program	Frequency	General Provisions
Retirement	In every state	A guaranteed amount (depending on length of service and contributions) on retirement; may include withdrawal privileges (with interest) of employee contribution for those who leave the system before retirement; disability and death benefits have become critical due to GASB regulations; some plans provide for investments in stocks and mutual funds that may offset any losses due to inflation. Some districts offer early retirement incentives.
Social security	Nationwide	Joint contributions; members pay part and the state pays part; available to employees. Federal program supplements state and local retirement; survivor disability, death benefits; guaranteed monthly income on retirement at proper age; employee takes benefits with him or her when moving from one state to another.
Sick leave	In nearly all districts	Full salary while employee is ill—up to a stipulated number of days, which are usually cumulative to some established maximum number. Required in some states; some districts pay teachers for unused sick leave days accumulated.
Personal leaves	In many districts	For emergencies other than illness; usually not more than 1 to 5 days per year; the circumstances of each request are usually considered on their own merits, rather than according to a universal policy.
Leaves of absence	Has become more widely accepted	Usually provides for extended leaves without salary for study or professional improvement, disability, political activity, travel, or maternity reasons. Some districts provide some compensation for sabbatical or improvement leaves for certificated employees.
Bereavement leave	In some districts	When a close relative dies, days are allowed to attend the funeral, arrange affairs, and travel.
Insurance	Widespread	Employer provides benefits without increasing employee's salary; usually provides group insurance: health and accident, hospitalization, dental, long-term disability, and life; becoming expensive—provided by fewer districts. Many districts provide liability insurance for tort action on all school employees.
Worker's compensation	Nationwide	Provides various options of benefits for injury and disability of all school employees; usually required by the states as protection for the risks of employment; mandatory in some states, optional in some, and not available in one or two others.

TABLE 15.8 A Summary of Benefits

Program	Frequency	General Provisions
Tax shelters	Nationwide	Federally granted privilege to public school teachers to invest part of their earnings in an annuity payable at a later time; delays income tax on these earnings until the benefits are received; since the retired teacher will probably be in a lower tax bracket, there will be tax savings. Some other flexible tax benefits are available.
Severance pay	In few districts	An infrequently used benefit; employee may get the value of his or her unused sick leave and other unused leave pay.
Income tax deductions	Nationwide	Provides income tax deductions (federal) for certain necessary and approved expenses while studying and otherwise improving and/or retaining their present position of employment; not available for the purpose of position advancement.

compensate workers. In today's competitive market, benefits have become part of the reward system of publicly as well as privately employed personnel (see Table 15.8).

Some of the positive aspects of these benefits as they apply to education are the following:

1. School boards, like private employers, have discovered that benefits rank next to attractive salaries and good working conditions as motivators of efficiency and maximum productivity.
2. Benefits serve a double purpose: First, they provide needed personal benefits that teachers often would not provide for themselves. Second, they do not involve the increases in income taxes that would accompany payment for the same benefits by the teachers themselves from increased salaries, although the federal government continues to analyze the prospects of taxing benefits.
3. Benefits help to increase job satisfaction and thus reduce disruptive changes resulting from faculty resignations and consequent replacements.
4. Some of the matching employer costs of retirement, insurance, and other benefits are now being absorbed as state rather than district expenditures, thus making such benefits available to the personnel of financially weak districts as well as all others.

In the twenty-first century, however, costs of benefits increased significantly. Salary increases are limited in order to pay for the various benefits. Skyrocketing medical costs have reached such proportions that some businesses and educational agencies are freezing salaries to pay for health care insurance coverage. Retirement benefits in businesses are becoming a thing of the past, as some employers expect employees to pay for their own retirement by individual planning and investment such as 401K and other similar plans. Social security contributions, as of 2007, up to a salary level of $97,500, are 15.3 percent of salary (7.65 percent by employer, 7.65 percent by employee). Leave benefits are becoming more expensive. Estimates for benefit costs to districts can range from 35 to 45 percent of salaries.

Some benefits have become somewhat controversial. One area involves benefits of same-sex partners and/or marriages. In 2000, Vermont became the first state to legislate same-sex unions, followed by courts in Alaska, Hawaii, and Massachusetts approving same-sex marriages. In *John Geddes Lawrence and Tyron Garner v. State of Texas* (Supreme Court Number 02-102, Decision Date, June 26, 2003), the Supreme Court, in regard to these issues, ruled that there "was a realm of personal liberty which the government may not enter." Those private organizations that have extended benefits to individuals thus defined may affect public entities, including school districts.[10] Another controversial issue is benefits to terminated employees. The Supreme Court ruled that employees do not lose their health, welfare, or pension benefits when terminated. Although the Court was addressing a specific statute, such a ruling may have implications to human resource benefits in education—especially in those districts with declining enrollments. At issue were termination rights motivated by an "employer's desire to prevent a pension from vesting" and "interfering with the attainment of any right to which a participant may become entitled."[11] The federal government may have an influence on benefits, declaring that such benefits are tantamount to income. For example, if one were paid for unused sick leave, then sick leave itself may be considered income, or if a teacher receives free tuition for dependents, that, too, may be regarded as income. In 2000, two innovative benefits were proposed in California. The Governor advocated that teachers not pay state income tax[12] and in San Francisco the Board of Education proposed building housing for educators.[13] Another problem related to benefits occurred when the Governmental Accounting Standards Board issued regulations about impending charges (see Chapter 13). Districts were informed that they should include the future costs of benefits, such as retirement and medical expenses that could be needed in the future, in current financial reports. Some districts are moving to compliance, and many educators retired, fearing that retirement benefits and medical needs would not be available when vested. This contributed to a critical teacher shortage in those districts that are adopting GASB's regulations.

Certification

Endemic to human resource administration is the fact that educators are professionals who require certification. Just as attorneys, physicians, and dentists are certificated, so are teachers. In public education, certification is handled by an agency in the various states' department of education. In some states, a requirement has surfaced that teachers must pass a competency test, similar to the bar examination for attorneys. This competency test has become a hot issue. The premise for the test is that a teacher should show a basic understanding of the core material that is to be taught—for example, math teachers should know math. The antithesis to this is the argument that no written test can determine the competency of a person to teach. Countering that viewpoint is that the bar examination for attorneys does not demonstrate their skill in the courtroom, but it does show a basic understanding of the law. Hopefully, a written competency test for teachers shows a grasp of the subject matter that is to be taught.

The competency test requirement has been adopted in some states, but is not required in others. The method of certification is being altered in certain areas of the country where many school districts and state departments of education are pursuing alternative certification programs. The process includes identifying and recruiting individuals with superior knowledge in such subjects as mathematics and science, coupled with a mentoring program that develops their pedagogical skills. The person recruited works under the direction of a certificated teacher for a given number of years until a competency of learning theory and instructional science can be demonstrated.

In 1987, the Carnegie Foundation for the Advancement of Teaching, perceiving that teachers were not properly prepared, recommended the creation of a National Board for Professional Teaching Standards (NBPTS). The mission of the organization was "to establish high and rigorous standards for what accomplished teachers should know and be able to do, to develop and operate a national voluntary system to assess and certify teachers who meet these standards, and to advance related education reforms for the purpose of improving student learning in American schools."[14]

The first certificates were awarded in 1995. Many states have used those certificates as a factor in determining additional compensation for teachers. However, research studies that have attempted to determine if there is a corresponding advancement in student achievement when taught by teachers who have been certificated thusly, have shown that there is no significant difference in pupil performance. In fact, in some studies the opposite has been the result.

Merit Pay

Merit pay and other provisions in salary schedules seldom satisfy teachers, school boards, or the general public. At the same time, the single-salary schedule has become harder to defend. Merit pay has received renewed attention nationwide because of the call for educational reform and accountability. Legislators, reflecting the attitude of the public, are expressing the opinion that salaries for teachers and administrators should be based on performance. Mere passage of time and additional education, without evidence of teacher improvement, as the criteria for salary increases, is increasingly attacked. Some career ladder programs have attempted to meet the criticism by tying performances to increased compensation.

The arguments have changed little in the last 50 years. Those who maintain that the salaries of teachers should be determined by merit have stated:

> Pay increases should not be based solely on time served in a position or the number of academic degrees held, but also on performance as measured by specific standards. In the case of teachers, that is an issue that has been raised by parents and educators for years. . . . President of the American Federation of Teachers, Albert Shanker, has said that "coursework

and seniority do not guarantee knowledge and skill." . . . The need for this kind of system is obvious . . . and the time to adopt it is now.[15]

Those who oppose merit pay have stated:

Merit pay won't work; it hurts those it purports to help. Anyone who promotes merit pay must believe that teachers are best motivated by financial incentives. They assume that teachers could do a better job, but they are holding back because there's not enough in it for them. Wrong. But the worst thing about tying pay to performance in education is that it leads to harmful practice for the very students that it purports to help. Merit pay would encourage divisive competition in a profession that requires cooperation and teamwork. Students learn best when teachers collaborate—not when teachers are forced to compete.[16]

The challenge in awarding merit pay comes in all parties agreeing on a scale and the subjective nature of evaluating performance. The topic will continue to be analyzed and the debate will be ongoing.

Additional Issues

Today, examination of certification, salaries, benefits, training, and other issues continue to be scrutinized by lawmakers and critics of education. The advent of the No Child Left Behind Act demands more stringent requirements for training, and may influence certification standards and call for more testing. Following are areas discussed in the literature that deserve scrutiny as they relate to human services and to school finance:

■ Studies reveal that accredited education schools are very effective in preparing candidates to meet today's teaching-content testing requirements. Graduates of accredited schools passed state licensing tests at a much higher rate than graduates in the liberal arts area and graduates of unaccredited schools. However, teacher certification procedures provide little information about whether the new teachers are ready to teach.

■ The No Child Left Behind Act requires a "highly qualified" teacher be in every classroom. Table 15.9 outlines the competencies necessary to meet the No Child Left Behind mandates of a "highly qualified teacher." The on-line journal *Education Policy Analysis Archives'* researchers indicate that students learn more from licensed teachers who have had formal training in both how and what to teach, than they do from uncertificated teachers.

■ A decentralized management program considers the role of the teacher in the district's professional development strategies and creating a comprehensive accountability model. Teachers are also involved in budget matters and personnel hiring. In programs where the concept has been introduced, because of its site-based approach, personnel undergo a comprehensive evaluation at least once every five years. Teachers are placed in categories patterned after college faculties, with five different levels of rank: apprentice, novice, career, advanced, and accomplished.[17]

TABLE 15.9   Defining a Highly Qualified Teacher

Certification	Competency	Schedule
Full certification, no waivers	Bachelor's degree	Students receive core content
Pass the state licensing test	Teach at proper level	2005–06 deadline/full
Alternate route/3 years	Content competent	certification
Charter school exception	Academic major	

▪ A performance-based compensation model is a means to pay teachers for their abilities in improving student achievement and other agreed upon criteria. Frequently used measures include parent satisfaction/involvement, teacher development, and teacher evaluations. Concerns with the approach are the subjective measurements where some biases and favoritism enter in. Individual differences of children, alternate cultural standards, and the ratio of achievement of the students become factors.[18]

▪ Knowledge and skill-based pay is being promoted in some districts to tie salaries to accountability. The system provides a mechanism to link pay to the knowledge and skills (and by extension, improved performance and increased student achievement) of teachers. Such skill dimensions may include National Board Certification, instruction abilities, assessment, self-reflection, family and community involvement, professional development, meeting individual differences, and course diversity. Opponents to the approach maintain that there is no legitimate rationale to extend knowledge and these skill dimensions to performance and student learning.[19]

▪ In the private sector, because of high medical insurance costs and other pressures in the economy, retirees are fearful that they will lose benefits. (In 2006, pension reform was a major issue in the U.S. Congress.) The same concern exists in education. A benefit for educators that is always on the bargaining table is the cost of health care and rising health insurance costs that continue to soar. Some are questioning the rationale of medical insurance. With tighter budgets, school districts and negotiating teams are analyzing the costs carefully.

▪ A few boards of education in districts that are losing enrollment are considering offering early retirement benefits to teachers as a revenue-saving method. Staff turnover saves the difference between better-paid experienced teachers and entry-level teachers. That policy is short-sighted, even though the microeconomics is plausible, as it perhaps saves money for individual districts. The macroeconomics of the issue causes concern when considerable costs are added to retirement systems. Also, educators may continue their careers in other localities, becoming "double dippers," which costs the overall education community.

▪ Urban/rural problems relating to hiring and retaining teachers remain difficult for educational administrators. In urban districts more teachers are leaving the profession because of working conditions. Furthermore, teacher transfer practices are of the nature that teachers often move to schools perceived to be better, have higher achievement levels, and have lower proportions of low-income and minority students. A similar issue is true in rural areas. Rural and small-town schools have difficulty in recruiting and retaining teachers. Professional isolation and chronically low salaries and benefits exacerbate the difficulty in attracting quality teachers to those schools.

■ Because of new testing demands, teachers report that the No Child Left Behind requirement to test is becoming so time consuming and burdensome that it leaves too little time for instruction. The advocates of testing—the federal government, state boards, and local school boards—assert that it is an essential element in the education process and provides for accountability and evaluation.

Teachers and School Finance

It is no secret that teachers as a group have not been particularly concerned or informed about the rudiments of school finance. Stories of teacher naiveté in this field have seldom been exaggerated. A few teachers received their initiation to the subject when their local or state professional organizations appointed them to teacher-salary committees, but the problem of financing education was of little interest to most classroom teachers.

The pendulum is swinging in the opposite direction. By choice, teachers are insisting on a stronger voice in decision making, particularly as it affects reward for service. Increased salaries, more substantial benefits, and better working conditions have accompanied greater power in professional negotiations. The teaching profession appears to be surprised and uncertain about the responsibilities accompanying such power.

Salaries and other benefits are not spontaneously generated. They must come from somewhere, and the normal budgets of most school systems are already overburdened. Teachers, who formerly viewed the fiscal affairs of schools as a foreign language to be learned only by administrators and boards of education, now find themselves among those who have an interest in seeking additional sources of school revenue. Further progress in providing for the still-rising costs of education is virtually impossible without the united efforts and sympathetic understanding of all large segments of the society in the United States, including the vast numbers of professional teachers who stand to receive important benefits in future years.

Only recently has the typical teacher begun to realize the potential benefits of understanding and skill in the field of school finance. Also, state legislative bodies have recently deemed it necessary to turn to the profession for assistance in finding new sources of revenue for schools. Only informed and interested people can respond successfully to this new challenge.

Thus, it seems that present-day human resource administration has reached the point where teachers must develop some acumen in school finance if the objective of teacher rights and participation is to be more than a mere platitude. Teachers, teacher organizations, and administrators face the task of providing the means and the motivation to raise the level of teacher knowledge so as to help find valid answers to the problems of financing education.

A number of avenues are open for fulfilling this need: required courses in the basics of school finance, in-service training projects, workshops, civic study groups, practical assignments to the members of negotiating teams, and many others. Teachers must understand that their participation in negotiations and salary disputes gives them a duty to understand the implications and the problems of higher salaries and benefits. They are citizens, too. Just as it is impossible for school boards to draw additional dollars out of depleted budgets, so it is impossible for an uninformed group to arrive at consensus on teacher salary demands. A beginning point can be established if the teachers themselves, particularly the career-directed ones, assume responsibility for learning principles of school finance.

The Changing Assignments of Teachers

In recent years, innovations of various kinds have changed the traditional pattern of teacher assignments. Computer instruction, flexible scheduling, large-group instruction, team teaching, closed-circuit television, individualized and continuous-progress instruction, and similar programs have accelerated the differentiation of staff assignments. State requirements of a college major in a subject other than education is now being imposed in some states for initial teacher certification. The inducement for such prerequisites is the belief that classes should be taught by teachers who are experts in the field. The improved use of qualified teaching personnel, with emphasis on specialization and expertise in instructional techniques, may utilize experienced teachers to mentor new teachers. Studies have shown that beginning teachers who receive such support focus on student learning much sooner and become more effective instructors. Additional requirements for teaching have become commonplace in many states by increasing internships and adding additional weeks to student teaching. This greater intensity of training has brought concomitant increases in salaries. Many of the chores that previously fell to the teacher can now be assigned to aides and clerks. The more difficult and technical aspects of education may then be left to professional teachers.

The Impact of Technology

Technology is accepted for what it is by educators—a potential supplement to upgrade and reinforce the instructional program. Computers are no longer considered luxuries; they are now part of the ongoing instructional program in every progressive school. States are now requiring skill in educational technology for teacher certification and recertification. State educational leaders believe that teachers should be able to use new technological tools in their instruction. It is hard to generalize about the implications of widespread adoption of educational technology, but use is a necessity.

With the exponential nature of technological advancements, teachers are finding new and exciting ways to present material to the learner. PowerPoint presentations, interactive lessons, and distant learning are examples of developments that are available to teachers. The sophisticated use of technology has, in some instances, made the classroom a "paperless" venue. Information from classroom presentations can be transferred to student computers; homework can be submitted and tests can be taken and corrected online, with immediate feedback for the student; and parents can be kept apprised of required homework. The technological evolution had its impact on teachers who found the *newness* of the computer age frustrating and retired rather than make the effort to modify their teaching methods. It is a necessity that this generation of teachers be aware of and utilize available resources for the improvement of instruction. It is the responsibility of educational leaders to find the revenue to keep pace with the changes.

Teacher Turnover

Retention of teaching personnel has always been a big problem. Relatively low salaries, lack of socioeconomic status, apathy of students, and little opportunity for advancement have combined to discourage many teachers and cause them to leave the profession. School districts have tried to stop this loss with greater rewards for service, employment of aides and teaching assistants, better leave policies, smaller classes and lighter workloads, and other such benefits,[20] but high teacher turnover persists. Teachers are among the most mobile of all professional workers. They tend to change positions often, always seeking but seemingly never finding the kinds of positions that they are willing to call permanent.

What are the ramifications of the problems of assignment and retention of teacher personnel from the financial point of view? What will be the net cost of paying higher salaries for the best professional teachers and lower salaries for various grades of assistants? What will be the fiscal result of the use of the vast array of technological devices that are part of the instructional program? What is the dollar effect of the extensive recruitment and in-service programs necessary to replace the large numbers of dissatisfied and itinerant teachers? The answers to these and related questions are of great concern in considering the problems of financing schools.

Where enrollments are soaring, teachers are being hired at an unprecedented rate. States that are losing teachers are forced to hike salaries, add signing bonuses, and beef up benefits packages. Schools will need to hire 2 million new teachers in this decade, thus exacerbating the teacher turnover problem. Many of the new hires will be replacing teachers "now in their 40s and 50s, who are expected to retire. At the same time, the demand for smaller classes means a number of districts will have to expand their staffs beyond current members."[21]

Administrative and Supervisory Salaries

Much of the information already discussed concerning teacher salaries, schedules, and benefits applies equally well to administrative and supervisory staff members. Professionally, all certificated personnel have much the same kinds of problems. Certainly they are all striving for the same goal—the education of the nation's children. There are some differences in how rewards for services are determined for administrative and supervisory personnel, however. The main ones are:

1. The salary of the chief administrator, the superintendent of schools, is most often decided by bargaining, ostensibly on the basis of training and past record; the extent of competition for the position may also have something to do with the salary offered to the successful candidate.

2. Salaries of the administrative and supervisory staff may not fit the teacher salary schedule. Such employees receive higher salaries, for several reasons: (a) their certification requirements are higher, (b) their positions require knowledge and skills in more fields, (c) they have responsibility for the actions of more people, (d) they serve for a longer period of time each year (11 or 12 months, compared to 9 or 10 for teachers), and (e) they are usually not tenured and serve at the pleasure of the school board.

3. In the minority of school districts in which administrative and supervisory salaries are related directly to teacher salaries, there are two common ways of determining them: (a) on the basis of a stipulated number of dollars above the salary for teachers with the same training and experience or (b) on the basis of a predetermined ratio or index involving such salaries.

4. Some districts determine the salaries on the basis of the teacher salary schedule plus additional amounts per teacher or per pupil, or both, in the school.

Noncertificated Personnel Salaries

Over the years, school administrators and boards of education have emphasized the importance of developing attractive salary schedules and providing good working conditions for certificated personnel, but they have often neglected similar conditions for noncertificated employees. The principal reason seems to be that since the purpose of the school is to provide instruction, this is where emphasis should be placed. Then, too, the qualifications of noncertificated personnel vary greatly.

An important difference is that all instructional or certificated personnel serve under contract for one or more years—service that usually results in tenure after a probationary period. No such arrangement exists for most noncertificated employees. They tend to serve with no written contract and no guarantee of salary increments based only on the passage of time. Resignations and replacements are commonplace.

Fortunately, the conditions in this area of human resources have improved. Large school districts, with their need for many such employees, increased job requirements, the unionization of many of these workers, and the gradual abdication of school boards interviewing and hiring all school employees has improved conditions in the employment, utilization, and retention of noncertificated personnel. These factors, along with inflation and higher taxes, have forced school districts to raise salaries and provide benefits similar to those that certificated personnel receive, thereby adding still another large increase to the costs of public education.

Payroll Policies and Procedures

The largest single classification of current expenditures involves payment of salaries to employees. All but one or two of the primary expenditure account categories in a school district's accounting system include provisions for the payment of salaries to employees. Only fixed charges and student-body activities would ordinarily not include salaries for personnel and under some circumstances even these may have salary related components. Collectively, almost 80 percent of the current expenditures of a typical school district are for salaries and benefits of employees.

The size and importance of a school's payroll dictates that sound principles and procedures of payroll accounting be followed. Most of these would apply to all payroll accounting, but there are some differences. Generally accepted policies and procedures to be followed include the following as a minimum:

1. Arrangements should be made and businesslike procedures followed to guarantee payment of salaries at a specified, regular, and acceptable time. No excuses are acceptable to employees when a payroll division is unreliable and uncertain in delivering salary payments. Only emergency factors beyond the control of the business office can be justified as legitimate reasons for delay or inconvenience in paying salaries.

2. Receiving the salary payment should be made as convenient as possible to the employee, including direct deposit. The onus for delivery should rest with the school district's business office, regardless of its size, not with the individual payee. The days of requiring school employees to go in person to the school board office or the clerk's home to receive a salary check, or just to wait for the convenience of the payroll division, are only a dim memory in most districts. Even when the district is temporarily short of funds, there is provision in the law for short-term borrowing on tax anticipation notes so that a school district may continue to operate on a businesslike basis.

3. All school employees should possess written copies of rules and policies concerning payroll procedures. The rules and policies should have been established by joint suggestion and approval of representatives of the employed personnel of the district, working with representatives of the board of education. Among other things, each school employee should have easy access to the following:

   a. A current salary schedule, with full explanation of increments and special provisions, if any.
   b. A statement of policy related to payroll procedures as they apply to the teacher on sick leave or on leave for other reasons. The policy should state how the teacher's salary is affected when a substitute is employed and any other conditions that are directly related to leave privileges.

    c. A written explanation of how all deductions required by law are calculated—federal withholding taxes, state withholding taxes, social security, and other legally imposed deductions such as garnishment of wages. The employee should be able to determine whether the amounts for such deductions are correct.

    d. A statement of policy concerning willingness of the district (and the conditions to be met) to withhold other deductions at the request of a school employee or a professional organization—such as membership dues in professional organizations, individual or group insurance premiums, tax-sheltered annuities, 401Ks, and other investment programs.

    e. An explanation of the options available to school employees as they relate to payroll dates for 9-month, 10-month, or yearly contracts. It is particularly important to clarify the school's policy concerning options that teachers on 9-month contracts may have concerning the summer salary payments.

    f. A statement in writing concerning the procedure to be followed by an employee in the event of a salary dispute or misunderstanding.

4. A well-understood procedure should be followed in reporting to the payroll division relevant information on all individual employees before the regular paying period—days of sick leave, other leave, salary changes, and dates of beginning and ending employment in the case of employees not under contract.

Governmental Influence

Recent occurrences demonstrate that some human resources functions are influenced by executive and judicial actions that occur outside the school program. Through the process of initiatives and referenda, laws affecting schools and school finance are emerging, and these laws impact human resources matters. An initiative is a method of obtaining positive law through a petition by citizens and approval by the voters. A referendum is a proposal generated by legislative action that subsequently allows the voters to have the final say. An initiative can be viewed as action instigated by the public; a referendum can be viewed as a response from voters on a proposal from the legislature.

In Florida, the state electorate, through an initiative petition, required that class size in the public schools be reduced. The governor and the legislature indicated that the state did not have enough money to meet the requirements of the initiative. The Supreme Court of Tennessee ordered the state legislature to level teacher pay among poor rural and richer school districts. The financial impact was staggering, with a price tag of hundreds of millions of dollars in a state that had raided the state's tobacco-settlement fund, borrowed from future state budgets, and had a three-day government shutdown.

In California, a state famous for ballot initiatives, voters approved spending increases for education and other programs and at the same time voted for a decrease in tax revenues. A recent dilemma was raised when government officials noted that required funds were not available to reduce class size. Voters passed an expensive after-school program initiative in spite of the warning that funds would not be available to provide for the program. Some proposals have required additional expenditures and others have demanded a tax reduction, which was the case with Proposition 13. Citizens in California favored increased funding for education and human services programs that made up 74 percent of the state's budget but also opposed higher taxes on income, sales, and automobiles.

Political scientists who see initiative and referendum procedures as elements of pure democracy have long praised them. Although well intentioned, the process has caused some bifurcation and problems in human resources.

Summary

Since the salaries and benefits provided for school personnel represent nearly 80 percent of the average school's current expenditures, it is obvious that the administration of human resources is a very important aspect of public school finance. The rapid rise of negotiations with teacher organizations and unions has helped make teacher salaries somewhat competitive with salaries in the private sector.

The extension of state- and district-financed benefits for school personnel in the last half of the twentieth century has done much to increase the job satisfaction of teachers. School districts should continue to provide benefits and do what they can to keep the significantly rising costs of such benefits manageable.

Teachers as well as school patrons would do well to become better acquainted with the problems states and school districts face in financing an adequate and equitable school program. When solving the difficult problem of procuring adequate funds and spending them wisely to provide the best possible education, there is no substitute for an informed public. Along with the numerous other groups that comprise society, teachers should provide enlightened understanding in this matter. The time when school finance problems were legitimately the responsibility of one or two small segments of society has long since passed.

Current issues in human resources include certification, constraints of time due to testing requirements, defining a "highly qualified teacher," early retirement, and extra-duty salary supplements. Questions raised include: Do students learn more from certificated teachers? How do schools get and keep teachers in urban and rural areas? and Should pay be determined by performance and skill bases? Some controversy exists about alternative certification, health care, postemployment benefits, and the role of the teacher in decentralized programs.

Trends in salary schedules in education include expanding the single-salary schedule. Technology, teacher assignment, and teacher turnover are important human resource administration concerns. Administrative noncertificated compensation with good payroll procedures for all employees are further items under consideration.

Government and other external agencies influence education. The initiative and referendum vehicles have particularly affected education's human resource activities.

ASSIGNMENT PROJECTS

1. Provide a definition for each of the following terms: *personnel, human resources, salary schedule, single-salary schedule, indexed salary schedule, steps, lanes, merit pay, salary, benefits, certificated, noncertificated, certification, retirement, career ladders.*
2. Analyze the human resource administrative procedures in your school district and make recommendations to improve present practices.
3. From the literature, determine current trends regarding merit pay for teachers and list the arguments for and against establishing such a practice in a district.
4. Interview several teachers at a local high school and determine their opinions concerning extra pay for supplemental duties.
5. Determine how administrative, supervisory, and classified personnel salaries are ascertained in your district and in surrounding districts.
6. Prepare a defense for the argument that teachers are overpaid because they only work nine months, have all major holidays off, including two weeks at Christmas, and only work from 8:00 A.M. to 3:00 P.M.
7. Research various career ladder proposals in the states and relate these plans to the salaries, benefits, status, and professionalism of teaching as a career.

Computer simulations and questions, research exercises, and website addresses relevant to this chapter can be found at

www.ablongman.com/edleadership

SELECTED READINGS

American School and University. Annual Compensation Issue (January 1993).

Bowin, Robert B. *Human Resource Problem Solving.* Englewood Cliffs, NJ: Prentice-Hall, 1987.

Campbell, Roald F., Luvern L. Cunningham, Raphael O. Nystrand, and Michael D. Usdan. *The Organization and Control of American Schools,* 6th ed. Columbus, OH: Merrill, 1990.

Collective Bargaining: A Critical Appraisal. Washington, DC: National Educational Association, 1991.

Conley, Sharon E., and Samuel Bacharach. "Performance Appraisal in Education: A Strategic Consideration," *Journal of Personnel Evaluation in Education, 3,* 1990.

Danielson, Charlotte, *Enhancing Professional Practice: A Framework for Teaching.* Arlington, VA: Association for Supervision and Curriculum Development, 1998.

Garfield, Rulon R., Gene J. Garfield, and J. D. Willardson. *Policy and Politics in American Education.* Atlanta, GA: St. Barthelemy Press, 2003.

Harris, Ben M. *Human Resource Management.* Fort Worth, TX: Harcourt Brace, 1999.

Ray, John, Walter G. Hack, and I. Carl Candoli. *School Business Administration Planning Approach,* 8th ed. Boston: Allyn and Bacon, 2005.

Rothwell, William H., and H. C. Kazanas. *Strategic Human Resources Planning and Management.* Englewood Cliffs, NJ: Prentice-Hall, 2001.

Taylor, Susan. *Public Employee Retirement Systems: The Structure and Politics of Teacher Pensions.* Ithaca: New York State School of Industrial and Labor Relations, Cornell University, 1986.

ENDNOTES

1. William B. Castetter, *The Personnel Function in Educational Administration,* 4th ed. (New York: Macmillan, 1986), p. 427.

2. American Federation of Teachers, annual survey of state departments of education, various years, overview, 2006.

3. Michael Podgursky, *Education News,* Hoover Institution at Stanford University; see *USA Today,* June 3, 2003, p. 9D.

4. Fredrecka Schouten, "Public School Teachers' Hourly Pay Tops Many Professions, Study Finds," *USA Today,* June 3, 2003, p. 9D.

5. Allan Odden, "Cincinnati's New Approach to Teacher Certification," *School Business Affairs,* May 2002, pp. 20–23.

6. Nancy Schilling and Stephen B. Lawton, "Performance-Based Pay: A Keystone for Improving Teachers' Salaries," *School Business Affairs,* November 2002, pp. 9–12.

7. Ibid.

8. Texas Education Agency, Search TEA's Site, www.tea.state.tx.us/school.finance/salary/sal107exp.html.

9. *The Profession Builder,* National Education Association, December 1996, p. 1.

10. Cheryl Gamble, "L. A. Board Considers Insurance for Unmarried Partners," *Education Week,* January 15, 1997, p. 17.

11. *Inter Model Rail Employees Association et al. Petitioners* v. *Atchison, Topeka, and Santa Fe Railway Company et al.,* Supreme Court of the United States, No. 96–491, May 12, 1997.

12. Bess Keller, "Calif. Leaders Balk at Tax Break for Teachers," *Education Week,* May 24, 2000, p. 21.

13. Jeff Archer, "San Francisco Schools to Build Housing for Teachers," *Education Week,* June 7, 2000, p. 3.

14. *The Profession Builder,* p. 1.

15. Clifford B. Janey, "Incentive Pay: A Logical Step toward Teacher Accountability," *Education Week,* November 6, 1996, p. 38.

16. Adam Urbanski, "Merit Pay Won't Work in the Schools, It Hurts Those It Purports to Help," *Education Week,* January 15, 1997, p. 48.

17. Allan Odden, "Cincinnati's New Approach to Teacher Certification," *School Business Affairs,* May 2002, pp. 20–23.

18. Nancy Schilling and Stephen B. Lawton, "Performance-Based Pay: A Keystone for Improving Teachers' Salaries," *School Business Affairs,* November 2002, pp. 9–12.

19. Ibid.

20. Julie Blair, "Districts Wooing Teachers Away with Bonuses, Other Incentives," *Education Week,* August 2, 2000, pp. 1, 17.

21. Barbara Kantrowitz and Pat Wingert, "Teachers Wanted," *Newsweek,* October 2, 2000, pp. 37–42.

16 The Road Ahead in School Finance

*The achievement of equitable and adequate financing of education
is a never-ending quest. When each and every child in the country
has received a quality education we will have made history.*
—Vern Brimley, Jr., and Rulon R. Garfield, 2007

Endemic to the passage of time is transformation. Civilizations have always been constantly challenged by change. In just the few short years since the previous edition of this text, a litany of changes in education have occurred—most of which have impacted school finance. The authors have a point-of-view that in the past two decades school finance has been reconstructed to such an extent as to indicate that a sixth period in the evolution of school finance has occurred. This period is highlighted by financing issues, tax-cut measures, and pressure for greater accountability for student learning and improved teacher competency. New players entering the arena have had an impact on public schools. Contracts to manage districts and individual schools were awarded to private companies and broader avenues for choice were given to parents through charter schools, vouchers, and tax credits.

The student is at the center of the educational enterprise that has a teacher as the most significant mentor other than the student's family. Different groups are attempting to become a part of that enterprise by influencing how educational funds are allocated and spent. One group has espoused, and some states have adopted, a concept that requires that at least 65 percent of revenue allotted to schools will be traced to instruction for students at the school level. Another consortium has recommended a new approach to the weighted pupil formula. A precise plan at this writing is undefined.

The notable "A Nation at Risk" narrative revealed that students in America's public schools were not receiving the product that was needed to compete in the world economic setting. The No Child Left Behind Act acceded to that view and added an assertion that there was a rift in the public school system. Although many schools are performing well, other schools, usually in disadvantaged areas, are not meeting expectations. Many parents express that they are generally pleased with their local school, but the perception, generally, is that the nation's schools are failing.

With the advent of the No Child Left Behind legislation, and eroding local control of the schools, the concept of federalism has been challenged by testing and oversight required by the federal goals. Federalism is the vertical diffusion of power among the three levels of government that create a strong federal government, strong state governments, and strong local governments, all part of one creative whole. In this national system, powers are assigned, shared, or denied among the three levels. The Tenth Amendment to the U.S. Constitution has been interpreted as legal sanction for state responsibility for education. Simply stated, in federalism the states are to have the major role for education—the structure being local control, federal interest, and state responsibility.

Various factors have affected the focus and funding of education. Continued emphasis is placed on equity and more attention has been given to adequacy. Both terms have proved difficult for the courts and legislatures to define in relation to language in state constitutions. In some states the courts believe it proper to designate to legislatures the amount of funds that must be spent to meet constitution requirements. Legislators question the courts' power in such action.

In this climate of change, certain socioeconomic truths have emerged that affect education generally and school finance specifically:

1. The United States is increasingly becoming a bilingual nation. Greater financial resources are needed to meet the needs of the population of students who speak English as a second language.
2. The U.S. population is growing older. A new emphasis on educational needs may be influenced by this fact. Educators seeking revenues for elementary and secondary schools will find competition for funds needed for entitlements from social security, Medicare, and other social programs. The emphasis on education may need to include programs for continuing education and life-long training for the aging population.
3. School enrollment is shifting as the general population is moving from the Midwest and Northeast to the South and West. The financial implications are astounding as new schools need to be built in one area while facilities are left empty and decaying in another. The capital outlay ramifications are extensive and operation and maintenance concerns are real. Shifting student enrollments affect the ability to provide students with the resources needed for an excellent pedagogical experience.

Changes in the accounting, auditing, and reporting of financial information have occurred. The Governmental Accounting Standards Board (GASB) is wielding great influence over government agencies, including public schools, requiring compliance with established practices. A comprehensive annual financial report (CAFR), expansive and voluminous in its coverage and presentation, is required from individual public agencies. Some of the information necessary for public schools' reporting is included in this text to provide students with a knowledge of some of the complexities that must be handled by a district business office. Small school districts that do not have a separate business office must still provide all of the required information.

The change from personnel functions to human resource development is more than a name change. Across the human resource spectrum, from hiring to separation, education leaders must focus on the growth and morale of teachers and supporting staff so that the educational process can function successfully. Some benefits have been curtailed in some regions of the nation, and need for additional salary increases to compete with other professions is a continual challenge to human resource specialists.

The increase of human capital is largely responsible for the remarkable social and economic development of the United States over the two centuries of its existence. The costs that are required to increase human capital through our education system are worthwhile. The most important producer of human capital is the public education system. It is the conduit that transfers resources from the private sector to education consumers, the future producers of the nation. The human capital generated in public schools and elsewhere is needed to ensure a dynamic economy, provide an adequate standard of living, reinforce domestic security, as well as sustain our nation's prominence in the world.

Educational investment benefits society through the greater production of goods and services. Education, the public must come to understand, creates a *virtuous circle.* The more quality education, the more wealth is developed, and the more funds are available for investment. The more investment, the greater amount is available for investment in physical and human capital. The increase in human capital generated by education allows for a better society and greater production of goods and services, not the least of which is education.

Emphasis must be placed on quality education so that the *diminishing marginal utility* is minimized. While striving for adequacy and equity in educational funding school personnel, its leaders especially must make certain that funds are expended wisely. Any additional expenditure must bring greater satisfaction, more worth, better pedagogy to the educational enterprise.

Consumer sovereignty has a role in education as well as in the broad economic picture. Unlike commercial enterprises where consumers will determine with their purchasing decisions what good and services will be provided, in education the consumers (students) generally do not pay for their education but payment decisions are determined in large measure by the wishes of government officials—school boards, legislatures, courts, governors, congressmen and women, even presidents. Each of these officials must be reminded that the well-being and growth of the pupil is paramount in the school endeavor. As the pupil advances through the school and college system, more *opportunity costs* are borne by the individual or the student's family. Those secondary and postsecondary college costs redound to the benefit of the student who delays entering the job market, for his or her long-term income will replace the income lost while pursuing more education.

Education allows for *free riders.* Those who are not or have not paid for education garner many benefits—lower social costs, greater tax revenues, and the development of the elements that expand the economy: resources, labor, capital technology, and management. Furthermore, every U.S. citizen is benefited from the noneconomic results of education—social mobility, the arts and culture, democratic processes, and scientific inventions.

It is incumbent on the taxpaying public to understand the necessity of providing revenue to accomplish the goals of education. To do so enriches the economic cycle.

Historically, the courts, particularly the United States Supreme Court, have disallowed direct financial support to private and parochial schools. In *Zelman* v. *Harris-Simmons,* the Court indicated that students may use vouchers to attend religious schools when aid is allocated on the basis of neutral secular criteria that neither favor nor disfavor religion and secular beneficiaries on a nondiscrimination basis. Over time, the trend in the courts has been to measure differences in per-pupil expenditures among school districts, and that thrust is expected to continue. More court cases are expected to test whether future voucher schemes comport to the caveats of *Zelman.*

One of the measures of an effective school is to provide for a protected place to learn and for teachers to teach. The world changed on September 11, 2001. Schools have been cautioned to be diligent in terrorism-preparedness efforts. They must plan, prepare, and practice for the worst possible incidents of violence. Providing for schools that are safe and secure in a terrorist environment will mean additional costs in an already tight school finance atmosphere.

Whether improvement in education can come about by changing the organizational pattern is a contemporary issue. Private contractors are becoming part of the public school scene. The number of charter schools, some of which have no connection to the typical public school organization, have significantly expanded in states, thus changing the public school structure. Revenues from the public treasury for students attending private and parochial schools, and providing an allowance for tax credits and deductions are elements that support the doctrine of those who believe that true reform can best come from outside the current public school system. Vouchers, tuition tax credits, and privatization are a reality. Many futurists insist that the concept will have a positive impact on the public schools. Whether reform takes the path of the existing school system or alternative programs, it will have a large influence on the way schools are financed.

Generally speaking, scholars in educational finance understand that there are many factors that have an impact on how well a student does in school. The makeup of the family influences that success or failure. Social indicators show dramatic changes in the family. Alterations in the typical family include children by teenage mothers, single-parents families, and latchkey students. Further, there has been an increase in after-school programs to meet the needs of latchkey children. Although there is controversy about the effect of money, most believe that additional funds positively affect student performance. Meeting the challenges of changing social patterns continue to have an impact on education funding.

In some states, obsolete and unfair methods of obtaining and allocating funds still discriminate against poorer school districts, and the revenues of some systems are still inadequate or inequitably distributed. Many scholars call for complicated funding formulas that confuse the public, as well as state legislatures. Other scholars call for nearly full state funding.

Education is a state responsibility, and financial support should come from that source, but local control should be maintained. A relatively uncomplicated approach utilizes local property taxes as the basis of a minimum support program, and all taxpayers throughout the state should be assessed a uniform levy. Whatever amount the local tax does not raise toward the minimum is supplemented by the state through other tax revenues. Money allocated on a weighted-pupil formula adds to the equity of the program. Local initiative is provided by allowing some reasonable board and/or locally voted leeway.

There has been extensive progress over the years in providing more equitable financing of education for children in the United States. Local property taxation, state nonequalizing grants, equalization programs with greater state participation and responsibility, district power equalization programs, lotteries, and funding education reform have provided progress in school finance that has been little short of phenomenal. During the history of the United States, state after state has moved from high-cost and largely private school education for a few to free and reasonably equitable public education for all its citizens, with reasonably equitable burdens for its taxpayers. This has been done for the most part without destroying the tradition of local control. People have been able to retain at least limited responsibility and control over the institutions that bring education to their children.

In the wake of *Serrano* v. *Priest*, equity for schoolchildren and equity for taxpayers became goals to which scores of states and millions of people previously had given no more than lip service. With the Supreme Court's decision in *Rodriguez*, equalization efforts were enhanced, with the responsibility resting at the state level. The need for reform in school finance plans was still apparent among the several states in relation to their meeting state constitution requirements. Groups of interested and knowledgeable citizens outside the realm of professional education began to apply their skills and their prejudices to improving the financing of education.

In the *Phi Delta Kappa/Gallup Annual Poll* (September 2006), the highest priority was that reform in the nation's public schools must be handled by the *public schools,* not some form of an *alternative* education structure. Certainly, at no other time in U.S. history have so many divergent groups worked with such enthusiasm, tenacity, and apparent success to improve the quality of the educational financing system of the various states. Extensive improvements have been made and greater progress is envisioned for the near future.

The Future of Public School Finance

Although the future of education, in general, and school finance, in particular, is hard to predict, America will rise to the challenge. With the past as just a prologue throughout its history, the United States has been able to forge forward in improving educational and school funding programs. In *Renaissance Trends for U.S. Schools* by Cetron and Gayle,[1] some trends are identified that relate to educational finance.

1. Education will continue to be viewed as the key to economic growth.
2. There is a growing mismatch between the literacy (vocabulary, reading, and writing skills) of the labor force and the competency required by the jobs available.

3. A wide spectrum of school finance initiatives and experiments will be undertaken. These will range from extreme centralization and financial control at the state level on one end, and privatization on the other.
4. Regional disparities of educational sources will increase.
5. The number of public school enrollments in the United States will increase.
6. Only 15 percent of the jobs will require a college diploma. More than half of all jobs will require postsecondary education and training.
7. Equity issues and adequacy concerns will become the major problems faced by policymakers. Legal challenges will increase as standards are raised.
8. Educational equity will be redefined, not in terms of access, but in terms of expenditures, and may include providing a "sound basic education."

Elusive forces that educational leaders must consider in determining the education structure includes analyzing the future in relation to these data:

1. *Demographics*
   a. *Enrollment:* will continue to increase
   b. *Enrollment shift:* certain states will lose enrollment and other states will gain it
   c. *Growth in urban areas:* with its attendant problems
   d. *Minorities:* major growth of numbers in the public schools
   e. *Immigrants:* providing education for them will be a challenge
2. *Interest rates.* Districts often depend on interest money for additional revenue to stretch tight maintenance operation budgets; interest rates will affect bonding in capital-outlay budgets.
3. *Tax limitation measures.* Some states will have limitations placed on their ability to tax.
4. *Federal deficit/surplus.* Past decades have resulted in an epic proportion of interest payments on the national debt. In 2003, the economy shifted from a surplus to a massive deficit and has continued. The 2007 national debt was $8.3 trillion.
5. *Risk management and safety measures.* Additional expenditures will be required to provide for safe and secure schools.
6. *Benefits.* Increases will be seen in health and accident insurance premiums, social security, and retirement benefits.
7. *Personnel needs.* In some states, there will be a teacher shortage; in others, there will be reductions in staff.

Unresolved Issues

All these facts raise questions such as: Who should be educated at public expense? To what grade level should free education be provided? Will the states cut back education programs if revenues diminish? Will the states provide adequate funds to sustain their current programs at their desirable or optimum levels? Should the federal government and states continue to increase their share of the revenue mix? Is inadequacy of funding a matter of lack of ability to pay, the problem of taxpayers' lack of willingness to pay, and/ or the demographics of a particular state? Other significant and relevant questions are:

1. What are useful innovative models for financing public education? How can the federal government, the states, and local school districts provide adequate, stable funding?

2. How can school finance systems be linked to performance?

3. How can states finance the costs of designing and implementing new assessment systems required by NCLB?

4. How can some states and local districts keep up with the demands for facilities created by rising enrollments? How can districts with declining enrollments maximize the use of schools that are being abondoned?

5. What is the impact of special education costs on general education budgets?

6. How can states increase local flexibility yet continue to exercise meaningful accountability for educational quality and equity?

7. What are the governance, finance, and management implications of the demographic and social changes shaping education?

8. How do investments in technology affect children's learning? Which technology investments are most cost effective? How can states and districts finance equitable access to technology?

9. What should be the responsibility for each of the three levels of government? How can policymakers with different philosophies more effectively coordinate local, state, and federal funding streams?

10. How can states monitor the operations and measure the quality of charter schools and choice schools? How cost effective are the various choice models? How do choice programs affect the quality, governance, demographics, and funding of public schools?[2]

These, along with many other related questions, now face the public school systems of this country. Crucial problems that schools face are not always clearly evident. The dilemma of finding sufficient revenues to finance public education will continue to plague many states. Education is considered by citizens of the United States to be of high priority and importance. Progress and improvement usually occur over time.

Some Characteristics of Educational Structure

Certain important elements must serve as the basis for all educational structures and solutions to the financial problems of the day. Education rests on several basic assumptions that receive general but not universal support. Some are more readily accepted than others; some rest on firm and long-accepted opinion and practice; and some seem destined to undergo periodic change. Various principles that this text has accepted include the following:

1. The perpetuation of the U.S. federal system of government is dependent on an informed citizenry, and that can only be attained by the operation of free public schools.
2. Education is a state function because of interpretation of the Tenth Amendment to the U.S. Constitution and the provisions in many state constitutions that declare education to be a state responsibility. Financing it is also a state responsibility, for the same reasons.
3. Education enhances the economic development of a country and is an investment in human capital.
4. Education helps protect individual freedom.
5. Education is no longer regarded as a privilege for those who can afford it.
6. Public funds used to establish or to aid operation of private schools must meet the *Agostini* tenets upheld in *Mitchell* v. *Helms,* and meet the criteria of the *Lemon* test and comport to *Zelman.*
7. Public funds cannot be used to prevent integration of minority groups.
8. School finance programs that provide equal dollars per student lack equity and fairness; weighted-pupil units are a fairer measure of need.
9. A state's and nation's efforts to support education are important for social and economic progress.
10. All but a few citizens should pay taxes for the services of government, especially education; some may miss one or more forms of taxation, but few should miss all forms.
11. The ability-to-pay principle of taxation and the benefit principle are both justifiable in providing funds for education.
12. Education is an investment in future generations.
13. Providing adequate funds for education will give a district or a school the opportunity to produce, but will not guarantee, a good educational program; inadequate funds, however, will guarantee a poor program.

School Finance Goals

School finance programs in the future should:

1. Support high-level education to provide programs appropriate to the unique needs and personal differences of children.
2. Provide a high degree of equity and equality of educational opportunity for all children.
3. Provide greater state financial support of education but at the same time leave much of its control in the hands of local school boards.
4. Clarify the role of each of the three levels of government in financing education and determine the proportionate share of cost that each should pay.
5. Assure that minority children attend 12 years of schooling in the same proportions as children from nonminorities, and close the achievement gap.

6. Provide school finance laws that recognize not only the problems and inequities in rural schools but also those in large city districts.

7. Eliminate the amount of adult and child illiteracy that continues to exist, in spite of the nation's free educational system.

8. Apply appropriate and legal allocations of public funds for the operation of non-public schools.

9. Make major improvements in the assessment and administration of the property tax.

10. Provide equitable practices in securing funds for capital outlays.

11. Eliminate fiscal dependence on other governmental bodies for those districts that still must operate under this handicap.

12. Provide financial support on an equitable basis for extension of the school year well beyond the nine months now used in many school districts.

13. Provide free education to adults who did not obtain it in their younger years but who now seek it for cultural and economic reasons.

14. Extend the years of formal education downward to include early childhood programs, particularly for the disadvantaged.

15. Educate people who are denied a fruitful life by a lack of education and vocational skills.

16. Prepare students to compete in the worldwide economy.

The Challenge

The twenty-first century is fraught with challenges for local boards of education and administrators who must determine the direction for education. There is greater involvement than ever before from forces that are influencing local decisions and in one way or another will affect the financing structure.

The National Institute on Educational Governance, Finance, Policymaking and Management released a document entitled *Meeting the Information Needs of Educational Policymakers.* The report was developed by a broad spectrum of leaders in various fields with an interest in the future of education. It is imperative that school administrators consider the relevance of these salient finance-related issues as they plan for "the road ahead."

1. Policymakers and educators are debating profound governance changes, including charter schools, vouchers, and other public or private choice options. Educators express frustration with the cumulative effect of state and federal mandates.

2. Improving instruction is the ultimate purpose of school reform. Therefore, ambitious reform agendas are unlikely to succeed unless they include strategies for providing professional development to current teachers and improving the preparation of prospective teachers.

3. Policymakers and education leaders are looking for effective ways to attract and retain the best new teachers, and to make coherent reforms in the whole enterprise of teacher preparation and professional development.

4. There is an emerging consensus that school reform must be a community-wide enterprise, carried out through partnerships with parents, business, social service agencies, and other community institutions.

5. Restoring public confidence in public education is a major challenge in an era when a minority of the voting public has children in school and more parents are looking to private schools and choice alternatives for quality education.

6. Although many citizens support education reform in general, they may disagree on the specifics or may be unprepared to accept the costs, discomfort, and time lines required to make significant changes.

7. Demographic and social changes are creating new governance, finance, and management challenges for education. Different kinds of children may require different methods of instruction to achieve at high levels.

8. Social problems—such as poverty, drugs, and crime—are affecting children's health, safety, and readiness to learn and are creating new demands for human services. Schools are already asked to do many things that divert energy and funding away from their main mission of teaching children.[3]

Educators in past generations may debate that these issues are no more critical than those they experienced. This may be true, for educational leaders, over the years, have solved significant school crises. Now, some of the finest minds and most capable persons are meeting the demands of educating the children and youths of this nation. There is much to be done to improve the financing of education in this country. No reasonable person expects that this will be achieved perfectly or that all the problems will be solved faultlessly. Educators, legislators, policymakers, and parents must have the vision, accept the responsibility, and take the challenge to work toward desirable and worthwhile goals. The price may be high, but the rewards are great, in terms of the future of millions of children.

Computer simulations and questions, research exercises, and website addresses relevant to this chapter can be found at

www.ablongman.com/edleadership

ENDNOTES

1. Marvin J. Cetron and Margaret Ebbons Gayle, *The Futurist*, September/October, 1990, pp. 33–40; list adapted from *Educational Renaissance: Our Schools in the 21st Century* (New York: St. Martin's Press, 1990).

2. The National Institute on Educational Governance, Finance, Policymaking, and Management, *Meeting the Information Needs of Educational Policymakers* (Washington DC: Office of Educational Research and Improvement, U.S. Department of Education, U.S. Government Printing Office, August 1997), pp. 4–8, 9, 12.

3. Ibid., pp. 7–11.

INDEX